Management
Accounting

••••••••••••••

Longman modular texts in business and economics

Series Editors: Geoff Black and Stuart Wall

Other titles in this series:

Marketing
Elizabeth Hill and Terry O'Sullivan

Introducing Human Resource Management
Caroline Hook and Margaret Foot

Business Economics
Win Hornby

Business Law
Ian Stirk and Helena McFarquhar

Financial Accounting
Christopher Waterston and Anne Britton

Management Accounting

David Wright

London and New York

Addison Wesley Longman Limited
Edinburgh Gate
Harlow, Essex CM20 2JE, England
and Associated Companies throughout the world.

*Published in the United States of America
by Addison Wesley Longman Inc., New York*

First published 1996

ISBN 0 582 26253 4 PPR

British Library Cataloguing-in-Publication Data

A catalogue record for this book is
available from the British Library

Library of Congress Cataloging-in-Publication Data

Wright, David, 1951 Apr. 4–
    Management accounting/David Wright.
    p. cm. - - (Longman modular texts in business and economics)
    Includes bibliographical references and index.
    ISBN 0-582-26253-4 (pbk.)
    1. Managerial accounting. I. Title. II. Series.

HF5657.4.W75 1996
658.15'11- - dc20

95–50909
CIP

Set by 30 in Stone Serif 9/12 pt

Printed in Great Britain by Henry Ling Ltd., at the Dorset Press, Dorchester, Dorset.

For my wife, Helen,
and my children, William and Beth.

Contents

Foreword ix
Acknowledgements xi

1 Introduction to management accounting 1
1.1 Introduction 1
1.2 The management decision-making, planning and control process 6

Part 1
Cost analysis techniques **15**

2 Cost ascertainment and costing techniques 17
2.1 Costs and cost accounting/costing 17
2.2 Absorption costing technique 23
2.3 Activity based costing technique 35

3 Cost behaviour and estimation techniques 43
3.1 Patterns of cost behaviour 44
3.2 Cost estimation techniques 52

4 Marginal costing technique 66
4.1 Marginal cost ascertainment 67
4.2 Concept of contribution 70
4.3 The problem of limiting factors/scarce resources 74

Part 2
Management decision accounting techniques **83**

5 Information for management decisions under uncertainty 85
5.1 Probabilities and management decisions 86
5.2 EMV criterion for management decisions 91
5.3 SEU criterion for management decisions 100
5.4 The nature and value of information 107

6 Cost-volume-profit (C-V-P) analysis 116
    6.1 C-V-P relationships 116
    6.2 Break-even analysis 121
    6.3 Limitations/assumptions of C-V-P analysis 128

7 Pricing decision techniques 134
    7.1 Optimal pricing technique 135
    7.2 Cost-plus and marginal pricing techniques 143

8 Capital investment appraisal/decision techniques 155
    8.1 Discounting investment decision techniques 159
    8.2 Non-discounting investment decision techniques 168
    8.3 Sensitivity analysis 173

Part 3
Management planning and control accounting techniques 179

9 Budgetary planning and control techniques 181
    9.1 Budgeting: building the budget 182
    9.2 Flexible budgeting 193

10 Control accounting through standard costing/variance analysis 204
    10.1 Analysis of variable cost variances 208
    10.2 Analysis of fixed overhead and sales variances 218

11 Control of divisional management performance 230
    11.1 Divisionalisation and responsibility accounting 230
    11.2 Measurement of divisional performance 233

12 Further management planning techniques/developments 243
    12.1 Linear programming (LP) 243
    12.2 Developments in management planning 247

Appendix 1a 252
Appendix 1b 253
Solutions to the self-check questions 254
Index 314

Foreword

Welcome to what I assume is your first study of management accounting. This book consists of twelve chapters. This makes it ideally suitable for a fifteen week semester which has for instance, at its end, two weeks devoted to revision and exam preparation with the final week set aside for examinations. During the other twelve weeks your studies might conveniently be based around a chapter topic per week. Even if your course of study is structured on a traditional academic year basis of terms rather than semesters, you will find the book's content is perfectly suited to providing you with a sound first experience of, and a robust introduction to, the subject of management (or managerial) accounting.

I have designed the structure of the book so that you progress smoothly and logically from learning about management accounting fundamentals to eventually being able to apply your understanding through a range of detailed managerial accounting techniques. The fundamentals are located in Part 1. They comprise several analytical techniques that might be described as costing, or cost accounting, principles. Your early assimilation of these cost analysis techniques is crucial as they underpin the subsequent use of accounting information for management planning, control and decision-making in Parts 2 and 3.

Every chapter begins with a clear statement of objectives indicating what you will be capable of doing after you have completed that chapter's study. You can perhaps use the objectives as a checklist against which you can chart your study progress. You will also find that you are often advised to hop around the text, both backwards and forwards, somewhat more than you are normally accustomed to. This is an intentional ploy on *my* part in order to develop *your* sense of active participation in the text which is so essential to your effective use of the book. With this aim in mind, I have also structured the whole text into main chapter sections and sub-sections for added ease of reference. Please ensure you follow up any such cross-references to enjoy maximum study benefit.

Finally, each chapter (except the first and last) contains activities which engage you *actively* in learning about the topic under consideration. You will recognise the purpose of an 'Activity' when you see the word '*Required*' which prefaces the action you will be involved in. Another feature is the occasional questioning 'slot' designed to stimulate your interest or involve you in a short task, such as 'How would you . . . ?'; 'Did you know . . . ?'; 'Can you think . . . ?' etc. Where there is a solution required, you will find a brief answer at the end of the question. Every chapter concludes with further study guidance and (again excepting the first and last chapters) self-check questions. Solutions to the self-check questions are at the end of the book. But remember: you can only benefit fully from the questions by *not* looking at their answers straight away, and not before you have made a serious and studied attempt yourself at their solution. Don't cheat – you'll only be cheating yourself! On that final word of advice, good luck with and enjoy your first learning experience of management accounting.

Acknowledgements

I would like to take this opportunity to briefly express my thankful acknowledgement to a number of people and institutions who have been importantly involved, to some degree or other, in my writing of this book. Firstly, the institutions deserving of thanks, for generously giving me permission to use a selection of their past examination questions, are the following professional accountancy bodies in the United Kingdom:

Association of Accounting Technicians
Chartered Association of Certified Accountants
Chartered Institute of Management Accountants
Chartered Institute of Public Finance and Accountancy

Several people I would also like to thank for being involved are: first and foremost my wife, Helen, for her unstinting devotion and uncomplaining support not only in the word processing of the whole book, but for providing me and my children with a warm and loving home life; next my beautiful children, William and Beth, whose noisy and playful antics often distracted but always encouraged me; third, my series title advisor, Carolyn Malinowski, for her constructive and helpful comments in reviewing many of the 'trickier' chapters in particular; and finally my colleagues Mike Edwards, Barry Corner and Suzanne Murphy, the latter for her unhesitating willingness to help type many of the self-check question solutions that appear at the end of the book. The editorial support of Chris Harrison, Lynette Corner, Geoff Black and Stuart Wall must also be acknowledged before this book can begin.

CHAPTER 1

Introduction to management accounting

Objectives

By the end of this chapter you should be able to:

▶ State a wide range of accounting information user groups, describing their information needs, interests and objectives.

▶ Differentiate between the branches of financial *vis-à-vis* management accounting.

▶ Understand and define clearly the management accountant's role as an accounting information source and provider to organisational managers.

▶ Describe in detail the *raison-d'être* of management accounting in the context of a general framework for managerial planning, decision-making and control.

The first few sections of this short introductory chapter concern the role of accounting and more specifically *management accounting*. Because there is no entirely satisfactory or wholly definitive explanation of its role you will be first given a taste of how several authoritative sources see it. All these views represent suitable definitions as they derive from either reputable accounting writers or recognised accounting institutions. Overall we will leave the question of definition as a rather open one. While no dogmatic assertion or prescription of its role is attempted, our aim is certainly not to leave you confused or in doubt as to its purpose, but merely to illustrate how wide the scope for definition is. In any case, for practical purposes we ultimately endorse one of the views in particular and adopt a 'working' definition.

The final sections of this chapter are then largely devoted to a general description of the process underlying managerial decision-making, planning and control before the remainder of the book goes on to consider chapter-by-chapter a broad range of specific management accounting techniques.

1.1 Introduction

An often quoted and, by now, very well established (1966) definition in the literature of accounting reads that accounting is: 'The process of identifying, measuring and communicating economic information to permit informed judgements and decisions by users of the information.' (American Accounting Association).[1] The definition is couched in rather general terms but nevertheless still gives strong emphasis to the importance both of the provision of information and, what is more, the subsequent effective use of that information. In particular the usefulness of accounting information is seen as helping to facilitate:

(a) the exercise of good judgement;
(b) the making of sound decisions.

However, the question then arises – exercising judgement and making decisions for what reasons and to what organised ends? Essentially two vital ingredients in the practice of any organised activity are *planning* and *control*. Such organised activity in need of planning and controlling is undertaken either by individuals for themselves or within organisations for which they operate. Returning briefly to the above definition, it casts its net very widely to include all 'users' of accounting information. But are we concerned here in this book with all manner of user of accounting information? Before we can decide that, we really need to consider the different types and variety of users or user group.

1.1.1 Accounting and its user(s) information needs

Two further questions at this early introductory stage now present themselves:

(1) What kind of individuals and/or organisations may require provision of accounting information to assist them in their judgements and decisions?
(2) What sort of situations can and do arise in which judgements and decisions need to be made to plan and control individual/organisational activities in the furtherance of their objectives?

There are numerous different types of user/user group, each with many and varied accounting information needs; Table 1.1 effectively summarises for you answers to both the questions posed above in its columns (1) and (2) respectively.

Although reflecting the main users of accounts information, you should appreciate that the list in Table 1.1 does not pretend to be wholly exhaustive – other users exist, e.g. environmental interest/pressure groups, competitors, etc. Moreover, the various individual user groups are of necessity likely to require access to different kinds of accounting information to further their objectives. For instance, HM Customs and Excise in the UK, acting on behalf of the government, will doubtlessly be more interested in whether the VAT (value added tax) and other duties have been paid rather than if the firm has recorded profits. But information reporting on the firm's income will be of immense interest to the organisation's shareholders in their planning, control and decision strategies regarding current and future investment in the firm. Management also will have specific information requirements when setting the prices to be charged for products or services (see Chapter 7) or finding out what level of operations is necessary to break even (see Chapter 6). Additionally, managers will find it useful to know the effect that changing activity levels will have upon costs incurred (Chapter 3 on cost behaviour analysis explores this important issue).

Generally speaking all the user groups in Table 1.1, with the exception of management, will look to having their informational needs satisfied by access to such sources as the organisation's annual report and accounts, regular/interim statements in the financial press (e.g. *Financial Times, Investors Chronicle*) and specialist information services/bureaux (such as Extel, Dun and Bradstreet etc.). This type of accounting information is often referred to as

table 1.1

Accounts' users and their respective objectives

(1) Type of accounts' user/user group	(2) Planning/control/decision situations where accounting information may help to further objectives
Trade unions	Wage and salary agreements; collective bargaining for terms and conditions of employment; industrial action.
Shareholders	Share dealings; investment strategies – hold/buy/sell.
Government	Environmental responsibilities of the organisation; tax adjustments and incentives.
Creditors	Level of credit facilities allowed – increase/decrease credit.
General public	National/local community effects (social and economic) of organisational activity.
Legal authorities	Fraudulent dealings – investigation and legal action.
Customers	Consume products/services provided by the organisation.
Lenders	Availability of loans (short and long-term) – advance/withdraw.
Employees	Stay/seek alternative employment opportunities.
Management	Pricing strategy for the organisation's products and services; levels of organisational activity – sales/production/research and development etc.

being derived from 'externally' available sources, whereas a firm's own management team are more than likely going to have accounts information needs geared specifically and in the main to the efficient 'internal' running of the organisation, both day-to-day as well as long term. Thus we can draw a convenient distinction between essentially two different forms of accounting information – *internal* and *external*.

1.1.2 Management (internal) versus financial (external) accounting

The start of the previous section presented an institutional definition of accounting in general provided by the American Accounting Association. Here, in order to focus perhaps a little more sharply on the 'internal/external' distinction, let us first of all consider another authoritative source. In distinguishing between the two branches of accounting Charles T. Horngren has been almost abrupt in his simplicity: 'Financial accounting and management accounting would be better labelled as external accounting and internal accounting respectively.'[2] In another of his works he has elaborated somewhat:

> 'the major distinction between them is their use by two different classes of decision makers. The field of financial accounting is concerned mainly with how accounting can serve external decision makers, such as stockholders, creditors, governmental agencies, and others. The field of managerial accounting is concerned mainly with how accounting can serve internal decision makers, such as managers.'[3]

Horngren thus has drawn a rather strict dividing line; he perhaps could even be accused of being over-dogmatic. Other reputable authorities, such as Arnold and Hope, are not quite so emphatic: 'The dichotomy between management and financial accounting is, in many ways, both unfortunate and misleading.'[4] However, despite expressing their apparent doubts about such a division within accounting, Arnold and Hope then still fall back on our basic distinction:

> 'management accounting is concerned with the provision of information to managers who make decisions . . . by contrast, financial accounting is concerned with the provision of information to users other than managers e.g. shareholders, customers and those who have loaned funds to an organisation'.[5]

Doubtlessly opinions will continue to differ. However, for our purposes here we shall carry on making use of the division, regardless of how sharply or how vaguely it might otherwise be made. This book is all about management accounting, *not* financial accounting. In spite of its scope continuing to expand as time progresses, financial accounting tends still to be preoccupied with the external aspects of reporting to the different types of user groups (excepting management, of course) discussed earlier. Many influences outside the confines of the organisation itself place strict and ever-increasing demands upon the accounting for, and reporting of, financial affairs. Particularly good examples of such requirements include statements of standard accounting practice (SSAPs) and financial reporting standards (FRSs) from the accountancy profession itself, as well as legal obligations imposed by government through companies acts, finance acts and so on. In the very different world of management accounting it is the internal aspects of managing an organisation which are predominant – indeed you should be aware that extremely few outside pressures ever dictate precisely what management accounting information is required beyond what is needed by managers themselves. Effectively this leaves the management accountant alone to get on with the job of structuring the managerial accounting information system in the most effective way possible to assist managers to plan, control and make wise decisions concerning the future efficiency and well-being of their organisation.

Planning, controlling and decision-making are critical management functions which have an essential orientation towards the future. Once more you need to appreciate how this differs significantly from one of the financial accountant's chief preoccupations – that of recording (via book-keeping) transactions which have already happened and then the subsequent reporting of these financial events through the vehicles of balance sheets and income statements along with other fiscal reports such as funds flow statements, showing the cash flows of previous accounting periods. An important difference between financial and management accounting involves the former's major aim of recording and providing figures which are accurate, objective and verifiable for, say, audit and tax purposes. Management accounting, on the other hand, contends that supreme accuracy, objectivity and verifiability may often need to give way to other virtues such as quickness, relevance and the immediate usefulness of information. There is the old adage for a management accountant that it is ultimately more advisable to be roughly right rather than exactly wrong! A summary of the relative attributes of management accounting in relation to financial accounting appears in in Table 1.2.

table 1.2
Management accounting and financial accounting compared

Financial accounting	Versus	Management accounting
External Reporting	Basic Application	Internal Reporting
Past Present	Time Frame	Present Future
Accuracy Verifiability Objectivity	Main Criteria	Relevance Speed Utility
Recording	Main Emphasis	Planning Decision-making Control
FRSs SSAPs Company law	Required By	Management

1.1.3 Role of management accounting

'What is management accounting?' asks Professor John Sizer. 'In the broadest sense', he replies, 'all accounting is management accounting.'[6] In other words, all manner of information supplied by accountants can, to some degree or other, be described as being of potential interest to managers. Further influential and rather weighty support for this same viewpoint is, in fact, provided by one of the leading chartered professional accountancy bodies in the United Kingdom, the Chartered Institute of Management Accountants (CIMA), which was established in 1919 specifically to promote the study and practice of management accounting. CIMA prescribes the following definition in explanation of what it perceives to be the detailed role of management accountancy.[7] Management accounting is: 'An integral part of management concerned with identifying, presenting and interpreting information used for:

▶ formulating strategy;
▶ planning and controlling activities;
▶ decision taking;
▶ optimising the use of resources;
▶ disclosure to shareholders and others external to the entity;
▶ disclosure to employees;
▶ safeguarding assets.

The above involves participation in management to ensure that there is effective:

▶ formulation of plans to meet objectives (strategic planning);
▶ formulating of short-term operation plans (budgeting/profit planning);
▶ acquisition and use of finance (financial management) and recording of transactions (financial accounting and cost accounting);
▶ communication of financial and operating information;

> ▶ corrective action to bring plans and results into line (financial control);
> ▶ reviewing and reporting on systems and operations (internal audit, management audit).'

Sceptics may well argue that CIMA's definition is inevitably reflective of a strong vested interest. Certainly, the almost all-embracing status ascribed by CIMA to management accounting might be seriously questioned and contested in other quarters. Even Professor Sizer eventually gives a definition of management accounting which attributes a very much more limited scope to its role – 'The application of accounting techniques to the provision of information designed to assist all levels of management in *planning*, in making *decisions*, and in *controlling* the activities of an organisation.'[8]

The management accounting techniques mentioned here fall into two distinct categories, being (a) decision accounting techniques; and (b) planning and control accounting techniques. Essentially, after dealing with some fundamental cost analysis techniques in Part I, the rest of this book is devoted to coverage of individual aspects or techniques of planning, control and decision accounting. The use of this categorisation will become apparent in section 1.2 which looks at the overall structure or process of managerial decision-making, planning and control.

A variety of viewpoints, both personal and institutional, have so far been presented. We now can adopt a 'working' definition for the role of management accounting which endorses most closely the view expressed by Professor Sizer above. Management accountancy in this book is therefore rather narrowly defined (especially when compared, say, with the generalist one suggested by CIMA.)

> Management accountings role lies with the utilisation of *decision-making, planning and control techniques* which provide information aimed at helping *management* to perform its role of planning and controlling the organisation's activities.

1.2 The management decision-making, planning and control process

The structural content of the process about to be described fundamentally consists of management's crucial activities of decision-making, planning and control. Such a process can be conveniently illustrated by a flow chart (Figure 1.1) depicting the different phases of the process.

Shown clearly in Figure 1.1 are not only the sequential relationships that exist between each individual phase I to VI as they progress from left to right but also the two important 'loop-back' effects, linking phases, which are known as *feedback* relationships. The essential ingredients of the overall structure in a general sense parallel the more specific role ascribed to management accounting at the very end of section 1.1. Also evident in the flow chart is the earlier-mentioned classification of management accounting techniques into the two branches of *decision accounting* and *control accounting*. (Note: Effectively speaking, the managerial function of *planning* is pervasive throughout all phases of the process. However, for practical purposes of the later arrangement of the book into Parts 2 and 3 it is, purely arbitrarily, more closely linked to control aspects/techniques rather than with decision-making.) By looking at the flow chart in Figure 1.1 we shall now proceed, phase-by-phase, to elaborate upon each constituent element within the process' overall structure.

figure 1.1
Structure of the management decision-making, planning and control process

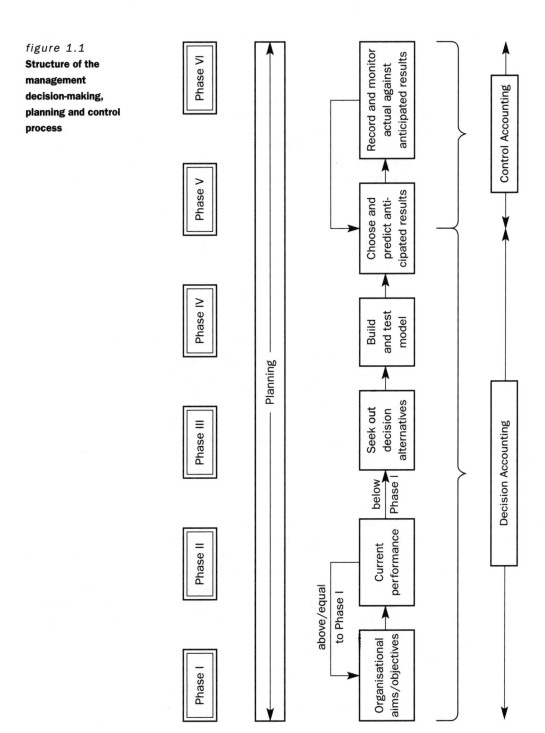

1.2.1 Flow chart – phase I

The first phase in the decision-making, planning and control process is concerned with establishing aims/objectives for the organisation. Put simply, the organisation needs to know where it wants to go. This is similar to setting out on a journey – it is advisable, if not indeed necessary, to know your desired destination (i.e. aim/objective) before beginning the trip. However, organisational aims/objectives are not always easy to determine, for various reasons. Consider here the range of different accounting information user groups presented to you earlier in the chapter in Table 1.1. To some degree these users are likely to have influence over the intended direction of the organisation, but inevitably will also have their own individual goals to pursue. For example, the shareholders who own the business may consider the aim of maximising organisational income and wealth to be of prime importance and largely consistent with their own ultimate likely objectives such as high dividend payouts, share value increases etc. But conflict may arise between other parties to the organisation (i.e. the various user groups) who will undoubtedly have vested interests of a different nature compared with those, say, of shareholders. Table 1.3 gives an indication of the types of individual aims and vested interests which other groups may consider paramount to the maximisation of the organisation's income and wealth.

In so far as survival of the business or firm is almost certainly going to depend upon income and wealth generation, then it might be argued that *all* user groups which are party to the organisation's continued existence will have an automatic interest in its future profitability and financial welfare. That may well be so but, to varying extents, such an interest will probably be of lesser importance compared to those sort of group interests relevant, for instance, to the users listed in Table 1.3. The last one of those user groups in particular, however, poses an interesting dilemma in that it is often taken for granted that management will instinctively strive to achieve the organisation's principal aim, say, of income and wealth maximisation. However, when the personal goals of managers functioning within certain types of organisation are observed, the assumption that they will be working in their firm's best interests can become open to doubt. One such type of organisation is the large, divisionalised, often multinational, company (or group of companies) whose divisional managers may in some circumstances be tempted to act in ways which best serve their own personal objectives at the expense of their organisation's. This sort of managerial behaviour is referred to as 'dysfunctional' or 'sub-optimal' behaviour, and it is this particular aspect of controlling divisional management performance which is explored in detail in Chapter 11 of this book. Other differing goals like those of environmentalist groups (i.e. 'green' objectives) can also perhaps influence the direction planned by an organisation. However, because it would be useful if we could settle upon a *single* particular objective, by and large the organisational goal adopted throughout the pages of this book is the one we mentioned first, i.e. that of income and wealth maximisation, regardless of whether income/wealth happens to be measured by cash flows, profits and losses, assets and liabilities.

table 1.3
Types of user group interest

User group	Aims/objectives/vested interests
Customers	Reliability of supply of organisation's products and/or services; type of credit facilities available.
Government	Collection of taxes and duties; enforcement of legal requirements.
Employees	Trade union activities; wage bargaining/settlements.
Management	Personal career ambitions; divorce of ownership from control; internal departmental struggles/conflict.

1.2.2 Flow chart – phase II

The process' second phase involves a continuous review of current operating performance followed by an immediate and subsequent comparison with the required performance as defined by the aims/objectives established in phase I. If it is found that current performance corresponds with the originally specified organisational goals, then two distinct eventualities present themselves:

(i) Management are satisfied that the original aims/objectives set out to be achieved are currently being attained or exceeded – and so the present strategy is continued in order to carry on reaching or exceeding the already established goals; *or*

(ii) Mere accomplishment/betterment of required performance (as per phase I) will only serve to raise management's level of expectations – and so the original organisational aims/objectives will be considered to be in need of upward revision.

Real problems arise, however, where current operating performance is discovered not to correspond with (i.e. falls below) the organisation's already stated aims/objectives. This is tantamount to the required performance level specified in phase I not being achieved. It then becomes necessary to look for other ways and means of attaining the original goals, which involves the decision-maker (management) proceeding to phase III of the decision accounting segment of the overall process. Before moving on it is worth noting that this act of discovering whether there is a correspondence (or not) between current and required performance is clearly reflected in the first of the two vital feedback relationships in the process, signified here by the loop linking phase II back to phase I. Also prior to considering phase III, it might prove useful, from a summary point of view, for you to capture the essence of the first two phases in the following sporting analogy which draws a parallel between the goals of an organisation and those of a 100-metres sprint athlete. Imagine that a UK-based international sprinter, specialising in the 100-metres event, sets a target of achieving this distance in ten seconds (i.e. this is his established aim/objective per phase I). Phase II is then about comparing performances. If he subsequently becomes capable of running a ten-second 100 metres, his reaction to his current performance being comparable with his planned/desired one will result in one of two things: he will either feel happy that he has reached his personal goal and not attempt to run any faster, *or* he will revise what he expects of himself and set a new target, for example, aim to achieve a time of 9.8 seconds for the 100 metres.

Subsequent performances are then compared with this newly established aim/objective . . . and so on. However, a real difficulty faces him if he finds he cannot manage to achieve a ten-second 100 metres, and this is the point in the process where the athlete must effectively move onto phase III! It is a tricky move because he will now need to look around and search to find some alternative way(s) of improving his performance to bring it up to his original goal of a 10-second 100-metres time. Preferably he will seek to do this by proper means such as changing his coach/trainer, or maybe looking to leave Great Britain for, say, the United States where training facilities and conditions are perhaps superior to those at home. A less desirable alternative, however, might be the temptation to consider more dubious means like deciding to use artificial aids or stimulants. Despite this alternative representing a highly undesirable (and indeed even illegal one in the eyes of athletics authorities) it is nevertheless still a very real option. Whatever the alternatives, phase III next involves the decision-maker (who will now revert back from being an athlete to being management) in the task of searching them out.

1.2.3 Flow chart – phase III

In this third phase of the process the organisation's management is seeking fresh alternative courses of action from which they must eventually choose the 'best', i.e. the one which serves to satisfy the maximisation aim of the decision-maker/management as set out in phase I's required organisational objectives. It is intended that the optimal decision alternative sought for will succeed in bridging the gap between the current sub-standard level of performance and the established goals the organisation is aiming to achieve. The search for decision alternatives will inevitably lead the organisation's management into investigating possibilities which bring them in touch with new environments – moreover, environments within which a great deal of risk and uncertainty might well exist. For example, to achieve its desired goals a firm may decide to replace outdated, obsolete plant and machinery in the factory with new 'high-tech' production facilities involving means such as computer-aided design and manufacturing (CAD/CAM) which employ advanced technical and automated equipment (e.g. robots) in preference to the more traditional labour-intensive modes of factory output. The risk/uncertainty factor may arise due to the firm having little or no previous knowledge and/or experience of such new systems including the range of potential suppliers of the equipment from which they must choose, i.e. the decision alternatives being the competing sources of supply. Alternatively an organisation, in attempting to reach its goals, may consider breaking new ground by entering into fresh markets for its products/services – markets previously alien, which might even prove to be hostile to it in the future, along with the chance of perhaps also encountering strong competition. Furthermore, and theoretically speaking, this phase of the process requires that, before deciding upon the best alternative, the decision-maker (management) must identify and assess all possible decision alternatives. This means in our examples, for instance, investigating every potential source of supply for new factory equipment or researching every possible market available for the firm to enter. In a realistic sense, in coming to its decision, management is unlikely to be quite so exhaustive in its considerations. (In Chapter 5, a perhaps more practical approach based upon acceptance of a satisfactory rather than 'perfect' alternative is suggested, in section 5.3.3, as a more feasible strategy for management decisions.) However, at this stage in the flow of the process, it is largely immaterial whether it is the ideal of establishing all possible alternatives or the rather more practical idea of a limited search involving not all possibilities is the one pursued. Quite simply, once a given range of decision alternatives has been established the decision-maker/management is then in a position to proceed to phase IV.

1.2.4 Flow chart – phase IV

The purpose behind building and testing a decision-making model is that it should help management to forecast the results or outcomes of the different decision alternatives established in phase III. Models can be highly sophisticated, technically and scientifically advanced 'tools' – excellent examples of this level of refinement are provided by the aerospace engineering and technology industries. Undoubtedly there must have been many years of developing and testing models/prototypes before, say, the first American space shuttle was launched successfully. Equally inevitably, there must also surely have been multitudes of occasions where models or prototypes were tested and discovered to be unsatisfactory or faulty, with the result that such malfunctions necessitated review and restructuring. No doubt major early failures and developmental disasters were kept firmly secret behind locked doors. You ought to remember, however, that models need not be quite so refined nor as sophisticated as those used in science and engineering. In the business world, for instance, many business models may effectively amount to being little more than simply tried and tested 'rules of thumb'. In the realms of accountancy, too, an accounting model can be as fundamentally straightforward as: *assets = capital + liabilities*.

By way of sharp contrast, however, highly developed computer corporate planning models are becoming increasingly common in both business and accountancy. Chapters 5 and 8 present you with various types of decision model both simple and more refined in terms of their use of probabilities and discounting techniques respectively. The essential role or intention of a decision model is that it helps management to foresee how much currently unsatisfactory performance can be improved by the different decision alternatives available, and to measure to what extent performance can then be brought up to an acceptable level consistent with original organisational objectives (see phase I). Once management have adopted a model tested suitable for its decision-making needs, then progress to phase V is possible.

1.2.5 Flow chart – phase V

Phase V is both an end and a beginning. Not only is it the final stage in the *decision accounting* segment of the overall process, but it is also the initial phase of the *control accounting* element of the flow chart. The first word in phase V is 'choose' – and it is the model (adopted per phase IV as the one most suitable) which provides management with its basis for choice, it is its decision tool. Use of the model will effectively rank the alternative courses of action open to management (remember, these were the decision alternatives established in phase III of the process). The order of preference in which the model will rank the alternatives will be the best combination/mix available to management in terms of correspondence with the organisation's original goals set out at the start of the process. Linear programming, for example, described in Chapter 12, is one technique out of a range of several, really quite sophisticated quantitative/operational research models which help management in its planning and decision-making by determining accurately the optimal mix or strategy to be followed to achieve maximum economy, efficiency etc. Another such model or technique is a planning tool used widely by managements of organisations which is known as 'materials requirements planning' – and this, too, is covered in Chapter 12 along with linear programming. Having thus chosen the best, i.e. optimal, plan then management's decision is made. This signifies the end of decision accounting in the process and heralds for you the start of control accounting. The initial requirement of the control process is that management establishes a formal statement based upon its prediction (see phase V wording after 'choose') of the results anticipated from adoption of the optimal plan. This formal statement appears in the shape of *budgets* which in themselves constitute the component parts of the budgetary control process of an organisation. Budgeting by its nature necessitates two things:

(i) the making of predictions or estimates (cost prediction/estimation is dealt with in Chapter 3); and
(ii) the consolidation of individual/subsidiary budgets into the master budget for planning and control purposes. Individual or subsidiary budgets are sometimes referred to as functional budgets because they set out the plans for the different functions of the organisation (e.g. sales, production, purchasing, research and development). These are combined together, i.e. consolidated, to form the master (or summary) budget which reflects the total plan for achieving the organisation's aims/objectives. This summarising of the various functional budgets provides a master budget for the firm consisting of a budgeted profit and loss account, budgeted balance sheet and a budgeted cash-flow statement. The budget period is normally an annual one, but can be shorter/longer according to the nature of the business (e.g. seasonal) or the industry (e.g. contracting). Much longer term budgets, say, five years and more will tend to be classified differently as strategic/corporate plans rather than the more short-term ones. (Budgeting is described in detail in Chapter 9).

1.2.6 Flow chart – phase VI

This is the last phase (but is one which is also linked in a feedback relationship, to phase V, signified by the second of the process's two important feedback loops.). If budgets are well constructed, i.e. neither too slack (too easily attainable) nor too tight (an impractical ideal which is realistically unattainable), then reaching budgeted targets can rightly be assumed as tantamount to achieving organisational objectives. To ascertain whether budgets have in fact been met, or not, necessarily entails the recording of actual results. Subsequent comparison of these actual results with those anticipated or planned (i.e. budgeted) constitutes the vital managerial function known as *monitoring* – the essence of this final control phase. Control statements, on both a routine as well as an *ad hoc* basis, will enable management to take necessary remedial action where variances from plan/budget are relatively significant ones, this being an indication that the system is potentially out of control. Typical examples of control statements are detailed analyses of variances which highlight any significant deviations from budget. Variance analysis is dealt with in Chapter 10 under standard costing. In standard costing systems the standards used are effectively the equivalent control measure to that of budgets in budgetary control. Generated by the monitoring process, these control statements are crucial to managers if they are to take quick and timely measures to bring control back to the system. Fundamentally speaking, the whole question of control hinges upon feedback which is illustrated in the flow chart by the second and final loop-back effect to phase V.

Progressing through the process, phase-by-phase, you may have noticed that nearly every subsequent chapter in the book has been mentioned at least once in passing through the flow chart. Whether you did or did not notice is really *not* important! However, the appearance of almost every chapter in the description of the process is indicative of how essentially it underpins all of the individual management accounting techniques that follow. Although not always easy to do, as you learn the *specific* detail of each technique try not to lose sight of the *general* 'scheme of things' *vis-à-vis* the intentions of the book overall. Having established the book's general theme, we next move on to consider a variety of different individual topics/issues with regard to the study of managerial accounting.

Notes
••••••••

1. American Accounting Association (1966) *A statement of basic accounting theory*.
2. Horngren, C.T. (1965) *Introduction to management accounting*, 1st edn, Hemel Hempstead: Prentice-Hall International.
3. Horngren, C.T. (1962) *Cost accounting: a managerial emphasis*, 1st edn, Hemel Hempstead: Prentice-Hall International.
4. Arnold, J. and Hope, T. (1990) *Accounting for management decisions*, 2nd edn, Hemel Hempstead: Prentice-Hall International.
5. Ibid.
6. Sizer, J. (1989) *An insight into management accounting*, 3rd edn, Harmondsworth: Penguin.
7. CIMA (1991) *Management accounting: official terminology*, Chartered Institute of Management Accountants.
8. Sizer, op cit.

Further study

Arnold, J. and Hope, T. (1990) *Accounting for management decisions*, 2nd edn, Hemel Hempstead: Prentice-Hall.

Drury, C. (1992) *Management and cost accounting*, 3rd edn, London: Chapman and Hall.

Glautier, M. and Underdown, B. (1994) *Accounting theory and practice*, 5th edn, London: Pitman.

Hopwood, A. (1974) *Accounting and human behaviour*, 1st edn, Hemel Hempstead: Prentice-Hall.

Horngren, C.T., Foster, G. and Datar, S. (1994) *Cost accounting – a managerial emphasis*, 8th edn, Hemel Hempstead: Prentice-Hall.

Horngren, C.T. and Sundem, G. (1993) *Introduction to management accounting*, 9th edn, Hemel Hempstead: Prentice-Hall.

Ryan, B. and Hobson, J. (1985) *Management accounting – a contemporary approach*, 1st edn, London: Pitman.

Scapens, R.W. (1991) *Management accounting – a review of recent developments*, 2nd edn, Basingstoke: Macmillan.

Sizer, J. (1989) *An insight into management accounting*, 3rd edn, Harmondsworth: Penguin.

PART 1

Cost analysis
techniques
....

CHAPTER 2

Cost ascertainment
and costing techniques

Objectives

By the end of this chapter you should be able to:

▶ Understand the purposes and means of ascertaining full unit product cost.
▶ Describe cost structures and the various ways in which to classify costs.
▶ Apply the ascertainment techniques of full absorption costing and activity based costing.
▶ Recognise and explain a wide range of fundamental/introductory cost accounting terms.

A key part of management accounting, and a necessary prerequisite to applying its techniques (in parts 2 and 3), is the study and analysis of costs. In fact a slightly expanded description that you might often encounter is *cost and management accounting*. Moreover, the specialist professional accounting body in this area, CIMA was previously called the 'Institute of Cost and Management Accountants'. The cost analysis techniques in Part 1 therefore provide a vital platform for you to move onto the application of managerial accounting techniques later. It is important to understand how, and by what means, costs have been determined (i.e. ascertained) before using them for the decision-making, planning and control accounting techniques employed by management. This first area of study – the techniques for analysing and ascertaining costs – is known as *cost accounting* or *costing*.

2.1 Costs and cost accounting/costing

Accounting for costs in the sense of recording, i.e. cost book-keeping, will not be covered in this book. This is because the focus of attention is specifically upon the application of useful techniques for management's purposes rather than the maintenance of accounting systems for the keeping of cost records. The aim is to impart an appreciation of techniques rather than mechanics. You should be aware, however, that the accounting numbers appearing throughout the book need of course to have come from somewhere, largely from information systems such as accounting databases or books of accounts which we assume already do exist and contain the relevant cost information. Costs held in these stores of information will be either:

▶ past costs (i.e. historic cost records in the accounts); or
▶ budgeted costs (i.e. embodied/predetermined in forecasts, estimates, standards, budget schedules etc.).

Indeed, all manner of expenditure can be identified as past *actual* costs which have already occurred or future *budgeted* costs planned for and expected to be incurred. As plans rarely (if ever) coincide exactly with what actually happens, there will virtually always be a difference between actual and budgeted cost – in cost accounting terms this is referred to as a 'variance' from budget (or standard) and is dealt with later in Chapter 10. In the case of overhead it may also be called an 'under/over-absorption' of cost which is covered in this chapter under the technique of absorption costing in section 2.2.1. In short, the description of expenditure as either historic or future is just one way of classifying costs. Further cost classifications, important cost concepts like cost centres and cost units, and techniques underpinning cost ascertainment now follow.

Opportunity, notional, environmental and social costs, which are particularly difficult to quantify, will not be dealt with in this book (with the exception of *opportunity cost* dealt with briefly on pages 150–1).

2.1.1 The object of cost ascertainment

What are we aiming to ascertain the cost of? From a management information viewpoint it is vital that accountants are in a position to provide managers with details about what it costs, for instance, to generate output, supply services, run processes and, in the final analysis, manage entire organisations. Management accountants have available to them a range of costing techniques through which they are able to offer such information. In this chapter two 'full' cost ascertainment methods are described – 'traditional' absorption costing in section 2.2 and activity based costing in 2.3. The meaning of the term *full cost* will soon become apparent, and it will be seen to contrast sharply with another costing technique dealt with later in the book – marginal costing (Chapter 4). But still the question remains: what specific object is it that the accountant, by applying a particular costing technique, is attempting to determine or ascertain the cost of? The short answer is: the cost of a *cost unit*. Perhaps the simplest way to bring to mind typical examples of what might comprise cost units is to think of the end-product of a business. In a manufacturing environment it would include the production or completion of items such as:

▶ consumer durables in a mass-production plant;
▶ batches of clothes/shoes in a clothing/shoemaking firm;
▶ barrels of oil, chemicals, beer etc. in a processing business;
▶ job orders in a factory;
▶ building contracts in the construction industry.

In the above cases each consumer durable, batch, barrel, job and contract would probably best be regarded as an individual cost unit in its own right.

Can you think ...? of further examples likely to be designated as cost units in the following organisations:

(i)   a hospital;
(ii) a computer hardware manufacturer;
(iii) a transport undertaking;
(iv) a printer or publisher;
(v)   a hotel caterer;
(vi) a college or university.

Answer

(i) Beds occupied/outpatient day-visits; (ii) Computer printer/keyboard; (iii) Passenger-mile/tonne-mile; (iv) Book/magazine; (v) Guest nights/meals served; (vi) Courses provided/full-time equivalent (FTE) students.

The whole point of cost ascertainment via a given suitable costing technique is to 'cost out' (either in 'full' or in 'marginal' cost terms) the value of a final product. Furthermore, we will see that not only the cost of finished items/goods can be costed by these techniques, but also that they offer means of valuing partially complete products – such units in an unfinished state are referred to as work-in-progress or work-in-process (W-I-P).

Finally, and perhaps most importantly, another objective of cost ascertainment is to provide, for income determination purposes, the figure for *cost of goods sold*. This figure, when deducted from sales revenue, gives the business's gross profit for a period. To summarise, unit cost ascertainment helps satisfy two vital accounting information needs:

(i)   Valuation of stocks of products – both finished articles as well as partly finished goods (W-I-P); and hence
(ii) Income determination – calculation of profit or loss.

This book will tend to concentrate almost exclusively on manufacturing environments rather than operations or services. In the alternative business environment of operations/service industries (e.g. transport, hospitals, education, hotels etc.) unit cost ascertainment is achieved relatively straightforwardly – by dividing total organisational costs by the number of operation/service units provided to arrive at *cost per unit*. For example, the total cost of a transport undertaking divided by the number of miles travelled would give the cost per mile – in the case of passenger transport: cost per passenger-mile; if freight transport: cost per tonne-mile.

2.1.2 The role of cost centres

To find their way to a specific cost unit, costs (particularly overheads) need to have a 'route' through which the product's unit cost can be ascertained. This route is provided by collection points or channels called *cost centres*. The flow of costs through the main arterial channels, i.e. cost centres, ending up in cost unit cost is shown in Figure 2.1.

figure 2.1
**Flow of costs into
unit cost**

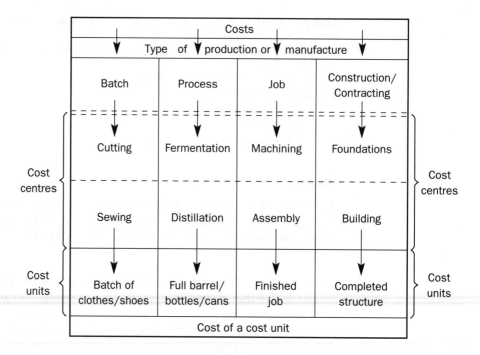

As a product travels through its stages of manufacture it attracts costs in each cost centre through which it passes. Cost centres are a vital ingredient in the costing system's aim to ascertain cost via application of a suitable technique, e.g. absorption costing (see section 2.2). Although Figure 2.1 shows, for illustration purposes only, a couple of cost centres for each type of production activity, in manufacturing environments there will inevitably in practice be many more. In a factory, for instance, jobs may require preparation, treatment, machining, assembling, trimming, painting, finishing . . . and so on.

Furthermore, cost centres will need to be established for other activities linked closely to production but not actually creating the end-product itself. Figure 2.1 only shows *production* cost centres that physically generate the product cost unit; but typical examples of these 'other activities linked closely to production' would include (once more, say, in a factory): maintenance, inspection, supervision, materials handling, production control, power, stores etc. Such kinds of cost centre are referred to as *service* cost centres which exist solely to support production rather than to generate cost unit output themselves. In short, all manner of manufacture-related cost centres can be described as being either:

▶ production cost centres – through which the product cost unit actually passes; or
▶ service cost centres – providing important support facilities to production but not producing *per se* (these are sometimes alternatively called 'utility' cost centres).

A little more remote from the activity of manufacturing itself there may also be other support amenities like canteens and boiler houses; however, these would still be recognised as qualifying for service cost centre status as they support production. But further removed from production we can clearly identify distinctly separate organisational functions such as marketing, administration, and research and development (R&D). Although these functional activities are absolutely vital to the business (and themselves could be broken down into cost centres, such as selling, distribution, warehousing etc.) generally their costing treatment will differ, and these costs will not end up as an ingredient in the ascertained cost of a product cost unit; reasons for this and a brief description of their different treatment are given in section 2.2.

2.1.3 Classification of cost

We have already seen that describing cost as being either 'future' or 'historic' was just one means by which costs might be *classified*. In the paragraph above, another possible way of classifying cost was described – into categories such as production, marketing, administration and R&D costs etc. This type of category is known as classification *by function*. The importance of classifying cost in this or some other way stems from its use in managerial planning, decision-making and control accounting situations. For cost information to be at all useful it needs first to be classified so that managers are able to understand it. Faced with an item of cost information a manager may, for example, wish to know whether it is an advertising or market research cost; a storage or distribution cost; a labour or materials cost; a direct or indirect cost; a fixed or variable cost . . . and so on. These kinds of cost classification will become increasingly apparent through this book. While there is virtually no limit to ways of categorising or classifying costs, here we will concentrate on the four most common and useful categorisations for management accounting purposes, that is cost classified by *function*, by *behaviour*, by *nature* and by *element* (see Figure 2.2).

Functional classification has already been explained above; categorisation by behaviour pattern will be dealt with in detail in Chapter 3; in the next section we look at classification by nature and by element.

figure 2.2
Cost classification

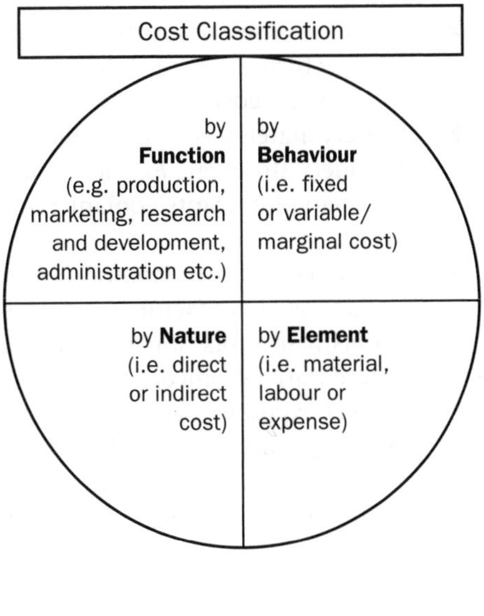

table 2.1
**Total cost structured
by nature and by
element**

Direct materials	+	Indirect materials	=	Total material cost
Direct labour	+	Indirect labour	=	Total labour cost
Direct expenses	+	Indirect expenses	=	Total expenses
Prime cost	+	Overheads	=	Total cost

2.1.4 Cost structures and build-up

Direct costs, assuming it is economically viable to do so, are those that can be readily identified with an individual cost unit, whereas indirect (overhead) costs cannot. Every item of cost can be recognised as being either direct or indirect cost – this is classification 'by nature'. All costs imaginable are also identifiable as material, labour or expense items – this is classification 'by element' of cost. By combining these two classification systems and also by introducing a couple of new terms (i.e. prime cost and overhead) we arrive at the twelve cost descriptions in the summary build-up in Table 2.1 – a structure of costs which is fundamental to any study of cost and management accounting.

In short, all direct costs are the *prime* costs of manufacture; together with *overhead* they make up the total cost of a product cost unit. To give a tangible idea of each of the terms in Table 2.1 combining cost element with nature of cost, consider the following further details:

▶ Direct material cost: raw materials, bought-in components, sub-assemblies, mainstream stores items etc. *Examples*: engines in cars; meat/vegetables in food processing; bricks in buildings; timber/metal in furniture; electronic components in technological/scientific hardware.

▶ Direct labour cost: production/manufacturing workers employed directly on the job, personal service direct to customer etc. *Examples*: labour force employees directly engaged in areas such as factory shop floors in manufacturing firms; assembly-line workers in mass-production organisations; counter staff in shops; building site workers in construction/contracting industries; drivers on buses and trains.

▶ Direct expenses: production royalties payable to holders of manufacturing/patent rights, hire of special machine tools for 'one-off' jobs etc. This category of cost is in practice very rare.

▶ Indirect material cost: consumable stores, maintenance materials, stationery stores etc. *Examples*: cleaning fluids and materials; office stationery; lubricants/coolants; minor adhesives, loose tools, nails, tacks, screws.

▶ Indirect labour cost: labour force employees not directly engaged in production/manufacture, processes, services, etc. *Examples*: progress chasers/inspectors; supervisory staff; maintenance/stores staff; sales representatives; office/executive staff.

▶ Indirect expenses: occupancy costs, capital and finance costs, legal and amenity/utility costs etc. *Examples*: rent and rates; depreciation/interest charges; insurances; telecommunications; heating/lighting; power for machinery/equipment; bank charges; fees and penalties/fines.

How would you ...? identify the following cost items classified into one (and only one!) of the above six categories combining element with nature of cost:

(i) glue in a clothes or furniture manufacturer to supplement or reinforce stitches and joints;
(ii) a laboratory assistant's salary in a chemical company/ordnance factory;
(iii) cast iron girders in an industrial crane manufacturer;
(iv) staples in a magazine printers;
(v) production company payment to an accountancy firm for an external audit;
(vi) hairdresser's wages in a hairdressing salon;
(vii) forklift vehicle driver's wages in handling and moving factory materials;
(viii) computer VDU screens in a PC manufacturer;
(ix) professional soccer player's wages in a football club.

Answer

(i) Indirect material; (ii) Indirect labour; (iii) Direct material; (iv) Indirect material; (v) Indirect expense; (vi) Direct labour; (vii) Indirect labour; (viii) Direct material; (ix) Direct labour.

To additionally reinforce your understanding of this important build-up/aggregate cost structure, go back to Figure 2.1 and consider its development into Figure 2.3. (Note: There is no chronological sequence involved, say, downwards in Figure 2.3. The diagram is not meant to indicate overhead cost being associated with cost units *before* prime cost. Cost ascertainment procedures involving prime cost and overheads occur simultaneously. The flow in Figure 2.3 represents a build-up of cost, *not* a passage of time.)

In product cost ascertainment direct/prime costs pose very few problems because they can easily be traced fully and accurately to the cost unit.[1] The real difficulty in ascertaining total (i.e. 'full') unit cost lies with the overheads/indirect costs of the product, and it is to this issue that the next two major sections are devoted. How, for instance, can a suitable portion of rent and rates be associated as a part-ingredient of the relevant overhead to be included in the full cost build-up of a product cost unit? The answer is that overhead can be identified with individual cost units via one of two full cost approaches, either:

(i) by a technique based on the use of absorption rates (section 2.2); or
(ii) by a technique which centres on the very activities which cause, or 'drive', the overheads themselves (section 2.3).

2.2 Absorption costing technique
....

The important principle underlying the absorption costing technique is that an amount of cost needs to be 'soaked up' by the product cost unit to cover (or, more correctly in an accounting sense, recover) production overhead attributable to that same cost unit. To this production overhead thus absorbed/recovered is added the product's prime cost in order to ascertain total or full

figure 2.3
**Flow of costs
(development of
Figure 2.1)**

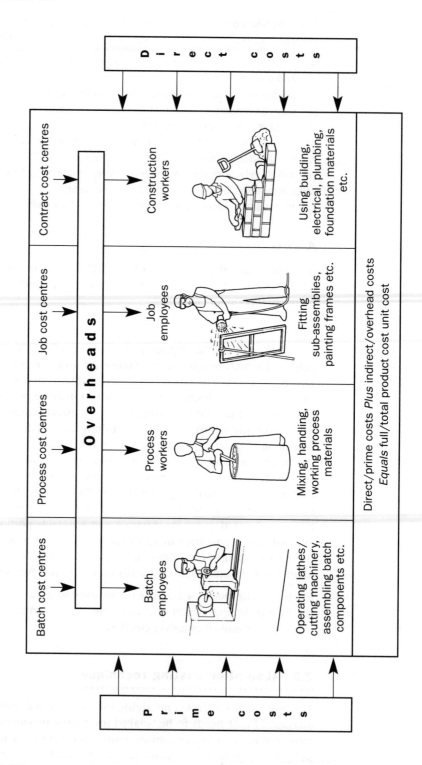

product unit cost – Figure 2.3 depicts this build-up. The terms 'absorption' and 'recovery' have precisely the same meaning in costing and are entirely interchangeable. Put simply:

prime cost + absorbed production overhead = full product cost

The first point to notice clearly is that the costing technique in this section will only absorb production overhead costs. There are occasions where it may be suitable to 'go the whole full cost way' and also absorb general overheads (such as marketing, administration and R&D costs) into unit cost too. But these occasions are rare, mainly for two reasons:

1   Production overhead comprises indirect costs of the function most closely concerned with the actual generation of the product cost unit. Other business functions, like marketing, are generally perceived to be more remote.

2   Reporting standards laid down by the accountancy profession[2] require that accounts show product stock valuations inclusive of relevant *production* overhead. Remember that valuation of stock is one of the key information objectives of product cost ascertainment (see discussion in section 2.1.1).

So, to the extent that absorption costing is known as a 'full cost' technique, the total product unit cost that it ascertains recovers only production overhead. This gives a full production cost per unit with general overheads being treated differently (briefly described in section 2.2.4 later). Furthermore, the overhead recovered by the absorption costing technique will in almost all cases be based on an estimated or *budgeted* amount.

2.2.1 Budgeted/estimated overhead

In section 2.1 it was said that 'all manner of expenditure can be identified as past *actual* costs which have already occurred or future *budgeted* costs planned for and expected to be incurred'. (Note that, as already mentioned in the first sentence of section 2.1.3, this distinction between 'past actual' and 'future budgeted' costs is yet another means of categorising or classifying cost.) You can safely assume that from hereon when full cost techniques are used to absorb indirect costs into product unit cost the overheads involved are budgeted overhead, i.e. instead of using actual historical costs, more relevantly budgeted figures for a future period or periods will be used.

This is more relevant because budgeted data derive from what accountants and managers estimate to be likely levels of cost in the future and are formally set out in the shape of cost forecasts, budgets and standard costs (these issues are dealt with in much more detail in Chapters 3, 9 and 10). Essentially the reason why absorption costing uses budgeted data is that actual information about overheads will nearly always become available only after, and sometimes well after, the costing period-end. Such actual historic data are far too late for management planning and control purposes like product pricing, production scheduling, compilation of product cost estimates etc. In

DID YOU KNOW ...?
that indirect expenses in the United States of America are often not referred to as overhead, but by the term **burden**. *This gives a rather colourful and vivid picture of costs that hang 'over the head' of the business placing a heavy load upon the organisation. The term is also commonly used in American subsidiary companies operating in the UK.*

addition they are also too late for many routine accounting functions such as customer invoicing.

For instance, take the case of a garage bill presented to a car owner for a respray job carried out in the garage's paint-spray shop. Although very often the actual invoice will not contain all costs in detail, separately and individually itemised, the price charged on the invoice to the customer will nevertheless need to cover all prime costs, such as:

▶ the paint used on the job – i.e. direct materials; and
▶ the spray painter's wages – i.e. direct labour.

In addition to the above prime cost of the job the price will also need to include an amount to recover the garage's indirect costs, i.e. overhead. The actual costs of paint used and the wage paid to the spray painter will be available immediately the job is completed. However, overhead costs incurred by the garage (such as the electricity bill for heating and lighting the spray shop) will only be known perhaps much later, when the electricity bill arrives.

The garage owner, on the other hand, is hardly likely to apologise to the car owner, saying 'I'm sorry but you'll have to wait till my bills for overheads come in before I can invoice you'! The invoice price charged will need to cover the actual prime costs of the job plus an estimated (i.e. budgeted) amount to allow for recovery of business overheads.

Under/over-absorption of overhead

Irrespective of how good estimates might be in approximating to what actually happens they are rarely (if ever) accurate to the penny, to the pound or even thousands of pounds, particularly in larger organisations. There is almost always bound to be a difference between estimated/budgeted and actual cost. In the context of overhead absorption this difference is known as an under/over-absorption. As a concept under/over-absorptions are extremely simple – they entail nothing more than a comparison of overhead actually incurred with the budgeted amount absorbed. This comparison produces the difference just mentioned and results in one of two things, namely:

(a) actual overhead is greater than the budgeted amount absorbed – this is an *under-absorption*; or
(b) actual overhead is less than the budgeted amount absorbed – this is an *over-absorption*.

In (a) above not enough overhead has been recovered while in case (b) above too much has been absorbed. The accounting treatment of under/over-absorptions is that under-absorptions are 'bad' and need charging against profits, i.e. *debit* profit and loss account (P&L) with the amount of the under-absorption. On the other hand over-absorptions are regarded as 'good' because they add to profits, i.e. *credit* P&L with the amount of the over-absorption. As briefly mentioned near the beginning of section 2.1, in standard costing (see Chapter 10) the now familiar 'difference' between actual and expected/planned cost (represented there by standard costs, which are virtually identical in principle to budgeted costs) is referred to as a 'variance'. You will notice in Chapter 10 that a similar cost accounting treatment is given to variances as is given here to under/over-absorptions. In the part of the book where overhead variances are analysed, under-absorptions are again recognised as a bad thing and being undesirable are called *adverse variances*. Conversely, over-absorptions are once more considered to be a good result being referred to as *favourable variances*.

2.2.2 Overhead absorption

In this and the next section (2.3) we are again concerned with overheads/indirect costs – and the absorption into unit product cost of such overhead. We have already said that direct/prime costs pose virtually no problems for the task of unit cost ascertainment. They can clearly and very easily be related to cost units such as jobs, batches, processes and contracts. You might take the opportunity here to look again at both Figures 2.1 and 2.3 which 'picture the scene' of costs passing through cost centres towards the final build-up of full cost unit cost. The important role played by cost centres has previously been discussed in detail (section 2.1.2) and their importance continues now because they not only represent collection points for prime cost to be associated with cost units, as the unit progresses through its stages of manufacture, but also because they act as channels in which indirect costs accumulate, to be treated in a way that results in the overhead finally being traced to individual product cost units by the process known as *absorption*. Technically speaking, overhead absorption into unit cost (via absorption rates) is the final step of a three-stage treatment process. The full costing procedure for treatment of overheads can be summed up by the '3 As': **A**llocate; **A**pportion; **A**bsorb.

Before we deal with the '3 As', you should first remember that we are concerned only with *production* overheads. Second, these overheads can be either included in product unit cost (as they are here through the absorption process) or be treated differently under an alternative principle known as the 'marginal costing' technique. What marginal costing does is recognise that the vast majority of overheads tend to be time-orientated (fixed or period) costs and therefore writes the whole of such overhead off against profit in the P&L account (i.e. not just the under/over-absorption as demonstrated at the end of section 2.1.1.) drawn up for the relevant cost accounting period in which the fixed overhead cost is incurred. This radically different treatment of fixed overhead cost will be described fully in the marginal costing chapter (Chapter 4) after the characteristic behaviour of fixed costs has been comprehensively detailed in Chapter 3. Now back to the '3 As'; first of all: *Allocation* and *Apportionment*.

2.2.3 Allocation and apportionment of overhead

During their manufacture, product cost units progress through various cost centres and the absorption costing technique ensures that each individual cost unit is allocated and/or apportioned (and finally absorbs) an equitable or proportional amount of cost centre overhead (see Figures 2.1 and 2.3). This fair measure of cost is achieved by using the cost centres as either:

▶ allocation points if a whole, discrete item of overhead cost can be identified in full with a single cost centre; or

▶ apportionment areas if an overhead item is incurred by a number of centres and needs, for the sake of fairness, to be shared between them.

As a general rule, allocate whenever and wherever possible. Allocation would be feasible, for instance, where a cost centre manager spends all his/her time in charge of just one single cost centre, say, the machine shop. The whole of the manager's salary, for example, could then be allocated in full (with no need for apportionment) to the machine shop cost centre.

Unfortunately, allocation of complete items of cost to one specific cost centre is often simply not possible. It would not be fair, for instance, to charge the whole of a supervisor's wage to only one centre if that supervisor carries out his or her supervisory duties over several cost centres; for example, half the time overseeing machining, and a quarter of the time each in supervising assembly and finishing areas. An equitable share-out of his or her wage would probably be to base it on time spent in the cost centres – in this case 50 per cent to the machine shop, 25 per cent to assembly and 25 per cent to the finishing area cost centres. This brings us to the next important issue, that is determining suitable and equitable bases of apportionment for different categories of overhead cost item that cannot be allocated wholly. To summarise, if allocation of whole costs is not fair or feasible, then you should apportion on some suitable/equitable basis.

Bases of apportionment

It is probably true to say that the major part of production overhead in practice comprises cost items that cannot conveniently be allocated as whole cost to a single, specific cost centre. Because of this it is important that the cost accountant determines fair bases upon which to carry out the exercise of overhead cost apportionment across cost centres. Also, because cost centre managers will be responsible for the control of costs incurred by their cost centres (often in addition referred to as *responsibility centres* – see Chapter 11), it will be vital to achieve a consensus of agreement amongst centre managers that the cost apportionment bases used are indeed fair to the managers themselves! Logically the bases, determined by mutual agreement with the cost centre managers involved, will be the ones that most suitably and equitably reflect the benefits gained by those managers' own individual centres from the overhead costs incurred.

For instance, if a manager's department occupies a proportionately larger area of the factory than any other centre, then that cost centre manager presumably could not logically argue against more rent and rates, say, being charged to his or her department relative to other centres, because floor area doubtlessly reflects best the benefit received from the cost of occupying that area. This example along with several others appears in Table 2.2, which contains various logical, relevant and fair bases for apportioning overheads that are typically evident in a production environment.

One final matter remains regarding allocation and/or apportionment and it again concerns cost centres. In section 2.1.2 manufacture-related cost centres were differentiated and identified as two types according to whether they:

▶ actually physically generated the output of cost units (i.e. *production* cost centres); or

table 2.2

Bases for overhead cost apportionment

Categories of overhead cost item	Apportionment bases	Categories of overhead cost item	Apportionment bases
Health and welfare of employees	Personnel numbers	Lighting and heating of buildings	Building size, i.e. volume (m³) of departments etc.
Operation of stores	Stores requisitions issued		
Works library and canteen	Personnel numbers	Insurance and depreciation of equipment, buildings, plant and machinery	Asset cost/book value
Rent and rates; occupancy costs	Floor area (m²) of departments etc.	Inspection, supervision and maintenance	Inspectors, supervisors and maintenance time/hours

▶ supplemented the actual production activity through offering important support facilities (i.e. *service* cost centres).

To complete the apportionment process it is necessary to clear out the overhead cost initially attributed to service cost centres – already achieved through the original (primary) allocation/apportionment exercise – by transferring, i.e. reapportioning the service cost centre overhead to production cost centres. This procedure is commonly known as *secondary* apportionment. The rationale behind it is that service centres do not themselves have actual product cost units to ultimately absorb the production overhead.

2.2.4 Absorption of production overhead

The last 'A' of the '3 As': after the service cost centre overhead has been reapportioned, again using a suitable and fair basis (see Table 2.2) for this secondary apportionment step, then the overhead cost now sitting solely in production cost centres can finally be absorbed into the product cost unit. This is achieved by means of *absorption rates* computed for each production cost centre. Once more a logical, commonsense approach needs to be adopted for calculating a relevant rate for each centre. The nature of the manufacturing work being carried out by the centre will determine how the absorption rate is arrived at.

For example, in a machine shop the predominant form of work carried out focuses upon and is based around the operation or running of machines; therefore the number of machine hours is relevant. Also (although manufacturing environments are rapidly changing – see section 2.3) in assembling products the dominant form of endeavour revolves, in traditional industries, around the direct use of labour to physically put the product cost unit together. So in an assembly area cost centre, direct labour hours (or even direct labour cost) would traditionally provide the most logical base for computing an absorption rate for that centre.

In the worked illustration that follows (Activity 2.1) you will in fact use these two types of absorption rate (a machine hour rate for machining, and a labour hour rate for assembly) in the final stage of the allocation, apportionment and absorption process for ascertaining product unit cost. You should, however, be aware of other possible bases for calculating relevant absorption rates that might be encountered in practice. They include the following:

▶ percentage of prime cost
▶ percentage of direct wages
▶ percentage of direct materials cost.

Note: Even the number of product cost units passing through the cost centres could be used as a base, but this is highly unlikely in practical circumstances.

Before embarking on Activity 2.1 remember from section 2.2.1 that all the figures (e.g. numbers of hours, overhead cost data etc.) will be entirely predetermined or budgeted amounts. Budgeted estimates, being the vehicle used to calculate absorption rates, will inevitably lead to differences arising when the estimated data are eventually compared with actual data after the end of a cost accounting period. The result of the comparison is an under/over-absorption of overhead, and as this matter was covered in some detail in section 2.2.1, refer back to that section now in order to refresh your memory. A final piece of information is to provide the general formula used for computing individual absorption rates for each production cost centre:

$$\frac{\text{Budgeted cost centre overhead}}{\text{Budgeted number of cost centre hours}} = \text{Budgeted absorption rate per hour}$$

ACTIVITY **2.1**

Midbatch & Co. Limited is an old-established manufacturing firm, using traditionally based batch production methods, specialising in the machining and assembly of batch components in just two main production cost centres – the lathe machine shop and a batch components assembly area. Supporting production is a single but large production control/maintenance department which is designated a service cost centre. Budgeted overhead costs and other estimates relating to the next cost accounting period are given below.

Cost centre information/estimates

| | [Production cost centres] | | [Service cost centre] |
	Machine shop	Assembly area	Control/maintenance
Equipment, buildings and plant and machinery book value (£ million)	12	8	4
Budgeted machine hours	5,000	–	–
Size of buildings/departments (m³)	12,000	24,000	16,000
Budgeted labour hours	2,850	3,750	2,850
Budgeted control/maintenance hours	1,710	1,140	(2,850)
Employee numbers	12	16	12
Floor area (m²)	6,000	6,000	6,000

BUDGETED OVERHEAD IS ESTIMATED AS FOLLOWS:

	£000
Equipment, buildings and plant and machinery depreciation	900
Light and heat	195
Rent and rates	750
Other occupancy costs	105
Insurances	150
Works canteen, health and welfare costs	300
Allocated costs (e.g. indirect labour, consumable materials etc.)	345
Total overhead budgeted for the period	2,745

Batches require 2 hours machining in the lathe machine shop and spend one hour in the batch components assembly area. Prime cost of direct materials and direct labour for a typical batch cost unit (serial number #4451) comprises £402 and £200 respectively.

Required: Prepare an overhead distribution schedule from which to calculate budgeted overhead absorption rates for both machine shop and assembly area, finally applying these budgeted rates to ascertain the full product cost of cost unit batch #4451.

Usually the most suitable starting point is for you to begin compiling the overhead schedule with the cost allocation items – this is the overhead amounting to £345,000 which is capable of being allocated straight to specific cost centres because this figure comprises whole, discrete items of cost (inclusive of such overheads as the particular cost centre managers' salaries; indirect materials issued specifically to individual centres etc.). Purely by coincidence the allocation amounts happen to be the same per centre. All other overhead you need to apportion, firstly across all cost centres (i.e. primary apportionment) followed by the control/maintenance service cost centre costs being 're-apportioned' over the two production cost centres (i.e. secondary apportionment) in accordance with the details you are provided with above. Your overhead distribution schedule will take shape as follows:

Overhead cost	Basis of apportionment	Production cost centres Machine shop (£000)	Assembly area (£000)	Service cost centre Control/ maintenance (£000)	Total (£000)
Allocated items	–	115	115	115	345
Depreciation	Asset book values	450	300	150	900
Rent and rates	Floor Area	250	250	250	750
Other occupancy costs	Floor Area	35	35	35	105
Insurances	Asset book values	75	50	25	150
Light and heat	Size/volume	45	90	60	195
Works canteen etc.	Number of employees	90	120	90	300
		1,060	960	725	2,745
Control/maintenance	Time/hours	435	290	(725)	
Overhead attributed to production centres:		1,495	1,250	–	

The final stage in the absorption costing technique procedure is to absorb the production cost centre overhead costs into the product cost unit (i.e. batch #4451) via application of a suitable absorption rate. In Midbatch's case, machine hours are taken to be the relevant base for the machine shop, and labour hours as the most suitable for the assembly area which is purely labour-intensive in nature. Your budgeted absorption rates for each of the production cost centres are computed thus:

	Machine shop	Assembly area
Budgeted cost centre overhead	£1,495,000	£1,250,000
Budgeted number of cost centre hours	5,000 hours	3,750 hours
∴ Budgeted overhead absorption rates =	£299 per machine hour	£333.33 per labour hour

When you apply (to the nearest £) the above rates to Midbatch's product cost unit, your full (absorption) production cost of finished components batch #4451 is ascertained as follows.

	(£)
Direct materials	402
Direct labour	200
Prime cost	602
Overheads absorbed:	
Machine shop (2 hrs @ £299/hr.)	598
Assembly area (1 hr. @ £333/hr.)	333
Full batch product cost unit cost	£1,533

Secondary apportionment with reciprocal services

In Activity 2.1 there existed only a single service cost centre (control/maintenance). If there were, say, another service centre (like a boiler house or power supply department for example) its costs too would need to be 'secondary' apportioned to the production cost centres. Furthermore, the situation known as *reciprocal servicing* may also arise where the service centres provide services for each other. The solution to this reciprocal problem situation is very straightforward. You simply need to follow a three-step process for its resolution, namely:

▶ Step 1: apportion one service centre's costs (for example control/maintenance) across all cost centres as you did in Activity 2.1, but now including the other service department (for instance, a power supply centre); then

▶ Step 2: apportion the accumulated costs, i.e. *inclusive* of step 1's apportionment, of the other service centre (e.g. power supply) to all other cost centres, making sure you include the first service centre (control/maintenance) in your distribution;

▶ Step 3: repeat this distribution procedure by continuously reapportioning service cost centres' costs until the figures involved become so small (this will usually happen, in examination questions, amazingly quickly) that they are materially insignificant – for example to the nearest 'pound'.

As the wording of step 3 implies, this process is referred to as the 'repeated distribution' or 'continuous apportionment' method of solving reciprocal servicing problems. An even simpler method is to merely ignore altogether the reciprocal services offered by service centres to each other, and just charge directly the relevant proportion of service costs straight to production cost centres, thus in effect bypassing the reciprocal problem. But as this approach is based on ignorance (for instance, do problems in real life simply disappear if you ignore them?) it is definitely not to be recommended; you should preferably follow the three-step apportionment procedure outlined above.

How would you ...? distribute the service cost centre overhead of the reciprocating services (boiler house and materials handling) to the production departments of cutting, fitting and pressing given the *primary* attribution (i.e. allocation/apportionment) data below:

	Production cost centres			Service cost centres	
	Cutting (£)	Fitting (£)	Pressing (£)	Boiler house (£)	Materials handling (£)
Primary overhead attribution:	28,570	12,600	8,830	4,000	10,000

You should apply the three-step repeated distribution/continuous allotment process just described, using the following agreed percentage charge-out rates for your *secondary* apportionment of overhead cost between centres:

Service cost centre	Production cost centres			Service cost centres	
	Cutting	Fitting	Pressing	Boiler house	Materials handling
Boiler house	40%	30%	20%	–	10%
Materials handling	40%	40%	10%	10%	–

Answer

Overhead distribution summary statement:

	Cutting	Fitting	Pressing	Boiler house	Materials handling
Primary Attribution	28,570	12,600	8,830	4,000	10,000
Secondary Apportionment of reciprocal service costs					
(Step 1) Boiler house (BH)	1,600	1,200	800	(4,000)	400

(Step 2) Materials handling (MH)	4,160	4,160	1,040	1,040	(10,400)
BH	416	312	208	(1,040)	104
MH	42	42	10	10	(104)
(Step 3) BH	4	3	2	(10)	1
MH	1	–	–	–	(1)
	34,793	18,317	10,890	–	–

Note: The final '£' has arbitrarily been charged to Cutting – equally it could have gone to Fitting.

Summary

In the absorption costing technique we can now see that the general aim of cost ascertainment has been achieved. More specifically let us first refer back to the two stated objectives mentioned in section 2.1.1 – that unit cost ascertainment helps to satisfy two important accounting information needs, stock valuation and income determination. To determine the gross profit or loss the cost of finished goods sold is deducted from sales revenue. In Activity 2.1 the full production cost of a finished batch of goods was ascertained to be £1,533 – this figure will be an important piece of input information in determining the company's income for the period. In addition it will be vital for valuing stocks of finished goods if left unsold at period-end.

Furthermore, the absorption costing technique facilitates valuation not only of finished goods stock but also of partially completed goods (i.e. W-I-P). For instance, if the batch in Activity 2.1 had been only half finished, i.e. machined but not assembled, then the work to that stage would have only absorbed overhead from the machine shop (£598) and its W-I-P valuation would not include the assembly overhead (£333) yet to be absorbed.

Absorption costing also satisfies the requirements regarding stock valuation currently laid down by the accountancy profession's financial reporting standards,[3] that relevant production overhead should be included in valuations of stock (both finished goods and W-I-P). As emphasised throughout this chapter, only *production* overhead cost has been the subject of absorption. There are ways and means of absorbing non-production overhead costs, often referred to as general overheads, such as administration, marketing and R&D, but they are not nearly as prominent in cost accounting as those used, and just demonstrated, for production – one important reason being they are not required by the profession's standards!

A possible way in which to absorb general overheads is merely to mark-up on production costs. For example, if a $33\frac{1}{3}$ per cent mark-up on production cost were to be accepted as a reasonable cover (i.e. recovery rate) for non-production overhead then, in the Midbatch case, £511 ($\frac{1}{3}$ of the £1,533 full production cost) would be absorbed into the product cost unit, i.e. each batch. This would result in a full unit cost of £2,044 per batch, as follows:

	(£)
Full production cost per batch	1,533
General overhead absorbed @ $33\frac{1}{3}$ % of production cost	511
Full absorption cost per batch	£2,044

Nevertheless, to reassert earlier comments, more often than not 'full' product unit cost will refer to the production cost of output rather than the value inclusive of other general overheads. Instead of associating general costs with products, overhead relating to marketing, administration, R&D etc. will be treated as costs of the accounting period (i.e. fixed overhead cost) and simply written off as a lump-sum amount against income for that period. This alternative treatment (of not absorbing fixed overhead) is at the heart of the marginal costing technique explained in some depth in Chapter 4. Also, because classifying/distinguishing cost as fixed – as opposed to variable – (i.e. by behaviour) becomes of paramount importance, Chapter 3 is devoted to cost analysis techniques founded upon this particular classification of cost by behaviour pattern.

One final point concerns a firm's pricing strategy. Often organisations, in order to fix a selling price, will look to the full cost build-up of the product cost unit and price their output using this value as a base. A suitable selling price may be determined by adopting again a 'percentage mark-up on cost' approach – this time to provide a desired profit margin for the product. For example, taking the full cost above of £2,044 (inclusive of general overhead) of Midbatch's product cost unit – then by deciding to mark-up on cost by, for instance, 25 per cent, management of Midbatch may price their output at £2,555 per batch, thus:

	(£)
Full product cost per batch	2,044
Desired % profit mark-up (25%)	511
Selling price per batch	£2,555

This approach is just one of several pricing methods available to help management decide upon what might constitute a suitable selling price, which will be described in detail in Chapter 7 in Part 2 of the book which discusses decision accounting techniques.

2.3 Activity based costing technique

Within many spheres of modern industry, manufacturing operations are becoming progressively less labour-intensive with the advent of developments such as computer integrated manufacture and robotics technology (see also, Chapter 12). As a result, in the case of such industries, reservations have been expressed as to the validity of continuing to use traditional direct labour measures, both in terms of cost (i.e. direct wages) and time (i.e. labour hours), to relate manufacturing overhead to products in order to ascertain unit cost. You saw earlier that the absorption costing technique, based on the use of rates in section 2.2, drew significantly upon such *labour-based* rates (amongst others) to determine unit product costs, as indeed do later chapters on, for instance, pricing decisions (Chapter 7) and also cost control techniques like variance analysis (Chapter 10). Rather than tracing overhead cost to products on the traditional basis of, for instance, labour hours in modern production environments it may be more logical to look for and search out other bases. The activity based costing (ABC) technique does this by identifying not, for example, the number of labour hours (i.e. volume of labour) involved in product manufacture, but by going further and recognising the very *activities* themselves which ultimately generate (or drive) the overhead costs.

ABC can be defined briefly as a technique which attributes cost to cost units on the basis of the indirect activities which drive/create overhead cost in the first place – activities such as the setting up of production runs, and testing quality of production output. Probably the best way to understand the technique is to work through a simple illustration in order to fully grasp its application. The scenario suggested is greatly simplified in order to concentrate on imparting to you the essential concepts underlying ABC, and to show how it differs in principle from the more traditional methods using labour-based absorption rates which figured so prominently in section 2.2 under the absorption costing technique. Activity 2.2 adopts the two examples of *cost drivers* just provided in the definition of ABC, i.e. setting up and quality testing.

ACTIVITY **2.2**

Minmax Limited manufactures two product cost units, the 'Min' and the 'Max', each requiring one direct labour hour of time in a single production cost centre. There are just two overhead generating activities in the cost centre: (i) computer-assisted setting up of production runs; and (ii) the carrying out of automatic quality tests of printed circuit boards which are inbuilt into each product unit. The following data apply:

	£
Computer-assisted setting up costs	30,000
Automatic quality testing costs	25,000
Total cost centre overhead	£55,000

	Total	Product 'Min'	Product 'Max'
Number of units:	5,500	500	5,000
Number of direct labour hours:	5,500	500	5,000
Number of quality tests:	50	20	30
Number of set-ups:	15	5	10

Required: Contrast (1) traditional absorption costing with (2) the ABC technique for ascertaining the cost of Minmax Ltd's product cost units.

(1) USING THE ABSORPTION COSTING TECHNIQUE

Calculation of direct labour hour rate $\dfrac{£55,000}{5,500 \text{ hours}} = £10$ per labour hour

	'Min'	'Max'
∴ Unit product cost via absorption costing (1 hour @ £10 per hour)	£10	£10

Applying traditional absorption costing: £5,000 and £50,000 of total overhead are traced to products 'Min' and 'Max' respectively using the labour hour rate of £10 per hour.

(2) USING THE ABC TECHNIQUE

	Activity cost	Cost driver	Cost per cost driver
Setting up:	£30,000	15 set-ups	£2,000 per set-up
Quality testing:	£25,000	50 tests	£500 per test

Cost attribution to products according to activity	'Min'	(£)	'Max'	(£)	Total (£)
Set-ups	5 @ £2,000	10,000	10 @ £2,000	20,000	30,000
Tests	20 @ £500	10,000	30 @ £500	15,000	25,000
		20,000		35,000	55,000

	'Min'	'Max'
	(£20,000 ÷ 500 units)	(£35,000 ÷ 5,000 units)
∴ Unit product cost via ABC	£40	£7

Applying ABC: £35,000 and £20,000 of total overhead are traced to products 'Max' and 'Min' respectively, reflecting the products' relative benefits derived from the cost centre activities of automatic quality testing and computer assisted setting up of production runs.

Although a much simplified situation compared with likely 'real-life' scenarios, Activity 2.2 was nevertheless a useful example clearly illustrating that both high-volume product 'Max' and low-volume product 'Min' are costed out, under traditional absorption means, to bear exactly the same amount of overhead cost per product, i.e. £10 each. But do you think this is fair to 'Max' which is responsible for ten times the output level of 'Min' yet only places twice the demand of 'Min' on the resource activity of setting up (10:5 ratio), and even less, at 1.5 times the demand of 'Min', on quality testing (30:20 ratio)? In aggregate terms 'Max' has attracted £50,000 of cost centre overhead compared with only £5,000 absorbed by 'Min' on the traditional basis of labour hours.

By way of stark contrast, ABC more equitably represents the two products' relative usage of resource centre activities by attributing only £35,000 of total overhead to 'Max' (resulting in a unit cost of £7) whilst tracing £20,000 out of the aggregate £55,000 overhead cost to 'Min' (i.e. a unit cost of £40). In short, high-volume products may suffer over-costing under traditional absorption methods by, in effect, cross-subsidising their lower-volume partners. ABC rectifies this inbuilt distortion by directing more of the overhead to low-volume product 'Min', in this instance, which is a relatively more complex product to manufacture in terms of setting up and testing. To summarise, ABC is likely to be a more suitable approach than traditional means in highly complex, diversified product environments where cost unit demands on resources are better reflected by unit costings based on the various activities which generate the overhead cost rather than a single volume measure such as labour hours.

Self-check questions

2.1 A company is considering changing from traditional overhead absorption based on labour hours to an activity based costing (ABC) approach. Budgeted details for the three products manufactured are as follows:

Product	B	A	Z
Output (units)	240	200	160
Costs per unit	£	£	£
Direct material	20	25	15
Direct labour	14	10	7
Labour hours per unit	8	6	4

The products are produced in production runs of 40 units and sold in batches of 20 units. The production overhead for the period under review has been analysed as follows:

	£
Assembly department costs	20,860
Costs of setting up machines	10,500
Costs of raw material storage	7,200
Costs of quality control	4,200
Costs of handling materials	9,240

The management accountant has identified the following cost drivers:

Cost driver	Cost
Production runs	Setting up machines/quality control
Requisitions	Raw material storage
Orders	Handling materials

Volume of requisitions raised was 20 for each product and the quantity of orders carried out was 30.

Required:

(a) Calculate the unit production cost for each product if all overhead costs are absorbed in the traditional manner.

(b) Calculate the unit production cost for each product using activity based costing.

(c) Explain briefly how activity based costing overcomes distortions in product costing which arise through conventional cost accounting.

(Accounting Degree)

2.2 A company with three production departments and two service departments has the following balances on a departmental distribution summary of expenses:

Production departments		Service departments	
Manufacturing	£24,000	Power	£3,000
Assembly	£21,000	Administration	£5,000
Finishing	£18,000		

The expenses of the service departments are charged out on the following basis:

Service department	Production department			Service department	
	Manufacturing	Assembly	Finishing	Power	Administration
Power	40%	25%	15%	–	20%
Administration	35%	30%	20%	15%	–

You are required to show the apportionment of expenses from the service departments to the production departments by an appropriate method.

(Association of Accounting Technicians)

2.3 Brainy College has three faculties (A, B and C) and a central administration department. Each faculty has its own overheads but is also charged with a share of the central administrative department's costs in the ratios A2: B3: C4. An overhead absorption rate is then determined for each faculty based on budgeted labour hours.

You are required to:

Complete the following 7 × 4 table, showing clearly how you have deducted the missing figures:

		Faculty			
		A	B	C	Total
(i)	Budgeted own overheads	8,000		6,000	
(ii)	Budgeted share of service department overhead	6,000			
(iii)	Total budgeted overheads		20,000		
(iv)	Budgeted labour hours		2,000		
(v)	Overhead absorption rate	2			N/A
(vi)	Actual labour hours	5,000			11,000
(vii)	Over/(under) absorption		2,000	1,000	

(Chartered Institute of Public Finance and Accountancy)

2.4 A company produces several products which pass through the two production departments in its factory. These two departments are concerned with filling and sealing operations. There are two service departments, maintenance and canteen, in the factory.

Predetermined overhead absorption rates, based on direct labour hours are established for the two production departments. The budgeted expenditure for these departments for the period just ended, including the apportionment of service department overheads, was £110,040 for filling, and £53,300 for sealing. Budgeted direct labour hours were 13,100 for filling and 10,250 for sealing.

Service department overheads are apportioned as follows:

Maintenance	– Filling	70%
	– Sealing	27%
	– Canteen	3%
Canteen	– Filling	60%
	– Sealing	32%
	– Maintenance	8%

During the period just ended, actual overhead costs and activity were as follows:

	£	Direct labour hours
Filling	74,260	12,820
Sealing	38,115	10,075
Maintenance	25,050	
Canteen	24,375	

Required:

(a) Calculate the overheads absorbed in the period and the extent of the under-/over-absorption in each of the two production departments.

(b) State, and critically assess, the objectives of overhead apportionment and absorption.

(Chartered Association of Certified Accountants)

2.5 The Isis Engineering Company operates a job order costing system which includes the use of predetermined overhead absorption rates. The company has two service cost centres and two production cost centres. The production cost centre overheads are charged to jobs via direct labour hour rates which are currently £3.10 per hour in production cost centre A and £11.00 per hour in production cost centre B. The calculation involved in determining these rates have excluded any consideration of the services that are provided by each service cost centre to the other.

The bases used to charge general factory overhead and service cost centre expenses to the production cost centres are as follows:

(i) general factory overhead is apportioned on the basis of the floor area used by each of the production and service cost centres;

(ii) the expenses of service cost centre 1 are charged out on the basis of the number of personnel in each production cost centre;

(iii) the expenses of service cost centre 2 are charged out on the basis of the usage of its services by each production cost centre.

The company's overhead absorption rates are revised annually prior to the beginning of each year, using an analysis of the outcome of the current year and the draft plans and forecasts for the forthcoming year. The revised rates for next year are to be based on the following data:

	General factory overhead	Service cost centres		Production cost centres	
		1	2	A	B
Budgeted overhead for next year (before any reallocation)	£210,000	£93,800	£38,600	£182,800	£124,800
% of factory floor area	–	5	10	15	70
% of factory personnel	–	10	18	63	9
Estimated usage of services of service cost centre 2 in forthcoming year	–	1,000 hrs	–	4,000 hrs	25,000 hrs
Budgeted direct labour hours for next year (to be used to calculate next year's absorption rates)	–	–	–	120,000 hrs	20,000 hrs
Budgeted direct labour hours for current year (these figures were used in the calculation of this year's absorption rates)	–	–	–	100,000 hrs	30,000 hrs

(a) Ignoring the question of reciprocal charges between the service cost centres, calculate the revised overhead absorption rates for the two production cost centres. Use the company's established procedures.

(b) Comment on the extent of the differences between the current overhead absorption rates and those you have calculated in your answer to (a). Set out the likely reasons for these differences.

(c) Each service cost centre provides services to the other. Recalculate next year's overhead absorption rates recognising the existence of such reciprocal services and assuming that they can be measured on the same bases as those used to allocate costs to the production cost centres.

(d) Assume that:

　(i) General factory overhead is a fixed cost.

　(ii) Service cost centre 1 is concerned with inspection and quality control with its budgeted expenses (before any reallocations) being 10 per cent fixed and 90 per cent variable.

　(iii) Service cost centre 2 is the company's plant maintenance section with its budgeted expenses (before any reallocations) being 90 per cent fixed and 10 per cent variable.

　(iv) Production cost centre A is labour intensive with its budgeted overhead (before any reallocation) being 90 per cent fixed and 10 per cent variable.

(v) Production cost centre B is highly mechanised with its budgeted overhead (before any reallocations) being 20 per cent fixed and 80 per cent variable.

In the light of these assumptions, comment on the cost apportionment and absorption calculations made in parts (a) and (c) and suggest any improvements that you would consider appropriate.

(Chartered Association of Certified Accountants)

Notes
....

1. Many good cost accounting textbooks that are more specialised than this one devote a significant amount of coverage to the technical procedures involved in costing for direct materials and labour costs. One such text is: *A practical foundation in costing* by D. Wright.
2. Accounting Standards Board, Statement of standard accounting practice #9: 'Stocks and long-term contracts'.
3. Ibid.

Further study
....

Drury, C. (1992) *Management and cost accounting*, 3rd edn, London: Chapman and Hall.

Drury, C. (1989) 'Activity based costing', in *Management Accounting*, September, Chartered Institute of Management Accountants.

Lucey, T. (1992) *Management accounting*, 3rd edn, D. P. Publications.

Pizzey, A. (1989) *Cost and management accounting*, 3rd edn, Paul Chapman Publishing.

Sizer, J. (1989) *An insight into management accounting*, 3rd edn, Harmondsworth: Penguin.

Wheldon, H. (1984) *Cost Accounting*, 15th edn, London: Macdonald and Evans.

Wright, D. (1994) *A Practical Foundation in Costing*, 1st edn, London: Routledge.

Cost behaviour and estimation techniques

In section 2.1.3, where various possible classifications of cost were discussed, one particular category identified was cost classification by behaviour pattern. Analysis of cost according to its pattern of behaviour, i.e. fixed or variable, is fundamental to any study of management accounting. Although other 'hybrid' patterns called *step* and *semi-variable* costs exist, the pivotal divide when classifying by behaviour focuses between variable or fixed. Throughout this and later chapters you will find it useful to consistently bear in mind the following important two-part 'golden' rule of cost behaviour:

▶ cost that is sensitive, and varies in proportion, to corresponding changes in the activity level is known as *variable* cost;

▶ cost that is insensitive to activity level fluctuations but is determined by the influence of time (and its passing) is referred to as *fixed* cost.

Over relatively short time periods fixed costs will remain constant and unchanged by fluctuating activity levels, hence fixed cost is frequently also called *period* cost. The time frame is the short-term and both accountants and economists tend to agree that the short-run time period takes into account passages of time up to and including one year.

The reference to passage of time hardly needs explanation as it is rather self-evident, but what exactly is meant by the term *activity level*? Many kinds of typical business activity would constitute suitable examples of activity level, for instance, numbers of orders/invoices processed through an office; goods produced in a factory; passenger-miles travelled on a transport undertaking; etc. In most cases, however, the activity level is expressed simply as 'units' of either:

▶ output (i.e. units manufactured/produced) or;

▶ turnover (i.e. units sold).

The generic term *units* will therefore tend to be used throughout to represent activity level. In management accounting a more frequently used expression for the activity level is 'volume' – and indeed the study of cost behaviour is widely referred to in the literature as cost-volume (C-V) analysis. In fact, the graphical forms of C-V analysis used extensively throughout this chapter will reflect cost on the vertical ('y') axis analysed in relation to activity/volume scaled on the horizontal ('x') axis.

Volume (or activity level) in units will, moreover, prove to be a key feature of many areas of your further study, for example, in section 4.1.2 of Chapter 4 on marginal costing and also throughout Chapter 6. The latter chapter expands the C-V relationships explored here to enable development of studies into the realms of cost-volume-profit (C-V-P) analysis using similar forms of written, graphical and mathematical/algebraic exposition as are employed now to describe the range of patterns underpinning the way in which costs are said to behave.

3.1 Patterns of cost behaviour

You will recall the first part of the cost behaviour 'golden' rule, i.e. that costs which vary in proportion to changes in activity/volume are variable costs. When we talk about activity level changes in connection with variable cost, we specifically mean *marginal* differences in volume, which excludes the possibility of massive fluctuations in activity that may cause there to be extreme and untypical effects upon the way costs behave. Because of this assumption, an alternative, and purely interchangeable, term for variable cost is 'marginal' cost (just as 'fixed' interchanges with 'period' as equally suitable descriptions of fixed overhead cost). Consider first of all the variable pattern of cost behaviour.

3.1.1 Variable cost behaviour

All prime cost (which, remember from the previous chapter, comprises direct material, direct labour and direct expense) because of the nature of direct costs is entirely *variable*. Classic examples of prime cost include:

▶ raw materials, for example, every car needs an engine – 1,000 cars will need 1,000 engines in total;
▶ production labour, for instance, construction workers – on days when no building activity takes place 'navvies' are not employed;
▶ direct expenses, for example, a royalty paid to an author or a composer – every copy and/or performance of the work incurs the royalty fee or charge.

Although it is true to say that most items of overhead cost tend to be fixed, there are nevertheless still many instances where overhead varies with activity, such as when:

▶ depreciation is *not* charged using one of the time-based methods (i.e. straight-line, reducing balance etc.) but where the asset is written down in value according to the extent to which it is used. This might, for instance, be the frequency with which a machine is operated – excellent examples include the duration for which heavy earth-moving equipment is used or the number (i.e. volume) of flight hours an airline operates its planes;

▶ sales commissions are paid to sales representatives working on a 'commission-only' basis – the level of earnings payable to such employees or agents will vary in proportion to the volume of sales achieved.

To summarise, variable cost comprises the following:

Variable overheads + Direct (prime) costs = Variable cost

(Note: Refer to section 4.1.1, Chapter 4 to see how this matches exactly the constituent ingredients of *marginal cost.*)

You can support the above largely narrative description equally well through both graphical and mathematical/algebraic means of illustrating variable cost behaviour which you now experience through Activities 3.1 and 3.2.

ACTIVITY **3.1**

Assume a firm employs sales agents selling encyclopaedias for 'commission-only' earnings door-to-door. Agents receive a commission of 10 per cent for each encyclopaedia sold. Encyclopaedias are priced at £40 each, therefore agents will earn a unit commission of £4 and commission earnings in total will vary in straight proportion to the unit sales volume attained.

Required: Provide graphical and algebraic expressions of this variable cost behaviour pattern.

The most obvious feature of Figure 3.1 is that the cost of paying agents' commission is a *linear* (i.e. straight line) function of the number of units sold. Unit volume therefore determines the cost level of agents' pay. Indeed, volume on the 'x' axis is referred to as the determining or explanatory variable because it explains the level of cost. Moreover, the cost-volume relationship is a perfectly proportionate one, giving rise to the mathematical/algebraic expression for variable cost as follows:

figure 3.1
Variable (linear) cost behaviour

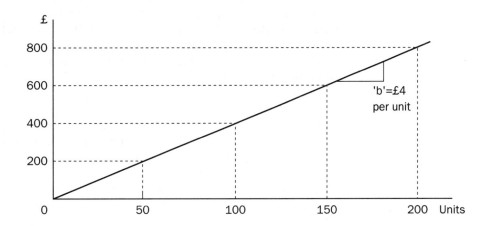

$$y = bx$$

where: 'y' is cost; 'x' is volume/activity; and 'b' is variable cost per unit.

As just mentioned, 'x' is the determining/explanatory variable which is in statistical language known as the 'independent' variable. Cost 'y' is itself also a variable, called the 'dependent' variable because its level is a function of (i.e. depends upon) independent variable 'x'. The other term in the equation or expression is 'b' which is the coefficient value attached to 'x' and is in this illustration £4 per unit. This unit variable cost of £4 is graphically represented in Figure 3.1 by the slope of the line (the linear function) and is the *marginal* rate of change in cost brought about by a unit change in volume 'x'. Hence, total variable cost is given by 'bx'.

A vitally important assumption both here and throughout the rest of the book (apart from the following sub-section) is that unit variable cost remains the same constant amount – no matter what the scale of volume. This assumption helps to simplify later analyses such as C-V-P analysis (Chapter 6) and pricing decisions (Chapter 7). Assuming the same £4 unit variable cost in our example, for any chosen level of volume, you could calculate total variable cost using the expression y = bx, for instance, for the four readings off the graph in Figure 3.1, thus:

$$£200 = (£4)(50 \text{ units}); £400 = (£4)(100 \text{ units});$$
$$£600 = (£4)(150 \text{ units}); £800 = (£4)(200 \text{ units}).$$

Nonlinear/curvilinear variable cost behaviour

Here we briefly relax the previous paragraph's important assumption of a constant variable cost per unit. Using the basic data from Activity 3.1's illustration of agent's commission, consider Activity 3.2.

ACTIVITY **3.2**

Required: Graphically and algebraically express the situation where agents move onto higher rates of commission for greater sales achieved.

For instance, a 25 per cent commission for sales above 200 encyclopaedias up to and including 400 units; then 40 per cent commission for any unit sales above 400. This expanded data would result in a series of segmental variable cost slopes, graphically speaking, with each subsequent linear function segment being steeper than the previous one. Figure 3.2 shows the graphical development of such a variable cost behaviour pattern.

The earlier mathematical/algebraic expression also needs developing to reflect the expansion of data into:

$$y = bx_1 + cx_2 + dx_3$$

where: 'y' and 'b' are as before; 'c' is £10 variable cost per unit (i.e. 25 per cent commission); 'd' is £16 variable cost per unit (i.e. 40 per cent commission); 'x_1' is volume range up to 200 units; 'x_2' is volume range 201–400 units; and 'x_3' is any volume level above 400 units.

Applying this expression you could calculate variable cost of commission for, say, (i) 250 units; and (ii) 500 units sales volumes respectively as follows:

figure 3.2
Variable (linear 'segmental') cost behaviour

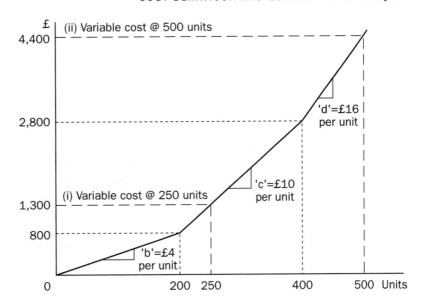

(i) £1,300 = (£4)(200 units) + (£10)(50 units);
(ii) £4,400 = (£4)(200 units) + (£10)(200 units) + (£16)(100 units).

Each functional segment of Figure 3.2 can be viewed as a unique *relevant range* within which a specific but constant unit variable cost applies. Some agents' operations may consistently fall into a single range, for instance, poor salesmen may never sell more than 200 encyclopaedias (and therefore never earn more than £4 per unit!).

figure 3.3
Curvilinear ('smoothed' non-linear) variable cost behaviour

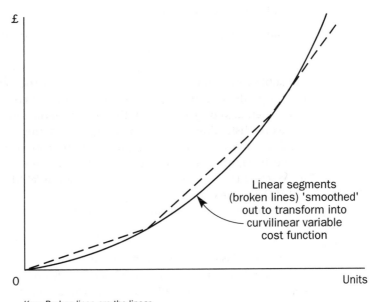

Key : Broken lines are the linear
segments from Figure 3.2

The segmental pattern in Figure 3.2 can effectively be 'smoothed' out to transform into a non-linear or curvilinear behaviour pattern as displayed in Figure 3.3.

This non-linear/curvilinear pattern of variable cost behaviour concurs with the economists' approach to cost analysis where it might be argued that the acquisition of greater supplies (i.e. higher volumes) of limited resources may necessitate paying increasingly higher rates/premiums for, say, scarce raw materials in order to fight off competition. Another economic theory (but one also widely observed in practice) is that of increasing returns to scale where, for instance, material supplies are plentiful and, by purchasing in bulk order quantities, discounts become available resulting in lower unit variable costs. Graphically this latter case would resemble opposite shaped functions to those in Figures 3.2 and 3.3 – i.e. progressively lower unit cost would be reflected by segments/curves becoming continuously less steep over increasing levels of volume.

It is important that you develop appreciation of wider issues, such as economists' *vis-à-vis* accountants' approaches to the treatment of cost. Indeed, Chapter 7 (pricing decisions) will again recognise the possible effects of economic forces of supply and demand in the different context of selling prices. However, having briefly been made aware of economic arguments concerning variable/marginal cost behaviour, you should from hereon assume *constant* unit variable cost irrespective of the range of activity, giving rise to simple linear functional relationships between cost and volume.

3.1.2 Fixed cost behaviour

Fixed (or period) cost is said to be fixed with respect to two factors:

▶ short-run time periods, i.e. up to and including a full year;
▶ volume (although under very extreme circumstances, such as complete shutdown where volume is sustained at zero, even fixed costs may change or be avoided entirely).

Excellent examples of fixed costs include: time-based depreciation methods (such as straight-line); insurance premiums; top executive salaries; rent and rates. Even economists would agree that these sort of costs in the short-term are not subject to change (despite arguing that over the longer run all costs or factors of production inevitably vary!). As all fixed costs are overhead they are often alternatively given the full title *fixed overhead costs*.

Notwithstanding the second of our determining factors above, even at zero volume/activity the graphical representation of fixed cost behaviour is, as illustrated in Figure 3.4, a constant linear function parallel to the 'x' axis and intersecting the 'y' axis at the fixed cost amount 'a' (this intersect point is often called the 'intercept').

The mathematical/algebraic expression could not be simpler:

$$y = a$$

where: 'y' is cost; and 'a' is a constant.

(Note: Independent variable 'x' does not feature in the equation because by definition volume does not in any way explain or determine the level of fixed overhead cost).

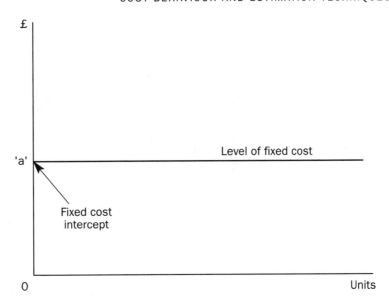

figure 3.4
Fixed cost behaviour

You should remember from the previous section how variable cost *per unit* is constant – well, to continue the conundrum, on a unit basis fixed cost is variable! Dispel any confusion for yourself by tackling the following question.

Can you calculate ...? for all of the three following periods the fixed cost per unit? Assume the fixed cost is a straight-line depreciation charge of £40,000 each period, and that the three consecutive periods reveal the following unit volumes:

Period	1	2	3
Volume (units)	30,000	40,000	50,000
Fixed cost per unit	(i)	(ii)	(iii)

Notice from your calculation how unit fixed cost varies – decreasing as the volume increases. This is simply because, as the periods progress, more units become available to soak up (or, technically speaking, 'absorb' – see Chapter 2, section 2.2) the constant fixed cost amount of £40,000. Hopefully, the conundrum now makes sense to you. Put simply, when we discuss cost behaviour we are talking in *total* (not unit) terms. Fixed overheads are constant/fixed in total, just as aggregate variable cost changes/varies in proportion to volume.

Answer

(i) £1.33 per unit; (ii) £1 per unit; (iii) £0.80 per unit.

3.1.3 Other patterns of cost behaviour

Certain types of costs do not behave in a way that can conveniently be described as either entirely fixed or, at the opposite extreme, fully variable. Such 'hybrid' versions take the form of *step* costs and *semi-variable* costs.

figure 3.5

Step cost behaviour

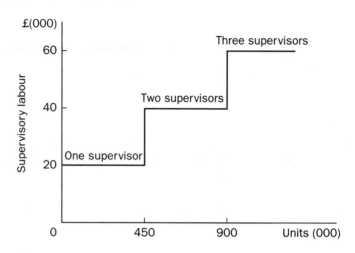

Step costs

On occasions a pattern of cost behaviour will be such that the cost remains constant for a given volume range before stepping up to a higher cost level at a specific, discrete point which signifies the end of the given range. Another range of volume then begins at the higher level of cost which stays constant again for the extent of the second range of activity at the end of which cost once again steps up, this time to a third and higher level . . . and so the pattern continues to be repeated. The characteristic behaviour of these step costs therefore is one of 'lump-sum' injections of a single cost amount at discrete points on the activity scale, similar to that depicted in Figure 3.5 which illustrates a common sort or variety of step cost, i.e. supervisory labour cost.

In Figure 3.5 supervisors in a firm are paid £20,000 per annum, each are able to control/supervise up to fifteen workers and a single worker produces 30,000 units per annum. Each plateau of cost spans a very wide range of activity, and because the cost remains at a constant amount throughout each range it can be treated as a fixed cost for that particular volume range. For example, it may be highly unlikely that the firm's annual output level ever falls below 450,000 units or rises above 900,000 units – in such a case the second plateau level can be regarded as the firm's relevant range of operations within which supervisory labour cost is fixed at a constant £40,000 (i.e. two supervisors' wages/salaries). For each relevant range the behaviour pattern is one of a fixed cost and can be represented mathematically/algebraically by the expression $y = a$ (as for a wholly fixed cost). This step pattern is known as *step-* (or *stepped-*) *fixed cost* behaviour.

A far less commonly observed category of step cost that you might encounter is that of a *step-variable cost*. This particular pattern exhibits very tiny step effects over such minutely narrow volume ranges that the step function can hardly be discerned and is therefore approximated to that of a linear variable cost. Because of this approximation the variable cost mathematical/algebraic expression, $y = bx$, is used to represent step-variable cost behaviour.

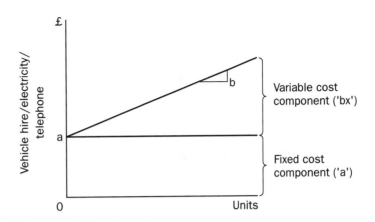

figure 3.6
Semi-variable cost behaviour

Semi-variable costs

An alternative name for semi-variable costs is *semi-fixed*.

All are suggestive of a variety of cost behaviour that includes in a single cost item *both* fixed and variable components of cost. Figure 3.6, which effectively combines the fixed and variable cost functions from sections 3.1.2 and 3.1.1 respectively, is illustrative of many common items of semi-variable cost, good examples of which are:

▶ vehicle hire – where a fixed hire charge is made for rental of the vehicle (irrespective of how many miles it will be run) but then, in addition to this fixed cost, a further variable charge may be made per mile operated;

▶ domestic electricity/telephone charges – where the consumer is billed for a fixed period (usually quarterly) charge even if, for instance, the telephone is not used for making calls, but in the more usual case of calls being made then an additional charge is levied which varies in proportion to the caller's use of the telephone.

Variants on Figure 3.6 are of course possible and often occur. For instance, in the example above of vehicle hire, the fixed rental charge may allow for free travel up to a given number of miles – here the fixed cost function would be drawn, as usual, horizontal/parallel to the 'x' volume axis up to the free miles on the activity scale, after which point the variable cost function would begin and continue to rise in proportion to the extra cost per mile charged in excess of the free miles. Watch out for many kinds of variant – remembering that all must contain both fixed and variable pattern features.

The final comment on patterns of cost behaviour rests with Figure 3.6. The cost function displayed in Figure 3.6 has a very important dual application. On the one hand it represents, as just described, the semi-variable cost pattern. Perhaps even more importantly, however, it is also a perfect reflection of an organisation's *total cost* function. Both these applications are mathematically/ algebraically represented by the same functional expression which simply combines the previous equations for fixed and variable cost into the following single cost equation:

$$y = a + bx$$

where all the terms are as before.

This total cost statement in one equation summarises all the four patterns previously discussed in detail. You need to keep aware that only *four* cost behaviour patterns exist and that they combine, as shown in Table 3.1, to constitute 'total cost'.

3.2 Cost estimation techniques

The two-variable linear cost equation $y = a + bx$ is at the root of all the techniques of cost estimation demonstrated in this second section of Chapter 3. Simply because this expression reflects both the semi-variable and total cost functions (see the penultimate paragraph of section 3.1) then the problem of estimating a firm or organisation's total costs, using the various techniques outlined in the rest of this chapter, is in fact the *same* problem as estimating the fixed and variable cost components of semi-variable cost. To differentiate between the two problems is just not relevant.

Briefly referring back to Table 3.1 you might first remember how the previous analysis determined that fully/step-fixed costs were defined by constant 'a' in the equation, while fully/step-variable costs were represented by coefficient 'b'. Secondly, recall how semi-variable costs were described as containing characteristics of both fixed and variable cost behaviour. It is with regard to the issue of segregation of the fixed from the variable components that resolution of the total cost estimation problem lies.

Many instances of semi-variable cost behaviour do not present any real segregation/estimation difficulty. Take the case of the earlier example of electricity/telephone costs – these may be easily split into their component parts because separate period (i.e. fixed) and usage (i.e. variable) charges are already displayed on the electricity/telephone bill or account itself. However, management may require estimates to be made for much wider classes of cost, such as, general office administration expense of which electricity/telephone costs may only be a tiny portion of the overall semi-variable costs involved in running office facilities.

table 3.1

Total cost structured by behaviour pattern

		Fixed cost		Variable cost
Four	*Variable* cost:	n/a		Fully variable
Cost	*Fixed* cost:	Fully fixed		n/a
Behaviour	*Step* cost:	Step-fixed		Step-variable
Patterns	*Semi* cost:	Fixed component		Variable component
	Total cost:	Total fixed	+	Total variable
	y =	a	+	bx

Key: n/a = Not applicable

Purpose of the estimation techniques

The following estimation techniques, by using available past data, aim to provide predictions/forecasts of future levels of cost likely to be incurred in areas of the business such as:

▶ non-manufacturing functions (for example, marketing, personnel, administration, R&D etc.);
▶ production activity (involving direct product manufacture and support services like inspection, delivery, maintenance etc.).

Indeed, estimating the total cost of operating the entire organisation itself may be the ultimate aim. Using the equation, $y = a + bx$, if individual values are found for 'a' and 'b' then the accountant can provide management with an estimate of future cost level 'y' by simply plugging into the formula the level of volume 'x' planned by management. For example, assume fixed costs of running a firm's order department are found to be £20,000 per month and variable ordering cost is 50p per order. For the month ahead, in which the order department manager expects 30,000 orders to be processed, the accountant can plug the planned volume into the cost equation ($y = £20,000 + £0.5x$) to arrive at £35,000 total cost estimate as follows:

$$£35,000 = £20,000 + (50p)(30,000)$$

Very shortly from your demonstration of the techniques in sections 3.2.1 – 3.2.3 you will see that they all determine a value for:

(i) intercept 'a' measuring constant fixed cost per period; and
(ii) coefficient 'b' measuring the slope of the line representing variable cost per unit.

Graphically, the above order department example would appear as in Figure 3.7.

A final point before dealing with the techniques is that each one will generate different values for 'a' and 'b' despite using the same data bank. This is inevitable as the results from applying any technique will only be as good as the quality of the technique itself. Activity 3.3. presents you with the basic data for practising each cost estimation technique followed by description of the techniques through the remaining three sections (3.2.1 – 3.2.3) of this chapter.

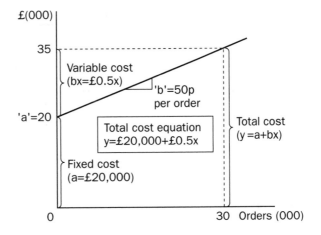

figure 3.7
Total cost estimation

ACTIVITY **3.3**

F. Else plc manufactures posters in very large unit quantities and, for the most recent four consecutive time periods, the following pattern of cost-volume data is revealed in Table 3.2.

Required: Using the F. Else plc data demonstrate/discuss the three cost estimation techniques of 'high–low' (section 3.2.1); 'scattergraph' (section 3.2.2); and 'regression' (section 3.2.3) analysis.

3.2.1 High–low ('two-point') estimation technique

As the technique's name implies, estimates for constant 'a' and coefficient 'b' are determined on the basis of the highest and lowest points observed in the data. Data for periods 4 and 1 respectively are therefore used and inserted into our now familiar two-variable linear expression, $y = a + bx$, to set up a pair of simultaneous equations which you then need to solve to arrive at values for 'a' and 'b', thus:

Highest: period # 4 – Equation (1)	$380 = a + 400b$
Lowest: period # 1 – Equation (2)	$240 = a + 200b$
Subtract equation (2) from (1)	$140 = \quad\quad 200b$

Therefore, value for 'b' calculated:

$$b = \frac{140}{200} = 0.7$$

Next, you substitute this value for 'b' into either equation (1) or (2) – it does not matter which equation as both will give you the same result to determine the value of 'a':

Equation (2) $240 = a + 200b$
$$\therefore 240 = a + (200)(.7)$$
$$= a + 140$$

Therefore:

$$a = 240 - 140 = 100$$

table 3.2
F. Else plc: production volume and total cost data

Accounting period (number)	Volume/ activity x (000 units)	Total cost y (£000)
1	200	240
2	300	340
3	250	280
4	400	380

So, using high–low as a means of estimation, the cost equation reads:

$$y = 100 + 0.7x$$

This equation informs management that the firm's total cost structure, broken down into its two components, is made up as follows:

(i) 'a' = 100: meaning, as total cost is scaled in £000s, that the constant element of the total is calculated to be £100,000 fixed cost per period;

(ii) 'b' = 0.7: meaning the marginal *unit* rate of change in cost, hence no scaling factor is required as variable cost is £0.70 per unit. When this unit cost of 70p is related to volume 'x' then the *total* variable cost element of the firm's overall total cost is determined.

You need to exercise a certain amount of care, however, when applying the high–low technique because the highest and lowest points need to be typical of the whole series of data for the result to be meaningful. A possible practical solution might be (rather than using the absolute highest and lowest) to instead take a 'high' and a 'low' reading which together better represent the nature of the data set. After all it is probably dangerous to take the absolute extremes of anything as being representative of the whole – witness, for example, how the 'far-right' and 'far-left' of politics do not often represent the mainstream body of political opinion.

3.2.2 Scattergraph ('visual fit/inspection') estimation technique

Compared with the previous high–low estimation technique, a scattergraph approach has at least one major advantage in that it uses the whole set of data observations rather than just two. Using again the data from Table 3.2, the coordinates (i.e. the data points) are plotted on graph paper, resulting in a points scatter over the face of the graph, which reveals a gradually ascending pattern representative of increasing total cost in relation to (i.e. correlation with) corresponding increases in volume. The variables 'x' and 'y' are said to be positively co-related (or correlated) as both move in the same direction together. Having plotted the scatter of points, the cost estimator (e.g. the management accountant), by visually inspecting the data, fits what is perceived to be the best line possible to the data coordinates. This is the reason for the alternative names of 'visual fit' or 'visual inspection' by which scattergraph is often known. The line (or function) fitted through visual means by the estimator is called the *line of best fit*.

A major reservation concerning the technique needs at this point to be emphasised. The method is highly subjective. Each individual estimator will probably think that he/she has fitted the best possible line to the data scatter. However, unless purely by very remote coincidence, no two lines will be exactly the same – hence readings of both the slope (coefficient 'b') and the intercept (constant 'a') will also differ between individual estimators. This is obviously a significant drawback to application of the technique. Fortunately, a more sophisticated and statistically sound technique is available and is reviewed in the next section – known as 'least-squares' regression analysis, it provides the line of best fit *statistically*, that cannot be disputed (as opposed to the *subjectively* argued 'visual' best fit used in the scattergraph method).

figure 3.8

Scattergraph

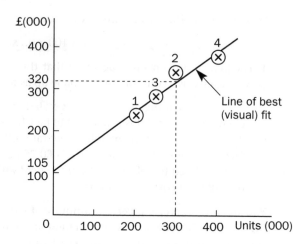

I assume that my line of best *visual* fit in Figure 3.8 is indeed the best fitted line possible. On this assumption, my reading of intercept 'a' as 105 is the best estimate available for fixed cost per period – and, as the 'y' axis is scaled in £000s, the constant period amount of fixed overhead is determined as £105,000. This is effectively the first step in applying the technique – the remaining steps concern determination of coefficient 'b' measuring the unit variable cost slope of the line of best fit.

To determine 'b', read off from the graph in Figure 3.8 a total cost value for any given level of volume – my reading is £320,000 at an arbitrarily chosen activity level of 300,000 units. As fixed cost is already determined at £105,000 deducting this amount from total cost will give the total variable cost for 300,000 units, thus:

		(£)
	Total cost @ 300,000 units	320,000
less	Fixed cost (intercept 'a')	105,000
	Variable cost @ 300,000 units	215,000

Simply dividing this total variable cost figure by the unit volume will provide the variable cost per unit, i.e. £215,000 ÷ 300,000 units = £0.7167. Thus $71\frac{2}{3}$p variable cost is incurred for every unit of volume produced, while period cost is fixed/constant at £105,000 irrespective of activity level. So, using the scattergraph as a means of estimation, my (not our!) cost equation reads:

$$y = 105 + 0.7167x$$

You will perhaps have noticed that values for 'a' and 'b' differ from those for high–low cost estimation in section 3.2.1. As mentioned previously (directly before Activity 3.3) this is inevitable – and we shall see different values again for 'a' and 'b' using the next technique for estimating costs, known as regression analysis. A final reminder to you before moving on is that regression as a statistical technique will provide unarguably the best measures for 'a' and 'b', whereas remember that the scattergraph values above are highly subjective –

they are, in fact, *my* estimates and you or any other cost estimator will (coincidences aside) generate different, perhaps only slightly different but nonetheless different, values for constant 'a' and coefficient 'b'.

3.2.3 Regression ('least-squares') analysis estimation technique

Regression and correlation are well-used statistical devices – both terms referring to how a range of variables (just two in our case, cost and volume) might be observed to behave in relation to how one affects the other. In other words, how they correlate. Correlation has already been mentioned briefly in the first paragraph of section 3.2.2 in connection with the scattergraph technique. The term *regression* means that by regressing one variable against another, through applying the 'least-squares' formulae, estimates of how our two variables might correlate to each other in the future can be obtained (again in the context of our very familiar two-variable linear expression, y = a + bx). Cost estimation using the least-squares regression technique ensures objectively and indisputably the line of best fit because the method is statistically proven and guaranteed correct. No attempts therefore will be made at proofs and/or derivations of the following formulae as they can be taken to be statistically sound – rooted as they are in the world of statistics rather than (management) accounting! You, as a student of accounting and related subjects, would always be provided with necessary mathematical tables/statistical formulae in examinations. Consequently, the 'tools' of least-squares regression analysis are now simply given you in the shape of what are described as the two *normal equations*:

$$(1) \quad \Sigma y = na + b\Sigma x$$
$$(2) \quad \Sigma xy = a\Sigma x + b\Sigma x^2$$

Note: Other alternative statistical formulae do exist which would also provide the same values for 'a' and 'b' as the normal equations approach does here – they would be available in examinations and it is immaterial which set of statistical 'tools' is used. Normal equations are adopted here because they bear the closest resemblance to our familiar expression y = a + bx, and you should therefore hopefully feel comfortable in their use.

table 3.3 **F. Else plc: data expansion (from table 3.2)**	Accounting period *n*	Volume (000 units) *x*	Cost (£000) *y*	(£ million) *xy*	(million units) *x²*
	1	200	240	48,000	40,000
	2	300	340	102,000	90,000
	3	250	280	70,000	62,500
	4	400	380	152,000	160,000
	Total	1,150	1,240	372,000	352,500
	n = 4	Σx	Σy	Σxy	Σx^2

To apply the above normal equations an expansion of our basic data from Table 3.2 becomes necessary. This is extended in Table 3.3 on the previous page.

To determine values for 'a' and 'b' you simply plug the data from Table 3.3 into the normal equations and solve them as a pair of simultaneous equations, thus:

$$(1) \quad 1{,}240 = 4a + 1{,}150b$$
$$(2) \quad 372{,}000 = 1{,}150a + 352{,}500b$$

Multiply equation (1) by a factor of 287.5 to get equation (3) in order to eliminate 'a':

$$(2) \quad 372{,}000 = 1{,}150a + 352{,}500b$$
$$(3) \quad 356{,}500 = 1{,}150a + 330{,}625b$$

Subtract equation (3) from equation (2):

$$15{,}500 = 21{,}875b$$

Therefore, value for 'b' calculated:

$$b = \frac{15{,}500}{21{,}875} = 0.7086$$

Substitute value for 'b' into equation (1):

$$(1) \quad 1{,}240 = 4a + (1{,}150)(.7086)$$
$$= 4a + 815 \text{ (rounded to whole number)}$$

Therefore:

$$4a = 1{,}240 - 815 = 425$$

Hence,
$$a = \frac{425}{4} = 106.25$$

So, using least-squares regression analysis as a means of estimation, the cost equation reads:

$$y = 106.25 + 0.7086x$$

Once, more, as constant 'a' is gauged in £000s then fixed cost per period is £106,250 while unit variable cost is 70.86p (which as coefficient 'b' when attached to volume 'x' will give total variable cost). Yet again another different set of values for 'a' and 'b' arises – this time from regression analysis. To conclude this chapter it is therefore appropriate to finally and briefly compare all three sets of estimates from sections 3.2.1 – 3.2.3, reminding you of what, overall, is the ultimate aim of the techniques described in detail throughout the chapter.

Comparison of the estimation techniques

To summarise and compare the three techniques reviewed, they are listed below in what might be regarded as an increasing level of sophistication.

High–low $y = £100{,}000 + £0.7x$
Scattergraph $y = £105{,}000 + £0.7167x$
Regression $y = £106{,}250 + £0.7086x$

The least preferable of the techniques is generally accepted to be the high–low method. You might have noticed how, in the Activity's case illustration of F. Else plc, high–low generates the lowest pair of values for both constant 'a' and coefficient 'b'. Hence it might be regarded here as consistently underestimating both fixed and variable cost levels. This is not necessarily always a feature of the technique; however, it is true to say that it is more susceptible to under/overestimation compared with others.

At the other end of the scale of sophistication, regression can claim to be superior to both the other two techniques. Because of its statistical rigour it is a more accurate and reliable 'tool' placed at the disposal of the cost estimator (e.g. the management accountant). Moreover, it is the only one of the techniques reviewed that lends itself further to statistical testing – but that area of analysis is outside the scope of this introductory text. On occasions, however, it may prove expedient to use a simple, 'rough-and-ready' means of estimation such as high–low for reasons of speed, cheapness, or ease of application. It can be argued, therefore, that there is a role for all of the techniques available.

In conclusion, remember the fundamental aim of cost estimation. It is to arrive at values for 'a' and 'b' in order that *future* likely levels of cost may be predicted. A final reference to our Activity data in Table 3.2 shows that is based on a four-period time frame. The four periods were consecutive, so period four is the most recent. Management may ask the cost estimator/management accountant for an estimate of likely total cost based on output for the coming period five. If, for instance, the production/works manager is in a position to provide planned works schedules for period five, then based on the planned future level of output the estimator/accountant can supply a total cost forecast.

For example, if plans were to produce 450,000 units of output in period five – then this future output level represents volume (independent variable 'x') from which estimates of future total cost (dependent variable 'y') for period five can be generated using our total cost functions determined earlier, thus:

High–low	£415,000 = £100,000 + (£0.7)(450,000)
Scattergraph	£427,515 = £105,000 + (£0.7167)(450,000)
Regression	£425,120 = £106,250 + (£0.7086)(450,000)

As explained earlier, values will always be different (unless pure coincidence occurs) and the resultant forecast is only as good a prediction of the future as the quality of the estimation technique used in the first place.

Self-check questions

3.1 (a) In economics, variable costs are often described as curvilinear whereas within cost accounting it is usual to assume variable costs have a linear function.

You are required to sketch two separate diagrams depicting:

(i) a curvilinear variable cost;

(ii) a linear variable cost.

(b) Explain and show by drawing two separate diagrams what is meant by:

(i) a semi-variable cost;

(ii) a stepped fixed cost;

and give one example of each.

(c) (i) Explain a method of depreciating an asset where the depreciation is not regarded as a fixed cost. Give the names of two common kinds of assets which may suitably be depreciated by the method you have stated.

(ii) You are required, ignoring inflation, to:

▶ comment on the following statement, and

▶ state whether, or not, you agree with it.

A business owning an asset with an estimated life of five years makes an annual provision for depreciation which is one fifth of the purchase price of the asset. Provided the asset lasts for exactly five years the business will, by making the depreciation entries, ensure that sufficient cash is available to replace the asset.

(Chartered Institute of Management Accountants)

3.2 The graphs on page 62 reflect the pattern of certain overhead cost items in a manufacturing company in a year. The vertical axes of the graphs represent the total cost incurred, whilst the horizontal axes represent the volume of production or activity. The zero point is at the intersection of the two axes.

You are required to:

(a) Identify which graph represents the overhead cost items shown below:

Ref.	Brief description	Details of cost behaviour
1	Depreciation of equipment	When charged on a straight line basis.
2	Cost of a service	£50 annual charge for subscription, £2 charge for each unit taken, with a maximum total charge of £350 per annum.
3	Royalty	£0.10 per unit produced, with a maximum charge of £5,000 per annum.
4	Supervision cost	When there is one charge hand for every eight men or less, and one foreman for every three charge hands and when each man represents 40 hours of production, thus:

	Hours	
	Under 320	one charge hand,
	321–640	two charge hands,
	641–960	three charge hands,
	etc.	plus one foreman.

Ref.	Brief description	Details of cost behaviour
5	Depreciation of equipment	When charged on a machine-hour rate.

6	Cost of a service	Flat charge of £400 to cover the first 5,000 units: Per unit £0.10 for the next 3,000 units £0.12 for the next 3,000 units £0.14 for all subsequent units
7	Storage/carriage service	Per ton £15 for the first 20 tons £30 for the next 20 tons £45 for the next 20 tons No extra charge until the service reaches 100 tons; then £45 per ton for all subsequent tonnage.
8	Outside finishing service	Per unit £0.75 for the first 2,000 units £0.55 for the next 2,000 units £0.35 for all subsequent units

(b) Give an example of an overhead cost item that could represent those graphs to which you do not refer in your answer to (a) above;

(c) Draw one graph of a pattern of an overhead item not shown and give an example of an overhead cost item that it would represent.

(Chartered Institute of Management Accountants)

3.3 (a) Explain the term 'cost behaviour'.

(b) The following table shows the production quantities and related total costs of a company manufacturing a single product

Period	Production units	Total cost
1	1,500	£2,600
2	1,800	£3,256
3	2,500	£4,560
4	3,200	£5,800

Using the index 100 to represent cost levels in Period 1, the following indices apply to succeeding periods

Period	2	110
	3	120
	4	125

On the basis of the foregoing you are required to calculate the total costs to be expected in Period 5 during which production of 4,000 units is planned and the cost level index is expected to be 135.

(Chartered Association of Certified Accountants)

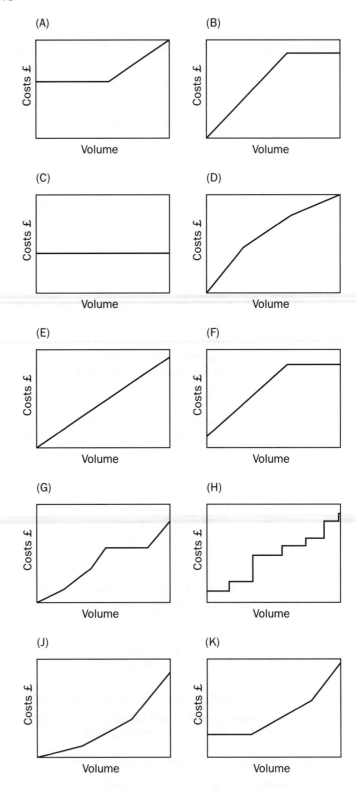

3.4 The following data relate to a company:

Sales	Delivery costs
£000	£000
80	16
85	11
115	21
160	16
205	23
280	18
290	27
330	32
390	30
450	37
470	25
550	35

You are required to:
(a) (i) plot these costs on a graph;
 (ii) draw on the graph the 'line of best fit';
 (iii) state the approximate level of fixed costs.
(b) state and explain a formula which may be used for predicting future delivery costs for any level of sales. (*Note:* figures are not required).

(Chartered Institute of Management Accountants)

3.5 (a) 'Management's knowledge of how a firm's costs actually behave is necessarily limited to an analysis of the results of *past* decisions, whereas planning requires estimates of *future* costs . . . Although costs cannot usually be predicted with absolute accuracy, it may be possible to identify a *cost function* which can be used to *estimate* the costs which the firm is likely to incur.' (J. Arnold and T. Hope *Accounting for Management Decisions*). *Required:*
 (i) State an algebraic cost function, explaining the role of each term in the formula, which 'can be used to estimate the costs which the firm is likely to incur'.
 (ii) Suggest and describe *three* methods of cost estimation which are based on the cost formula you have stated in (i) above.
(b) The cost behaviour patterns illustrated on the diagrams below represent nine cost-volume relationships. They have been constructed on the following bases and assumptions:
 (i) Cost is the dependent variable on the 'y' axis.
 (ii) Activity is the independent variable on the 'x' axis.
 (iii) Axes intersect at zero.
 (iv) Period under review is a year.
 (v) Each relationship which is represented should be interpreted as being independent of those shown on other diagrams.

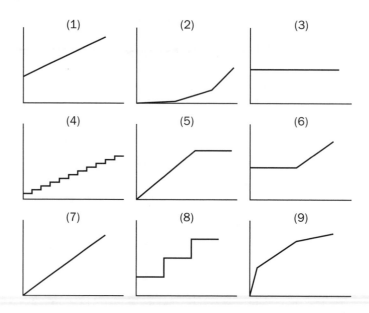

Notes: (i) Diagram No. 4 represents small, frequent changes in cost over a relatively narrow range of activity.

(ii) Diagram No. 8 represents significantly large, infrequent cost level changes over very wide ranges of activity.

Required:

Indicate (by use of the relevant number given) which diagram is illustrative of each of the following examples of cost items below. Place alongside each of your letters (a) to (k) the number you have chosen, and also indicate clearly whether the cost is: fixed; variable; semi-variable; step-fixed; or step-variable. A diagram may be used more than once or not at all.

Example	Cost item
(a)	Rent and rates.
(b)	Small pieces of glass cut from larger individual sheets of glass (i.e. cost of a whole sheet incurred irrespective of either just one or several pieces being cut).
(c)	Supervisory labour.
(d)	Total cost of running a firm/organisation.
(e)	Car rental (i.e. where agreed hire charge includes a free mileage allowance but above which extra charges are levied per additional mile).
(f)	Service engineer's maintenance calls charged: @ £7/hour between 0–3 hours; @ £10/hour between 3–6 hours; and @ £12/hour for calls longer than 6 hours.

(g)   Royalty/patent right payable according to how often the right is utilised, but with agreed maximum over which no payment made.

(h)   Depreciation (i.e. straight-line method).

(i)   Telephone and electricity charges.

(j)   Building/property insurance premiums.

(k)   Raw materials (e.g. screens in televisions; engines in cars; etc.).

(c) Norman Ltd. produces Fandangoes for the export market. Over the past five years output and total costs have been as follows:

Year-end	Tons output	Total costs (£)
19 x 4	1,800	4,467
19 x 5	2,000	4,522
19 x 6	2,400	4,746
19 x 7	2,100	4,410
19 x 8	2,800	5,145

Required:
Determine a regression equation from the above data and from it:
(i) Estimate the level of fixed costs that Norman Ltd. will incur in the production of Fandangoes in 19 x 9.
(ii) Estimate the variable cost per Fandango in 19 x 9.

(Accounting Degree)

Further study

Arnold, J. and Hope, T. (1990) *Accounting for management decisions,* 2nd edn, Hemel Hempstead: Prentice-Hall.

Baggot, J. (1977) *Cost and management accounting – made simple,* 2nd edn, London: Heinemann.

Carsberg, B. (1979) *Economics of business decisions,* 2nd edn, London: Pitman.

Horngren, C.T., Foster, G. and Datar, S. (1994) *Cost accounting – a managerial emphasis,* 8th edn, Hemel Hempstead: Prentice-Hall.

Lucey, T. (1992) *Management accounting,* 3rd edn, D.P. Publications.

Morse, W. and Roth, H. (1986) *Cost accounting,* 3rd edn, Wokingham: Addison Wesley.

Wright, D. (1994) *A practical foundation in costing,* 1st edn, London: Routledge.

CHAPTER 4

Marginal costing technique

Objectives
....

By the end of this chapter you should be able to:

▶ Apply the technique of marginal costing for the purpose of product cost ascertainment.
▶ Understand and develop the application of the fundamental management accounting concept of 'contribution'.
▶ Prepare marginal costing information for managers in order that they might make optimal use of scarce resources in a single limiting factor context.
▶ Appreciate the use of the marginal costing/contribution approach in helping management make effective decisions (such as solving an optimal product mix problem).

Let us begin this chapter with a reminder of a quote from the chapter which dealt with the *alternative* to marginal costing as a technique for cost ascertainment, that is Chapter 2's coverage of full absorption costing. In order to effectively contrast the 'full cost' technique of absorption costing with that of marginal costing, section 2.2.2 stated that 'what marginal costing does is recognise that the vast majority of overheads tend to be time-orientated (fixed or period) costs'. Absorption costing doesn't pay any attention to this particularly interesting characteristic of overhead costs and simply absorbs all manner of overheads, both fixed and variable, into unit product cost. This chapter now focuses sharply upon, and develops, what is an intuitively appealing view of cost analysis, centering on the distinctly different patterns of cost behaviour discussed in detail in the previous chapter. We saw there that the incidence of cost is impacted upon fundamentally by two differing influences – the level of business activity and the passage of time.

Fixed overhead costs are subject to change only with time and are not affected by marginal variations in the scale of business operations, i.e. they are *fixed* relative to changes in activity level. A good example is the cost of business rent and rates which may change over time but not because of a marginal change in the level of, for instance, production output. Marginal, or variable, costs such as raw materials and sales commissions (items of direct cost and variable overhead respectively) do, however, tend to *vary* with changes in the level of activity. This distinction between fixed and variable costs is especially crucial when management decisions about marginal changes in the level of business operations need to be made. Indeed, it is in the realms of management decision-making that marginal costing often plays a vital role. This is borne out later, for instance, in the decision accounting techniques part of the book (Part 2) particularly with regard to the topics of cost–volume–profit analysis (Chapter 6) and pricing decision techniques (Chapter 7).

4.1 Marginal cost ascertainment

The operation of marginal costing as a technique depends upon the separation of cost into its fixed and variable components. Several techniques for determining how this split of total cost is achieved were dealt with at some length in Chapter 3, so now we can assume that the division into fixed and variable cost is already satisfactorily made.

4.1.1 Ingredients to ascertain marginal cost

Variable cost and marginal cost are one and the same thing. The two terms can be used interchangeably, and will be throughout the rest of this book.

Essentially speaking, there are just two ingredients in the build-up of variable/marginal cost – they are: *prime cost* and *variable overhead*. This structure, however, can in addition be seen to consist of four ingredients if prime cost is further broken down into its own elements of cost (also look at section 2.1.4 again for extensive examples of the three basic ingredients of prime cost). Figure 4.1 clearly displays this structural build-up of ingredients.

As prime cost by its nature can be directly identified with, and easily traced to, specific individual cost units then it is not hard to imagine prime cost varying in direct proportion to the number of units produced or provided. Chapter 2 in general demonstrated how straightforward it is to ascertain product unit prime cost and Figure 2.3, in particular, clearly illustrated this. In addition to obvious examples of direct/prime cost such as raw materials, production

figure 4.1
Ingredients of marginal cost

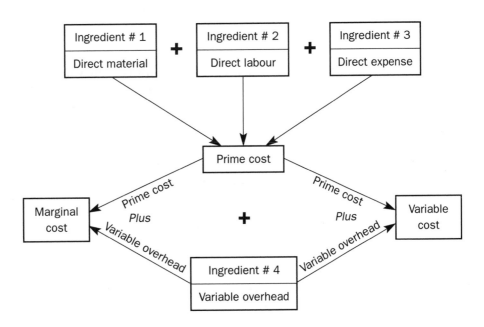

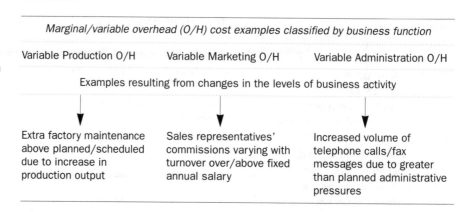

table 4.1
**Functional
marginal/variable
overhead breakdown**

Marginal/variable overhead (O/H) cost examples classified by business function		
Variable Production O/H	Variable Marketing O/H	Variable Administration O/H
Examples resulting from changes in the levels of business activity		
▼	▼	▼
Extra factory maintenance above planned/scheduled due to increase in production output	Sales representatives' commissions varying with turnover over/above fixed annual salary	Increased volume of telephone calls/fax messages due to greater than planned administrative pressures

labour and royalties, the composition of marginal cost can be extended even beyond the four ingredients in Figure 4.1 if, say, a functional overhead breakdown were presented (in Table 4.1) containing some perhaps less obvious examples of marginal/variable overhead cost to be added to those of prime cost.

In the balance of ingredients between prime cost and variable overhead to ascertain unit marginal cost the former (direct) cost element will virtually always be greater, sometimes immensely higher, than the variable overhead part. This is largely due to the nature of overhead cost. You might recall the quote from Chapter 2 right at the beginning of this chapter which stated that marginal costing recognises 'that the vast majority of overheads tend to be time-orientated (fixed or period) costs'; there are relatively few overheads which are variable in their behaviour. The treatment of fixed overhead costs in marginal costing will be dealt with shortly. But here it is sufficient to remind you that they are not in total affected by activity level changes, being time or period-related costs. The amount of total marginal cost, however, *is* related to and determined by the level of business activity – so we now consider this issue.

4.1.2 Marginal cost and the activity level

This section focuses upon, and consists entirely of, Activity 4.1. After completion you ought to ensure that you are completely familiar with its features as it will appear again in the next section as well as section 4.2 in the discussion of the concept of contribution.

ACTIVITY **4.1**

Product X is just one of a range of products manufactured by XYZ plc and its marginal cost profile consists of the following ingredients:

Product X: Unit marginal cost

	Unit cost	
	(£)	(£)
Direct costs		
Direct materials		3.00
Direct labour		2.00
Direct expense		0.50

Prime cost		5.50
Variable overheads (O/H)		
Variable production O/H	1.00	
Variable administration O/H	0.40	
Variable marketing O/H	0.80	2.20
Marginal cost		7.70

The management of XYZ plc is deciding on what level of activity to plan the manufac-turing output of product X. The original business plan is to manufacture 10,000 product cost units. But the company's management also wish to consider the effect on cost if marginal variations, say 10 per cent, around the original plan were to occur. The impact on cost may influence the decision as to whether to produce at business activity levels above or below the original plan.

Required: Advise XYZ plc's management, in suitable form, of the likely cost results of such activity level variations from the original plan.

The following schedule summarises the marginal cost effects of the three levels of business activity:

	Original plan	*Decision to produce marginal 10% above original plan*	*Decision to produce marginal 10% below original plan*
Activity level (units)	10,000	11,000	9,000
Unit marginal cost (£)	7.70	7.70	7.70
Total marginal cost (£)	77,000	84,700	69,300

Thus it can clearly be seen that there is an impact on marginal costs and that *in total* they vary directly in proportion to the level of activity – this is not the case, however, with fixed overheads. Any fixed cost commitments incurred by XYZ plc would not be affected by whichever of the three activity levels were decided upon because of the underlying nature of fixed overhead cost behaviour (see Chapter 3). Hence your attention is turned now to the treatment of such fixed overheads. (Note: You might also remember from Chapter 3 the 'conundrum' that variable/marginal cost *per unit* is a constant or fixed amount (£7.70 in above schedule) while fixed cost will vary per unit. In terms of cost behaviour, the descriptions 'fixed' and 'variable' relate to total cost *not* to unit cost.)

4.1.3 Marginal costing treatment of fixed costs

The crucial difference between the two alternative principles of full/absorption costing (see Chapter 2) and marginal costing here lies with their divergent approaches to the treatment of fixed, or period, costs. Marginal costing writes such overhead costs off as a single, lump-sum total amount charged against income (i.e. profit) in the profit and loss account for the cost accounting period in which the overhead is incurred. Full/absorption costing on the other hand recovers/absorbs fixed overhead costs (as well as variable costs) into the product cost unit, i.e. it breaks fixed cost down over products so fixed overhead becomes a part of the cost of goods sold figure in the trading account and hence is also absorbed into opening/closing product stock valuations. Under marginal costing, both stock values and the cost of sales figure include *only* variable costs.

Unit product cost ascertainment need not always be on a full/absorption costing base – although it must be for financial reporting purposes determined by the accounting profession[1]. Unit costs used for other purposes, like managerial decision-making, can be structured on a marginal costing base. This was the situation in the case of product X in Activity 4.1 where management may be deciding at what level of business activity to pitch operations and the marginal cost build-up of £7.70 per unit included no fixed overhead cost whatsoever. In addition to prime cost, only variable overheads were included in the unit product cost valuation of product X. It is also worth noting here that all fixed costs are bound to be overhead. Because prime (direct) cost consists only of variable costs, then all fixed costs must by necessity be indirect, i.e. overhead.

Finally, in many respects it is intuitively appealing to attach to product cost units only those type of costs which owe their very existence to that of the product – these are the variable costs. They will only be incurred (i.e. exist) if the product exists. Alternatively, they will not be incurred if the product isn't made. Hence they are *product-related*. By similar intuition, some costs have little or nothing to do with whether, marginally speaking, another product more (or one less) is brought into existence. These are fixed overhead costs like business rent and rates, and insurance premiums. Because they arise typically due to, say, monthly or annual charges, then instinctively you would relate them not to the existence of individual marginal product cost units but to the passage of time. Marginal costing treats them accordingly as *time-related*, writing them off fully in the costing period which incurs them and thus accounting for them as 'time' not 'product' cost.

4.2 Concept of contribution

The previous section talked about charging/writing off fixed overheads in the accounting period in which the overhead cost is incurred – but writing them off against what? The beginning of section 4.1.3 indicated a charge or write-off against 'income/profit' but more strictly and technically speaking it is against *contribution*. This notion of contribution is a brand new concept, hitherto unmentioned, but one which is pivotal to the operation of the marginal costing technique. It is of vital importance, arising as it does out of the crucial distinction between fixed and variable cost.

4.2.1 The contribution margin

The contribution margin is a measure of the difference between the two variable elements on the left-hand side of the following fundamental accounting relationship/equation:

Sales revenue – (Fixed cost + Variable cost) = Profit or loss

Both sales revenues and variable/marginal costs will vary in total according to changes in the level of business activity (see section 4.1.2). It follows that the amount of contribution which is the result of the difference between sales revenue and marginal cost will also vary in proportion to the activity level. As long as unit selling price is higher than unit marginal cost – the more activity, the more contribution. Contribution is calculated (in equation form) as follows:

Sales revenue – Marginal cost = Contribution

The very word itself – 'contribution' – has not simply been dreamed up. It actually is meaningful. The meaning is that the contribution margin figure from the above equation will initially *contribute* towards paying for the fixed costs of the firm (which will not change according to activity) and thereafter, once fixed overhead is covered, towards making profits. Expressed again in equation form:

Contribution = Fixed cost + Profit

Be careful never to confuse contribution margin with profit margin. Profit margins will invariably contain an element of accounting for fixed overhead absorbed into the cost of sales and opening/closing stock figures (see again first paragraph of section 4.1.3). Remember, marginal costing accounts for fixed costs differently by ascertaining a contribution margin first, as demonstrated above, against which fixed overhead is charged as one lump-sum amount (so no element of fixed cost is attributed to individual product cost units as would be the case with full/absorption costing). Any contribution remaining after fixed overhead costs are paid for is pure profit.

In summary, once unit marginal cost has been covered by the selling price of a cost unit then a contribution is made towards: (i) fixed overhead; and, afterwards, (ii) profit.

4.2.2 Contribution/marginal costing profit statements

Recall the product cost unit from Activity 4.1 – product X. You need to consider again its marginal cost structure and now also assume that it sells for £10 per unit, again remembering that sales revenue in total (like total variable cost) will vary in relation to the level of sales activity achieved – see start of section 4.2.1

table 4.2
Product X:
summary contribution
statement

	Per unit		In Aggregate/total (10,000 units)	
	(£)	(£)	(£)	(£)
Sales revenue:		10.00		100,000
Prime cost	5.50		55,000	
Variable overhead	2.20		22,000	
Marginal cost:		7.70		77,000
Contribution:		2.30		23,000

table 4.3
**Contribution/
marginal costing
profit statement**

	Product cost units			
	X	Y	Z	Total
Activity level (units)	10,000	11,000	4,000	25,000
	(£)	(£)	(£)	(£)
Sales revenue	100,000	88,000	80,000	268,000
Marginal cost	77,000	66,000	40,000	183,000
Contribution	23,000	22,000	40,000	85,000
		Fixed overhead cost:		60,000
		Profit:		25,000

again. We can now construct in Table 4.2 a typical summary contribution statement for product X in both 'per unit' as well as in 'aggregate' (i.e. total) terms given a level of activity of, say, 10,000 units (as was XYZ plc's original plan).

Now consider further a *multiple* product range of cost units. You might recall that product X in Activity 4.1 was just one of a range of products manufactured by XYZ plc. Assume that the wider product range offered by XYZ plc now extends to three product cost units – X, Y and Z. We can then prepare a multi-product contribution/marginal costing profit statement (as provided in Table 4.3) given that products Y and Z have different marginal cost structures (£6 and £10 respectively) and selling prices (£8 and £20 respectively) to those of product X. You also need to note that each product in the expanded contribution/marginal costing profit statement in Table 4.3 has, in addition, differing assumed levels of activity as well as the varying selling prices and marginal cost profiles. Finally, assume that XYZ plc's fixed overhead cost commitments amount to £60,000 per period.

We can see clearly from Table 4.3 that the three products earn at different rates of contribution. A rank order of earnings/profitability potential can therefore be established, thus: Z–X–Y. In this way the concept of contribution assists XYZ plc's management to decide which product type ought to be concentrated upon. In short, a basic *decision criterion* can be said to emerge from management's need here to rank alternative products. At this point you would benefit from quickly looking ahead to the introductory paragraphs at the very start of Chapter 5 which briefly describe the use of decision-making criteria, sometimes referred to as decision 'models', 'rules' etc.

4.2.3 Contribution/marginal costing criterion

The contribution/marginal costing product information for XYZ plc's management contained in Table 4.3 could alternatively, and perhaps more effectively, be summarised further in the slightly briefer product contribution/marginal costing profit statement provided next in Table 4.4.

table 4.4
**Product
contribution/
marginal costing
profit statement**

Products:	X	Y	Z	Total
Sales level (units):	10,000	11,000	4,000	25,000
	(£)	(£)	(£)	(£)
Unit contribution:	2.30	2.00	10.00	
Product contribution	23,000	22,000	40,000	85,000
			Fixed overhead cost:	60,000
			Profit	25,000

Through focusing sharply upon unit contribution Table 4.4 emphasises a little more clearly than Table 4.3 the rank order of management preference for the company's products, *viz.*:

Product cost unit	Unit contribution	Order of ranking
Z	£10.00	First
X	£2.30	Second
Y	£2.00	Third

Production and sale of one extra marginal unit of any of the firm's products will realise additional contribution (towards XYZ plc's profits because fixed costs are already covered) – but product Z will earn another £10; product X an extra £2.30; and product Y only an additional £2.00. On the other hand, the marginal loss of one product cost unit will reduce overall contribution by those same unit amounts. The decision criterion is a simple one: *maximise profits by concentrating resources upon the product offering the greatest contribution*. At this point it is important to realise that this decision criterion assumes no scarcity of resources (i.e. limiting factors). Scarce resources/limiting factor problems will be discussed in the next section of this chapter.

XYZ plc's management would consider it worthwhile to carry on making and selling all three products X, Y and Z because they each show a positive contribution towards fixed overhead costs and profit. Conversely, a negative contribution figure shown by any product would indicate to management that, on financial grounds at least, that particular product line should be discontinued. Moreover, in considering XYZ plc's products in Tables 4.3 and 4.4, there might be very good reasons why only 4,000 out of 25,000 units made and sold are of the highest ranked product Z. Reasons may include the possibility that Z is a bulky product and warehousing capacity for its storage is restricted, or that 4,000 units is simply the extent of market demand for Z.

Nevertheless if it were feasible, given no such limiting factors, to concentrate the entire 25,000 unit activity level on manufacturing units of Z in accordance with the decision criterion stated above, then XYZ plc's profits would increase from £25,000 (see Tables 4.3 and 4.4) to a maximum amount of £190,000, thus:

	£
Optimal contribution (25,000 units @ £10)	250,000
(less) Fixed overhead costs	60,000
Maximum profit	190,000

Exactly what is occurring with the above optimal/maximising strategy is this – an extra 21,000 unit contributions of £10 (£210,000) from Z, less the lost contributions from X and Y (comprising £23,000 + £22,000 = £45,000) is generating an additional profit of £165,000, which when added to the existing profit of £25,000 gives the maximum profit of £190,000.

This section now concludes with a summary reminder of the treatment of fixed overheads under marginal costing.

In the case of XYZ plc's product range, no attempt whatsoever was made to allocate, apportion and absorb (recall the three 'As' from Chapter 2?) the fixed overhead of £60,000 into the firm's product cost units as would have happened under full/absorption costing. Remember that fixed costs are alternatively referred to as *period* costs and the contribution/marginal costing technique treats them precisely in that manner, that is by writing them off against contribution as a single lump-sum total amount in the accounting period for which they are incurred.

4.3 The problem of limiting factors/scarce resources

When productive resources are in scarce supply such shortages can place severe limits on the manufacturing capacity of an organisation. Moreover, the management of organisations affected in this way will naturally, in the interests of maximum efficiency, wish to make optimal use of the precious scarce resources that the firm does possess. Scarce resources are alternatively referred to as *limiting factors* – and in further analysis later in the book (linear programming in Chapter 12) they will be known as 'constraints' on the activities of the firm. Whatever they are called you need to be aware that their effect is the same. Classic examples of scarce resources (from now referred to only as limiting factors) include:

▶ Shortage of raw materials.
▶ Limited number of machine running hours available (i.e. plant capacity).
▶ Restricted storage space in the factory/warehouse.
▶ Skilled labour market constraints causing restriction on number of skilled labour hours available.

The marginal costing technique, however, still holds the key to solving decision problems in situations where a limiting factor exists.

Can you think ...? of any further good examples of scarce resource constraints that would be considered as serious limiting factors to an organisation's operational activities?

Answer

(i) Market/sales demand for an organisation's product or service; (ii) Availability of money/capital to fund organisational operations (sometimes called 'capital rationing'); (iii) Limited number of service channels/points in an organisation etc.

4.3.1 Marginal costing solution to limiting factor problems

In the previous section we demonstrated the usefulness to management of a certain decision criterion, central to the application of marginal costing as a technique, embodied by the concept of 'contribution'. The same marginal costing decision criterion still applies but is now in need of a little modification. The notion of maximising profits through optimisation of contribution remains, but instead of looking at straight contribution there is a subtle, but vitally important, shift of emphasis when a limiting factor prevails. Emphasis must now be upon a slightly changed requirement to that of the decision criterion established in section 4.2.3 which simply prescribed maximisation of contribution. The change is to develop that simple criterion to now read: *maximise contribution per unit of limiting factor*. Application of this further refinement to the decision criterion is via the use of the following ratio:

$$\frac{\text{Unit contribution (in £s)}}{\text{Quantity of limiting factor (in units)}}$$

The importance of this ratio to managerial decision-making under conditions of resource constraint or scarcity is demonstrated in Activity 4.2.

4.3.2 Product mix decisions

Section 4.2.3 earlier concentrated on the use of straight contribution to rank products. The refined decision criterion just stated, and expressed further in ratio form above, builds upon this approach to enable management to achieve an optimal mix of the firm's products in order to maximise profits. This section is now wholly devoted to Activity 4.2.

ACTIVITY **4.2**

W. Vuts Limited has the facility to manufacture a varied range of five products – S; T; U; V; and W. Due to frequent limitations in the skilled labour market from which Vuts draws its production labour force, the firm often has to decide on an optimal mix between its products which may exclude manufacture of one or more of them. Vuts incurs total fixed overhead costs of £1.5 million per period. The following information is available for the coming period:

Product	S	T	U	V	W
	(£)	(£)	(£)	(£)	(£)
Selling price	200	360	280	240	320
Marginal cost	176	328	160	156	160
Contribution	24	32	120	84	160
(i) Hours of skilled labour time (hours)	12	8	40	24	32
(ii) Market sales demand (units)	10,000	4,000	5,000	8,000	6,000
∴ Total hours required [(i) x (ii)]	120,000	32,000	200,000	192,000	192,000

Required: Advise Vuts' management as to its product manufacture decisions in the separate cases of:

(a) where there exists no production labour limit;
(b) where there exists a skilled labour availability of only 480,000 hours in the period.

Your advice to W. Vuts Ltd's management would need to be consistent with the decision criteria we have discussed so far; therefore the following decision advice would be offered:

Case (a): In the ideal situation of no limit on skilled labour available, then the answer is simple – manufacture *all* products, as they each make a positive contribution.

Case (b): If production labour is limited to 480,000 hours, there arises a need to *rank* the products to achieve an optimal mix for the period. Moreover, the ranking order needs to be in accordance with the decision criterion of concentrating upon the products that 'maximise contribution per unit of limiting factor'. The relevant order of ranking is indicated in the following schedule:

Product	Unit contribution	Unit hours	Contribution per hour	Rank order
S	£24	12	£2	Fifth
T	£32	8	£4	Second
U	£120	40	£3	Fourth
V	£84	24	£3.5	Third
W	£160	32	£5	First

To manufacture all five products would require 736,000 hours (120,000 + 32,000 + 200,000 + 192,000 + 192,000) but only 480,000 skilled production hours are available. Therefore, consistent with the decision criterion to concentrate on the products that yield the greatest contribution per unit of limiting factor, your advice to Vuts' management would be to manufacture in the rank order above that maximises contribution per hour. Start with the highest ranked product, and continue through the order of manufacture to satisfy market sales demand until all the units of limiting factor (i.e. 480,000 skilled labour hours) are exhausted. The following optimal product mix thus emerges:

Labour hours (h) available	Usage of hours (h) at contribution per limiting factor	Optimal product mix at contribution per product unit	Total Contribution (£000)
480,000 h:	192,000 h @ £5 =	6,000 W @ £160 =	960
288,000 h:	32,000 h @ £4 =	4,000 T @ £32 =	128
256,000 h:	192,000 h @ £3.5 =	8,000 V @ £84 =	672
64,000 h:	64,000 h @ £3 =	1,600 U @ £120 =	192
		Maximum contribution	1,952
		less *Fixed overheads*	1,500
		Optimal profit	452

The final product amount in the mix (product U) is determined by the balance of limiting factor units still available/remaining (i.e. 64,000 hours) utilised to manufacture as many (1,600 units) of that product as possible – although this falls short of satisfying its market demand (of 5,000 potential sales units). No units of product S would be advised for manufacture.

A final confirmation of the rationale behind this logical optimisation procedure would be to suggest that if product S were to be made instead of U, then such a decision would be sub-optimal, proved thus:

Transfer 40 hours from production of one U: £120 lost contribution

To production of $3\frac{1}{3}$ units of product S: £80 gain in contribution

Thus, assuming fractional manufacture of S is feasible, to produce $3\frac{1}{3}$ of S instead of one U would only succeed in reducing total contribution by £40 (i.e. £120–£80). On the basis of your decision advice, W. Vuts Limited could not do better than make a maximum £452,000 profit from the suggested optimal product mix.

Summary

Management's decision strategy based on maximisation of contribution per unit of limiting factor is only able to cope with situations where a *single* binding constraint limits operations. Often, however, in practice there will exist concurrently quite a number of different limiting factors. Under these circumstances, and where linearity is valid as a reasonable assumption, then a more sophisticated aid to managerial decision-making is offered by the operational research technique known as 'linear programming' (LP). This more advanced technique identifies optimal solutions to product mix decision problems where several, or even a multitude of, limiting factors exist. It is one of the further planning techniques detailed in Chapter 12.

We have assumed throughout that managers are inherently 'maximisers/ optimisers' or in the specific context of this section, management's aim has been to achieve the greatest (maximum) profit by devising and deciding upon the best (optimal) mix of products. In Chapter 5 amongst the many issues that it addresses, we discuss situations where managers prefer to adopt non-maximisation/non-optimisation decision strategies. Finally, as much of the thrust of the last couple of sections, 4.2 and 4.3, has been concerned with managerial decision-making, it is a natural development that Part 2 of this book is entirely devoted to *decision accounting techniques*.

Self-check questions

4.1 The following information has been extracted from the books of the My Heir Company by its proprietor concerning a new product that he put into production at the commencement of the period just completed:

Sales	10,000 units sold at £5 each
Production	15,000 units which were produced at the following cost:

	£
Direct materials	15,000
Direct labour	30,000
Variable expenses	6,000
Fixed expenses	12,000

The proprietor of the company has two sons, both of whom are studying accountancy, but at different colleges. He sends each of them a copy of the figures and asks them to produce a statement showing their calculation of the company's profit for the period and the value of its closing stock.

One of the sons, having just been taught full-cost product costing, prepares a statement following that method. The other, who has just learned all about period costing, produces his statement on that basis.

When the father receives the two statements he finds that they provide different profits and stock valuations. Therefore he returns a copy of both statements to each of his sons, asking them to make a check and to find out which one has made a mistake.

Required:
(a) Formulate the **two** statements, presenting these in tabular form, showing the different ways that the sons were likely to have produced their statements.
(b) Explain why these two methods gave different results. In your discussion, use data from the two statements to illustrate your answer as appropriate, and briefly provide the arguments for and against these different approaches.

(Chartered Association of Certified Accountants)

4.2 The management of Springer plc is considering next year's production and purchase budgets.

One of the components produced by the company, which is incorporated into another product before being sold, has a budgeted manufacturing cost as follows:

	£
Direct material	14
Direct labour (4 hours at £3 per hour)	12
Variable overhead (4 hours at £2 per hour)	8
Fixed overhead (4 hours at £5 per hour)	20
Total cost	54 per unit

Trigger plc has offered to supply the above component at a guaranteed price of £50 per unit.

Required:

(a) Considering cost criteria only, advise management whether the above component should be purchased from Trigger plc. Any calculations should be shown and assumptions made, or aspects which may require further investigation should be clearly stated.

(b) Explain how your above advice would be affected by each of the two **separate** situations shown below.

(i) As a result of recent government legislation if Springer plc continues to manufacture this component the company will incur additional inspection and testing expenses of £56,000 per annum, which are not included in the above budgeted manufacturing costs.

(ii) Additional labour cannot be recruited and if the above component is not manufactured by Springer plc, the direct labour released will be employed in increasing the production of an existing product which is sold for £90 and which has a budgeted manufacturing cost as follows:

	£
Direct material	10
Direct labour (8 hours at £3 per hour)	24
Variable overhead (8 hours at £2 per hour)	16
Fixed overhead (8 hours at £5 per hour)	40
	90 per unit

All calculations should be shown.

(c) The production director of Springer plc recently said:

'We must continue to manufacture the component as only one year ago we purchased some special grinding equipment to be used exclusively by this component. The equipment cost £100,000, it cannot be resold or used elsewhere and if we cease production of this component we will have to write off the written down book value is which £80,000.'

Draft a brief reply to the production director commenting on his statement.

(Chartered Association of Certified Accountants)

4.3 A market gardener is planning his production for next season and he asked you, as a cost accountant, to recommend the optimal mix of vegetable production for the coming year. He has given you the following data relating to the current year.

	Potatoes	Turnips	Parsnips	Carrots
Area occupied, in acres	25	20	30	25
Yield per acre, in tonnes	10	8	9	12
	£	£	£	£
Selling price per tonne	100	125	150	135
Variable costs per acre:				
fertilisers	30	25	45	40
seeds	15	20	30	25
pesticides	25	15	20	25
direct wages	400	450	500	570

Fixed overhead.
per annum £54,000

The land which is being used for the production of carrots and parsnips can be used for either crop, but not for potatoes or turnips. The land being used for potatoes and turnips can be used for either crop, but not for carrots or parsnips. In order to provide an adequate market service, the gardener must produce each year at least 40 tonnes each of potatoes and turnips and 36 tonnes each of parsnips and carrots.

(a) You are required to present a statement to show:
   (i)   the profit for the current year;
   (ii) the profit for the production mix which you would recommend.
(b) Assuming that the land could be cultivated in such a way that any of the above crops could be produced and there was no market commitment, you are required to:
   (i)   advise the market gardener on which crop he should concentrate his production;
   (ii) calculate the profit if he were to do so.

(Chartered Institute of Management Accountants)

4.4 Z Ltd is a retailer with a number of shops selling a variety of merchandise. The company is seeking to determine the optimum allocation of selling space in its shops. Space is devoted to ranges of merchandise in modular units, each module occupying seventy square metres of space. Either one or two modules can be devoted to each range. Each shop has seven modular units.

Z Ltd has tested the sale of different ranges of merchandise and has determined the following sales productivities:

	Sales per module per week	
	1 Module	2 Modules
	£	£
Range A	6,750	6,250
Range B	3,500	3,150
Range C	4,800	4,600
Range D	6,400	5,200
Range E	3,333	3,667

The contribution (selling price – product cost) percentages of sales of the five ranges are as follows:

Range A	20%
Range B	40%
Range C	25%
Range D	25%
Range E	30%

Operating costs are £5,600 per shop per week and are apportioned to ranges based on an average rate per module.

Required:

(a) Determine the allocation of shop space that will optimise profit, clearly showing the ranking order for the allocation of modules.

(b) Calculate the profit of each of the merchandise ranges selected in (a) above, and of the total shop.

(c) Define the term 'limiting factor', and explain the relevance of limiting factors in planning and decision-making

(Chartered Association of Certified Accountants)

Note
. . . .

1. Accounting Standards Board, Statement of standard accounting practice #9: 'Stocks and long-term contracts'.

Further study
. . . .

Glautier, M. and Underdown, B. (1994) *Accounting theory and practice*, 5th edn, London: Pitman.

Morse, W. and Roth, H. (1986) *Cost accounting*, 3rd edn, Wokingham: Addison Wesley.

Pogue, G.A. (1984) 'Contribution analysis for decision-making' in *Management Accounting*, February, Chartered Institute of Management Accountants.

Sizer, J. (1989) *An insight into management accounting*, 3rd edn, Harmondsworth: Penguin.

Wheldon, H. (1984) *Cost accounting*, 15th edn, London: Macdonald and Evans.

Wright, D. (1994) *A practical foundation in costing*, 1st edn, London: Routledge.

PART 2

Management decision
accounting techniques

Information for management decisions under uncertainty

Objectives
··············

By the end of this chapter you should be able to:

▶ Understand the role of probabilities in helping facilitate effective management decision-making under conditions of business risk and uncertainty.

▶ Differentiate between simpler non-probabilistic decision-making models and the more advanced probabilistic decision criteria.

▶ Apply probabilities in using the superior decision models of expected monetary value (EMV) and subjective expected utility (SEU).

▶ Describe an alternative to maximisation decision criteria and explain the role of information analysis in managerial decisions.

Whilst the general topic area of the whole of Part 2 is about management decision accounting, this chapter largely concerns itself with management's use of accounting information specifically for decision-making under conditions of business risk and uncertainty. It begins with the use of probabilities and the application of different criteria in decision-making, and it ends with a brief description of the nature and value of information for management decisions.

At the very start of the book (in Chapter 1) two main branches of management accounting (decision and control accounting) were described in the context of an overall planning, decision-making and control process. If you were to refer to the section of Chapter 1 dealing with decision accounting, you would be reminded of the fundamental way in which managers can be said to go about their decision-making activities. They are necessarily involved in searching out and evaluating alternative courses of action from which they might choose. A technique or tool of choice in that decision-making process was described as a *model*.

Much of the context of this chapter describes for you the use of particular models which managers may find useful as a guiding rule upon which to base their decisions. In many branches of science and technology the use of complex and highly sophisticated models is widespread. For example, in the aeronautical and astronautical engineering divisions of the aerospace industry, miniature versions and prototypes of air and spacecraft are used for developing the 'real thing'. The types of model dealt with in this chapter are somewhat different.

Use of the word 'model' in this book is solely intended to convey to you the idea of applying a particular criterion or approach to resolving decision problems. As such the model approach to problem solving here essentially involves the use of a range of decision criteria (described later) as possible bases from which management may be advised as to what is likely to be their best or optimal course of action. In short, the expression *decision criterion* is used as a perfectly interchangeable term for what may also be described as a 'decision model', 'decision technique', or even 'decision rule'.

5.1 Probabilities and management decisions
....

Decision-making is largely concerned with the future and, in a more specific sense, the choice which lies between likely alternative future events and their associated possible courses of action. Depending on one's personal point of view, it can be construed as either a fortunate or unfortunate fact of life that it is notoriously difficult to predict what the future holds. But why is prediction of the future such a problem? The simple answer is uncertainty. Managers, like everyone else, live and work in a world which is riddled with *uncertainties*. Moreover, out of the constant and inevitable presence of uncertainty another additional element arises, that of *risk*.

5.1.1 Risk and uncertainty

Is it possible to draw a distinction between risk and uncertainty, and if so is the difference an important one in this context of managerial decision-making? In essence, the usual differentiation made is that measures of risk are based to some extent upon the existence of past evidence to support the level of risk attributed to the likelihood of similar future occurrences arising again. Uncertainty, on the other hand, is characterised by the distinct lack of support-ive evidence or information about the different degrees of likelihood of a future event happening or not.

Another way of looking at this essential difference, and one which may serve to make the distinction more apparently obvious, is depicted in Figure 5.1. Here the further notion of levels of objectivity/subjectivity is introduced, representing the degree to which accurate evidence exists, or does not exist, to support the measure of risk and/or uncertainty.

The 'span' of risk and uncertainty in Figure 5.1 indicates the degree of relia-bility or exactness with which a probability may be attached to an event occurring. For example, it is known exactly that a coin has a one-in-two chance of showing 'heads', and that a die has a one-in-six probability of showing a 'four'. The supporting evidence in this instance lies with the well-established statistical law of averages. This law of statistics dictates that, in the long-run,

figure 5.1
Span of risk and uncertainty

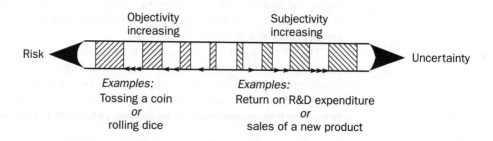

Risk ◄— Objectivity increasing   Subjectivity increasing —► Uncertainty

Examples:
Tossing a coin
or
rolling dice

Examples:
Return on R&D expenditure
or
sales of a new product

the throwing of a die or the tossing of a coin will be reflected by a risk frequency of one-in-six and one-in-two respectively.

Levels of risk might be said to be capable of being more precisely measured by the probability attached than might levels of uncertainty (i.e. the risk, as opposed to uncertainty, of losing or winning on the toss of a coin is exactly 1:1). If you refer again to Figure 5.1 the degree of precision involved in attaching probabilities to possible outcomes becomes less and less as movement is made sideways towards the right of the span. As the degree of subjectivity increases and movement continues further into the realms of uncertainty rather than risk, then probabilities attached to likely outcomes become increasingly more in the nature of *subjective credibility estimates*. Indeed, practically all business situations fall to the right of this span and lie somewhere within the uncertainty/subjectivity range or area. It is impossible to predict precisely such things as: (a) the probable future returns to be made from current investment in research and development; or (b) the future possible levels of sales to be generated from a newly launched product. Estimates therefore of the probabilities to be attached to the varying levels of such returns or sales are likely to be highly subjective in nature.

Can you think ...? of a further suitable example in addition to those just mentioned (appearing in Figure 5.1) of (i) objective risk; and (ii) subjective uncertainty.

Answer

(i) Objective risk – spinning a roulette wheel; (ii) Subjective uncertainty – chance of football team being relegated/promoted next season.

Let us return briefly to the question posed earlier in the section as to how important (or not) it is to make a clear-cut distinction between risk and uncertainty in the overall context of management decisions. In the light of the aims of this chapter, the straightforward reply is that the difference is *not* a vitally important one. In other more detailed and perhaps more advanced texts on probability and decision theory a finely drawn dividing line may well be of particular significance. However, for the present purposes of meeting the practical information requirements of managers in their decision-making activities, such a fine distinction is not considered to be critically relevant. What *is* of importance is that this brief discussion of risk and uncertainty has hopefully introduced you to the essential nature of probability, which is that probabilities attempt to measure risk/uncertainty and that some estimates of probability are more reliable (or objective) than others.

5.1.2 Probability estimates of risk/uncertainty

In objective terms, on the toss of a coin there is a '50/50' chance of a head or tail (i.e. probability = 0.5). Or, on the roll of a die there is a $16\frac{2}{3}$ per cent chance of the number four, or any other of the six faces, turning up (i.e. probability = 0.167). Alternatively in the world of management decision-making the marketing manager may make the subjective evaluation that the launch of a new product line has a 75 per cent chance of success (probability of 0.75) which implies a 25 per cent chance of failure (probability of 0.25). The probability estimates attached by the manager will not be as reliable as the 0.5 chance of a head or the 0.167 chance of a four. In fact, they may represent estimates virtually 'dreamed up' by the manager, due to perhaps a total lack of previous experience of past trends of similar new product launches to act as supportive evidence of the degree of new risk involved. Once again, such an estimate would be regarded as a highly subjective evaluation of a possible outcome.

At this point you might ask the question: 'How are probability estimates determined in the first place?' By now it should be fairly obvious where the coin and the die probabilities emanate from, but how are the more subjective measures of probability arrived at? If our marketing manager, for example, had actually dreamed up the 75:25 chance estimate of new product success/failure then the probabilities had been determined literally off the top of his or her head! Other different and more sophisticated methods do exist (e.g., the Delphi technique; equivalent gambles) but their detailed description is beyond the scope of this introductory level text.[1] It is sufficient in the current context of this chapter to simply say that various ways and means of determining probabilities are available, and that they range quite widely in the degree of sophistication to which they provide subjective estimates of probability values. In all subsequent business decision situations presented here the probability estimates required will be 'given' as part of the overall information set made available to management.

5.1.3 Scale of probability

Probabilities are expressed on a scale which starts at zero (no chance) and runs up to a maximum of 1 ('unity' or 100 per cent). An outcome with a probability of 1.00 represents the only possible outcome – because it is 100 per cent certain to occur. No uncertainty about other possible outcomes exists. The probability of Tuesday following Monday is equal to 1.00 – the possibility does not exist that another day of the week may sometimes follow Monday (which would only serve to reduce Tuesday's probability below that of unity!). It also follows

table 5.1 **Probability summation to unity**	Toss of a coin		Roll of a die						Marketing manager's estimates for new product launch	
Outcome	Head	Tail	One	Two	Three	Four	Five	Six	Success	Failure
Probability	0.5	0.5	0.167	0.167	0.167	0.167	0.167	0.167	0.75	0.25
Unity (Σ)	1.00				1.00				1.00	

table 5.2
Refinement of marketing manager's probability estimates

Success (= above 10,000 units)		Failure (= below 10,001 units)	
Sales in units	Probability	Sales in units	Probability
Above 50,000	0.25	2,001–10,000	0.20
25,001–50,000	0.40	0–2,000	0.05
10,001–25,000	0.10		0.25
	0.75	Σ Probability = 1.00	

that the summation of (Σ), of all individual probabilities, must add up to 1.00. Table 5.1 uses the simple instances of probability estimates given to you so far in this section to illustrate the 'sum total to unity' rule:

From Table 5.1, the marketing manager's subjective probability estimates could perhaps be a little further refined to reflect differing levels of possible success/failure as expressed, for example, in various expected sales levels (see Table 5.2) where sales in excess of 10,000 units are taken to equate to 'success', whilst sales below 10,001 units represent 'failure':

Note that such developments or refinements within the range of probability estimates in Table 5.2. can occur because of the highly subjective nature of the marketing manager's estimates; whereas the purely objective probabilities related to throwing dice and tossing coins are not open to such manipulation having no scope for manoeuvre within the probability range.

5.1.4 Types of management decision model/criterion

Perhaps the simplest description of probability would be to say that it is a measure of *expected* outcome. The statistical meaning of 'expected' is the long-run average or mean. For example, if a die is rolled six million times, it is to be expected that each surface of the die will statistically on average show up about one million times each. However, this book as a whole is concerned not with statistics but with accounting – and principally with management accounting. In particular this chapter primarily deals with the usefulness of accounting information as an aid to management decisions. In short the role of managerial accounting information is the general theme throughout, and the commonest way in which such information is presented is in the form of *monetary values*.

When the notion of expected outcome (which is measured by probability) is applied to accounting, which uses monetary values as its measure, the combined result may be said to be the *expected monetary value* (EMV) model. The use of EMVs represents one way in which management may be provided with decision-making information incorporating uncertainty. In addition to EMVs, other approaches of varying degrees of simplicity or sophistication exist as devices to aid management in the decision process. Two of these are dealt with in the next section, and as such represent models which managers may find useful for carrying out their decision-making activities. The use of models for decision purposes was briefly mentioned at the start of this chapter, as well as in Chapter 1 where their role in the overall planning, decision-making and control process was discussed. Using decision models is one means by which decision-makers (managers) may logically and rationally approach problem-solving situations. In so far as they represent ways of providing management with useful information to help them take decisions, then appropriate models may be said to act as *decision-making tools/techniques* designed to assist managers in choosing between alternative courses of action.

The EMV approach is a type of decision model. Various decision models exist. Some are relatively crude and simplistic whilst others reflect a rather more sophisticated view of management decision-making. In the following sections three different types of model will be dealt with. Firstly, the simplest forms of decision model will be discussed, known as the 'maximin' and 'maximax' criteria or approach. Somewhat wider coverage will then be given to the EMV model, followed by a review of a slightly more refined approach to managerial decision-making referred to as the 'subjective expected utility' (SEU) model or criterion.

5.1.5 Simple criteria for management decisions

A suitable starting point for our description of decision criteria is first to provide a brief outline of one or two of the less sophisticated approaches. Often in practical situations managers simply do not have the time and resources to make use of the more advanced techniques available to them. In such circumstances, it may be more expedient for the management accountant to advise managers of their best alternative course of action on the basis of really quite simplistic criteria which nevertheless are easily and readily applicable. These criteria will be explained for you using the following example:

A manager must choose one course of action out of A or B. The pay-off (monetary outcome) of each course of action will depend on the economic conditions, as follows:

Action	Conditions	Pay-off
A	Favourable	£15,000
	Unfavourable	£2,000
B	Favourable	£10,000
	Unfavourable	£4,000

One crude and simple approach is to use a decision criterion called 'maximin'. The actual name itself derives directly from the strategy employed, which is: to *maxi*mise the *mini*mum pay-off from various alternative actions. Maximin takes a pessimistic view of likely monetary outcomes or pay-offs, and assumes the worst possible results will occur from each course of action, i.e. Action A will result in a pay-off of £2,000 and Action B will result in a pay-off of £4,000.

Based on the maximin approach, a manager would choose 'the best of the worst' and adopt Action B. Managers who prefer to use the maximin criterion are pessimistic in their business outlook. Not surprisingly, maximin is often referred to as the 'criterion of pessimism'.

The opposite approach is known as the 'maximax' strategy, which assumes the best possible results will occur from each course of action, i.e. Action A will result in a pay-off of £15,000 and Action B in a pay-off of £10,000. Using this criterion, the manager chooses the course of action which *maxi*mises the *maxi*mum pay-off, i.e. this manager would choose Action A. A manager adopting this approach is an inveterate optimist, and maximax can be regarded as the 'criterion of optimism'.

In the next section (in Activity 5.1), both these equally simple decision criteria of maximin and maximax are further exemplified along with the statistically more sophisticated EMV approach to decision-making. (Other relatively crude/simple decision rules such as the 'minimax regret' criterion exist, and you are referred to a more specialist text.[2])

5.2 EMV criterion for management decisions

The EMV model/criterion was very briefly introduced to you previously in section 5.1.4 by combining the notion of *expected* outcomes (as measured by probabilities) with the fact that accounting is primarily concerned with *monetary values*. Such a combination of notion and fact results in a more sophisticated approach to management decision-making than the simple criteria dealt with so far. Often simply called the expected value criterion, EMVs represent a way in which the management accountant can adopt a more scientific, or at least statistical, approach to providing accounting information to managers to help them make better decisions more effectively. Essentially the use of expected values enables management to incorporate the problem of uncertainty (inherent to most business situations) into their decision-making.

5.2.1 Meaning and application of EMV criterion

An effective way of explaining precisely what is meant by an EMV is to define it. The Chartered Institute of Management Accountants (CIMA) in its official terminology uses the term 'expected value' and defines it as 'the financial forecast of the outcome of a course of action multiplied by the probability of achieving that outcome. The probability is expressed as a value ranging from at least 0 to 1.'[3] Practical application of the EMV criterion requires that management adopt the following basic decision rule, *viz*.:

'Choose the alternative course of action which serves to maximise EMV'

The expected values requiring to be maximised are likely to be in the form of either cash flows or profits. If the accounting measure used is one of cash flow then, for example, a £2,500 cash inflow may be expected to arise from a 75 per cent chance of benefiting from a cash surplus of £10,000 *less* a 25 per cent chance of incurring a cash cost deficit of £20,000. In this instance the relevant accounting expression is:

Equation (1): $E(F) = E(B) - E(C)$ (where F = Cash flow
B = Cash benefits
C = Cash costs.)

The prefix (E) is formally referred to as the 'expectation function', and when placed before the terms in the expression means that the given related probabilities have been applied to each relevant term. In other words:

$$\text{Expected cash inflow} = 0.75(£10,000) - 0.25(£20,000)$$
$$\therefore E(F) = £7,500 - £5,000 = £2,500$$

Alternatively, if profit rather than cash flow is used as the accounting measure then the expectation function may be applied in the following expression:

Equation (2): $E(P) = E(R) - [E(V) + E(F)]$ (where P = Profit
R = Sales revenue
V = Variable costs
F = Fixed costs)

You are at this point looking at an expression which assumes only profit and not loss is made. You will become distinctly more familiar with it in Chapter 6 on cost-volume-profit (C-V-P) analysis, but without the expectation function. Extracting (E) gives the classic accounting equation below:

Profit = Sales revenue – (Variable costs + Fixed costs)

With only slight rearrangement the above expression can be transformed into the following accounting equation particularly useful for purposes of C-V-P analysis:

Sales – Variable costs = Fixed costs + Profit

In equations (1) and (2) above EMVs are reflected by either expected cash or expected profit. To summarise, when adopting the EMV criterion a manager simply chooses the option which realises the greatest EMV. In other words, the manager's decision rule is to maximise either E(F) or E(P). Whether in the form of cash or profits EMVs are commonly calculated and presented in one, or both, of two different formats:

(a) pay-off matrices; and/or
(b) decision trees.

5.2.2 Calculation techniques: tabular (matrix) method

At this very fundamental level of decision theory a pay-off matrix may be regarded as little more than a tabular statement showing relevant cash flows, revenues, costs, profits, sales and production levels. When the appropriate probability estimates are applied to the values in the table (or matrix) a final column then shows the expected money outcome of the different possible alternatives. The manager will then be able to make his or her decision on the basis of information which thus incorporates a measure of the uncertainty attached to taking different courses of action. To further appreciate not only the use of a tabular, or matrix, approach to presenting EMVs but also the maximin and maximax decision criteria (mentioned in section 5.1.5) which do not attempt to allow for uncertainty, undertake the following Activity:

ACTIVITY 5.1

E.N. Anderson is the owner-manager of a chain of town-centre disc, tape and video stores. Anderson started his business with a single record shop in Manchester many years ago and as the business flourished he opened up new outlets in and around the North West. In recent years he has also expanded his retailing operations to other parts of the country and now owns and manages a number of stores in the North, Midlands and South of England. For several years Anderson has also been involved with managing a local Manchester-based group called 'Maine Trafford' who have just released a new record, and Anderson is deciding whether or not to embark upon an extensive advertising campaign to promote sales of the new record through all his branches. It is uncertain how well the record will sell. Demand could be high, average or low with respective probabilities of 0.2, 0.5 and 0.3. Because of local popularity Anderson believes that, even without advertising, positive net cash flows would still result at all demand levels, i.e. £16,000 if sales were high; £2,800 if average; and £400 even if sales were low. If, however, Anderson were to take the risk of advertising the record widely throughout his branches then net cash flows could be as high as £32,000 if it sells well, and £8,000 if demand for the record is average. Alternatively, if sales turn out to be low then a net cash outflow of £2,000 would occur as a result of the expenses involved in the advertising.

Required: Using a tabular/pay-off matrix presentation to show the information, advise Anderson as to whether or not he should advertise the new record, on the bases of: (i) maximin; (ii) maximax; and (iii) EMV decision criteria.

Table 5.3. and the advice which follows together satisfy this requirement. *Management advice to Anderson*:

(i) Maximin reflects a wholly pessimistic approach to decision-making and assumes with 100 per cent certainty that the worst outcome will happen. Effectively it attributes a probability weighting of 1.0 to the lowest level of demand. Because the given probabilities are not used it is referred to as a *non-*

table 5.3
E.N. Anderson: tabulation/pay-off matrix

Decision	Demand	Net cash flows	Probabilities	Expected monetary values
Advertise	High	£32,000	0.2	£6,400
	Average	£8,000	0.5	£4,000
	Low	(£2,000)	0.3	(£600)
			1.0	£9,800
Not advertise	High	£16,000	0.2	£3,200
	Average	£2,800	0.5	£1,400
	Low	£400	0.3	£120
			1.0	£4,720

probabilistic decision model/criterion. Advice to Anderson would be not to advertise because even at worst a positive cash flow of £400 would be achieved (as opposed to a negative £2,000 cash outflow if he chose to advertise).

(ii) Maximax is also a non-probabilistic decision criterion with its wholly optimistic decision strategy placing l00 per cent certainty upon the best outcome eventuating, i.e. high demand. Advice to Anderson would be to advertise because this choice would realise twice the cash amount when compared with the alternative (a maximum of £32,000 as opposed to £16,000).

(iii) EMV is a *probabilistic* decision model/criterion which takes account of given relative degrees of prevailing uncertainty. Advice to Anderson would be to advertise because this alternative course of action has the higher overall likely expectation (an expected cash value of £9,800 compared with £4,720 from not advertising). It is well worth noting, however, that this EMV advice ignores the fact that Anderson may not want to risk the 30 per cent chance of losing £2,000, and he may instead choose not to advertise as this alternative always gives a positive cash return despite only offering the lower EMV. With such an apparently contradictory (in terms of EMVs) decision Anderson would be expressing a subjective attitude to the taking of risks which is something the EMV criterion, in its purely objective fashion, cannot cater for. This aspect of decision-making is further explored in section 5.2.4, when EMV's limitations are discussed.

5.2.3 Calculation techniques: decision tree method

Decision trees provide the decision-maker with an alternative to using the tabular, or matrix, approach for presenting and solving EMV problems. Use of this decision tree method will *not* result in contrasting advice being offered to management. Both approaches merely represent different means of arriving at the same solution to a decision problem. Decision trees possess three basic ingredients or elements in their structure:

(i) Branches – these indicate the lines of alternative actions and outcomes;

(ii) Decision nodes – these indicate a decision point (conventionally shown as a box: □);

(iii) Event/outcome nodes – these indicate the different possible results/ outcomes of a decision (conventionally shown as a circle: o).

Before embarking on Activity 5.2 involving you in the use of these decision trees as a way of presenting EMVs, consider the written definition of a decision tree provided by the CIMA. It is 'an analytical tool for clarifying the choices, risks, objectives, gains and information needs involved in different courses of action. It can be non-quantitative for planning purposes, or quantified for decisions.'[4] Figure 5.2 allows you to see the essential nature and appearance of a decision tree before using the method to solve the decision problem in Activity 5.2

figure 5.2
Decision tree
illustration

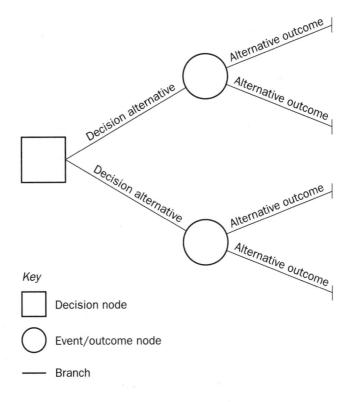

Key

☐ Decision node

◯ Event/outcome node

— Branch

ACTIVITY **5.2**

Lilywhite plc is involved in the manufacture of sports hardware and the company's management team consists of the production, marketing, finance and managing directors. The directors have to decide for the coming football season whether to produce 5,000 or 10,000 units of a special 'limited edition' batch of silver souvenir tankards for the local football club Phoenix FC's centenary year celebrations. The marketing director has advised the managing director that the optimal price for selling tankards will be £40 each. Meanwhile the production and finance directors have collaborated to determine that certain types of costs will vary directly with output and these will work out at exactly half the tankard's selling price (i.e. a variable cost of £20 per unit). Furthermore, on the basis of advice from his management accountant, the finance director has also ascertained that the fixed costs involved with either size of batch will total £80,000. Together the managing and marketing directors have estimated that although market demand for tankards amongst the club's supporters is uncertain, basically it will result in sales being either good or poor. They expect that there is only a 40 per cent chance of demand being good when 10,000 tankards would be sold. On the other hand, they believe that there exists a greater probability of 60 per cent that only half that number (i.e. 5,000 tankards) would be bought by supporters. (It can be safely assumed that any unsold units would not realise either further profit or loss for Lilywhite plc.)

Required: Using a decision tree to formulate and solve the decision problem, advise Lilywhite's management team, on the basis of the EMV criterion, as to which of the two levels of batch manufacture to undertake.

figure 5.3
**Decision tree
(Lilywhite plc)**

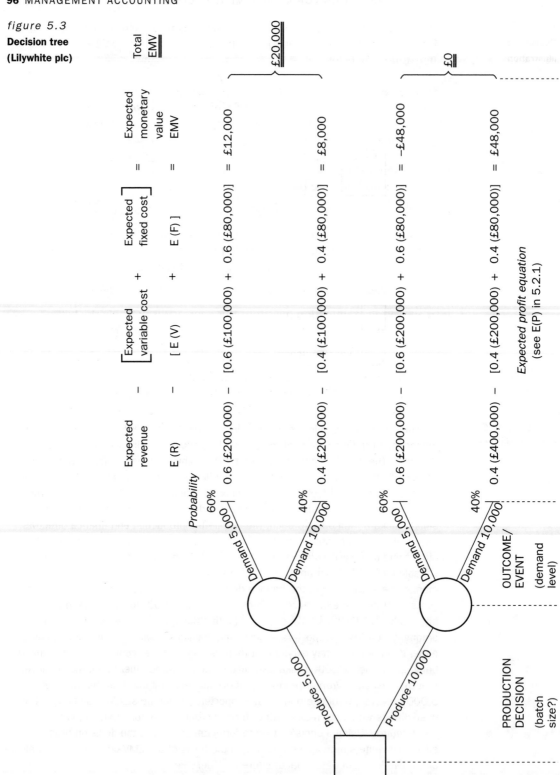

Via application of equation (2) which was presented in section 5.2.1, the above requirement is satisfied by both Figure 5.3 and the brief advice immediately following below.

Management advice to Lilywhite plc: In accordance with the EMV criterion the course of action which will lead to maximum EMV is chosen. This means Lilywhite will be best advised to decide upon a batch of 5,000 tankards as this unit production level realises the higher total EMV of £20,000.

Alternatively, and preferably from the viewpoint of greater economy of calculation, each branch of the decision tree in Figure 5.3 could be evaluated as follows instead of using the expectation equation:

$$\text{Sales} - (\text{Variable cost} + \text{Fixed cost}) = \text{Profit} \times \text{Probability} = \text{EMV}$$

The above avoids you having to apply the individual probability repeatedly for each expectation (E). Instead the profit (or loss) outcome is weighted just once, for example taking the first branch of Figure 5.3's tree:

$$£200,000 - (£100,000 + £80,000) = £20,000 \times 0.6 = £12,000$$

In answering examination questions this approach is probably the better, quicker way of performing the EMV calculations involved. You will often find that when two separate means of solving a problem are available to you (as in 5.2.2 and 5.2.3) you come to master one technique more quickly and efficiently than the other. You then feel more comfortable and confident in using that method. However, by using both methods you may find that your understanding of how to solve the problem is reinforced. The advice given here, particularly for examination purposes, is that if you find the use of two differing approaches only serves to confuse the issue, then you should obviously concentrate on the method with which you feel more sure and at ease. Alternatively, you may feel equally 'at home' with either approach, and are largely indifferent as to which one you adopt. But you should be careful to present the examiner with *one* clear solution to the problem and perhaps, time allowing of course, use the other method as a means of checking the answer. This also serves to make the examiner aware of your wider understanding and appreciation of the problem. However, always clearly indicate to the examiner which answer is offered as the one to be marked.

5.2.4 Limitations of the EMV criterion

Where and whenever resources allow it, choice between decision alternatives by managers on the basis of the EMV criterion is to be preferred to the simpler approaches (such as maximin) by virtue of the fact of EMVs attempt, through the use of probabilities, to provide for the ever-present uncertainties which pervade most business decision-making situations. Why not then apply this single criterion to all uncertain business situations which require a decision to be made by management? The basic answer is that, as with many management accounting techniques (break-even analysis, for example, see Chapter 6), certain practical limitations exist which restrict its usefulness and application. Only under the following particular circumstances is it appropriate to use EMVs:

(i) where the business project or investment opportunity under consideration is itself small in relation to both the organisation's overall size and also to the total set of projects/opportunities being considered;

(ii) where there are a large number of similar, relatively small and statistically independent projects or opportunities already being undertaken on a large number of occasions;

(iii) where managers hold a neutral attitude towards the taking of risks, they are neither risk-seekers nor risk-avoiders.

To explain each circumstance a little further consider limitation (iii) first. Use of the EMV criterion contains an in-built assumption that managers who make decisions are *risk-neutral* and have no particular risk preferences as such. The meaning of 'risk neutral' will become clear as you work through Activity 5.3.

ACTIVITY **5.3**

Manager A offers manager B the opportunity of gaining or losing £1 in a gamble between each other – the gamble being on the single toss of a coin. 'Heads I win, tails you win' says A, and B accepts.

Required: What is the EMV (to manager A) of such a decision to gamble?

The worked solution below also develops Activity 5.3 into a further 'decision-to-gamble' situation.

Outcome	Gain/(Loss)	Probability	EMV
Heads	£1	0.5	£0.50
Tails	(£1)	0.5	(£0.50)
			0

(Note: Obviously the same total EMV of zero would also apply to B's situation.) Having seen them gamble, an observer, manager C, feels that the other two managers have got the 'gambling bug' into their systems! Manager C now suggests that A offers B a further gamble and the opportunity to win or lose £4,000. Again, what is the EMV?

Outcome	Gain/(Loss)	Probability	EMV
Heads	£4,000	0.5	£2,000
Tails	(£4,000)	0.5	(£2,000)
			0

Quite simply, the EMV criterion, by producing the same net value of zero, does not differentiate between the two 'decision-to-gamble' situations. However, is it likely that the managers themselves will be equally indifferent (i.e. neutral) to taking the risk? It is highly probable that both managers A and B (unless extremely wealthy!) will turn down manager C's suggestion that they take on the second opportunity to gamble. And by so doing they would not be exhibiting a risk-neutral attitude to the decision opportunity but would be adopting a risk-averse (or risk-avoiding) stance.

Advice to the managers via the EMV criterion, however, does not reflect such an attitude to risk. It assumes that the managers are risk-neutral, and prescribes that they should hold no preference for gambling £1 or £4,000 on the toss of a coin.

Returning to the basic three limiting circumstances, consider condition (ii) where it is stated that to appropriately use the EMV criterion it is necessary that a large number of independent, similar and relatively small projects are undertaken extremely regularly. No further elaboration on this condition is really necessary other than to cite the familiar commercial example of the insurance business. Insurance companies exist largely on the strength of a willingness to take on multitudes of individual risks simply because there are so many, and because there is a likelihood of misfortune occurring only in a relatively small number of the cases. Furthermore the individual incidence of mishaps occurring are taken to be wholly unrelated to each other, i.e. they are statistically independent.

Last of our necessary prevailing circumstances is condition (i) which dictates that the individual project/opportunity should be small relative to the size of the organisation and its entire set of projects and opportunities. To exemplify this point a little further, refer again to the £4,000 'decision-to-gamble'. If one of the managers A or B happened to be an enormously wealthy millionaire to whom £4,000 represents a relatively insignificant proportion of overall personal monetary resources, then his/her inclination may well be to take the gamble as it merely represents a 'drop in the ocean' compared with total personal wealth.

Finally, and to still further illustrate condition (i), take the case of a small business where perhaps the loss of a few thousand pounds may result in bankruptcy and collapse. If the manager of such a small business were to adopt the EMV criterion in considering a business opportunity which, for example, was estimated to have a 70 per cent chance of realising £10,000 profit but a 30 per cent probability of making a £10,000 loss – what should the manager's course of action be? On EMV grounds there is no doubt what the right decision should be:

$$0.7 (£10,000) + 0.3 (-£10,000) = £4,000$$

A positive EMV of £4,000 indicates that the manager should accept the opportunity as it is expected to increase the wealth of the business by £4,000. However, the business's manager may decide that even a 3-in-l0 chance of bankruptcy (assuming that losing £10,000 would have a bankrupting effect on the business) is too great a risk to take and, so in order to ensure the continued survival of the business, the opportunity is rejected. Such a decision contradicts the EMV's risk-neutral recommended course of action, but instead reflects the practical reality of a manager adopting a quite understandable risk-averse attitude. (Here you might also find it useful to quickly re-read the similar considerations briefly mentioned in advice item (iii) of Activity 5.1).

Despite the principal limitations discussed in this section, which illustrate EMV's possible shortcomings as regards its practical application, the EMV approach still provides managers (in situations where it is applicable) with a 'rule of thumb' for making decisions which is preferable to the earlier simplistic criteria of maximax and maximin. The existence of uncertainty in business situations represents to the manager probably the single most difficult condition which prevails upon, and militates against, effective decision-making. EMV's probabilistic approach offers the manager a tool which goes a long way towards measuring and incorporating the ever-present uncertainties involved in choosing one course of action as opposed to another. In the appropriate circumstances outlined above, choice of the alternative which maximises EMV will provide the manager (decision-maker) with the best possible course of action in the light of prevailing uncertainty. However, the assumption that management will be entirely risk-neutral in deciding between alternatives is a rather strict assumption to make, and another criterion is suggested next which does effectively cater for the practical reality of managers having different attitudes towards the taking of risk. This further approach, known as the *subjective expected utility* (SEU) criterion, is described in detail in section 5.3.

5.3 SEU criterion for management decisions

Application of the subjective expected utility (SEU) criterion represents one way of overcoming probably the most serious of EMV's criticisms, that is its complete disregard for differing risk attitudes. The very word 'subjective' in its description is a clear indication of an attempt to recognise individual differences, as opposed to the EMV criterion's purely neutral and objective approach. Once more, as with EMVs, use is made of *expected* measures which simply means that probabilities are again applied in order to reflect the particular uncertainties that might prevail. The specific measure about to be used here, however, does not appear in terms of money values but is now expressed as *utility*. Recall the earlier EMV decision rule (from the start of section 5.2.1). It very slightly modifies now to include utility instead of EMV and the decision rule becomes:

'Choose the alternative course of action which serves to maximise utility'.

5.3.1 Utility and utility functions

As accountants in their dealings tend to be primarily concerned with monetary measures, a brief description and illustration of the term 'utility' is called for. Utility is essentially a measure which reflects the usefulness of something (e.g. money) to someone in terms of the satisfaction derived by the individual from using it. Additionally, and most importantly in the current context, utility also serves as a measure which reflects the attitude of individual decision-makers towards either seeking out, or alternatively, avoiding risks. Furthermore, such respective risk-aggressive or risk-averse attitudes can be indicated by differing utility functions. What then is meant by 'utility function'?

Earlier in the book (Chapter 3) you were presented with quite an array of various sorts of cost function in order to describe different patterns of cost behaviour. These cost functions were depicted as being either linear or curvilinear and reflected the types of relationship existing between cost and volume/

activity levels. Further functional relationships will be presented in later chapters. Chapter 6, for example, extends the study of cost-volume (C-V) relationships by adding the extra dimension of a sales function enabling C-V-P analysis to be carried out. Other chapters will also deal with the interrelationships between differing levels and mixes of costs, sales, production units and the like. The purpose here behind mentioning these other functional relationships is merely to emphasise that a function, be it either mathematical in the form of an equation or graphical in the shape of a curve or line on a chart, is basically no more than a 'mapping out' of how different things react with each other. Hence, the following use of utility functions in applying the SEU criterion will involve firstly a graphical and then a numerical illustration. The relationship mapped out here is one between utility and money, and is one which incorporates a measure of the opposing risk attitudes that may be adopted by different decision-makers. It has been stated already that the SEU approach, by reflecting individual risk preferences of aversion or aggression overcomes EMV's principal shortcoming of assuming risk neutrality. How might this be explained a little more fully? Carefully consider the following two Figures 5.4 and 5.5.

The utility function in Figure 5.4 takes the form of a *parabola* (similar to the curvilinear variable cost functions discussed in section 3.1.1 of Chapter 3 on cost behaviour). In this instance, the curve indicates the relationship between utility (u) and money (m). When a change in the level of money is made, a reading from the curvilinear function can be taken which reflects the corresponding change in utility derived from the change. The form of utility function in Figure 5.4 can be used to quite clearly illustrate what is meant when a decision-maker is said to be adopting a risk averse stance or attitude. First of

figure 5.4

Parabolic (risk-averse) utility function: (SEU) graphical model

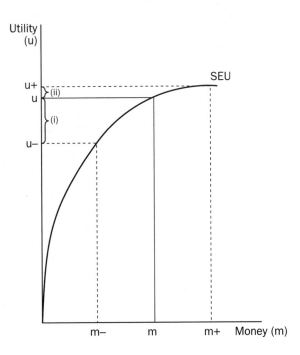

figure 5.5

**Linear (risk-neutral)
utility function:
(EMV) graphical
model**

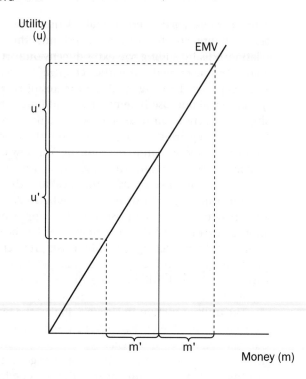

all, take the case of where it is equally likely that a manager's decision will result in the same amount of money either flowing into (m to m +) or flowing out of (m to m –) the business. If the manager is a risk avoider, then he or she will experience a subjective loss in utility (indicated by (i) in Figure 5.4) from losing money (m to m –) which is relatively greater than the corresponding gain in subjective utility derived from having the equal amount (m to m +) flowing in – as indicated by (ii) in Figure 5.4. So although it is just as likely that business wealth will increase as decrease by that amount, the manager is *not indifferent* to taking that 50/50 risk because of the disproportionately greater loss of subjective utility. In practical terms, the loss of that amount of money may be so significant as to, say, bankrupt the business, and therefore the 50/50 chance would not be taken in the interests of the continued financial safety of the business. Such a cautious decision, despite the 'evens-chance' attached to the outcome, is clear reflection of a risk averse strategy. At this point you may also find it useful to compare this decision situation with Activity 5.3. A risk-aggressive attitude would be represented by a concave utility function as opposed to the convex (risk-averse) function in Figure 5.4.

In Figure 5.5 a typically risk-neutral stance, being representative of the EMV approach, is illustrated. Here, changes in utility levels would vary exactly (i.e. equally proportionately) in accordance with corresponding changes in money flows, revealing no relative preferences or aversions to the taking of business risks involving potential monetary loss or gain. Utility functions can also be expressed by mathematical means; e.g., for a parabola the form of expression is the following:

$$U = a + bm + cm^2 \ldots nm^n$$

(For a corresponding explanation of the above terms you should refer to the description of curvilinear variable cost functions in section 3.1.1 of Chapter 3.)

Individual decision-makers' subjective utility functions can present themselves in many varied shapes (graphical) and forms (of mathematical expression). This book will not enter into the subject of how the many differing types of utility function are derived or determined. For present purposes the utility function will simply be taken as 'given'. What is important to realise is that any given mathematical expression is, in essence, a numerical/algebraic reflection of the graphical form of the function. Just as, for example, the above mentioned expression: $U = a + bm + cm^2 \ldots nm^n$ is the relevant equation describing the type of function known as a parabola – the shape of which appears in Figure 5.4. Various other types of utility function exist (e.g. logarithmic, negative exponential, etc.) but we cannot cover them all in an introductory-level text.

5.3.2 *Practical application of SEU criterion*

Probably the best way to demonstrate the practical application of SEUs in the making of management decisions is by means of a worked example. Using the same basic data as for the EMV illustration (Lilywhite plc) in Activity 5.2, work through Activity 5.4.

ACTIVITY **5.4**

Assume the same decision problem (i.e. to produce 5,000 or 10,000 tankards) is facing the management of Lilywhite plc as it did in Activity 5.2. However, suppose now that the four directors on the management team have also determined that the team's attitude to risk-taking is summarised in the following subjective utility function:

$$U = 4 \left(\frac{m}{10,000} \right) - \frac{1}{4} \left(\frac{m}{10,000} \right)^2$$

(where values for 'm' are in '£s' of monetary profit or loss).

Required: Advise Lilywhite's management team, on the basis of the SEU criterion, as to which of the two levels of batch manufacture to undertake.

In Activity 5.2 the problem as to whether to produce a unit batch of either 5,000 or 10,000 tankards was solved by using the technique of decision tree analysis. Alternatively, the decision confronting Lilywhite's team of directors could have been presented in tabular (or matrix) form, as in Table 5.4:

Making a decision based on EMV you have already seen, in Activity 5.2, that the directors would be best advised to schedule production of a 5,000-unit batch of tankards (because it generates the higher EMV). But now, by 'plugging' the same data into the SEU function provided, advice can be offered to Lilywhite's management on the different basis of greater utility (rather than monetary value). The figures resulting from applying the utility function will obviously not be in '£s', but instead are expressed in a utility measure referred to as *utiles* or *utilities*. The result from the team's SEU function when applied to each decision alternative (A) and (B) is as follows:

table 5.4
Lilywhite plc:
tabulation/pay-off
matrix

Decision	Demand	Sales revenue	Variable costs	Fixed costs	Profit/ (loss)	Probability	EMV
(Units)	(Units)	(£000)	(£000)	(£000)	(£000)		(£000)
Produce	5,000	200	100	80	20	0.6	12
5,000	10,000	200	100	80	20	0.4	8
						1.0	20
Produce	5,000	200	200	80	(80)	0.6	(48)
10,000	10,000	400	200	80	120	0.4	48
						1.0	0

(A) Decision alternative: produce 5,000 units:

(1) There is a 0.6 probability of £20,000 profit: $4\left(\dfrac{20,000}{10,000}\right) - \dfrac{1}{4}\left(\dfrac{20,000}{10,000}\right)^2$

(2) There is a 0.4 probability of £20,000 profit: $4\left(\dfrac{20,000}{10,000}\right) - \dfrac{1}{4}\left(\dfrac{20,000}{10,000}\right)^2$

Sum the probabilities by adding together the two utility expressions:

$(1) + (2) = 0.6[4(2) - \frac{1}{4}(2)^2] + 0.4[4(2) - \frac{1}{4}(2)^2]$

$= 0.6[8 - \frac{1}{4}(4)] + 0.4\,[8 - \frac{1}{4}(4)]$
$= 0.6(8 - 1) + 0.4(8 - 1)$
$= 4.2 + 2.8$
$= \underline{7 \text{ utiles/utilities}}$

(B) Decision alternative: produce 10,000 units:

(3) There is a 0.6 probability of £80,000 loss: $4\left(\dfrac{-80,000}{10,000}\right) - \dfrac{1}{4}\left(\dfrac{-80,000}{10,000}\right)^2$

(4) There is a 0.4 probability of £120,000 profit: $4\left(\dfrac{120,000}{10,000}\right) - \dfrac{1}{4}\left(\dfrac{120,000}{10,000}\right)^2$

Again, sum the probabilities by adding together the two utility expressions:

$(3) + (4) = 0.6[4(-8) - \frac{1}{4}(-8)^2] + 0.4[4(12)\frac{1}{4} - (12)^2]$

$= 0.6[-32 - \frac{1}{4}(64)] + 0.4[48 - \frac{1}{4}(144)]$
$= 0.6(-32 - 16) + 0.4(48 - 36)$
$= -28.8 + 4.8$
$= \underline{-24 \text{ utiles/utilities}}$

Management advice to Lilywhite plc: In accordance with the SEU criterion, Lilywhite's team of directors would be best advised to schedule manufacture of a 5,000-unit batch of tankards as this strategy realises a *positive* utility value of seven (as compared with a *negative* utility value of 24 from the other alternative course of action of producing 10 000 tankards).

In Activity 5.4, therefore, once again (as was the case in Activity 5.2) management's optimal choice would be to opt for the 5,000-unit production level. The fact that the same alternative batch quantity is recommended by both the EMV and SEU criteria is entirely coincidental. It must be stressed that it does not necessarily follow that the use of one criterion will always result in the same management advice being offered as with the other! (If both criteria consistently resulted in the same decision advice, what would be the point of having two separate probabilistic approaches to problem-solving situations in the first place?)

So far, recommendations to managers indicative of what might be their best or most likely 'correct' decision have been based purely on the alternative which provides the greatest or highest return. However, do you think that such an approach is always going to be the most suitable and most relevant in all practical circumstances? In the next section a possible alternative strategy to management decision-making is described for you, it is one *not* based on optimising or maximising criteria.

5.3.3 A possible alternative to optimisation criteria

A range of different decision criteria spanning various degrees of sophistication have been mentioned so far. Partly to introduce this section, and partly as a timely reminder of the relevant decision rules/techniques for management decision-making, consider the following brief three-point summary:

1. Choose the alternative which maximises either the worst or the best possible outcomes. This is the non-probabilistic, relatively unsophisticated and crude approach to decision-making adopted by the maximin and the maximax criteria (see section 5.1.5).
2. Choose the alternative which maximises EMV. This is a more sophisticated and probabilistic approach incorporating risk and uncertainty, but risk neutral in its disregard of managerial preferences and attitudes to the taking of risks (see section 5.2).
3. Choose the alternative which maximises SEU. This is an even more refined probabilistic approach incorporating risk preferences and attitudes of risk aversion/aggression (see sections 5.3.1 and 5.3.2).

It should be fairly obvious to you that there is one single recurring theme common to all these criteria, irrespective of how simplistic or developed the approach happens to be. The common element lies with the assumption that the decision-making manager at all times adopts a strategy of maximisation or optimisation. How true a reflection do you think this is likely to be, however, of the approach of practical business managers in their routine, daily decision-making activities?

Assumptions/limitations of 'rational economic behaviour'

Except for the cruder approaches (which only consider the worst/best sets of possible outcomes) the criteria dealt with up to now have assumed that the decision-maker will undertake a thorough and rational assessment of all available alternatives, and then consistently choose from the alternatives available the opportunity which maximises either money values or utility. Such a pattern of decision-making clearly reflects the behaviour of *rational economic man*, and furthermore both the EMV and SEU decision criteria can be said to generally typify the approach of the 'rational economic-minded manager'. The notion of this form of behaviour was mentioned at the start of the book. Refer back to Chapter 1 – particularly to phase III in the decision process (Fig. 1.1 and section 1.2.3) where it was suggested, even at that early stage, that individual decision-makers will assess all possible alternative courses of action before selecting the one which best fulfils (i.e. maximises) his or her stated goals and objectives.

It is natural that managers in their decision-making would like to feel that they have adopted such a comprehensive, all-embracing strategy to the problem of choosing the 'right' option. The more practical manager, however, may alternatively point to certain stringent and severely demanding assumptions which necessarily form the foundation upon which such rational, economic-minded managerial behaviour is based. These principal assumptions, which ultimately reflect the limitations of such optimal behaviour, include:

(a) Maximisation: maximum money values or utility will always be sought by management;
(b) Omniscience: management possess complete and comprehensive knowledge about all available alternatives;
(c) Consistency: management will be consistent in their choice between alternatives (e.g. if strategy X is preferred to Y, and Y preferred to Z, then X will be preferred to Z);
(d) Human information processing capability: managers have sufficient mental capacity to utilise the 'total information set' assumed in (b) above in order to evaluate available alternatives.

Managers are individuals, and as individuals they are limited by many factors, including environment, education, mental capacity, and society in general. In summary, possibly the most severe shortcoming of the more refined optimisation criteria described in this chapter (i.e. EMV and SEU) is that they both can be accused of failure to recognise the individual manager's limited capacity to behave effectively in a rational economic context.

A more practical alternative – 'bounded rationality'?

Because it may be observed that limiting factors such as societal, mental and environmental conditioning are both prevalent and dominant in 'real-world' situations, and that managers might not in practice come to their decisions via optimisation models of behaviour, a very different approach has been suggested as being rather more practical and feasible. This alternative approach has been termed *bounded rationality* and is in direct contrast to the 'rational economic man' school of thought.

Bounded rationality (proposed and developed principally by Herbert A. Simon from the 1950s) recognises the importance of constraining factors that may serve to limit management decision-making strategy to something appreciably far short of the optimal. Simon developed the notion of bounded rationality as a way of describing individual and managerial decision-making activity in terms of 'satisficing' behaviour (as opposed to optimising behaviour).[5]

The satisficing approach implies primarily that in practice:

(i) Non-maximisation strategies with regard to money values and utility are adopted by managers;

(ii) Information 'overload' is avoided by managers through the screening, sifting and consequent rejection of whole sets of information;

(iii) Managers limit their search for alternatives, thereby only evaluating a restricted number of alternative courses of action.

Whatever the level of study (introductory, intermediate or advanced) it is important that you should not only be aware of different decision-making techniques used in management accounting, such as the various criteria dealt with in this chapter, but also of the wider implications arising from the fact that managers are human and that a large part of their work is dealing with other human beings who naturally have human failings (e.g. limited mental capacities) and human needs (e.g. motivation and reward).

To return again to the main purpose of this chapter on information for management decisions, refer back to the satisficing implication (ii) above. *Information overload* is a very real danger in many decision-making situations. It is important, therefore, that the information which may end up being discarded (for the practical reasons already mentioned) should not be useful or valuable information. Such information, as far as possible, ought to be filtered and separated from other less useful or valuable information (and also any useless data) and then retained. This reference to information which may be useful and/or valuable leads us naturally into the final section of this chapter – a description and illustration of the *nature* and *value* of information for management decisions.

5.4 The nature and value of information

In the modern world the communication and supply of information comes about through rapidly developing and increasingly more sophisticated means. The impact of *information technology* in the form of both hardware (personal computers, micro-processors etc.) and software (i.e. computer programs.) is being felt throughout the worlds of business, commerce and industry and also in the domestic environment of the home. Channelled through advanced fibre optics cable technology, people all over the globe are rapidly linking into and accessing the information 'superhighway' for their information needs. Information presents itself in may varied shapes and forms generated from a multitude of sources, both new and traditional:

▶ Mass media – press, television, radio, books and magazines, discs and videos etc.;

▶ Conversation – interaction with people (social, domestic and business);

▶ Work – management reports, production schedules and summaries, computer print-outs.

5.4.1 Information and the nature and value of its content

What do you think is the essential nature of information? It is possible to draw a sharp distinction between *information* and *data*. Data can be said to comprise the entire range of words, pictures, facts and figures which assail everyone in daily business, social and domestic life. The vast majority of such data, however, ends up being relatively useless. It is only that small part of the entire set of data which proves *useful* to an individual that can correctly be recognised as having information content. Briefly speaking, whereas data can be found to be both useful and useless; information may be said to consist only of useful data (i.e. it is a sub-set of data.).

Both in general terms and in relation to decision-making, information may be loosely described as a message which changes the expectations and beliefs of a decision-maker. To elaborate, first of all imagine the following simple example set in the strictly non-business context of a pleasurable pre-football match drink in the pub! The match is scheduled to begin at 3.00 p.m. on Saturday afternoon. Ken is in a pub having a drink at 2.00 p.m. and is aware that the game starts at 3.00 p.m. Consider the following three separate situations:

1 Situation 1: Ken's brother, Dave, walks into the pub and tells him that the match starts at 3.00 p.m. This is a piece of useless data to Ken. Here there is no information content in the message as Ken fully expects the game to start at 3.00 p.m.

2 Situation 2: Dave walks into the pub and tells Ken that the start of the match has been delayed by half an hour and will start at 3.30 p.m. This message does have information content because it changes the prior belief/expectations of the recipient, Ken. But if Ken has no intention of going to the game, the information has no value to Ken as it won't change his plans – nevertheless it is still useful. Consider the position of a bystander, Taff, who overhears the message concerning the half-hour delay. Taff is going to the match and the likely effect of the overheard piece of information will be that it may change his intended course of action. To summarise this second situation:

   (i) the message is *useful* information to Ken because he has used it to change his prior expectations and now believes something different, i.e. the game starts at 3.30 p.m;

   (ii) the message is both *useful* and *of value* to Taff because it has not only changed his prior belief/expectations but it may also have altered his planned actions.

3 Situation 3: Ken now intends to go to the game. He gets his brother Dave's message that the start is delayed by half an hour. Here the information is both *useful* and *of value* to Ken if he changes his planned course of action.

For example, he may decide to have another drink before he goes; or he may choose to go elsewhere for half an hour; or he may even decide not to go to the match at all (because it might now be finishing too late and he would miss a favourite television programme).

(Note that Ken's position in situation 3 becomes effectively identical to that of Taff in situation 2.) A concise summary of the above example of Ken and the football match would be to say that: 'Prior' beliefs/expectations of a decision-maker can be conditioned (i.e. changed) by messages with information content to produce 'Posterior' (or after-the-event) beliefs/expectations. Or we can summarise it in another way:

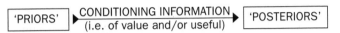

In short, the content of information received is said to be *useful* if it changes the prior beliefs of a decision-maker. However, it can only be said to be *valuable* information if it also changes the planned course of action (the decision) of a decision-maker.

5.4.2 *The cost and monetary value of information*

Information is very often of such value that a price has to be paid for it (for instance the price of a market research survey). Because information frequently has to be bought, a cost can be attached to the acquisition of it. The cost of information needs to be offset against its value to the decision-maker, i.e. would buying, say, survey information be worthwhile? For instance, given a particular set of information, a business manager may have decided to embark upon a course of action which he or she believes to be optimal. If further information becomes available which will change the manager's prior belief and cause the manager to revise the optimal plan to a more beneficial one, then the information undoubtedly has value (as it would be changing a planned course of action). The information may also have a cost. If this is the case, then the increase in optimality needs to be weighted against the cost – and if this still results in a net benefit, then the information is worth buying.

To conclude this last section and also the chapter, the approach of using expected monetary values (EMV) in management decision situations will be adopted once again. Three summary points can be identified from what has been discussed so far in this section:

(a) Information has value if it changes a planned course of action (e.g. a management strategy or business decision).

(b) The benefit derived from such information, based on an EMV approach, will be equal to:

> EMV of acting with information
> *less*   EMV of acting without information
> *equals*   Gross value of information

(c) Information is worth buying if the benefits in (b) above (i.e. the 'gross' value) exceed the cost of the information. Deduction of the information's cost from its gross value gives the 'net' value of information, *viz*:

> Gross value of information
> *less*   Cost of information
> *equals* Net value of information

Finally, as an illustration of the gross and net values of information, consider once more the basic EMV data used in Activity 5.2 and work through Activity 5.5.

ACTIVITY 5.5
············

Given below in Table 5.5 is a summary of the detail (from Activity 5.2) to be used here in terms of monetary profit/(loss) values together with the relevant probabilities attached to alternative outcomes:

As you have already seen from your experience of Activity 5.2 the rational management decision, on the basis of EMVs, was to adopt a production strategy of 5,000 units which realises an expected profit of £20,000. The marketing director of Lilywhite plc now intervenes and reveals that he knows of a market research agency which has a vast amount of experience and success in researching and forecasting possible future levels of sales demand within the existing market. The agency's 'track record' indicates that the information they can provide after a research survey will be entirely accurate. The results of the survey, however, will only be made available by the agency for a fee of £30,000.

Required: Is it worthwhile for the management of Lilywhite plc to buy the information contained in the survey?

If the survey were to indicate a demand level of only 5,000 units then management would decide to produce 5,000 units thereby making a profit of £20,000. If, however, the survey were to indicate sales of 10,000 units then the decision would be to manufacture 10,000 units with a resultant profit of £120,000. When the respective probabilities for each state of market demand are applied, the EMV *with* the market research survey information is calculated thus:

$$0.6 (£20,000) + 0.4 (£120,000) = £60,000$$

table 5.5
**Lilywhite plc:
summary tabulation/
pay-off matrix**

Demand:	5,000 units	10,000 units
Production:		
5,000 units	£20,000	20,000
10,000 units	(£80,000)	£120,000
Probabilities:	0.6	0.4

Using the procedure described in 'summary points' (b) and (c) immediately prior to this Activity, the gross and net values of the survey information can be determined as in (i) and (ii) respectively below:

(i) Gross value of information

		£
	EMV with information:	60,000
less	EMV without information:	20,000
		40,000

∴ the gross value of the survey is £40,000.

(ii) Net value of information

		£
	Gross value of information:	40,000
less	Cost of information:	30,000
		10,000

∴ the net value of the survey is £10,000.

Conclusion: It would, therefore, be worthwhile for the management of Lilywhite plc to decide to buy the market research survey information, because even after paying for the information an increase in EMV of £10,000 would be achieved.

The nature of the survey information in Activity 5.5 (as implied by the phrase 'will be entirely accurate') is that of *perfect* information. The analysis would become somewhat more complex if only imperfect information sources were available. Perfect information has intentionally been used to keep the illustration simple so that the chief features of the analysis might be demonstrated as clearly as possible. If you are keen to pursue further the consequences of only imperfect information being attainable you are recommended to refer to more advanced managerial accounting texts.[6]

Self-check questions

5.1 One of the publications carried by a certain store is *Motorvan* weekly magazine. The dealer pays 15 pence per copy and sells it for 25 pence per copy. Copies unsold at the end of the week cannot be returned and thus have no value. The probability distribution for demand is shown below:

Demand (number per week)	Probability
10	0.05
12	0.1
14	0.15
16	0.3
18	0.2
20	0.15
22	0.05

Use each of the following decision criteria to determine the optimal number of magazines to stock:

(a) Maximin criterion

(b) Expected values

Which criterion do you consider the most sensible one for the dealer to adopt?

(Chartered Association of Certified Accountants)

5.2 The managing director of a British aircraft company is reviewing his company's policy in the light of various statements by the government that they may enter the space race. The government has made it clear that, if it does enter the race, it will either attempt to land space craft on the moon (a) without French collaboration; (b) with French collaboration; or (c) attempt landing on some other, as yet unspecified planet.

In the managing director's judgement the probabilities of these three events are 0.5 for (a), 0.1 for (b) and 0.4 for (c).

If either (a) or (b) is attempted the company can use American experience. To reach some other planet, however, a completely new space craft would have to be designed and, depending on government action, this may be done with or without French help at company level.

The managing director believes that his company has three possible strategies:

A. To remain an aircraft company which would provide them with an expected profit of £2m, regardless of any government decision on (a), (b) or (c).

B. To invest in building space craft capable only of reaching the moon.

C. To invest in designing and building new space craft.

The latter two may be undertaken with or without French collaboration and the table below shows the various payoffs (in £m) that may occur:

Table of payoffs

	(a)	(b)	(c)
(B)	40	40	− 30
(C)	− 100	20	80

Using the criterion of expected value which decision would you recommend?

(Accounting Diploma)

5.3 Recently two potentially attractive business opportunities have been brought to the attention of the management team of Sanderone plc (toy and games manufacturers) who are now in the process of deciding which of these two new ventures they should embark upon. Both involve the manufacture of a new product from patent rights already owned by Peggy Palmer, a renowned inventor of family indoor board games. Peggy is willing to sell for £1,000 the rights to one, but not both, of her new games – 'Cornix' and 'Solitaire'.

Manufacture and a sale of either game would be a risky proposition, and the likely business success or failure of each game has been measured in terms of expected pay-offs (which are summarised in the table below). Cornix is expected to be moderately successful whatever the outcome. However, estimates for

Solitaire range from it failing to make any positive return at all (i.e. a negative pay-off or just breaking even) through to it generating the highest expected pay-off of either opportunity. Probability estimates attached to the likely 'gross' pay-offs for each new game are:

Probability	Gross Pay-offs (£000)	
	Cornix	Solitaire
0.2	7	(5)
0.5	16	–
0.3	27	40

Sanderone's management team have summarised their attitude to risk-taking with regard to new business ventures in the following subjective utility function: $U(M) = 2(10 + M)^{\frac{1}{2}}$.

Notes: (i) 'M' in the expression represents net monetary values in £000s.

(ii) Net pay-offs from each game are arrived at by adjusting the gross monetary values in the table above to allow for the cost of purchasing the patent rights from Peggy Palmer.

Required:

(a) On the basis of subjective expected utilities (SEU model) advise Sanderone's management team as to which venture's manufacturing and patent rights to purchase.

(b) 'The SEU model typifies the approach of rational economic man to decision-making.' With regard to this statement:

(i) Briefly describe the principal advantage held by the SEU decision criterion over the expected monetary value (EMV) model;

(ii) State *three* of the major limiting assumptions upon which the SEU approach is based.

(c) Suggest and briefly discuss an alternative approach to both SEU and EMV models which claims to overcome their strict limitations.

(Accounting Degree)

5.4 Inglestone Ltd can purchase the patent and the manufacturing rights of any one of three products. The costs of the rights are:

Product A	£130,000
Product B	£190,000
Product C	£200,000

At a meeting with three of Inglestone's directors, the management accountant stated:

'We are all agreed on the facts. Each venture is a very short-term project. The fixed manufacturing and advertising costs of each venture will be:

	A (£000s)	B (£000s)	C (£000s)
Fixed manufacturing cost	120	20	20
Advertising costs	50	30	20

Sales and production will, once known, dovetail and there will therefore be no stock build-up. The sales prices and variable costs per unit are:

	A	B	C
Sales price per unit	£340	£190	£130
Variable cost per unit	£140	£110	£70

However the sales volume is the crunch question.

We do not know what the sales level will be but we do know the various possibilities of what the sales levels could be. Product A could be a complete flop, it could sell well, or it might sell very well. B is also quite variable whereas with C the range of outcomes is quite small. The various possible sales volumes and their associated probabilities are:

Product					
A		B		C	
Sales volume Units	Probability	Sales volume Units	Probability	Sales volume Units	Probability
zero	0.1	3,000	0.1	7,000	0.8
2,500	0.4	4,000	0.3	8,000	0.1
4,000	0.5	6,000	0.3	9,000	0.1
		8,000	0.3		

Based on the assumption that the above facts are all completely accurate, and we agree with this, all we need do is make the decisions as to which one product to undertake. What are your views, gentlemen?'

Required:

(a) Calculate the expected money value of each product and on the basis of this advise Inglestone of the best course of action.

(b) List and briefly comment on three other factors which may be relevant in a practical situation to the final choice between the three available courses of action.

(c) Consider only product A for this section. The marketing manager agrees that the subjective probabilities assigned to sales levels given are as accurate as it is practical to assess, however, he suggests that if a market research study was undertaken then it would be possible to ascertain with complete accuracy exactly which of the sales levels specified would be effective, i.e. it would indicate whether the sales would be zero, 2,500 or 4,000 units. This market research would cost £20,000 and could be undertaken before deciding whether to purchase the patent and manufacturing rights. Assuming the fixed manufacturing costs are all avoidable if no production takes place then is it worthwhile to undertake the market research?

(Chartered Association of Certified Accountants)

Notes

1. For a description of these other such methods refer to a suitable text on probability and decision theory such as *The anatomy of Decisions* by P.G. Moore and H. Thomas.
2. Ibid.
3. *Management Accounting: Official Terminology*, CIMA, (1991).
4. Ibid.
5. Two publications representative of H.A. Simon's influential work and ideas are: *The New Science of Management Decisions*, Harper and Row, (1960), and 'Theories of Decision-Making in Economics and Behavioural Science', *American Economic Review*, Volume 49, (1959).
6. Such a text is: R.W. Scapens (1991) *Management Accounting – A Review of Recent Developments*, 2nd edn, Basingstoke: Macmillan.

Further study

Arnold, J., Carsberg, B. and Scapens, R.W. (1980) *Topics in management accounting*, 1st edn, Philip Allan.

Arnold, J. and Hope, T. (1990) *Accounting for management decisions*, 2nd edn, Hemel Hempstead: Prentice-Hall.

Brookfield, B. (1988) 'Probability as an aid to decision-making', in *Management Accounting*, March; May; September, Chartered Institute of Management Accountants

Carsberg, B. (1979) *Economics of business decisions*, 2nd edn, London: Pitman

Drury, C. (1992) *Management and cost accounting*, 3rd edn, London: Chapman and Hall.

Harper, W. (1995) *Cost and management accounting*, 1st edn, London: Macdonald and Evans.

Hopwood, A. (1974) *Accounting and human behaviour*, 1st edn, Hemel Hempstead: Prentice-Hall.

Lucey, T. (1992) *Management accounting*, 3rd edn, D.P. Publications.

Moore, P.G. and Thomas, H. (1978), *The anatomy of decisions*, 1st edn, Harmondsworth: Penguin.

Ryan, B. and Hobson, J. (1985) *Management accounting – a contemporary approach*, 1st edn, London: Pitman.

Scapens, R.W. (1991) *Management accounting – A review of recent developments*, 2nd edn, Basingstoke: Macmillan.

CHAPTER 6

Cost-volume-profit (C-V-P) analysis

Objectives
....

By the end of this chapter you should be able to:

▶ Understand the relationship effects brought about by volume changes upon costs and revenues.

▶ Express these C-V-P relationships through both graphical and mathematical/algebraic forms of analysis.

▶ Appreciate the various applications of C-V-P analysis for purposes of management decision-making.

▶ Describe the major C-V-P assumptions/limitations underpinning break-even analysis.

In Chapter 1, Figure 1.1's diagrammatic illustration of the management planning, decision-making and control process highlighted organisational aims and objectives as phase one of the process. The ultimate aim/objective we decided upon was that of income and wealth maximisation. To achieve this ultimate goal it is important that a firm's management considers the combined effect on both its cost and revenue structures of changes in the level of activity, i.e. volume. (You might recall that, as in previous chapters, most notably Chapter 3, the two terms 'activity level' and 'volume' can, and will, be used interchangeably as their meaning is precisely the same.)

In effect, we now superimpose (sales) revenue functions onto the (total) cost functions previously described in detail in Chapter 3. This development then enables us to investigate the ways in which cost-revenue relationships in total behave over different and changing levels of activity. From hereon your study of these relationships will cease to be referred to by the term 'cost-revenue' but will be given their more usual description of cost volume profit (C-V-P) relationships or, even more commonly and simply, *C-V-P analysis*.

As the analysis of C-V-P relationships in this chapter is essentially an expansion/development of the underlying cost volume (C-V) relationships analysed in Chapter 3, then your understanding of, and familiarity with, the content of Chapter 3 is necessarily assumed throughout.

6.1 C-V-P relationships
....

The second paragraph above mentioned superimposing a total sales revenue (TR) function (i.e. a TR line on a graph) onto a total cost (TC) function. Both TR and TC lines or functions are shown clearly on Figure 6.1. This picture is presented for you starkly and simply because it lies at the root of all graphical

figure 6.1

**Cost-revenue
relationships**

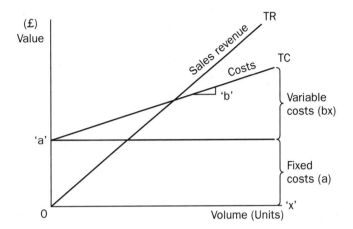

C-V-P analysis. (In Chapter 3 we saw that volume/activity is always scaled on the horizontal ('x') axis in units, and value in '£s' on the vertical ('y') axis; this convention will continue to be used throughout this and the next chapter.)

You will notice also how the TC function on Figure 6.1 is a perfect replica of the semi-variable cost behaviour pattern depicted by Figure 3.6. In fact, it is very important here, before we progress further, that the final couple of paragraphs in section 3.1 and the first paragraph in section 3.2 are carefully re-read. These three short paragraphs explain and remind you of the vital dual role of the cost structures displayed in both Figures 3.6 and 6.1 (i.e. the TC component of the latter).

6.1.1 C-V-P equations and calculations

Chapter 3 dealt solely with cost-volume (C-V) relationships, i.e. only *cost* values were represented on the vertical axis of graphical illustrations. However, we expand the analysis in this chapter to incorporate both *revenue* as well as cost values on the vertical axis of Figure 6.1. Nevertheless, first of all just concentrate on the cost (TC) function on Figure 6.1. and its relevant equation and calculation.

Total cost equation and calculation
A final reference back to Chapter 3 is to Table 3.1 at the very end of section 3.1. That table shows you very clearly how an organisation's total cost overall comprises fundamentally of two essential ingredients – total *fixed* cost plus total *variable* cost. Having classified all cost items (via the means and techniques detailed throughout Chapter 3) as being either fixed or variable, the following simple linear equation can now be used again to represent the total cost function of the firm:

$$y = a + bx$$

where: y is total cost; a is fixed cost per period; b is variable cost per unit; and x is volume.

A set of sample data for the firm of G. Mutchpen plc will be used for the remainder of this chapter's analysis, so you ought to familiarise yourself closely with the basic items of data that follow:

Variable cost	£12 per unit.
Fixed cost in total	£48,000 per period.
Selling price	£20 per unit.

In an accounting period Mutchpen produce and sell on average 8,000 units of output; all of the ensuing C-V-P analysis is based on this normal (average) level of activity.

ACTIVITY **6.1**

Required: Using the total cost equation above and by applying the data to the expression   calculate Mutchpen's anticipated total cost (TC) for a typical period.

Your calculation and solution follow a restatement of the basic equation, thus:

Equation: $y = a + bx$
Calculation: $y = £48,000 + (£12 \text{ per unit})(8,000 \text{ units})$
Solution: $TC = £48,000 + £96,000 = £144,000$

Therefore, at whatever level of activity Mutchpen's management decide to operate (it may on occasions be above or below the 8,000 unit average) you can make a total cost calculation very straightforwardly by applying the TC equation, given a specific volume of output that is higher or lower than the 'norm'.

Total revenue and profit equation/calculation

Mutchpen's selling price of £20 per unit was not used above (because sales revenue is not involved in a cost calculation) but that C-V computation of £144,000 TC can now be expanded into a C-V-P calculation when unit selling price is introduced to generate total revenue (TR) and consequently income, i.e. profit or loss.

Basic business logic dictates that if an item is sold for less than it cost, then a loss results. Alternatively, and more positively perhaps, the same basic logic informs us that if sold for a higher price than cost, a profit is reaped. Concentrating on the latter more favourable outcome, consider the expansion of our analysis into the realm now of C-V-P relationships. The following statement in the style of a profit equation represents this underlying logic of business:

Sales revenues – [Total fixed costs + Total variable costs] = Profit

A more fully developed statement reflecting the same logic is:

[Selling price per unit x units] – [Fixed cost per period
    + (Variable cost per unit x units)] = Profit

Once again using algebraic terminology in equation form, the above statement becomes:

Equation: $px - (a + bx) = \pi$

where: p is selling price per unit; π is profit; and a, b and x are as before.

Calculation: (£20 per unit) (8,000 units) – [£48,000 + (£12 per unit) (8,000 units)]

= <u>£16,000</u>

In an average or typical period Mutchpen would make a business profit therefore of £16,000. This pattern of C-V-P relationship can be highly condensed into a simplified profit equation which not only summarises the above-mentioned business logic but is one that lies at the heart of all accounting:

Equation: TR – TC = Profit (or loss)

Summary calculation: £160,000 – £144,000 = £16,000

Before we move on, take a brief look back to Figure 6.1. You will notice that where the TR function is above the TC line a profit occurs measured by the difference between the two sloping lines. The gap between the two functions will also gauge losses but in this case in the area where the TC line lies above TR. The point at which the two functions intersect is where the firm breaks even; this is the focus of analysis in section 6.2. In deciding at what activity level to operate, the firm's management are in a position to take readings of profit (or loss) from a chart such as the one in Figure 6.1. We will take a more detailed look at such types of chart in section 6.2.'s break-even analysis later.

Just as the above expression, TR – TC = profit/loss, has been said to be at the fulcrum of accounting in general, then an equally important concept occupying a central place at the core of *management* accounting in particular is the notion of 'contribution'.

6.1.2 Contribution analysis

Contribution as a concept was encountered previously in section 4.2 and elsewhere in Chapter 4. Its role is as important now in C-V-P analysis as it was pivotal then to the technique of marginal costing. Essentially it embodies the idea that the difference between selling price and variable cost provides an amount that 'contributes' towards fixed costs. This amount is called the *contribution*.

As variable cost is alternatively known as marginal cost (see Chapter 4) then contribution can equally well be said to be the difference between sales revenues and marginal costs in total. Contribution is thus measurable either 'per unit' (unit selling price less unit variable cost) or in total 'aggregate' terms, i.e. total sales revenue (TR) less total marginal/variable cost (TVC).

With each unit made and sold Mutchpen needs £12 to cover the sort of cost which varies in accordance with how many units are manufactured (i.e. variable cost). Given Mutchpen's £20 selling price, then £8 remains to pay for the other type of costs that have to be covered regardless of the firm's volume of activity (i.e. fixed cost). Whereas the variable cost will be avoided if the unit is not produced, the fixed cost will not simply disappear if fewer (or indeed increase if more) units are manufactured. In the case of Mutchpen, the latter type of cost is the total fixed cost (TFC) of £48,000 per period which will be incurred irrespective of volume of output/sales. Consider next the impact of this question of volume.

At Mutchpen's normal period volume of 8,000 units, the first 6,000 units (each contributing £8) are required to pay for the firm's fixed cost commitments of £48,000 per period. Hence a period volume of 6,000 units is the point on the activity level at which Mutchpen is said to break even (analysis of break-even issues comprises the whole of section 6.2). However, there are, in an average period, still 2,000 units left beyond this point; in other words 2,000 more lots of £8 contribution! Once fixed cost is covered, what then does this £16,000 (£8 unit contribution × 2,000 units) contribute towards? The answer is simple – *profit*, pure profit!

Total and unit contribution equations/calculations

You might recall the profit equations from the previous section, now re-stated thus:

$$TR - TC = P \qquad (1)$$

or, slightly disaggregated, as:

$$TR - [TFC + TVC] = P \qquad (2)$$

where: P is profit and the other abbreviations are as already indicated.

Contribution is represented by the two variable elements on the left-hand side of the above equation, i.e. both TR and TVC will vary in relation to volume changes. Consequently contribution itself, being the difference between TR and TVC, is variable in nature. Provided unit selling price is higher than unit variable cost, then the greater the volume the more contribution is generated; less volume results in less total contribution.

In both 'unit' and 'total' terms, and using equations again, contribution is described by the following expressions:

Unit: Selling price – Variable cost = Contribution (3)
Total: TR – TVC = Contribution (4)

Substituting the Mutchpen data into equations (3) and (4):

(3) £20 – £12 = £8 unit contribution
(4) £160,000 – £96,000 = £64,000 total contribution

Total contribution towards what? Initially towards TFC and subsequently towards P, expressed in equation form:

Total contribution = TFC + P (5)

Substituting the Mutchpen data into equation (5):

(5) £64,000 = £48,000 + £16,000

Finally, cross-checking with earlier equations (1) and (2):

(1) £160,000 – £144,000 = £16,000
(2) £160,000 – [£48,000 + £96,000] = £16,000

Can you calculate ...? both (i) contribution and (ii) profit for each monthly period, given a £15,000 period fixed cost together with unit values of a £5 selling price and £3 variable cost, and volume levels for the months January to March as follows:

	January	February	March
Sales *Volume* (in units):	5000	7500	10000

Answer

	January	February	March
(i) Contribution:	£10,000	£15,000	£20,000
(ii) Profit/(loss):	£(5,000)	–	£5,000

6.2 Break-even analysis

The idea of an organisation or firm breaking even has already been alluded to a couple of times. Here it now becomes the sole focus of analysis. One means of conducting the analysis is through the use of graphical techniques. In fact, Figure 6.1 was itself a form of break-even chart although not referred to specifically as such at that early stage in the proceedings. It graphically represents the nature of C-V-P relationships as analysed throughout this chapter. However, before resorting to graphical aids of analysis (in section 6.2.2), let us first continue with the more mathematical or algebraic analytical techniques, again using equations, which concluded the previous section.

6.2.1 Break-even point calculations/formulae

Remember in the paragraph just prior to performing the contribution calculations by the use of equations in section 6.1.2 that G. Mutchpen plc's *break-even point* was identified (without the technical means demonstrated here) as 6,000 units on the company's scale of activity, i.e. 2,000 units below the firm's average or normal volume of 8,000 units. A firm is said to break even at the point where total costs incurred are exactly covered by total sales revenues generated. In short the break-even point (BEP) is where TR = TC; (in Figure 6.1 the precise point at which the TC and the TR lines/functions intersect. At this point neither profits nor losses are made).

Several formulae are available for calculating the BEP. The first one to be considered emanates from this idea of TR/TC equality, and utilises probably the most familiar algebraic expression to appear in the entire book. Recall once more the TC equation:

$$y = a + bx$$

where all the terms are as before (see section 6.1.1).

Also, as before, TR is represented by px (selling price × volume). As the BEP is where TR = TC, then substituting 'px' in place of 'y' in the above TC equation gives:

$$px = a + bx$$

This formula therefore provides the BEP as px (TR) is here the same value as y (TC). Apply Mutchpen's data in the formula:

$$20x = 48{,}000 + 12x$$
$$\therefore \quad 8x = 48{,}000$$
$$\therefore \quad x = 6{,}000$$

Alternatively as BEP is where neither profit nor loss occurs, then setting profit (π) equal to zero in the earlier profit equation we get:

$$px - (a + bx) = \pi$$
$$20x - (48{,}000 + 12x) = 0$$
$$\therefore \quad 8x - 48{,}000 = 0$$
$$\therefore \quad x = 6{,}000$$

Using either formulaic approach, Mutchpen's BEP is clearly 6,000 units. Perhaps an even simpler BEP formula for you to apply comes in the shape of the following:

$$\frac{\text{Fixed cost}}{\text{Unit contribution}} = \frac{£48{,}000}{£8} = 6{,}000 \text{ units}$$

If the BEP is required in *value* rather than the above volume amounts, then you simply multiply the numerator in the above formula by the unit selling price thus:

$$\frac{\text{TFC} \times p}{\text{Unit contribution}} = \frac{£48{,}000 \times £20}{£8} = £120{,}000$$

Or, alternatively, apply the following 'total' formula:

$$\frac{\text{TFC} \times \text{TR}}{\text{Total contribution}} = \frac{£48{,}000 \times £120{,}000}{£48{,}000} = £120{,}000$$

(NB: Although the total revenue and total contribution figures used above happen to be the BEP values, *any* chosen aggregate level of sales and corresponding contribution would result in the same BEP sales value – you might try one or two examples for practice.)

The above range of formulae are not the only ones available to you for calculating BEP – a further one is suggested in section 6.2.3. Finally, although not strictly a break-even issue, if a firm's management decide on a targeted level of profit desired, say, for a future period, then the BEP formulaic approach can be adapted/developed a little to useful effect. For example, assume that Mutchpen's management team decide, for whatever reasons, that in the coming period the firm should plan on reaching a minimum target profit (P) of only

£8,000, compared to the average/normal profit of £16,000. Simple addition of this targeted figure to the fixed cost numerator of the BEP formula will inform management of the activity level needed to achieve the target, thus:

$$\frac{\text{TFC} + \text{Target P}}{\text{Unit contribution}} = \frac{£48,000 + £8,000}{£8} = 7,000 \text{ units}$$

In short, Mutchpen's management will need to decide upon a unit volume of 7,000 to generate this minimum target £8,000 profit. Proof is provided by applying the data to one of the very first fully detailed C-V-P equations that appeared back in section 6.1.1. This brings the calculatory approach in C-V-P analysis 'full circle' thus:

[Unit selling price x units] – [Fixed cost per period + (Unit variable cost x units)]
= Profit
[(£20/unit)(7,000 units)] – [£48,000 + (£12/unit)(7,000 units)] = £8,000

Can you identify ...? using the Mutchpen plc data, the necessary unit sales volumes to: (i) achieve profits of £19,200; or (ii) suffer losses of £6,400.

Answer

(i)   8,400 units (i.e. 2,400 units *above* BEP @ £8/unit contribution = £19,200, or)

$$\frac{£48,000 + £19,200}{£8} = 8,400$$

(ii)   5,200 units (i.e. 800 units *below* BEP @ £8/unit contribution = £6,400, or)

$$\frac{£48,000 - £6,400}{£8} = 5,200$$

6.2.2 Break-even charts

A break-even chart in skeleton outline appears in Figure 6.1. We now develop the picture, embellishing it with numbers and terminology to produce graphs or charts that can aid management in decision-making activities such as profit (or loss) estimation, graphical identification of the BEP, and choice of the appropriate level of volume at which to operate.

ACTIVITY **6.2**

Required: Applying the Mutchpen data again but on this occasion for graphical purposes, construct a C-V-P chart of the type commonly known as a *conventional* form of break-even chart.

The conventional break-even chart
Because the charts in this section all use straight line functions (i.e. they are *linear* graphs) their construction is very straightforward in that only two points

(coordinates) are necessary to plot each line or function. The construction process required to build a 'conventional' break-even chart involves the following elements and results in the graph appearing in Figure 6.2.

▶ The origin (0) of the graph automatically provides you with one coordinate for the sales (TR) function. It is linked with a straight line to a second coordinate plotted, for instance, at the point where volume of 8,000 units is represented by £160,000 sales value, i.e. at the extremes of both the axes which, with our data on Figure 6.2, coincide at the top right-hand corner of the chart. Other points could have been chosen – the only requirement being to ensure that TR corresponds with the relevant activity level, for example 7,000 unit volume and £140,000 TR may have been used. (Note that other possible points could also be used for the TC coordinates plotted next, rather than the specific ones chosen here in this Activity.)

▶ For the fixed cost function you need to draw a line horizontal and parallel to the 'x' axis. This line needs to intersect the vertical axis at the value representing the firm's TFC – using our data this is £48,000, and is the intercept point ('a' in the TC expression: y = a + bx). It informs management that even at zero volume the firm still incurs fixed costs in the short-term of £48,000 per period.

▶ Begin to plot variable cost at the fixed cost intercept with the vertical axis, in effect adding the variable cost on top of fixed cost to form the TC function. Don't be tempted to plot variable cost from the graph's origin in break-even charts of this type. The intercept point is thus the first coordinate. Next you choose any unit volume (e.g. 8,000 units), multiply it by the unit variable cost (£12) and add this TVC value (£96,000) onto the TFC figure (£48,000) to plot the second coordinate which represents TC when joined to the TFC intercept/first coordinate. In our illustration, like TR, the second coordinate lies at the extreme of the volume range, reflecting a TC value of £144,000. TVC of £96,000 at an 8,000 unit activity level is given by 'bx' in the TC expression:

y = a + bx (inserting our illustrative data: TC = £48,000 + (£12)(8,000) = £144,000).

All the terms in Figure 6.2. are by now known to you apart from one – the *margin of safety*. This key indicator in C-V-P analysis informs management of the amount by which sales exceed the BEP. It can be expressed in either unit volume or sales value, which in Figure 6.2 are 2,000 units and £40,000 respectively. A clear indication is sent to management of exactly to what extent any leeway exists, if indeed one does, for the firm to tolerate losses in sales before the threat of becoming a loss-maker in money terms occurs too. For example, take the instance near the very end of section 6.2.1, where Mutchpen adopted a minimum target profit figure of £8,000 which would imply target sales of 7,000 units worth £140,000. Such a target halves the existing safety margin to only a thousand units (£20,000) which may prompt management to decide on a revised minimum target. In short, the margin of safety is a simple but effective 'tool' to heighten management's awareness of how changing volume levels impact upon profits. It is perhaps best considered as a key indicator of a firm's potential to weather the storm in economic adversity, such as, when serious recessions occur.

figure 6.2
**Conventional
break-even chart**

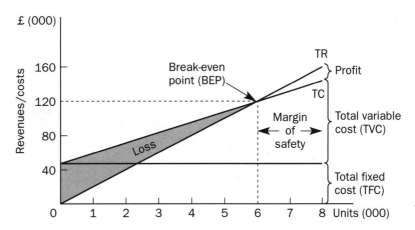

Finally, another key indicator, and one already mentioned, is the BEP. Figure 6.2 clearly shows management that a decision to operate at levels below 6,000 units (£120,000) will only result in losses being suffered, the extent of which is high-lighted by the shaded area on the graph. Whatever the level management decided upon for production and sales activity it should very clearly be beyond the BEP and provide as wide a margin of safety as possible.

ACTIVITY **6.3**

Required: Applying the Mutchpen data once more, and again for graphical purposes, construct a C-V-P chart of the type generally referred to as a profit-volume chart (although personally my preference is to describe it as a form of *contribution*, or 'contribution-volume', chart for reasons that should become apparent to you as you progress through this Activity).

The profit-volume (P/V) chart

Profit-volume (P/V) charts are simpler, and in several ways more useful, than the conventional form of break-even chart. Their construction is certainly simpler as only one sloping line needs to be plotted in relation to the graph's two axes which themselves appear differently – see Figure 6.3. The layout of the P/V chart differs in that the 'x' axis, instead of lying horizontal at the base of the graph, now moves part-way up the vertical axis but still lies horizontal with a 90 degrees intersect at zero on the vertical scale. This structure accommodates profits above the horizontal 'x' axis and losses below it. Because construction is of a single line/function you only need to plot two coordinates joined by a straight line as follows:

▶ At zero volume a maximum loss is suffered equal to the amount of the firm's fixed costs. Therefore one coordinate is plotted, using the fixed cost figure, on the negative section of the vertical axis below zero, i.e. £48,000.

▶ If you have already calculated the BEP, using one of the BEP unit formulae in section 6.2.1, the other coordinate can be plotted at the point on the 'x' axis representing the firm's break-even volume (6,000 units). Failing this, a profit (or loss) calculation for any chosen activity level would provide the other coordinate. For example, at 8,000 units TR (£160,000) less TC

figure 6.3
**Profit-volume (P/V)
chart**

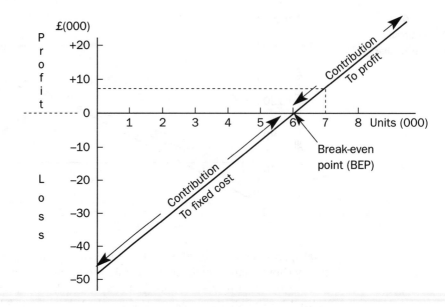

(£144,000) equals a profit of £16,000, giving the other coordinate above the horizontal where value of £16,000 corresponds to unit volume of 8,000. In examinations such profit (or loss) information may be readily available to you from data provided in the question, rendering a calculation unnecessary.

The P/V chart provides management with a simpler and more exact picture of the profits/losses that arise from decisions to operate at different levels of volume. 'More exact' because it's often not easy to derive absolutely precise profit/loss readings from conventional break-even charts which, after all, only show profits/losses as an *area* of the chart lying between the slopes of two lines (the TR and TC functions). Because the P/V chart largely overcomes this problem by effectively combining the sales and cost functions into a single sloping line, then very accurate *point* derivatives can be drawn from the single line/function itself. For instance, you might consider yet again the case at the end of section 6.2.1 where Mutchpen's management decided on a minimum target profit figure of £8,000 for a future period.

If a particular level of profit is decided upon – for example, Mutchpen's target profit of £8,000 – then the P/V chart in Figure 6.3 gives virtually at a glance (see the broken lines) the exact volume necessary (7,000 units). Remember that the firm's current margin of safety is 2,000 units; the target profit of £8,000, however, represents a reduced safety margin of only 1,000 units above BEP. Note that each one of these 1,000 units generates an £8 contribution, hence the profit of £8,000. This raises an important point; the single sloping function on the chart is a direct graphical representation of the rate at which contribution is earned. The sloping line is often, wrongly, referred to as the graph's profit line. It is actually the *contribution function*, because below the horizontal axis it is a *loss* (not profit) line. To summarise then, above zero volume initially a contribution rate of £8 per unit provides funds for covering the firm's fixed costs – this is the case up to a volume level sufficient to break even. Beyond BEP any further volume contributes £8 per unit towards profits. Before developing the analysis of rates of contribution a little further, a final comment relating to break-even charts is necessary. Other types of chart are available to help management in their decisions – one such chart is the contribution break-even chart. Although not described in detail here, it resembles very closely the conventional type of chart. The only real difference is that the variable costs are plotted first (from the origin of the graph) with the fixed cost function then running parallel and on top of the variable cost line – giving of course the same TC function overall. Its essential use is that it emphasises the concept of contribution; a matter which we now pursue through the application of the *profit-volume (P/V) ratio* (alternatively often called the *contribution-volume* or *contribution-sales* ratio).

6.2.3 Profit-volume (P/V) ratio

Although most widely in practice and examinations referred to as the P/V ratio, a better descriptive term is the contribution (either 'contribution-sales' or 'contribution-volume' ratio). This term is preferable because the slope of the function on the P/V chart is, as just mentioned to you above, a precise reflection of the rate that contribution is generated over ranges of sales volume. The steeper the slope, the higher the rate of contribution (and vice-versa). As a ratio it measures the relationship between the two variables, i.e. contribution and sales. Hence its calculation is based on these two ingredients; contribution is the numerator and sales price is the denominator, thus:

$$\text{P/V ratio} = \frac{\text{Contribution per unit}}{\text{Selling price per unit}}$$

Employing once more our Mutchpen data:

$$\text{P/V ratio} = \frac{£8}{£20} = \underline{40\% \text{ (or 0.4)}}$$

This means that contribution is earned at a rate of 40 per cent (or 0.4) of sales, and the steepness of the gradient of the sloping function in Figure 6.3. graphically represents this fraction/percentage rate. Obviously the steeper the slope (the higher the fraction/percentage rate) the better for the firm.

Consider now one of the P/V ratio's most useful and practical applications. It was mentioned in section 6.2.1 when dealing with BEP formulae/calculations that other formulae existed; a particularly appropriate one utilises the P/V ratio. If the firm's fixed costs are simply divided by the P/V ratio, the BEP in sales value is given.

$$\text{BEP} = \frac{\text{Fixed costs}}{\text{P/V ratio}} = \frac{£48,000}{0.4} = \underline{£120,000}$$

DID YOU KNOW ...?
*that the idea of **break-even** can also be applied to a product's or project's very life cycle pattern. The point in its life at which a product/project 'breaks even' is identified and discussed for you in section 8.3 of Chapter 8.*

The entire analysis so far of C-V-P relationships has been conducted on the basis of various important underlying assumptions being applied. Some, such as *linearity*, may have been more obvious to you during the C-V-P analysis than others were. The next section now lists several of the most important of these assumptions. It subsequently goes on to relax the application of one in particular which then leads naturally onto the topic of the next chapter, pricing decision techniques.

6.3 Limitations/assumptions of C-V-P analysis

Break-even analysis, as a technique to help managers in their decision-making activities, needs to be considered in the light of its limitations, which themselves are mainly imposed by the very assumptions that break-even analysis makes about C-V-P relationships.

6.3.1 C-V-P analysis assumptions

A range of assumptions underpin C-V-P analysis. The major ones include:

▶ *constant fixed costs* over the range of activity – although you need to be aware that on occasions fixed costs may become 'stepped'. Step- (or stepped-) fixed cost behaviour patterns were described for you in detail in section 3.1.3.

▶ *single product analysis* – or, if not, then a constant product sales mix applies.

▶ *volume as the only independent variable.* In our familiar TC function $y = a + bx$, the independent variable 'x' is deemed to be the only factor determining or influencing cost levels. In practice, other additional factors may partly affect the level of cost too, such as technology. Where further variables go towards explaining cost levels, extra independent variables need to be added to the simple two-variable regression ($y = a + bx$) causing it to expand into a multiple regression form, i.e. $y = a + bx_1 + cx_2 \ldots nx_n$ (where each 'x' represents a partial explanation for cost level 'y').

▶ *production equals sales* or that changes in stock levels are relatively insignificant, and therefore do not create important disparities between volumes of output and corresponding sales levels. Alternatively, profit computed on a marginal costing basis (see Chapter 4) as opposed to absorption costing profit (see Chapter 2) nullifies the effect of any sales/production inequalities distorting C-V-P relationships.

▶ *variable/fixed cost components* have been accurately determined and segregated from each other. Several techniques for identifying and separating the variable from fixed elements of total cost were detailed for you fully throughout section 3.2.

▶ *linearity* – of both cost and revenue functions.

This list is not wholly comprehensive and exclusive as other assumptions do exist, but it is a summary of the most important ones. An instance of a further assumption applying is, for example, the existence of *certainty* that all the data input to the basic C-V-P model can be relied upon and will not change significantly for the period and range of analysis. We now look more closely at the last of the assumptions in the above list.

6.3.2 Non-linear/curvilinear revenue functions

The last on the list of assumptions also mentions, in addition to revenue, cost function linearity. The matter of non-linear or curvilinear cost functions will not be addressed here explicitly because it has already been discussed in some detail in Chapter 3's analysis of cost behaviour patterns (see section 3.1.1). We concentrate instead upon *revenue*. When an assumption is held not to reasonably apply, it is said to be 'relaxed' for purposes of further analysis – here we relax the assumption of linearity of the total revenue function, TR.

Earlier in the chapter both Figures 6.1 and 6.2 showed the TR function as an ever-increasing straight line over the scale of activity. This TR linearity implies a constant unit selling price – for example, £20 per unit in the case of our G. Mutchpen plc data, irrespective of whatever level of sales volume applied. It is often argued (in particular by economists) that TR will not necessarily follow a linear pattern. Unit sales price might not stay constant but may need to fall to sell higher volumes of output – basic economics dictates 'the lower the price, the higher the demand' (and vice-versa). This is a result of, for instance, the market saturation effect where supply is plentiful and only lower prices will enable further amounts of product to be sold. The eventual outcome of this classic economic behaviour, as embodied in traditional supply and demand theory (and practice), is that TR may well be reduced by actually selling more.

To illustrate this phenomenon for you, consider a very simple example. An organisation may be able to sell 15,000 units of its output at a selling price of £7 per unit, thus generating TR of £105,000. However, to expand sales beyond 15,000 units, say up to 17,000 units – unit sales price may need to fall to, say £6 per unit. In such a case TR will actually fall (from £105,000) by selling more, as only £102,000 (£6 × 17,000 units) revenue will be realised at the lower price, which, however, creates higher demand. In short, the increase in demand is not sufficient to compensate for the reduction in sales price. Figure 6.4 highlights graphically this kind of functional behaviour where TR is now non-linear/curvilinear, becoming gradually less steep and eventually taking a downturn (due to continued price-cutting) resulting in TR actually being reduced at greater levels of sales volume.

In the context of C-V-P analysis the non-linear/curvilinear effect on TR in Figure 6.4 also has further break-even implications. Note the second sentence in this chapter – 'the ultimate aim/objective we decided upon was that of income and wealth maximisation'. Assuming then that profit maximisation is management's chief goal, consider the profit situation depicted prior to Figure 6.4 according to all of the break-even charts encountered so far, i.e. Figures 6.1–6.3. Each chart shows the same (economists argue unrealistic) picture of forever increasing returns (profits) over continuously expanding levels of volume after the BEP has been reached. The gap between TR and TC on Figures 6.1 and 6.2 beyond the BEP simply gets wider and wider ... *ad infinitum*! This means that the maximum profit level is therefore never attained – or, in practical terms at least, it lies

figure 6.4

Multiple break-even point (BEP) chart

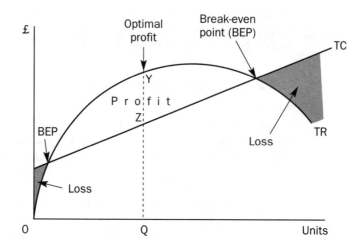

at the extreme upper reaches of the scale or range of volume. This is purely the result of linearity. In those earlier break-even charts, management faced with the problem of deciding at what level to fix business operations in order to max-imise/optimise profit would simply decide on the highest level of volume possible. Moreover, the effect of linearity is that there will only ever be one unique BEP.

Finally, consider again the very different non-linear/curvilinear picture dis-played by Figure 6.4. A second BEP is seen to emerge, hence Figure 6.4 might be referred to as a *multiple* break-even point chart (another type to add to those in section 6.2.2). On this kind of chart it now becomes feasible to determine an optimal profit point other than merely at the top end of the activity range; this is represented on Figure 6.4 by point 'Q' on the scale of activity/volume. Indeed, at higher levels of volume losses are seen to occur again. It is obviously important to management to be able to pinpoint precisely the volume of opera-tions to decide upon that will maximise or optimise profits. Given this objective, the fundamental decision problem is to accurately identify the loca-tion of point 'Q' on Figure 6.4. where distance YZ on the chart is at a maximum (i.e. at the point of optimal profit).

At this suitable juncture we leave C-V-P issues and move onto pricing deci-sion techniques in which *optimal pricing* strategies are just one of several methods of pricing available to management. In Chapter 7, the multiple BEP chart model is again presented as a basis for resolving and identifying, through mathematical means (i.e. application of elementary calculus/simple differentia-tion), this precise optimal volume point 'Q' on Figure 6.4 in the context of changing price-demand relationships.

Self-check questions
....

6.1 Hammond and Evans are a firm of publishers involved in the production of popular 'H & E' paperback novels. The firm's management are planning a future publication which would follow on as a sequel to one of its already well established romantic novels, *Passion Play*. Budgeted production cost and revenue details of the proposed sequel, tentatively entitled *Passion Play II (PPII)*, are as follows:

(i) Irrespective of how many copies of *PPII* are produced, 'setting-up' costs of typesetting, editing and photographers' and author's fees are to be budgeted at £40,000.

(ii) Budgeted printing costs for a production run up to and including 70,000 copies of *PPII* are estimated to be £800 per 1,000 copies.

(iii) No matter how many copies come from the print run, binding and finishing of *PPII* is budgeted at a cost of 20p per copy.

(iv) Retail stockists such as bookstores and newsagents will be supplied with *PPII* at a budgeted selling price of £2 per copy.

Required:

(a) (i) Construct a conventional break-even chart and read off the break-even point.

   (ii) Verify the accuracy of your break-even point reading by calculation.

   (iii) If actual sales of *PPII* are expected to be in the region of 55,000 copies what would you give as an approximate estimate of the publication's margin of safety?

(b) Hammond and Evans still have in stock 10,000 copies of another paperback novel which did not sell as well as expected and are not now likely to be sold. A local market trader has offered £1,800 for them. Give reasons why Hammond and Evans' management should or should not accept the offer. Would their decision be affected if the copies have not yet been bound and finished? (Assume an identical cost structure to *PPII*).

(Accounting Degree)

6.2 Shown below is a typical cost-volume-profit chart:

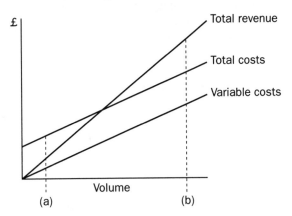

Required:

(a) Explain to a colleague who is not an accountant the reasons for the change in result on the above cost-volume-profit chart from a loss at point (a) to a profit at point (b).

(b) Identify and critically examine the underlying assumptions of the above type of cost-volume-profit analysis and consider whether such analyses are useful to the management of an organisation.

(Chartered Association of Certified Accountants)

6.3 (a) Define, and briefly explain, the following costing terms :
   (i)   Break-even Point.
   (ii) Margin of Safety.
   (iii) Profit/Volume (or Contribution/Sales) Ratio.
   (iv) Contribution Break-even Chart
   (b) From the following data, construct a P/V chart, from which you are required to clearly state the break-even point and margin of safety:

Marginal costs	£000	Fixed costs	£000
Direct materials	85	Fixed production overhead	40
Direct labour	55	Fixed administration overhead	20
Direct expenses	10	Fixed marketing overhead	15
Variable overhead	25		

   Sales revenue is £300,000   (Unit cost and unit sales data is not available).

   (c) Calculate the P/V (or contribution/sales) ratio from the above data, and use it to verify (by calculation) the break-even point which you derived from the P/V chart in (b) above.
   (d) List, and briefly describe, *four* of the main limitations/assumptions of break-even analysis.

                                        (Accounting Diploma)

6.4 ZED plc manufactures one standard product which sells at £10.
   You are required:
   (a) to prepare, from the data given below, a graph showing the results for the six months ended 30th April and to determine:
   (i)   the fixed costs;
   (ii) the variable cost per unit;
   (iii) the P/V ratio;
   (iv) the break-even point;
   (v)   the margin of safety;

Month	Sales units	Profit/(Loss) £
November	30,000	40,000
December	35,000	60,000
January	15,000	(20,000)
February	24,000	16,000
March	26,000	24,000
April	18,000	(8,000)

   (b) to discuss the limitations of such a graph
   (c) to explain the use of the relevant range in such a graph.
                          (Chartered Institute of Management Accountants)

Further study

······················

Arnold, J. and Hope, T. (1990) *Accounting for management decisions,* 2nd edn, Hemel Hempstead: Prentice-Hall.

Drury, C. (1992) *Management and cost accounting,* 3rd edn, London: Chapman and Hall.

Glautier, M. and Underdown, B. (1994) *Accounting theory and practice,* 5th edn, London: Pitman.

Horngren, C.T., Foster, G. and Datar, S. (1994) *Cost accounting – a managerial emphasis,* 8th edn, Hemel Hempstead: Prentice-Hall.

Scapens, R.W. (1991) *Management accounting – a review of recent developments,* 2nd edn, Basingstoke: Macmillan.

Wheldon, H. (1984) *Cost accounting,* 15th edn, London: Macdonald and Evans.

Wright, D. (1994) *A practical foundation in costing,* 1st edn, London: Routledge.

CHAPTER 7

Pricing decision techniques

Objectives
·············

By the end of this chapter you should be able to:

▶ Appreciate the difference between theoretical (economists') pricing techniques and the more pragmatic (accountants') type of approach to price determination.

▶ Perform graphical and/or mathematical analyses in order to determine a suitable price.

▶ Compare and contrast the individual techniques within the range of practical, 'accountant-type' methods of pricing.

▶ Offer relevant decision advice to management as to the most suitable of the techniques to adopt in different business circumstances.

The range of methods available to help management decide on a suitable selling price for the organisation's product reflects a span from the more practical (often more simplistic) pricing approaches to the more finely developed, theoretically based pricing techniques. In general, the more practically orientated methods are:

▶ Full-cost ⎫
▶ Rate of return ⎬ i.e. *cost-plus* pricing techniques
▶ Marginal (or, alternatively, *contribution margin*) pricing.

The first two methods above are approaches to pricing based on the absorption costing technique (see Chapter 2) while the third method uses the marginal costing technique (see Chapter 4) as a basis for making pricing decisions. Alternatively, at the opposite end of the spectrum, a more theoretically based approach to deciding on price is offered by: *optimal* pricing techniques. This approach to price determination makes use of graphical and mathematical means (e.g. elementary calculus and simple differentiation) harnessed to economic considerations of price-demand relationships, i.e. classical economic theory. Such a theoretical approach nonetheless holds important implications for price management in practice.

Because the latter rely and draw heavily upon economic argument and theory, the approach is often referred to as the 'economists' view of pricing, whereas the former more pragmatic techniques, derived from their use of absorption and marginal costing, are frequently known as the 'accountants' approach to pricing. Despite embodying decidedly different emphases, both approaches ought to be regarded in positive fashion by management as complementary techniques. This chapter's analysis of pricing decision techniques commences with the economics-influenced approach of optimal pricing.

7.1 Optimal pricing technique

An important simplifying assumption that has often applied to the analysis (of 'cost' in Chapter 3 and 'cost-revenue' behaviour in Chapter 6) is that of *linearity*. Cost linearity will continue to be assumed here (for additional details of economic forces that alternatively cause cost non-linearity/curvilinearity, you need to refer back to section 3.1.1 of Chapter 3). On the other hand, the economists' contention that revenue does not behave in a linear fashion will be observed in this section, giving rise to the non-linear/curvilinear total revenue (TR) functions that occur throughout. You should remember first that a constant selling price per unit is bound to result in a linear TR (as in, for instance, Figures 6.1 and 6.2 – where the latter TR line represented £20 per unit regardless of the activity level/volume). From now on in this section, however, the analysis is based on the economic argument that to sell more (i.e. to increase sales volume along the 'x' axis) it may be necessary to reduce unit selling price – the effect being to create a non-linear/curvilinear TR function such as that which appeared earlier in Figure 6.4. Before progressing onto section 7.1.1 study again the nature of the total cost-total revenue (TC–TR) relationships presented in Figure 6.4, also quickly reread section 6.3.2 on *non-linear/curvilinear revenue functions* which form the basis of the TR function in optimal pricing.

7.1.1 Price-demand behaviour

Prior to dealing with sales revenues (and costs) in total – i.e. TR (and TC) – consider first of all selling price behaviour *per unit* with respect to demand level. A 'motto' born out of classic economic theory has an important application in this context:

'The higher the unit selling price, the lower the demand,
the lower the price, the higher the demand.'

In some extreme circumstances (e.g. high prestige/luxury goods of an ostentatious nature) the above motto does not strictly always apply, but in general it is a truism of economic behaviour.

In graphical terms, the motto translates into Figure 7.1. As already mentioned to you, cost linearity that results from a constant variable cost per unit will be assumed throughout – however, selling price/demand sensitivity represented by changing prices relative to varying demand (i.e. volume) levels will now be a feature of the analysis. The inverse proportional relationship implied by economics is exhibited in the following sample data of J. Gooch Limited that will be used for both graphical and mathematical means of illustrating optimal pricing decisions for the remainder of this section.

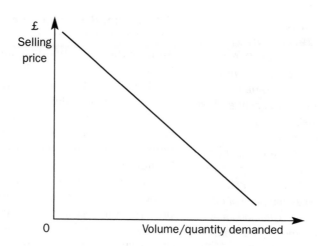

figure 7.1
**Price-demand
relationship**

J. Gooch Ltd incurs fixed overhead costs of £37,000 per period. The firm's product
has a variable (i.e. marginal) cost structure of £2.50 per unit, and the market sensitivity of changes in volume demanded in relation to variations in product selling price
(i.e. the firm's price/demand function) is given by the following schedule:

Selling price per unit (£)	Volume/quantity demanded (000 units)
2	80
3	60
4	40
5	20

Required: Help J. Gooch Ltd's management to decide upon an optimal level for
business activity and the related optimal price via both graphical (section 7.1.2) and
mathematical (section 7.1.3) means of analysis.

7.1.2 Graphical optimal solution method

The above data for J. Gooch Ltd can be plotted on a graph to produce a *multiple
break-even point chart* (similar in form to the one you have already seen in Figure
6.4 as part of Chapter 6's analysis of types of break-even chart) – see Figure 7.2.

Gooch's management, assuming its objective is to maximise/optimise
profits, will want to identify point 'q' on Figure 7.2 as this is where profit
distance YZ on the chart is greatest. Activity level 'q' (of 35,000 units here) is
said to be optimal. A decision by Gooch to produce and sell at this level of
activity will generate maximum profit YZ. Table 7.1 also shows the
quantity-related optimal price to be £4.25.

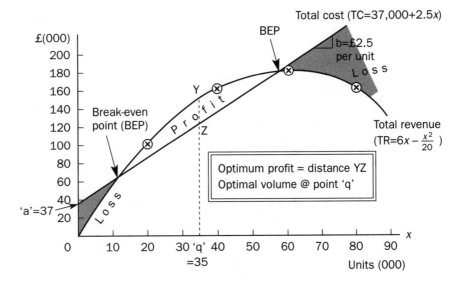

figure 7.2
Optimal pricing technique – graphical method

Instead of employing the more precise mathematical means detailed next in section 7.1.3, you can use non-linear/curvilinear break-even charts such as Figure 7.2. effectively to *estimate* this optimal point 'q'. Often your estimated reading, because of the physical limitations of constructing a perfect graph, will not be irrefutably accurate. However, where approximations to optimality are sufficient for management's decision purposes, then reliance on graphical identification of point 'q' is acceptable.

The laws of economics dictate that optimal point 'q' is described as the position where marginal revenue (MR) is equal to marginal cost (MC). In applying this law, economists make use of such mathematical devices as elementary calculus and simple differentiation. Consider now the *written* description of the use of these mathematical tools in conjunction with the graphical analysis embodied in multiple BEP charts in general and Figure 7.2 in particular.

Through the process of differentiating (d) TR with respect to volume 'x' (a process expressed as $\frac{dTR}{dx}$) the slope of TR can be measured. Similarly, a measure

table 7.1
Optimal price/quantity by linear interpolation

Selling price per unit (£)	Volume/quantity demanded (Units)
2	80,000
3	60,000
4	40,000
4.25	35,000
5	20,000

Optimal (via linear interpolation)

Key: $*\frac{1}{4}$ into range of £1 : 20,000 units
$\varphi\frac{3}{4}$ into range of £1 : 20,000 units

of the slope of the TC function is given by differentiating TC with respect to volume ($\frac{dTC}{dx}$). In the simplified cost case of a single constant unit variable/marginal cost, MC is simply the unit cost amount (for example, £2.50 in the Gooch illustration). The differentiated measures reflect MR and MC respectively, being the rate at which the slopes of the lines change. As elementary calculus may be used to provide an exact measurement of the slopes of TR and TC, the point at which TC becomes steeper than TR can be precisely located or determined. This is the economist's optimal point, that is where MR = MC (and is point 'q' on Figure 7.2).

For as long as TR remains steeper than TC, increases in volume are worthwhile because TR is increasing at a faster rate than TC. Where MR = MC, the TR curve ceases to be steeper than TC – the slopes become equal. The value of 'q' in Figure 7.2 which equates MR and MC is optimal, and is where:

$$\frac{dTR}{dx} = \frac{dTC}{dx}$$

At volume levels above 'q' on Figure 7.2, TC becomes steeper than TR and any expansion of business activity above optimal 'q' is simply not worthwhile. Any profit readings taken from the chart in Figure 7.2 above activity level 'q' will reveal a lower profit than the measure of profit between YZ. This mathematical process of differentiation to determine an optimum has been described so far for you without the aid of numbers, but the following section works through the mathematics involved using the Gooch data provided at the start of your Activity 7.1.

7.1.3 Mathematical optimal solution method

In carrying out the mathematics throughout this section a basic understanding of the mechanics of simple differentiation is necessarily assumed. The algebraic representation of how the differentiation process 'crunches the numbers' is given by:

$n\beta x^{n-1}$ (where 'n' is the power function number and 'β' is the coefficient value attached to volume 'x').

Specific application of this generic expression firstly to illustrate differentiation of both TR and TC functions with respect to 'x' (to determine MR and MC respectively) is done using the previous Gooch data. Secondly, the profit function/equation from the data is differentiated to provide a cross-check with the first derivation of the optimum. The ultimate aim of the calculations is to determine the optimal price, so the initial step is to establish the price equation from the data.

To create the price equation we need to identify its parameters. The first one is its lower bound, the base parameter, representing the price at which no demand (zero quantity/volume) exists. As the trend of the Gooch data reflects a perfectly proportionate inverse relationship between selling price and demand, we can extrapolate to a £6 price at which there would be nil volume sold/demanded. This occurs because each £1 increase in sales price reduces demand by 20 (in thousands – all calculations will be maintained in thousands). Moving up from a £5 price to £6 would decrease quantity/volume (x) by 20 – from 20 @ £5 down to zero @ £6. Therefore six is the first, lower parameter in the price equation. Because demand is generated as a result of any reduction from six, then this parameter of six is linked to the second (and final other) parameter with a minus sign.

The second parameter reflects the relationship that exists when quantity/volume is demanded by changing (i.e. reducing) the selling price from six – in short, it is the price:demand ratio. This is written as price over demand:

$$\frac{\Delta \text{ Price}}{\Delta \text{ Demand}} \qquad \text{(i.e. change in price)} \\ \text{(i.e change in quantity/volume demanded)}$$

From the Gooch price-demand schedule this is obviously $\dfrac{£1}{20 \text{ units}}$

As this is the relationship between the change in quantity brought about by price change, the expression needs to be multiplied through by quantity/volume, i.e. 'x', thus becoming:

$$\frac{1}{20} \text{ x} \quad \text{or, simply,} \quad \frac{x}{20}$$

This being the second parameter established, the complete price (p) equation can be set up, written as follows:

$$\text{Price (p)} = 6 - \frac{x}{20}$$

Next step is for you to develop the total revenue (TR) equation from the above price equation; this is achieved simply by multiplying selling price (p) by volume (x), thus:

$$\text{TR (px)} = 6 \text{ x} - \frac{x^2}{20}$$

Because ultimately we want to equate MR with MC to determine the optimum, the above TR equation requires differentiating to give MR. Differentiation of TR is performed, as already mentioned, by applying the $n\beta x^{n-1}$ operator:

$$\frac{dTR}{dx} = 6 - \frac{x}{20} = MR$$

If you find that the above calculation is not immediately apparent consider the following slightly more detailed application of $n\beta x^{n-1}$ to the TR equation which can be re-stated more fully as:

$$TR = 6x^1 - \frac{1}{20} x^2$$

Apply $n\beta x^{n-1}$ to carry out the differentiation of TR with respect to x:

$$\frac{dTR}{dx} = (1)(6)\, x^{1-1} - (2)\left(\frac{1}{20}\right) x^{2-1}$$

$$= 6x^{\circ} - \frac{2}{20}\, x^1$$

$$= (6)(1) - \frac{1}{10}\, x$$

$$= 6 - \frac{x}{10}$$

Note that anything raised to the power function zero (here, x°) is equal to unity, i.e. = 1. Optimality is where the above MR measure is set equal to MC, and as variable cost per unit of £2.50 is Gooch's MC, then the equation for an optimum can be stated very directly and simply as:

$$6 - \frac{x}{10} = 2.5$$

However, for a fuller explanation once again using the $n\beta x^{n-1}$ operator, a more detailed derivation of MC is to differentiate TC with respect to x. Recall from earlier analyses (in Chapters 3 and 6) our familiar TC equation, y = a + bx; where 'y' is TC; 'a' is constant fixed cost per period; and 'b' is variable cost per unit. With the Gooch data inserted it is: TC = £37,000 + £2.5 x. Restated more suitably for differentiation purposes:

$$TC = 37,000 + 2.5\, x^1$$

Apply $n\beta x^{n-1}$ to carry out the differentiation of TC with respect to x:

$$\frac{dTC}{dx} = (1)(2.5)\, x^{1-1} = 2.5\, x^{\circ} = 2.5 = MC$$

You will have noticed that under differentiation any constant (e.g. fixed cost amount of £37,000) disappears. This is because, when cost is differentiated *with respect to* x, only variable cost's rate of change is marginal and related directly to x; fixed cost has nothing to do with (i.e. is not affected by) changes in x and it has no role to play in measures of marginal rates of change.

Obvious by now, the optimal point on the activity level x is where:

$$MR = MC$$

$$6 - \frac{x}{10} = 2.5$$

$$\therefore 6 - 2.5 = \frac{x}{10}$$

$$\therefore 3.5 = \frac{x}{10}$$

$$\therefore 35 = x \text{ (i.e. optimal volume)}$$

As the volume/quantity demanded throughout has been scaled in thousands, Gooch's optimal level of operations is 35,000 units (see the optimal point 'q' determined graphically in section 7.1.2).

Rather than differentiating both TR and TC and setting them equal to each other, because TR minus TC equals profit (π), an alternative approach would be to differentiate π with respect to x and set that term equal to zero to determine the optimum, *viz*:

$$\frac{d\pi}{dx} = 0$$

Assuming you have developed greater ease of calculation now in using differentiation, apply the Gooch data:

$$TR = 6x - \frac{x^2}{20} \text{ and } TC = 37,000 + 2.5\,x$$

Deducting TC from TR gives the profit equation:

$$\pi = 6x - \frac{x^2}{20} - (37,000 + 2.5\,x)$$

$$= 3.5x - \frac{x^2}{20} - 37,000$$

Apply $n\beta x^{n-1}$ to carry out the differentiation of π with respect to x:

$$\frac{d\pi}{dx} = 3.5 - \frac{x}{10}$$

For an optimum, set $\dfrac{d\pi}{dx} = 0$:

$$3.5 - \frac{x}{10} = 0$$

$$\therefore x = 35 \text{ (i.e. 35,000 units optimal volume)}$$

Finally, having derived the optimal level of business operations in order to maximise profit, as stated earlier, the ultimate goal is to use this to determine the optimal price for the firm's product or service. This is achieved by simply substituting the optimal volume level x, already ascertained, back into the price equation set up as the initial step earlier on in this section, thus:

$$p = 6 - \frac{35}{20}$$

$$= 6 - 1.75$$

$$= \underline{4.25}$$

Hence, the optimal price for Gooch to sell its output is £4.25 per unit. You might take the opportunity here to cross-check this solution with Table 7.1, where it was arrived at by interpolation in the graphical solution.

Can you determine ...? both optimal volume and optimal price given the price equation, marginal cost (£) and fixed cost (£) data in the following two cases:
(i)   Price (P) = 400 – 2x; Marginal cost (MC) = 120; Fixed cost (FC) = 111,000.
(ii) Price (P) = 10 – 0.0001x; Marginal cost (MC) = 2; Fixed cost (FC) = 55,000.

Answer

(i)   P = 400 – 2x ∴ Total revenue (TR) = 400x – 2x²

Marginal revenue (MR) by differentiating TR with respect to x

$$\frac{dTR}{dx} = 400 - 4x$$

Optimal point is where MR = MC:

   400 – 4x = 120

   ∴ 4x = 280   ∴ x = 70

By substitution in P:

   P = 400 – (2)(70) = 400 – 140   ∴ P = 260

Hence, optimal volume: 70; and optimal price: £260.

(ii) P = 10 – 0.000lx ∴ Total revenue (TR) = 10x – 0.000lx²

Total cost (TC) = FC + (MC × x) = 55,000 + 2x

Profit (π) = TR – TC ∴ π = 10x – 0.0001x² – (55,000 + 2x)

Optimal profit by differentiating π with respect to x:

$$\frac{d\pi}{dx} = 10 - 0.0002x - 2$$

$$\text{For optimum, set } \frac{d\pi}{dx} = 0:$$

   8 – 0.0002x = 0   ∴ x = 40,000

By substitution in P:

   P = 10 – (0.0001)(40,000)
      = 10 – 4   ∴ P = 6

Hence, optimal volume: 40,000; and optimal price: £6

A final question you might ask is: 'Why, if we have determined the best (i.e. optimal) price, might an organisation price its output differently in comparison with this optimum?' The short answer is that often price will be set not in accordance with elegant theory but rather instead with a view to other non-theoretical/non-maximisation influences such as:

▶ *Competitors' prices*: the optimal price may be out of line with nearest competitors.
▶ *Price image*: a firm may wish to create, say, a 'low-cost/high-sales' volume image.
▶ *Psychological factors*: desire for increased prestige may induce a high-price/high-status demand.
▶ *Strategy*: perhaps a short-term, selective 'loss-leader' range of output priced below cost.

Such issues also need to be considered in conjunction with the more pragmatic/practically orientated ('accountants'-type') approaches discussed in the next section.

7.2 Cost-plus and marginal pricing techniques

Marginal pricing is often referred to as the 'contribution margin' pricing technique and is considered in section 7.2.3. It derives from the marginal costing principles detailed in Chapter 4, whereas the *cost-plus* techniques for deciding on a suitable selling price have their roots in the absorption costing technique discussed at length in Chapter 2. Thorough knowledge on your part as to the content of both Chapters 2 and 4 is therefore necessarily assumed throughout the rest of this chapter. Cost-plus pricing methods consist essentially of two main approaches to price determination, namely, 'full-cost' pricing and 'rate of return' pricing.

7.2.1 Full-cost pricing technique

This cost-based approach is founded upon the establishment of total (i.e. *full*) cost via the conventional application of absorption costing principles seen in Chapter 2 for cost ascertainment of products, services etc. Because of this, the technique is often called 'absorption cost' pricing. A mark-up percentage (profit percentage) on the ascertained full absorption cost is then added to the figure for total cost to determine a selling price. A typical build-up of full cost leading to a price using the absorption cost ascertainment technique from Chapter 2 is provided for you in the example below of a full-cost price calculation.

Direct costs		
Raw materials	22,000	
Production labour	17,600	
Direct expenses	800	
Prime cost		40,400
Overhead		
Production overhead (absorbed @ 100% of direct labour cost)		17,600

Production cost	58,000
Marketing and administration overhead (absorbed @ 40% of full production cost)	23,200
Total/full cost	81,200
Profit mark-up (@ 20% of total/full cost)	16,240
Selling price	£97,440

Notice that the selling price decided upon via the full-cost technique here incorporates recovery (i.e. absorption) of other general overhead costs such as marketing and administrative expenses as well as production overhead. In this context an absorption rate (40 per cent of production cost) was used to account for all manner of overhead in addition to just production which itself is recovered using a percentage (here 100 per cent) of direct wages/labour cost. Application of a wide range of different types of overhead absorption rate has already been covered in Chapter 2. With regard to this issue of accounting for non-production overhead such as marketing and administration, you will find it useful at this juncture to refer back to the summary considerations at the very end of section 2.2. Also for reasons previously given only production overhead will be seen to be absorbed into full production cost to generate a price in Activity 7.2.

A further point worth noting is that although use of the cost-plus technique is here restricted purely to absorption cost-plus, there is nothing whatsoever to preclude management choosing an *activity based cost-plus* approach as an alternative to pricing consistent with the ABC technique for cost ascertainment/treatment of overhead detailed in section 2.3.

Finally and before embarking on our Activity 7.2, in addition to the problem of management through the cost accountant having to decide, somewhat arbitrarily, on what suitable overhead absorption rate to adopt from the range available, there is also the further complication of deciding (again often arbitrarily) upon the appropriate profit percentage mark-up for an individual organisation. The percentage rate will differ widely depending on and according to the nature of the business. For instance, fast-moving consumer goods such as foodstuffs and tobacco will have a relatively low profit margin compared with, say, luxury goods.

ACTIVITY **7.2**

A motor vehicle repair and maintenance company, which we will call Grindrod's Car-Care and Repair Factory, carries out on its garage premises a wide variety of maintenance and repair work on heavy commercial vehicles as well as on domestic, privately owned cars. Its repair factory tackles jobs ranging from routine maintenance and servicing of family cars to major overhauls and repairs to heavy trucks and lorries. One job currently being undertaken to a customer's specific requirements is job number HRW 40:

Job HRW 40: This job is already partially complete and all necessary parts and materials, costing £69, have been used.

It is particularly labour-intensive and, although the job is only 50 per cent complete as regards the mechanics' time, the direct labour cost has already reached £140. Additionally a specialist tool has been needed and has been used only once so far at a hire charge of £25. It is expected that Grindrod's will have to rent the tool twice gain, at the same hire charge each time.

Required: Given that Grindrods recovers its repair factory overhead using a predetermined/budgeted absorption rate based on 50 per cent of direct labour costs, what is the current work-in-progress (W-I-P) valuation of job HRW 40 and what is the estimated price that will have to be charged to the customer to give a final repair factory profit of 25 per cent on full cost when the job is completely finished?

Consider and work carefully through Table 7.2 below to determine both these requirements for a W-I-P valuation and an estimated 25 per cent cost-plus price for Job HRW 40.

7.2.2 *Rate of return pricing technique*

When required organisational (and also divisional – see Chapter 11) performance levels are based on a measured rate of return on capital employed, then management may well decide to fix a sales price calculated on just such a basis. Perhaps link this with your financial accounting studies as this relationship between return (i.e. profit) and capital employed is the primary ratio used in financial accounts analysis. Sometimes called 'return on investment' it is an important financial measure of profitability, as well as here providing a convenient platform for managers to choose an appropriate selling price for the firm's (or division's) output.

For such a calculation, three essential elements are involved:

▶ total organisational costs budgeted;
▶ level of the firm's capital employed;
▶ the required rate of return targeted.

table 7.2
Grindrods Car-Care and Repair Factory: Job HRW 40

	W-I-P Valuation		Price estimate	
Prime costs:	(£)	(£)	(£)	(£)
Direct materials (currently 100% complete):	69		69	
Direct labour (currently 50% complete):	140		280	
Direct expenses (currently 33⅓% complete):	25	234	75	424
Production overhead (absorbed)				
Repair factory O/H (recovered @ 50% of direct labour cost):		70		140
Current W-I-P valuation:		304		564
Required 25% (on cost) repair factory profit for job HRW 40:				141
Estimated selling price of job HRW 40:				705

This approach to pricing may not so obviously be seen as a cost-plus technique, but it is! Its method of calculation is slightly more obscure when compared with that of the straightforward full-cost approach. Nevertheless the *mark-up on cost* principle at the root of all cost-plus pricing is still clearly evident. The appropriate mark-up on cost percentage figure is (perhaps more circuitously) determined by applying the above three ingredients of this technique into the following formula:

$$\frac{\text{Capital employed}}{\text{Total budgeted cost}} \times \text{Required (i.e. 'target') rate of return}$$

ACTIVITY 7.3

Utilising the given formula and based on the following sample data for Target plc:

▸ budgeted costs in total = £8 million
▸ capital employed = £6 million
▸ required/target rate of return = 20 per cent

Required: Calculate the appropriate percentage mark-up on cost necessary to arrive at a selling price that will satisfy Targets plc's desired rate of return on capital of 20 per cent.

Firstly, consider what profit figure is implied by Target plc's requirement of a 20 per cent return on capital employed. The target profit is:

£6 million x 0.2 = £1.2 million

Next, substitute Target plc's data into the formula:

$$\frac{6}{8} \times 20\% = 15\%$$

Therefore, a mark-up on total cost of 15% will determine the required selling price.

Proof: Total budgeted costs x 15% = Target profit
£8 million x 0.15 = £1.2 million

In conclusion, management of Target plc would be best advised to decide on a 15 per cent cost mark-up on its product output to fix a selling price that will achieve its profit objectives.

Summary and the limitations of cost-plus methods

Although inferior in a conceptual or theoretical sense to the optimal pricing techniques we discussed in section 7.1, cost-plus methods of price setting are very widely used in practice. This may be due in the main to their inherently simpler and more straightforward nature. However, you need to be aware of the *shortcomings* of cost-plus pricing methods which can seriously limit their application. For instance, the rate of return technique does not really avoid the largely arbitrary decision inherent in full-cost pricing (as mentioned in section

7.2.1) as to what should be the relevant mark-up percentage figure. It merely transfers it to the required 'target' return rate on capital employed.

Perhaps even more importantly, and in stark contrast particularly to optimal pricing criteria, market demand conditions are ignored entirely as price fixing becomes a purely cost-based function. Unlike, and again contrasting sharply with, the marginal pricing technique dealt with next in section 7.2.3, cost-plus methods are basically not suited to short-run strategic pricing decisions because of their inbuilt lack of flexibility (although they may be useful serving more as a long-term pricing measure). In an attempt to partially counteract this severe limitation, in practical pricing situations a degree of flexibility may often be incorporated via the cost-plus methods being regarded by management as essentially just a 'first stage' in the price-fixing process. Managers will often, subsequent to a cost-plus determined price being achieved, decide to alter the fixed mark-up percentage figure though more informal and intuitive assessments and judgements of such conditions as market demand, output capacities, and business competition levels.

Finally, neither cost-plus method overcomes the problem of using what are predominantly arbitrary means of allocating, apportioning and absorbing (remember the 3 'A's from Chapter 2!) fixed overheads into total cost. The arbitrariness of choosing or adopting one fixed overhead absorption rate as opposed to another is, intrinsically speaking, a problematic feature of all absorption costing systems (upon which cost-plus pricing is based) in general. This final comment leads us conveniently to the last pricing technique to be considered in this chapter.

7.2.3 Marginal/contribution margin pricing technique

The marginal (or contribution margin) approach to pricing overcomes certain of the limitations just mentioned. For example, no allocation, apportionment or absorption of fixed overhead is involved in deciding upon the selling price – fixed costs are treated as a lump sum, period cost amount and written off against the contribution for the accounting/costing period in question (see Chapter 4). Short-term pricing strategy is better served by this approach, which possesses a greater degree of flexibility in price fixing, because no automatic/mechanical addition (i.e. mark-up) to cost is made in arriving at a suitable selling price. After marginal/variable cost is ascertained contribution is maximised by fixing a sales price based on demand conditions, level of market competition etc.

Marginal costing therefore is the principle underlying the marginal pricing technique in which *only* variable costs are considered and the difference between such variable cost and the sales price results in a contribution being made towards covering fixed costs. There are many occasions in practice where it proves wiser to attract business by not charging full unit cost (which might deter customers) and charging less than full absorption cost, i.e. a cut-price marginal cost rate. Anything charged above marginal/variable costs will yield a positive contribution (no matter how small) towards paying for the often very high levels of fixed overhead in, for example, many service industries.

Good examples of applying this marginal principle in practice include:

▸ Off-peak transport fares to attract people to fill what would otherwise be under-utilised spare capacity, i.e. empty seats.

▸ Out-of-season/'bargain'/midweek rates (i.e. differential price tariffs) in holiday resort hotels, guesthouses etc.

▸ Cut-price meals in restaurants, cafes, pubs, etc. at lunch-time to fill what would otherwise be empty tables. As long as a meal's variable costs (the food itself, power and fuel for cooking, direct staff wages, etc.) are covered, a contribution will be made to paying for the organisation's fixed costs such as rent, rates and insurances which are incurred regardless of how full the tables are.

In defence of full absorption cost pricing it needs to be stressed that in the long run any successful business must cover *all* its costs. Short-term sporadic losses may be tolerable, but no commercial enterprise can survive persistent loss making. In the long term, *both* fixed and variable costs need to be covered. This is where the absorption cost pricing technique has perhaps its most vital practical application. The full cost of a cost unit tells management what minimum price needs to be charged to make profits in the long run. However, the short term and one-off situations may dictate otherwise and allow a different price from full cost to be charged as a minimum.

For example, and prior to undertaking Activity 7.4, take the case of pricing a book; published by Sportbooks Limited, it is a soccer publication entitled *Big Boot* written by former Ireland international footballer, Roy O'Rover and retailing at £28.00 per copy. The full absorption unit cost build-up for a single copy of the book is demonstrated in Table 7.3.

A full unit price of at least £25.00 must be charged to ensure recovery of all costs, while a £28.00 selling price, perhaps based on a 12 per cent mark-up on full costs, gives a normal retail profit of £3.00. As *Big Boot* must be sold for more than £25.00 per copy for long-term continued profit-making, the full absorp-

table 7.3 **Sportbooks Ltd: 'Big Boot' unit cost statement**		
Direct costs (all variable by nature):		(£)
Direct/raw material:		12.60
Direct production labour:		3.00
Direct expenses (10% royalty):		2.80
Prime cost:		18.40
Indirect costs: (all assumed to be fixed):		
Production overhead absorbed:		4.10
Production cost:		22.50
Administration and marketing overhead absorbed:		2.50
Full unit absorption cost:		25.00

tion cost information is of significant value to Sportbooks' management when deciding what normal retail price to charge.

The absorption costing principle of recovering all costs can in this situation be said to be appropriate for pricing decisions. However, other circumstances may arise where covering the full cost of £25.00 and advising a recommended retail price of £28.00 would be imprudent.

Examining more closely the full cost build-up of £25.00 shows that every copy of *Big Boot* produced directly incurs £18.40 of prime cost. In other words these are the direct costs that will vary according to how many books are printed, as prime cost is entirely variable.

The physical material in the book, the wages of direct workers making the book, and the 10 per cent royalty paid to Roy on every book printed are all either:

▶ unavoidable if another book is made; or
▶ not incurred if one less book is produced.

If there are no variable overhead costs then the marginal cost of *Big Boot* is £18.40; the extra cost incurred or saved by making one more or one less book respectively.

This instance assumes all overhead to be fixed, although this is obviously not always the case and some variable overhead usually does exist (e.g. salesperson's commission). But for the purpose of this illustration let us assume production overhead is entirely fixed and that general overheads (i.e. administration and marketing) too are wholly fixed. By definition, no matter whether another 1, 10, 100, or even 1,000 are made, the total fixed costs of Sportbooks Ltd. will not change or vary. This holds implications for the pricing of *Big Boot*.

Imagine further that Roy retires – perhaps on the strength of royalties – from domestic football and goes to live in an exotic faraway tropical land where soccer is in its infancy, but is nevertheless gaining fast in popularity. Roy sees this as a new challenge and resumes playing in his new homeland, rapidly becoming a national hero.

Sportbooks Ltd., however, does not know how long the hero worship will last (it may be very short-lived) but a great demand arises for Roy's book. The home market is highly unlikely to be affected by this new demand and *Big Boot* will continue to be sold at £28.00 domestically. But at what price could the book be offered for sale in Roy's new home nation, where people are generally poor?

A one-off strategy would be to sell at any price as long as direct marginal costs are covered – i.e. anything over £18.40. Charging such a price will make a marginal contribution towards paying for Sportbooks' unchanged fixed costs at home. Obviously as much over £18.40 as can be charged will give a greater contribution but, money being scarce, demand may be very price-sensitive. But even if only, say, £21.40 is charged, which is £6.60 less (unit overhead of £4.10 plus £2.50) than full price, then £3.00 per unit is still being earned as contribution. In short a marginal cost of £18.40 becomes more important and relevant than the absorption cost of £25.00 in this sort of short term, one-off pricing decision which effectively ignores recovery of fixed overhead. Fixed costs in other words are taken to be entirely irrelevant to the decision – they are not a *decision variable* as are the prime costs.

Which technique to apply?

The point of the above simple illustration is to show that the accountant's choice of which pricing/costing technique to adopt, when providing management with cost information, should be tailored as closely as possible to fit the relevant circumstances.

Sometimes full absorption cost will be relevant, whilst on other occasions it is more prudent to use marginal costing/pricing. The *ad hoc* pricing decision above is just one example – a multitude of others exist, (including the one comprising Activity 7.4 which concludes this chapter on pricing decision techniques).

ACTIVITY 7.4

The 'Curry House' is a town-centre Indian restaurant renowned for its unique speciality curry dish (the only meal that the Curry House offers) which is served at varying strengths to suit all tastes, from mild 'korma' to very hot 'vindaloo'. Each dish, irrespective of strength, sells at a standard price of £6.00 and the Curry House's current level of business is 200 meals per day. The marginal cost of providing each meal is £2.50 per dish, and fixed costs of operating the restaurant amount to £500 per day. However, the Curry House is not operating to its normal available capacity as it has the potential to serve up to 250 dishes daily.

Toni Singh (an ex-management accountant and now proud owner/manager of the Curry House) recently turned down a special offer from an old business colleague, Ricki Heppolette, managing director of a nearby factory site-cum-office block which has neither its own factory nor office canteen facilities. The offer rejected by Toni was to guarantee to provide Ricki's workforce with an absolute daily minimum of 100 dishes at a specially reduced price of £4.00 per meal. Ricki is furious with Toni because he has just witnessed the Curry House willingly cater for a coach party of 50 pop fans returning from a concert who offered £200 for a special one-off order. Ricki shouts at Toni: 'That works out per meal at exactly what I offered you – what do you think you're playing at?! Have you no business sense at all?

Required: What was Toni Singh's rationale behind refusing Ricki's offer but accepting the coach party offer of £200 for 50 meals?

Toni Singh's management accounting background has enabled him to come to a logical and sound business decision via the following rationale:

Ricki's special offer would generate a contribution of £150 (100 meals at a selling price of £4 less marginal cost of £2.50) but it would also have resulted in Toni having to turn away 50 regular full-price customers paying the standard £6 because the restaurant's daily spare capacity is only 50 meals (i.e. normal available capacity of 250 minus current business activity of 200). The lost contribution, plus possibly loss of goodwill, from turning down regularly priced business amounts to £175 (50 meals at £6 less £2.50). Ricki wants at least 100 places per day reserved and therefore Toni cannot merely use up the 50 meal spare capacity like he did with the coach party. If Toni had accepted Ricki's offer he would have sacrificed a net benefit (i.e. incurred a net opportunity cost) of £25.00 a day. The concept of *opportunity cost* is introduced here and can be described as the value of a benefit sacrificed for some other chosen alternative course of action or, even more succinctly, the value of the 'displaced alternative'.

	£
Gross opportunity cost – 50 'displaced alternative' meals (@ a lost contribution of £3.50 per dish):	175
less Contribution from Ricki's special offer (- 100 meals @ £1.50 per dish)	150
Net opportunity cost (i.e. net benefit sacrificed/net contribution lost)	25

Note that at the present level of business, fixed cost per unit is £2.50 – i.e. £500 ÷ 200 meals. Therefore full absorption cost of a meal/unit = £5, made up of variable plus fixed unit costs both being £2.50 each meal. At a standard price of £6 per meal and at the current activity level, the Curry House is presently more than breaking even (see Chapter 6). Because any contribution beyond break-even point is wholly profit then meals served, using spare capacity, at any price above marginal cost of £2.50 simply add to the restaurant's profits. Illuminated by this Activity, the accounting/pricing logic and economic good sense behind weekday, low-price business lunches is explained. Even where a business is making a loss, given spare capacity, any revenue above marginal cost will contribute towards meeting the usually very high fixed overhead costs (e.g. rent and rates) of operating, say, a town-centre business.

However, also beware of the dangers of consistently pricing below full absorption cost. It cannot be stressed too strongly that fixed costs in the long-run must still be met to ensure continued business survival. Continually pricing all business on nothing but a marginal cost base will not provide for covering fixed costs over the long-term and will inevitably/eventually prove to be a recipe for commercial disaster. In essence, marginal pricing as a decision-making tool ought to be reserved for short-term marginal decisions, such as the one-off pricing strategy in Activity 7.4 and the Sportbooks *Big Boot* example prior to it. To conclude it might be appropriately claimed that marginal pricing can loosely be viewed as a much closer approximation to fixing optimal prices than cost-plus techniques could ever be.

Self-check questions
....

7.1 Woody Limited manufacture a range of three wooden products using a series of machine operations.

House: Saw the wood to size, shape on a lathe, paint and assemble.
Horse: Saw, shape and assemble.
Hellefump: Saw, shape, drill, paint and assemble.

Woody Limited currently operate a system whereby labour and overhead costs for all products are absorbed into product units at 150 per cent of direct material costs which are £80, £120 and £100 for the House, Horse and

Hellefump respectively, and result in profit/losses of £20 profit, £20 loss and £10 profit respectively.

For the coming year the following apply:

(i)

Machine operation	Fixed labour and overhead (total) £000	Variable labour and overhead per unit £
Saw	92	25
Shape	138	10
Drill	48	30
Paint	360	20
Assemble	184	22

(ii) Production/sales units

House	10,000
Horse	5,000
Hellefump	8,000

(iii) Material prices will rise by 10 per cent.

(iv) Selling prices will rise by 5 per cent.

(v) Fixed costs for each machine type will be absorbed at a rate per unit based on the aggregate number of units budgeted to pass through that machine type.

You are required to:

(a) Prepare a summary for the coming year which details for each product:

(i) Fixed and variable costs by machine operation.

(ii) Contribution earned per unit and in total.

(iii) Net profit or loss per unit and in total.

(b) Comment on the likely effects that the change in absorption bases will have on costing and pricing decisions.

(Chartered Institute of Public Finance and Accountancy)

7.2 (i) 'Maximise the contribution' has been said to be the golden rule of pricing. Explain and comment on this statement.

(ii) The marketing manager of your company has estimated that demand for a new product with a marginal cost of £20 would be as follows:

Price	£40	£38	£36	£34	£32	£30	£28
Demand	2,000	2,400	3,000	3,800	4,800	6,000	7,500

Machines will be acquired which will each produce 500 units per year at an annual fixed cost of £2,000.

How many machines should be acquired and at what price should the product be sold? (Show workings in a suitable format.)

(Chartered Institute of Public Finance and Accountancy)

7.3 Set out below is information taken from the production plan of Archaic plc for 1994, relating to the manufacture and sale of central heating valves.

PLANNED LEVEL OF PRODUCTION AND SALES		**120,000**
		(£)
Selling price		20
Variable costs	materials	8
	labour	7
Allocation of fixed overheads		2
Planned profit per unit		3

Required:
(a) Plot the cost and revenue information on a graph and calculate
 (i) the break-even point;
 (ii) the amount of profit if sales fell to 100,000;
 (iii) the level of sales required to generate a profit of 20 per cent of sales.
(b) Compare the accountant's and the economist's approaches to break-even analysis, and state what you consider to be the main limitations of cost-volume-profit analysis.
(c) The company has now received information from market research which suggests that price and demand for valves are related as follows:

Price (£):	16	18	20	22	24
Quantity demanded (in 000s):	180	150	120	90	60

Calculate whether Archaic has chosen the optimal level of production for the year and advise management on production for the year and the related price that should be charged.

(Accounting Degree)

7.4 Scenic Snaps Ltd produces a number of products, with cameras being produced in Department C. The company draws up budgets for each department based upon the fullest practical capacity. For the year commencing 1 Jan. 19X9, the following budget has been formulated for Department C from budgeted sales of 40,000 units.

	£000
Direct costs	
Material	120
Labour	80
	200
Production overheads	200
Factory cost	400
Administrative and marketing overheads	100
Full cost	500
Profit	100
Revenue	600

Production overheads are absorbed on the basis of 100 per cent of direct costs. However, half are fixed, while the remainder are related to the machining of the materials. The administration and marketing overheads are based on 25 per cent of factory costs and do not vary within wide ranges of activity. For each department, a profit margin of 20 per cent is applied to the 'full costs', as this is felt to give both a fair return on assets employed as well as providing a fair reward to entrepreneurial effort. This also results in a price which appears to be fair to consumers.

Halfway through the budget period, it became obvious to the management of Scenic Snaps Ltd that there was going to be a shortfall on sales which could be expected to be 25 per cent below those forecast. At about the time that this shortfall in sales became evident, a chain of photographic shops became interested in purchasing 10,000 units of a special camera which would be stripped down to bare essentials and sold under the chain's brand name AREMAC. If Scenic Snaps produced such a model, there would obviously be a saving on the usual material and labour unit costs. The management accountant of Scenic Snaps estimated that materials costing £24,000 and labour of £16,000 would be required to produce the 10,000 cameras. As the production could take place within the firm's existing capacity, fixed costs would not be affected.

Required:

(a) Computations showing the price that should be quoted for the order based on:
  (i) full costs plus pricing, on the current basis;
  (ii) a price which would enable the original budgeted profit to be attained;
  (iii) overheads being absorbed on a unit basis, with profit applied on the current basis.

(b) Your advice to the management of Scenic Snaps Ltd on a pricing policy for this quotation. Discuss any factors that you feel should be brought to management's attention when they consider the pricing strategy for this special order.

(Chartered Association of Certified Accountants)

Further study

Arnold, J., Carsberg, B. and Scapens, R.W. (1980) *Topics in management accounting,* 1st edn, Philip Allan.

Arnold, J. and Hope, T. (1990) *Accounting for management decisions,* 2nd edn, Hemel Hempstead: Prentice-Hall.

Lucey, T. (1992) *Management accounting,* 3rd edn, D.P. Publications.

Ryan, B. and Hobson, J. (1985) *Management accounting – a contemporary approach,* 1st edn, London: Pitman.

Sizer, J. (1989) *An insight into management accounting,* 3rd edn, Harmondsworth: Penguin.

CHAPTER 8

Capital investment appraisal/decision techniques

Objectives
....

By the end of this chapter you should be able to:

▶ Apply both discounting as well as non-discounting decision techniques in appraising capital investment project opportunities.

▶ Understand the reasons behind, and the 'mechanics' of, discounting cash flows to present value terms.

▶ Compare and contrast the relative merits and shortcomings/problems associated with the range of decision techniques available for capital investment appraisal purposes.

▶ Appreciate the assumptions and limitations of the decision analysis and understand the role of sensitivity analysis.

In Part 2 of the book on management decision accounting techniques, the types of managerial decision situations we have considered so far have mainly been in the nature of short-run operating decisions. But now we turn to longer term *investment decisions* about project opportunities that often involve considerable sums of capital outlay. The basic decision or question we need to ask is: 'Do the benefits/returns from investment make the outlays worthwhile?'. In the short term it is not strictly necessary to account for the time value of money. Over the long run, however, it is important to consider the fact that money does possess *time value*. (In accounting (as well as economics) the short run is generally regarded as any period up to, and including, a full year – the long and/or medium-term being time periods in excess of a year.)

Time value simply means that it is preferable to have money sooner than later – even with zero inflation – because of the earlier opportunity of investing it in order to earn interest at a rate often called, in investment appraisal, the organisation's cost of capital (i.e. the firm's discount rate). The economic phenomenon known as inflation, generally experienced to varying degrees by modern societies and business environments, merely exacerbates the problem of money losing value over time. Some capital investment appraisal decision techniques do take account of time value through a process referred to as the *discounting* of future money cash values back to *present value* amounts, whereas other simpler techniques (for example, payback) do not. Because investment appraisal can become quite complex in more advanced areas of analysis, this chapter's predominantly introductory level of study will be conducted in the context of several simplifying assumptions. Some of these could be seen as rather sweeping assumptions, but they are the ones generally applied to the analysis prior to it becoming more involved at more advanced study levels. The main assumptions are:

▶ No inflation and no shortage of capital (i.e. no capital rationing).
▶ No uncertainty (at least until the last section of the chapter when this assumption is relaxed to illustrate uncertain project life cycles).
▶ Linearity, which has often been assumed, for example for C-V-P analysis (Chapter 6) and cost estimation techniques (Chapter 3), and will be again at the later stages in the book (e.g. linear programming in Chapter 12).
▶ Cash flows arise at the end of a year and are orthodox (i.e. initial cash outlays are followed by subsequent inflows of cash).
▶ Annual interest/discount rates apply – others are possible as long as the level of rate relates to the length of period; for example, in the case of personal credit cards an interest rate of, say, 2 per cent charged per month.
▶ Cost of capital (i.e. interest/discount rate) is both known and given, whereas in more advanced studies calculation of the rate (e.g. a weighted average cost of capital) may be required of you.

Present value calculation via discounting

Discounting is a mathematical process involving the application of a discount rate (the organisation's cost of capital, i.e. interest rate) to cash flows that occur in the future to reduce them to a present value (PV) amount. The rate, or cost of capital, is essentially the interest rate at which funds might be borrowed by an organisation, for example, to invest in capital projects in the hope that the future cash return from investment will exceed its net cash cost.

Furthermore, the annual rates applied throughout are *compound* interest rates. This means that £1,000 invested now at a compound rate of interest of (say) 20 per cent will grow to a future value (FV) at the end of one year of £1,200 (£1,000 × 1.2) which will become, at the end of the second year, £1,440 (i.e. £1,200 × 1.2) . . . and so on. This can be expressed as a compound interest equation:

$$FV = PV(1 + i)^n$$

where: 'i' is the cost of capital/interest/discount rate; and 'n' is the period number. Applied to our simple example above, your calculation using this equation is:

$$FV = £1,000(1.2)^2$$
$$= (£1,000)(1.44)$$
$$= £1,440$$

Replacing FV, and by inversion, the above equation transforms into the following basic/general mathematical formula that underlies the function of discounting:

$$PV = \Sigma \ \frac{Cn}{(1 + i)^n}$$

where: 'Cn' is the period cash flow; 'i' and 'n' are as before; and 'Σ' means summation (i.e. the sum of . . .).

(*Note:* Periods are normally years (y), and y = o is taken to mean the present time, i.e. the *start* of the first year (year 1); y = 1 represents the *end* of year 1; y = 2 is the end of year 2; . . . and so on).

A computer, given values for 'n' and 'i', can be used to generate detailed discount/compound interest tables representative of the specific application of the above general formulaic expression. Appendix 1 provides you with the relevant tables. Discount factors, reflecting different rates of interest related to (annual) time periods, are easily extracted from these discount or compound interest tables which are published for statistical/mathematical uses and widely adopted for business purposes by insurance and investment companies, banks and building societies. You might conveniently think of discounting as effectively compound interest in reverse! The formulae just given above clearly reflect this reverse/inverse relationship. After initially using *both* the general PV formula as well as specific discount factors, for illustration, you are advised to concentrate solely on the application of discount factors for further calculation purposes as they are a lot more manageable than applying the full formula each and every time. A PV discount factor can be symbolised as either:

▶ an 'individual' yearly amount: V_{n7} (this is Appendix 1a's table); or
▶ a 'repeated' annuity amount: A_{n7} (this is Appendix 1b's table).

(*Note:* V_{n7} and A_{n7} are pronounced V *angle* n and A *angle* n respectively.)

A written description of PV to support its formula and table versions would be: 'the effective value *now* of all future cash flows whether they be *different singular* amounts at future points in time (apply V_{n7} per Appendix 1a) or the *same annual* sum repeated at future points in time (apply A_{n7} per Appendix 1b).' Notice that the discount factors in Appendix 1b are merely those of Appendix 1a in cumulative form.

Consider the next couple of illustrations for practice prior to encountering the various appraisal techniques themselves in sections 8.1 and 8.2.

Two cash flows (£4,000 at the end of year 2 and £1,000 now) given a 25 per cent cost of capital would be discounted using both formula and factors as follows:

Year:	0........................		2	Σ
Apply formula:	$\dfrac{£1,000}{(1.25)^0}$	+	$\dfrac{£4,000}{(1.25)^2}$	
PV (i.e. sum of all discounted amounts):	$\dfrac{£1,000}{1}$	+	$\dfrac{£4,000}{1.5625}$	
∴ PV	£1,000	+	£2,560	= £3,560
Alternatively, apply V_{n7} discount factor:	$(£1,000)(V_{07})$	+	$(£4,000)(V_{27})$	
Apply factor from 25% discount table:	$(£1,000)(1)$	+	$(£4,000)(.64)$	
∴ PV	£1,000	+	£2,560	= £3,560

(*Note:* y = o (V_{07}) often does not appear in discount tables as the factor is 1 (see, for example, Appendix 1b), reflecting the fact that cash flows occurring now/immediately are already in present value terms and not in need of discounting.)

Discounting was described before as compound interest in reverse . . . consider here the year 2 £2,560 PV above. Having to wait two years renders the £4,000 equivalent to only £2,560 in PV terms. Think of investing the £2,560 as available now at 25 per cent compound interest – it would grow at a compound rate over two years to equal £4,000; thus:

		£
	Invest capital amount (y = o):	2,560
add	Year 1's interest @ 25%:	640
	Accumulated sum (y = 1):	3,200
add	Year 2's interest @ 25%:	800
	Accumulated sum (y = 2):	£4,000

Note that *simple* (as opposed to compound) interest works differently in that the interest would be withdrawn/excluded from the calculation at the end of a year, just leaving the capital sum invested to earn annual interest (i.e. £640 each and every year in the above example).

Can you calculate ...? again using a 25 per cent rate, and both by formula and discount factor, the PV of the following profile of cash flows:

Year:	0	1	2	3	4	Σ
Cash flow:	£1,000	£5,000	£4,000	£1,000	£2,000	?

Answer

Year	0	1	2	3	4	Σ

Apply formula:

$$\frac{£1,000}{(1.25)^0} + \frac{£5,000}{(1.25)^1} + \frac{£4,000}{(1.25)^2} + \frac{£1,000}{(1.25)^3} + \frac{£1,000}{(1.25)^4}$$

PV (i.e. sum of all discounted amounts)

$$\frac{£1,000}{1} + \frac{£5,000}{1.25} + \frac{£4,000}{1.5625} + \frac{£1,000}{1.953,125} + \frac{£2,000}{2.44,1406}$$

$\therefore$ PV = £1,000 + £4,000 + £2,560 + £512 + £820 = £8,892

Apply discount factor: $(£1,000)(V_{07})+(£5,000)(V_{17})+(£4,000)(V_{27})+(£1,000)(V_{37})$
$\qquad + (£2,000) (V_{47})$

Apply factor from discount tables: $(£1,000)(1)+(£5,000)(.8)+(£4,000)(.64)+(£1,000)(.512)+(£2,000)(.41)$

$\therefore$ PV = £1,000 + £4,000 + £2,560 + £512 + £820 = £8,892

To summarise, the principle behind the discounting process is that it penalises later cash flows. This is done by rewarding earlier cash flows which are discounted less heavily (or not at all in the case of y = o), thus being consistent with the idea that it is better to have money sooner rather than later. A final PV illustration for further practice now utilises the annuity (A_{n7}) function/discount factor given a repeated annual cash flow of the same amount, i.e. £1000, at a rate again of 25 per cent:

Year:	0	1	2	3	4	Σ
Cash flow:	£1,000	£1,000	£1,000	£1,000	£1,000	
Apply A_{n7}:	£1,000	+	($£1,000)(A_{47}$)			
Apply discount factor @ 25%:	($£1,000)(1$) +		($£1,000)(2.362$)			
$\therefore$ PV	= £1,000	+	£2,362			= £3,362

So although in 'hard cash' terms £5,000 will have flowed, in PV terms the 5,000 'physical' pounds sterling will only be equivalent to 3,362 present value pounds sterling.

Four separate calculations could have been performed for each of the years 1 to 4 employing the relevant V_{n7} factors (which incidentally accumulate to 2.362) to achieve the same result, i.e. PV of £3,362. The above annuity approach, however, is much quicker and is to be preferred particularly where the same annual amount repeats over a large number of years – for example 20 or 30 years would require 20 or 30 separate computations using V_{n7}. You might also notice that formulae and symbols have not been resorted to above, and will indeed cease to be used from this point onwards; all subsequent discounting mechanics will simply apply discount factors extracted from the PV tables in Appendix 1.

Sections 8.1 and 8.2 now deal with four of the major decision techniques of capital investment appraisal – two of them utilise discounting whilst the other two, being simpler (and less preferable), are non-discounting methods for deciding on the worthwhileness, or not, of capital projects. The exhibit at the start of section 8.1 illustrates, in summary form, all four techniques, categorising them not only as to whether they discount or not, but also according to the money base they adopt. Cash flows are regarded as the superior money base over income (i.e. profits/losses) for reasons given in section 8.2.

8.1 Discounting investment decision techniques

Discounting/ non-discounting	Investment decision technique	Money base
Discounting	D.C.F. Net present value (NPV)	Cash flows
	D.C.F. Yield: Internal rate of return (IRR)	
Non-discounting	Payback	
	Accounting rate of return (ARR)	Income

(*Key:* D.C.F. = Discounted cash flow technique)

table 8.1

**Bethnell plc: future
project cash inflows**

Year Project:	1 (£000)	2 (£000)	3 (£000)	Total (£m)
W	1,000	–	–	1
X	500	500	500	1.5
Y	150	450	1,200	1.8
Z	1,000	300	300	1.6

8.1.1 Net present value (NPV) technique

So far only PV has been described and illustrated for you, but what is *net* PV? It simply means the result, the sum (Σ), of netting off all negative cash outflows against positive cash inflows expressed in present value terms. In the examples just prior to this section, you were given little indication as to whether the cash flows were cash in or out. Now we consider a bank of sample data (to be used for illustration of all four decision techniques) which clearly indicates flows of cash both in and out.

The management of Bethnell plc wish to rank four alternative capital investment project opportunities in order of their acceptability. All four projects (W, X, Y and Z) involve an initial capital investment cash outflow of £1 million each immediately, and will generate future cash inflows as shown in Table 8.1.

Bethnell's cost of capital is 20 per cent. You might also notice here that Table 8.1's pattern of cash inflows in conjunction with the immediate £1 million per project cash investment outlay constitute an *orthodox* cash-flow pattern (see the fourth assumption on p. 156) in that it is non-erratic. Erratic, unorthodox patterns of cash flow can cause serious analysis problems (in particular with the IRR technique) but such scenarios will not be investigated at this essentially introductory level of investment appraisal. Other more advanced texts[1] pursue such issues in depth. For now, however, undertake Activity 8.1.

ACTIVITY **8.1**

Required: Using the NPV decision technique, how and in what order would you advise Bethnell's management to rank the four capital project opportunities under consideration?

A typical presentation in which you might lay out the decision problem is similar to that adopted in the discounting examples illustrated earlier, *viz.*:

Year Project:	0 (£000)	1 (£000)	2 (£000)	3 (£000)	NPV (£000)
W	–1,000 + (1,000)(.833) +		0 + 0		= –167
X	–1,000 + (500)(.833)	+ (500)(.694)	+ (500)(.579)		= +53
Y	–1,000 + (150)(.833)	+ (450)(.694)	+ (1,200)(.579)		= +132
Z	--1,000 + (1,000)(.833)	+ (300)(.694)	+ (300)(.579)		= +215

(*Note:* Calculations to the nearest £000).

Alternatively, and preferably in terms of speed of calculations, you could have computed project X's cash inflows utilising the annuity discount factor (Appendix 1b), thus:

$$(500)(A_{47}) = (500)(2.106) = 1,053 - 1,000 = +53$$

Hence, the rank order of preference (on the basis of NPV) that you would advise to Bethnell's management regarding the four capital investment project opportunities is as follows:

RANKING:
1st – Z;
2nd – Y;
3rd – X;
4th – W.

Technically speaking, however, you would not include project W in your rank order advice to Bethnell particularly when the investment is considered in the light of the following general decision rule for applying the NPV appraisal technique:

▶ Accept all projects with *positive* NPVs.
▶ Reject all projects with *negative* NPVs.

The management advice consistent with the NPV decision rule in Activity 8.1 would be for Bethnell to undertake three of the project opportunities (X, Y and Z). One of our basic assumptions (see p. 156) is of central importance to this advice, i.e. that Bethnell experiences no shortage of capital. The firm is assumed not to have a limited finite supply of capital available to allocate over competing projects and can therefore undertake all three. Consider for a moment the alternative case where Bethnell had, for instance, only £1 million available for investment purposes. Then the competing projects X, Y and Z would be said to be *mutually exclusive,* as acceptance of one project, costing £1 million, would automatically preclude the other two. In this simplified situation the answer is obvious in that you would advise Bethnell's management to adopt the top-ranking project Z as it gives the highest net discounted cash return of £215,000. Often the analysis, with capital rationing and mutual exclusivity applying, will become more complex and lies beyond the scope of this book.

Finally, before moving on to the next appraisal technique, you ought to be aware of the underlying rationale behind NPV. The fundamental logic underpinning the decision rule is that by accepting projects X, Y and Z because they have positive NPVs, Bethnell will in each case be better off (i.e. in terms of wealth). If, for example, Bethnell had to borrow the £1 million capital per project to undertake each investment then, even after paying off the interest charged at the compound rate at which Bethnell is able to borrow funds (i.e. the firm's cost of capital of 20 per cent), each project would still realise a cash surplus equal to its respective and positive NPV amount. Bethnell's increase in corporate wealth would be greatest from project Z (£215,000); then Y (£132,000); and finally X (£53,000).

8.1.2 Internal rate of return (IRR) technique

Sometimes referred to as the 'yield' technique for appraising potential investment in capital projects, the IRR is a rate which, when applied to the relevant
cash flows of a project, discounts the flows to give a zero NPV for the project.
IRR is often criticised for being a rather unwieldy technique by virtue of the fact
that its determination is based on 'trial and error'. The method involves trying
different discount rates until two are found – one which gives a positive NPV
and the other a negative NPV. Then a process of *linear interpolation* is carried out
(remember, one of our assumptions is that of linearity) by either graphical or
mathematical means in order to determine the IRR that results in a zero NPV
for the project being appraised. This description of how the IRR technique operates will perhaps become more meaningful when the Bethnell plc data is once
again used in Activity 8.2.

ACTIVITY **8.2**

Required: Using the IRR technique, how and in what order would you advise Bethnell's
management to rank the four capital project opportunities under consideration?

Again calculating to the nearest £000, consider first how you would identify the
IRR *graphically*. Your illustration here only demonstrates determination of project X's IRR because its cash flows lend themselves to the speedier use of the
annuity (A_{n7}) discount factor. As you have previously, in Activity 8.1, tried
Bethnell's cost of capital of 20 per cent in applying it to calculate project NPV
(i.e. +53 for X) you already know a rate that produces a positive NPV. You also
need to identify a rate that gives a negative NPV. Obviously the rate will need to
be higher than 20 per cent to discount the cash flows more heavily to a lower
and negative NPV. So try another rate above 20 per cent – if it still results in a
positive NPV, then try again until you succeed in achieving a negative NPV
figure. For illustration assume a 25 per cent rate, which appears below with the
20 per cent rate you have already applied in Activity 8.1:

	Present value (£000)		Capital investment (£000)		NPV (£000)
Try 20%: (500)(A_{37}) = (500)(2.106) =	1,053	*less*	1,000	=	+53
Try 25%: (500)(A_{37}) = (500)(1.952) =	976	*less*	1,000	=	–24

Then construct a graph of project NPV plotted against discount rate.
The graph's structure is identical to one you have already seen in Chapter 6 –
that of the P/V graph, Figure 6.3. However, rather than profits and losses on the
vertical, you need instead to show positive and negative NPVs respectively.
Interest rate replaces volume on the horizontal which meets the vertical axis at
zero. You need finally to plot the NPV coordinates determined above, which are
+53 @ 20 per cent and – 24 @ 25 per cent interest rates. The picture emerges as
in Figure 8.1 on page 165, and by linear interpolation (joining the coordinates
with a straight line) you can read off, at the intersect point with the horizontal,

the percentage rate which gives zero NPV. This rate is the project's IRR: 23 per cent in the case of project X.

You may alternatively determine the IRR for project X *mathematically* through the following calculation:

$$IRR = 20\% + \left[\frac{53}{7} \times 5\% \right] = \underline{23\%}$$

A 5 per cent change in discount rate (from 20 per cent to 25 per cent) has produced a change of 77 in NPV (+ 53 to – 24), thus overall NPV change being the denominator of the fraction in the 5 per cent range bracket. The numerator in the fraction is the NPV reduction required through heavier discounting (above 20 per cent) necessary to bring the positive NPV (+53) down to zero, thus identifying the project IRR; 23 per cent for project X.

Can you find ...? mathematically the IRRs for the other remaining projects W, Y and Z?

Answer

Because project W's future cash inflows are exactly equal to its present cash outflow, then W gives no return on capital invested and its IRR is zero. The other project calculations in (£ooos) follow:

Project Y:
Try 20%: From your Activity 8.1. this discount rate produced an NPV = +132

Try 30%: –1,000 + (150)(.769) + (450)(.592) + (1,200)(.455) = –72

$$IRR = 20\% + \left[\frac{132}{204} \times 10\% \right] = \underline{26\%}$$

Project Z:
Try 20%: From your Activity 8.1. this discount rate produced an NPV = +215

Try 40%: –1,000 + (1,000)(.714) + (300)(.51) + (300)(.364)   = –24

$$IRR =\quad 20\% + \left[\frac{215}{239} \times 20\% \right] = \underline{38\%}$$

The very final step is to compare each project's IRR with Bethnell's cost of capital, but not before you have identified the rank order of preference (on the basis of IRR) that you would advise to Bethnell's management regarding the four capital projects as follows:

RANKING:
lst – Z (38%);
2nd – Y(26%);
3rd – X(23%);
4th – W(0%).

Comparison with Bethnell's 20 per cent cost of capital reveals only project W to be unacceptable in the light of the following general decision rule for applying the IRR appraisal technique:

▶ Accept all projects with IRRs *greater* than the firm's cost of capital.
▶ Reject all projects with IRRs *less* than the firms cost of capital.

Comparison of IRR with NPV

You will have noticed that the order of preference of the projects according to the IRR technique is consistent with that of NPV – but this is only coincidental in terms of the *ranking* of the projects, given that the cost of capital is 20 per cent (elaboration upon this issue will follow shortly). No such coincidence is evident, however, when the decision rules of IRR and NPV are considered, compared and summarised below (in Table 8.2) in terms of *accept/reject* advice where the consistency stems from true agreement between the techniques rather than mere coincidence.

What if a project's IRR is the *same* rate as the firm's cost of capital? The answer is that this is the 'mirror-image' of the project's NPV being zero. This is because the cost to the firm of borrowing capital for instance (i.e. at that interest rate) plus the capital sum itself invested in the project *equates* to the cash flow returns from the project back to the investor. Thus the firm/investor is neither better nor worse off in such an instance because it costs as much to borrow and invest the borrowed sum as the future cash inflows generated by the investment. In our Activities we have clearly seen that the opportunity to invest in project X, for example, is worth accepting because it gives a return (its IRR) 3 per cent in excess of Bethnell's 20 per cent cost of capital. This means that even after discounting project X's future cash flows at 20 per cent there still remains a positive cash value (its NPV) which itself signals worthwhile acceptance of the project opportunity. The converse is obviously the case with projects (for example project W) showing negative NPVs reflecting the fact that their IRRs are below the cost of capital. If management were to decide to invest in them the firm would be worse off by the amount of the negative NPV, i.e. the percentage shortfall of IRR below that of the firm's cost of capital.

table 8.2
Summary of discounting decision technique rules

Technique	Decision	Accept project	Reject project
NPV:		Positive	Negative
IRR:		> Cost of capital	< Cost of capital

In short, with the 'accept/reject' type of investment decision both NPV and IRR techniques will *always* give management consistently the same advice (i.e. signal) as to the worthwhileness, or not, of projects. This is not the case necessarily, however, with the 'ranking' type of decision. With the Bethnell plc data in Activities 8.1 and 8.2 you have already seen that the project ranking order, applying both NPV and IRR, just happens to be the same at Bethnell's cost of capital of 20 per cent, but this is no more than a coincidence which occurs given the 20 per cent rate! If you were to rework the data you would find that the picture might be different at another discount rate, say 10 per cent – your calculation (to the nearest £000) being as follows:

Year Project:	0 (£000)	1 (£000)	2 (£000)	3 (£000)	NPV (£000)
W	– 1,000 +	(1,000)(.909) +	0 +	0	= –91
X	– 1,000 +	(500)(.909) +	(500)(.826) +	(500)(.751) = +243	
Y	– 1,000 +	(150)(.909) +	(450)(.826) +	(1,200)(.751) = +409	
Z	– 1,000 +	(1,000)(.909) +	(300)(.826) +	(300)(.751) = +382	

Alternatively, and preferably, project X's cash inflows could be computed by applying the relevant annuity discount factor from Appendix 1b, thus:

$$(500)(A_{37}) = (500)(2.487) = 1,243 – 1,000 = +243$$

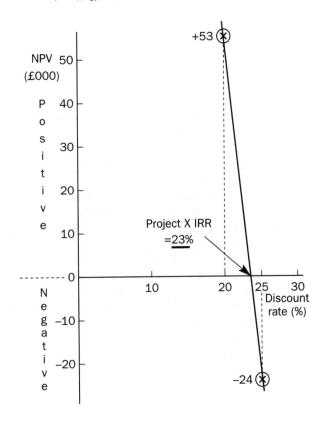

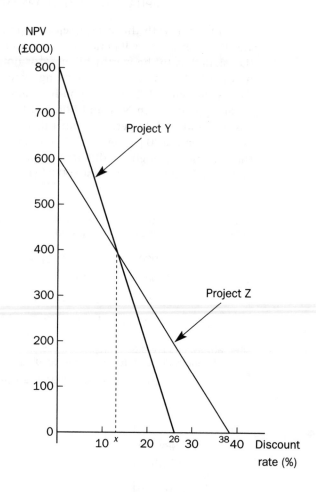

You will now notice that project Y is preferable to Z, at a 10 per cent discount rate, because of its higher NPV – and the ranking order between Y and Z reverses compared with a 20 per cent rate! Hence management's, perhaps arbitrary, choice as to which technique to use becomes of vital importance, and particularly so if Y and Z are mutually exclusive (because, say, of capital shortages). Notice, too, how a lower discount rate penalises future cash flow less heavily, and the negative NPV (project W) is lower while the positive NPVs (X, Y and Z) are higher than at 20 per cent in Activity 8.1. Furthermore the inevitable accept/reject decision consistency is still, and will always be, evident in that projects with IRRs greater than the cost of capital are acceptable, while a project IRR less than the firm's cost of capital signals rejection (see Activity 8.2). But how has the apparent change in the order of ranking projects Y and Z at different discount rates occurred? A graphical explanation of the situation is provided in Figure 8.2.

Unlike in Activity 8.2 the project NPV profile lines for Y and Z are extended to meet the zero per cent intercept with the vertical axis. The project coordinates on the vertical axis are, of course, simply the projects' *undiscounted* cash flows, i.e.:

	Total inflow	less	Capital investment	=	Total cash flow
Project Y	£1.8 million	less	£1 million	=	£800,000
Project Z	£1.6 million	less	£1 million	=	£600,000

The other coordinates, to plot the project NPV profile lines, lie on the horizontal axis at the projects' percentage IRRs equating their *discounted* cash flows to zero NPV. The answer to why project Y is ranked above Z at 10 per cent (and vice-versa at 20 per cent) should now be obvious from studying Figure 8.2. Up to a point (i.e. 'x' : 13 % approximately) project Y has the greater NPV and is preferable on an NPV basis despite having a lower IRR. After that point 'x' project Z has both higher NPV as well as its greater IRR. The steepness of the project profile lines is the clue to the problem of ranking inconsistency. The entire rationale behind discounting is that the process penalises later cash inflows *vis-à-vis* earlier inflows, and the extent of the penalty increases as the level of discounting (i.e. the percentage rate) becomes heavier. Because two-thirds of project Y's cash flows (£1.2 million ÷ £1.8 million) happen 'late' (in year 3) compared with Z's relatively 'early' (mainly year 1) inflow, i.e. £1 million out of £1.6 million total, then Y suffers more from the discounting process. Project Y generates more net cash in *absolute* terms (£800,000 compared with Z's £600,000) and this is recognised at lower rates of discounting (i.e. prior to point 'x'). Project Z's earlier (but less net absolute) cash is rewarded in *discounted* terms with a higher NPV after point 'x'. In short, the 'timing' of cash-flow patterns is all-important. However, given that the NPV and IRR techniques' advice can on occasions be in conflict (for instance, before point 'x' in Figure 8.2's example) in ranking decision situations, how then might management choose the most suitable *discounting* investment decision technique? The answer is that NPV is generally considered to be the better technique, and this section now explains the principal reasons why.

In broad terms, NPV is preferred because it is an 'absolute' measure providing a monetary result which reflects the scale of the project decision, whereas IRR is only a 'relative' measure (i.e. a percentage rate) that gives no indication as to the actual size of money amounts involved. For instance, a 50 per cent return could just as easily be £1 from a £2 outlay as £1 million from a £2 million investment! Other reasons for the general recognition that NPV is superior to IRR include:

▶ IRR can suffer serious technical problems; for example, multiple IRRs for a single, individual project or even no meaningful IRR at all (for further detail you might refer to a more advanced text[2] than this one).

▶ NPV is easier to calculate (compared with IRR's rather cumbersome 'trial and error' approach).

▶ NPV provides unambiguous decision information even with unorthodox/erratic project cash flows.

▶ Non-financially/quantitatively minded managers may feel they get a clearer 'signal' from NPV as it is conceptually easier to grasp in terms of the firm being 'better or worse off' from capital investment decisions.

8.2 Non-discounting investment decision techniques

One of the two non-discounting techniques we consider in this section is based on monetary cash flows (i.e. payback) whilst the other technique uses accounting income (profits/losses) as the appropriate money measurement base. The latter technique is known as the accounting rate of return (ARR). Once again the Bethnell plc sample data from Table 8.1. is used for purposes of illustration.

8.2.1 Payback investment decision technique

Although it is a non-discounting technique and is therefore less sophisticated than those reviewed in section 8.1 *payback* is nonetheless a very popular one in practice. This is probably because of its very straightforward nature and its ease of comprehension by non-accounting members of management. Activity 8.3 bears this out.

ACTIVITY **8.3**

Required: Using the payback decision technique, how and in what order would you advise Bethnell's management to rank the four capital project opportunities under consideration?

Unlike previous techniques whose results were presented either in the form of a cash figure (i.e. NPV) or a percentage rate (i.e. IRR), payback advice to management is expressed in terms of a *period* of time. The simple calculation is that you work out how long it takes for the initial capital outlay on investment in a project to be paid back without discounting the cash returns. In Bethnell's case of investing £1 million capital, the payback periods are as follows:

Year Project:	1 (£000)	2 (£000)	3 (£000)		Payback period (time)
W	1,000			=	1 year
X	500	500		=	2 years
Y	150	450	1,200	=	3 years
Z	1,000			=	1 year

If we were to relax the assumption of cash flows only arising at the *end* of a year, then (assuming an even cash flow throughout the year) a 'fractional' year solution for project Y would be thus:

Year	1 (£000)	2 (£000)	3 (£000)		Payback period (time)
Project Y	150	450	400	=	$2\frac{1}{3}$ years

The £1,200 cash flow in year 3 would generate the additional £400 (needed for paying back the £1,000 cash outlay) a third of the way (400 ÷ 1,200) through year 3 (figures in £000s).

Therefore the rank order of preference (on the basis of payback) that you would advise to Bethnell's management regarding the four project opportunities, being consistent with the subsequent decision rule, is as follows:

RANKING:
Joint 1st – W and Z;
3rd – X;
4th – Y.

The general decision rule for applying the payback appraisal technique is, like the method itself, very simplistic:

▶ Accept projects with the *quickest* payback period.
▶ Reject projects which do *not* pay back the cash investment.

Because payback disregards the timing of cash flows it is considered inferior to the discounting techniques in section 8.1. Also, management often need to take care with use of the technique, adopting a 'common-sense' approach to investment situations such as presented by project W. Despite ranking joint first with Z, project W only just pays its £1 million investment back. Rather than wait a year for the £1 million cash return, management would intuitively consider other investment opportunities instead which would return interest on the investment. However, this intuitive approach nevertheless incorporates the time value of money concept (i.e. interest on capital) which payback, as a non-discounting technique, does not. Other disadvantages you can associate with the payback technique are seen in the following areas constituting serious drawbacks to its use:

▶ No consideration is given to cash flows beyond the payback period. For instance, although projects W and Z rank equally in Activity 8.3, Z is obviously preferable as it generates further cash flows *after* the end of the one-year payback period whereas W does not.
▶ No regard is paid to the timing of cash flows even *within* the payback period.

How would you ...? rank projects M and N below, applying the payback capital investment technique, if both projects involve a £600,000 outlay and subsequently generate the following cash inflows:

	Project M (£000)	Project N (£000)
Year 1	300	100
Year 2	200	200
Year 3	100	300

Answer

You should rank the above projects M and N equally according to the payback criterion; however, M is of course preferable (but this natural, logical conclusion once more embraces the time value notion of preferring money sooner than later which payback does not incorporate). Despite not reflecting the wider overall worthwhileness of project opportunities, payback is nevertheless capable of easy understanding by all breeds of manager – this is perhaps why it is so widely used in practical business circumstances.[3] Also and finally in its favour, payback's approach inherently places greater emphasis on speedy project cash returns which in itself is an aid to improving liquidity within organisations.

8.2.2 Accounting rate or return (ARR) technique

ARR is the only capital investment decision technique using a money base of accounting income (i.e. profit/loss rather than cash flow) and is not to be recommended as a project appraisal method. This is largely due to the inbuilt *subjectivity* of income measures – profits/losses merely being a set of results influenced significantly by whatever accounting conventions and policies happen to be arbitrarily followed by the organisation's accountants and management – for example, depreciation policy. Depreciation charges against income will often have a profound effect upon profit/loss but depreciation can be calculated on various bases, for example, the 'reducing balance' method. For the following (unrelated to Bethnell plc) illustration of how profit/loss might be 'distorted' by different depreciation methods two other means of capital item depreciation will be used, i.e. 'straight-line' (SL) and 'sum-of-the-years' digits (SYD) – assuming a capital/fixed asset cost of £60,000 and annual operating cash flows of £24,000 thus:

	Year 1 (£000)	Year 2 (£000)	Year 3 (£000)
Operating cash flows	24	24	24
Depreciation (SL)	20	20	20
Operating profit	4	4	4

	Year 1	Year 2	Year 3
Operating cash flows	24	24	24
Depreciation (SYD)	30	20	10
Operating profit/(loss)	(6)	4	14

(*Note*: SYD calculation is to add up the years' digits, i.e. $1 + 2 + 3 = 6$, then depreciate $\frac{3}{6}$ first year; $\frac{2}{6}$ second year; and $\frac{1}{6}$ final year.)

It should be clear from the above example how profit/loss figures can be open to manipulation (sometimes called 'window-dressing') through varying accounting policies, such as depreciation, to create different income figures (have you heard of 'creative accounting'?!). In short, whereas income is highly subject to other influences, a preferable money base for investment appraisal purposes is cash flow, which is a wholly *objective* measure. A net cash flow computation of simply 'cash in' less 'cash out' is not susceptible to clever manipulations or massaging of figures such as illustrated above (notice the cash flow is the same and unaffected in both sets of calculation, unlike the income figures).

The ARR technique is virtually identical to the important primary ratio you may be familiar with from your financial accounting studies called the 'return on capital employed' (ROCE), sometimes referred to as 'return on investment' (ROI – also see Chapter 11). Instead of cash returns being the money base used in the appraisal/decision techniques so far, we now have return measured by profit. In Activity 8.4 the level of capital employed will be taken to be the *average* investment in projects. Another reason for ARR not being an advisable investment decision criterion is that one could argue for the appraisal to be carried out using, for instance, 'total' investment (i.e. £1 million per project in Bethnell's case). So as well as profit being an unsatisfactory money base for analysis purposes, we now also have the amount to be used as the investment level possibly open to different interpretations; there is no definitive formula for what constitutes 'capital employed' (you may also have previously experienced this problem in the area of financial accounting studies known as ratio analysis).

ACTIVITY **8.4**

Required: Using the ARR decision technique, how and in what order would you advise Bethnell's management to rank the four capital project opportunities under consideration?

Like IRR previously, the result from ARR computation presents itself in the form of a percentage rate. Your calculations might be conveniently laid out in the following way:

Project	Average operating cash flow (£000)	Average (SL) depreciation (£000)	Average profit (£000)	Average investment (£000)	Return on investment (%)
W	1,000	1,000	–	500	–
X	500	333	167	500	33%
Y	600	333	267	500	53%
Z	533	333	200	500	40%

Notes: 1 Calculations to the nearest £000.
  2 Project W has only a one-year life cycle so its average cash flow and depreciation is the same as its total.
  3 Average investment could be calculated simply as:

$$\frac{\text{Opening investment value} + \text{Closing investment value}}{2} = \frac{£1,000 + £0}{2} = 500$$

or, more long-windedly, as the mid-point written down book value (WDV) of the investment, thus:

	(£000)
Opening value:	1,000
Year 1 depreciation:	333
End of year 1 WDV:	667
Half year 2 depreciation:	167
Mid-point WDV:	500

[4] It is assumed that the only non-cash adjustment to convert cash flow to profit is the depreciation charge (in reality there may be other non-cash items to account for).

The rank order of preference (on the basis of ARR) that you would advise to Bethnell's management regarding the four projects is therefore as follows:

RANKING:
lst – Y;
2nd – Z;
3rd – X;
4th – W.

Once more (as with NPV) technically you would not include project W in your rank order preferences to Bethnell's management as you would advise rejection of W consistent with the following general decision rule for application of the ARR capital investment appraisal technique:

▶ Accept projects with the *highest* percentage return on capital invested.
▶ Reject projects with *no* return from investment.

As mentioned from the outset, ARR is not a recommended decision technique for purposes of capital investment appraisal. A couple of reasons why have already been suggested to you, but a 'points-listing' summary of ARR's disadvantages (including those previously given) provides a convenient conclusion to this section. ARR:

▶ disregards the time value of money (as it is a non-discounting technique);
▶ being similar to IRR, provides a relative (rather than absolute) measure with no indication as to the actual size or scale of the project opportunity;

▶ incorporates different conflicting definitions of what constitutes capital employed, e.g. average or total investment?;

▶ includes highly subjective income (profit/loss) measures – whereas cash flows are preferable as a money base, being purely objective.

8.3 Sensitivity analysis

In this final section of the chapter we relax the second of the assumptions that were listed on p. 156, i.e. that of *certainty*. So far only certain 'single point' estimates of project variables have been considered, for example, definite cash flow; single cost of capital/interest rate (20 per cent for Bethnell plc); and a certain project life cycle (one year for W and three years for X, Y and Z). In practical circumstances, however, it is likely that some or even all of these factors will be subject to change (i.e. a fluctuating discount rate, varying project life and unreliable cash flows). Sensitivity analysis, by flexing project variables up and/or down, gives an indication of how *sensitive* the project outcome (for instance, its NPV) is to changes in key factors/variables, and furthermore which of these factors/variables are relatively the most critical when liable or likely to change.

> **DID YOU KNOW ...?**
>
> *that sensitivity analysis is often simply referred to as **what if** analysis and is carried out by asking the question, for example, 'what if the interest/ discount rate were to rise (or fall) by 2 per cent?'.*

To date certainty has been assumed in connection with one of the above mentioned key project variables in particular, i.e. the length of a project's life cycle. As with the other examples of key variables, the time factor of project life span involved can also be subjected to the sensitivity analysis approach. For illustration we take the certain life cycle estimate for project X, in the Bethnell case, of three years (see Table 8.1). You might consider later changing other projects and variables for your own further practice. Bethnell's management may be concerned about the possible impact of project X proving to have a shorter life of, for example, only two years. As a reminder of the Bethnell data, with a definite life cycle of three years project X showed a positive NPV of £53,000, indicating X's recommended acceptance and worthwhileness, calculated as follows:

Annual cash flows	Capital investment	NPV (£000)
(£500,000)(2.106)	less £1,000,000	= +53

If Bethnell's management's worst fears of only a two-year life span for X were to be realised, then its NPV would need to be re-estimated using the now relevant two-year 20 per cent annuity discount factor of 1.528. A negative NPV of – £236,000 results, signalling that X is not worthwhile:

Annual cash flows	Capital investment	NPV
		(£000)
(£500,000)(1.528) *less* £1,000,000		= −236

Bethnell can therefore plan on a break-even project life for X of somewhere between two and three years. The precise life-cycle break-even point is located at the moment in time when X's NPV equates exactly to zero, the point at which Bethnell is indifferent to the worthwhileness, or not, of X. This exact life-cycle break-even point can be accurately determined by interpolation between year two and year three based on the overall change in X's NPV from its negative – £236,000 at the end of year two to its positive £53,000 at end of year three. Project X's NPV has changed overall by £289,000 (i.e. −£236,000 to + £53,000) and the interpolation calculation is as follows:

$$2 \text{ years} + (\frac{236,000}{289,000} \times 1 \text{ year}) = \underline{2.817 \text{ years}}$$

Thus X's life-cycle break-even point is 2.817 years. Furthermore, and finally, from this Bethnell's management can detect that, in terms of sensitivity, project X is highly sensitive to any possible future change in the length of its life cycle. Its safety or sensitivity margin for error in estimation, given its current life-cycle estimate of three years, is as low as 6 per cent. This safety/sensitivity margin percentage figure is computed thus:

$$\frac{3 - 2.817}{3} = 0.06 \times 100 = \underline{6\%}$$

Although sensitivity analysis is a useful management technique, its major draw-back is that only a single key variable/factor is flexed at one time, and in isolation from others (which are held constant). This is perhaps a little unrealistic in so far as multiple changes in variables/factors are likely to occur at the *same* time in practice.

Self-check questions
....

8.1 The Countess of Elder has just received the results of a survey which shows that there is oil on her estate. The oil could be produced by one of three different rock types (A, B or C). The probability of occurrence and annual revenues associated with each rock type are given below:

Rock type	Probability of occurrence	Annual revenue
A	0.5	£20,000
B	0.3	£40,000
C	0.2	£80,000

Each rock type will produce oil for ten years, and production of oil will start immediately after special pumping equipment has been purchased. This equipment will cost £95,000 and has a ten-year life expectancy, whichever rock type is found. The equipment will have a zero scrap value after ten years. At the end of the ten years, the Countess will have to spend £40,000 to restore the estate to its former beauty. The Countess also estimates that the oil production will cause a drop in her annual tourist income of £10,000.

The Countess estimates her cost of capital to be 10 per cent p.a. and asks you to assume that all cash flows are orthodox.

Required:
(a) Compute the expected monetary value of the annual revenue from oil production.
(b) Using the result from part (a), calculate by how much the Countess' wealth measured in net present values (NPV) is expected to increase if oil production is undertaken.
(c) Determine by how much her economic wealth (i.e. NPV) would change if rock type A is present.
(d) Given that a special survey could identify with perfect accuracy if rock type A is present, calculate the maximum amount that the Countess should pay for the survey information.
(e) Discuss the limitations of using expected monetary values for this type of decision.

(Accounting Degree)

8.2 A company is considering which of two mutually exclusive projects it should undertake. The finance director thinks that the project with the higher NPV should be chosen whereas the managing director thinks that the one with the higher IRR should be undertaken especially as both projects have the same initial outlay and length of life. The company anticipates a cost of capital of 10 per cent and the net after-tax cash flows of the projects are as follows:

		Project X £000	Project Y £000
Year	0	– 200	– 200
	1	35	218
	2	80	10
	3	90	10
	4	75	4
	5	20	3

Required:
(a) Calculate the NPV and IRR of each project.
(b) Recommend, with reasons, which project you would undertake (if either).
(c) Explain the inconsistency in ranking of the two projects in view of the remarks of the directors.

(d) Identify the cost capital at which your recommendation in (b) would be reversed.

(Chartered Institute of Management Accountants)

8.3 The cash flows for two projects are given below:

	£ Project X	£ Project Y
Year 0	− 5,000	− 8,000
Year 1	+ 2,500	+ 1,500
Year 2	+ 1,000	+ 2,000
Year 3	+ 1,000	+ 2,500
Year 4	+ 500	+ 1,000
Year 5	+ 1,500	+ 1,000
Year 6	+ 1,000	+ 2,500

Required: (assuming a discount rate of 12 per cent):
(a) Calculate the payback period for each of the above projects, stating which is to be preferred on the basis of the payback investment criterion.
(b) Calculate the net present values (NPV) of both projects indicating whether or not they are acceptable on the basis of the NPV investment criterion.
(c) Find the internal rate of return (IRR) for project X by graphical means.
(d) Explain why the accounting rate of return (ARR) is not a recommended measure.
(e) Briefly compare the relative merits of each of the investment appraisal techniques mentioned in parts (a) to (c) above.

(Accounting Degree)

8.4 The following data are supplied relating to two investment projects, only one of which may be selected:

	Project A £	Project B £
Initial capital expenditure	50,000	50,000
Profit (loss) year 1	25,000	10,000
2	20,000	10,000
3	15,000	14,000
4	10,000	26,000
Estimated resale value end of year 4	10,000	10,000

Notes:
1. Profit is calculated after deducting straight-line depreciation.
2. The cost of capital is 10 per cent.
3. Present value £1 received at the end of
Year 1   0.909
Year 2   0.826
Year 3   0.751
Year 4   0.683
Year 5   0.620

Required:
(a) Calculate for each project :
    (i)   average annual rate of return on average capital invested,
    (ii) payback period,
    (iii) net present value.
(b) Briefly discuss the relative merits of the three methods of evaluation mentioned in (a) above.
(c) Explain which project you would recommend for acceptance.

(Association of Accounting Technicians)

Notes
········

1. An advanced text specialising in the further details and complexities of investment appraisal is *Investment Appraisal – a Guide for Managers* by R. Dixon.
2. Ibid.
3. A detailed research survey of 141 medium-sized UK companies revealed that 80 per cent of them used payback compared with, say, internal rate of return (only 28 per cent) as a means of appraising capital investments. These findings were reported in a CIMA article by N. Coulthurst and A. McIntyre entitled 'Planning and Control of Capital Investment in medium-sized U.K. Companies', *Management Accounting*, March 1987.

Further study
················

Allen, A. (1992) 'DCF: Elegant theory or sound practice?', in *Management Accounting*, September, Chartered Institute of Management Accountants.

Arnold, J. and Hope, T. (1990) *Accounting for management decisions*, 2nd edn, Hemel Hempstead: Prentice-Hall.

Dixon, R. (1994) *Investment appraisal – a guide for managers*, revised 1st edn, London: CIMA/Kogan Page.

Drury, C. (1992) *Management and cost accounting*, 3rd edn, London: Chapman and Hall.

Dugdale, D. (1991) 'Is there a "Correct" Method of Investment Appraisal?', in *Management Accounting*, May, Chartered Institute of Management Accountants.

Glautier, M. and Underdown, B. (1994) *Accounting theory and practice*, 5th edn, London: Pitman.

Harper, W. (1995) *Cost and management accounting*, 1st edn, London: Macdonald and Evans.

Horngren, C.T., Foster, G. and Datar S. (1994) *Cost accounting – a managerial emphasis*, 8th edn, Hemel Hempstead: Prentice-Hall.

PART 3

Management planning and control accounting techniques

······················

CHAPTER **9**
················

Budgetary planning and control techniques

Objectives
··············

By the end of this chapter you should be able to:

▶ Explain the purpose and rationale that underpin the budgetary process.

▶ Perform the 'mechanics' associated with the budget-building exercise of preparing functional/subsidiary budgets and summary/master budgets.

▶ Understand the limitations within which both management and accountants apply budgetary planning and control techniques.

▶ Construct flexible budgets as well as describe the principal reasons behind flexible budgetary control.

It is a truism that management needs to be provided with good-quality information to help make sound decisions (see Part 2 of the book for that particular aspect of management activity), but managers in addition need to foresee the way ahead. This involves forward *planning* of future operations, similar, for example, to the way in which a wise traveller would plan his or her route in advance before embarking on a journey. Having made their plans, managers will still need to know whether actual events are in accordance with their planning. Comparison of actual with planned, sometimes referred to as the 'monitoring' of feedback information, is central to the vital management function of exercising *control* over the business or organisation. Thus, Part 3 of the book is concerned specifically with both of these crucial management activities of planning and control accounting. This chapter looks closely at *budgetary techniques* – showing initially how plans (or perhaps route-maps using again the travel analogy) for the future of the business or organisation may be drawn up. The building or drawing up of management's plans is manifested in the shape of budgets – subsidiary/functional budgets eventually combining to form the overall master/summary budget of the business organisation.

The control aspect emerges from the subsequent comparison of budgeted with actual results. This might be achieved either on a business-wide basis (i.e. 'macro' in an economics sense) by comparing actual costs and revenues with whole organisational budgets, or (on a 'micro' level) through a more detailed comparison of predetermined/established standards for individual product costs and revenues with actual data. This latter type of comparison which results in variances from plans (i.e. standards) is the subject of Chapter 10 on control accounting, and is our primary focus for comparative analysis rather than using budgets as the comparator in this chapter. (Before progressing any deeper into this chapter you would find it worthwhile devoting a few moments to reviewing the final two phases of Chapter 1's structural framework introduction, depicted in Figure 1.1, and re-reading sections 1.2.5 and 1.2.6.)

9.1 Budgeting: building the budget
....

At the very core of budgeting lies the notion of controlling activities through the operation of a predetermined plan or preconceived objective. Ideas behind budgetary planning and control are not entirely new to you, however. The establishment of predetermined 'budgeted' overhead rates in Chapter 2, for example, featured there as an important element in applying the absorption costing technique. Nor is the idea of budgeting alien to ordinary people in managing their own personal finances. The budgeting of an individual's domestic or personal financial situation generally involves the planning and control solely of cash resources (often a scarce, or even negative, resource unfortunately in the case of student finances!). Throughout this chapter, however, budgetary matters are discussed more in the context of business issues rather than personal or domestic affairs. Budgeting in such a business context will develop way beyond just planning for cash as budgetary control procedures extend to all aspects of the business' operation including production, marketing, and administration. Nevertheless, the cash budget itself will also be seen (in the form of a summary budget) to be an integral part of the overall master budget-building process.

Standards or budgets?

Standard costs and revenues rather than budgeted data will be used extensively in the next chapter where expectations (i.e. plans) are monitored against actual results to facilitate control accounting through the analysis of variances from standard. The question therefore begs: is there any significant difference between the use of *standards* as opposed to *budgets*? The short answer is that there is little or no difference. What distinguishes a standard from a budget is in essence a matter of perspective; a sense of proportion or scale differentiates the two. Budgetary systems in comparison to standard costing systems can be said to focus on very different aspects of organisational control. Borrowing once more from the language of economics, budgeting tends to assume a *macro* role in that budgets are established and controlled in the wider context and against a broader spectrum of planning the operations of entire departments, sections, divisions and, ultimately, the whole business. This is the budget building process or system and it comprises functional/subsidiary budgets (see section 9.1.1) which generate the summary/master budgets (in section 9.1.2). In sharp contrast to this, standard costing systems, based on the setting of standard costs and revenues, lie closer akin to a more narrowly defined *micro* context. This implies a different perspective – one of analysing individual product cost units in meticulous detail, breaking down the component parts of a unit into what its material, labour and overhead elements are planned to cost, and what price the cost unit is expected to be sold for. In brief, standard costing might be said to be a 'breaking down' unit-based concept as opposed to budgetary control's function-based, budget 'building up' process!

In terms of practical guidance in answering examination questions, despite the above important differentiation between the two, whether the data given is described as 'budgeted' and/or 'standard', simply treat the descriptions as synonymous – both are meant to represent the *planned/expected* costs, revenues, output levels etc. for use in the question. Prior to embarking upon the detailed exercise of budget building, study the visual (rather than 'number-

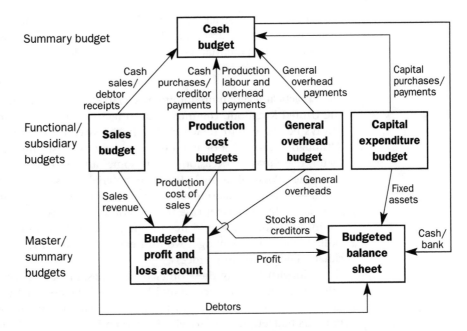

figure 9.1
Budgetary planning and control information flow through subsidiary/ functional and master/summary budgets

crunching') dimension of budgetary planning and control systems provided by the budgetary information flow diagram illustrated in Figure 9.1.

9.1.1 Functional/subsidiary budgets

How might we begin the entire process of budget building? At the outset it is of paramount importance for management to identify what factor will place the most critical constraint, or limit, on the budgetary activities that lie ahead. Whatever it is that is identified by management as the over-riding limitation to the future plans of the business is referred to in budgeting as the *principal budget factor*. The idea of the presence of a similar sort of constraining factor has in fact already been encountered in Chapter 4, in the guise of the 'limiting factor' (section 4.2.2) problem. Moreover, it will reappear again when, in Chapter 12, the quantitative planning technique known as linear programming is seen to operate within a framework of 'binding constraints' (section 12.1) which place a limit upon business activity. Both concepts, of *limiting factor* and *binding constraint*, are in principle identical to that of the principal budget factor.

Can you think ...? of good examples (before reading further and without either looking back to Chapter 4 or forward to Chapter 12!) of limiting factors/binding constraints that might be paralleled with the notion of a 'principal budget factor'.

Answer

Examples include (i) Limited productive capacity (for example, machine time and plant hours); (ii) Scarcity of skilled labour (for example, trade skills);

(iii) Limited storage space (for example, warehousing facilities); (iv) Scarce materials (such as natural limitations or limitations imposed by law); (v) Limited sales potential (for example, market demand constraints).

On a practical level, in predominantly market-driven economies such as that of the United Kingdom, the most crucial factor in building budgets will almost always be the extent to which the business can sell its product or service. Although sales/market demand is most likely to constitute the principal budget factor, there may be occasions where some other business ingredient over-rides even sales. Possibilities include where materials are scarce due to import restrictions, or where the labour supply is limited owing to the nature of particular work skills. In the former case the materials budget would be the principal constraining factor and would need to be prepared first. In the latter situation a skilled labour hours budget would herald the start of the *functional* (i.e. subsidiary) budget building process.

Notwithstanding these other possibilities, market demand in a consumer-orientated society and economy like ours will be assumed to be the principal factor in determining the starting point at which management will begin to build its budget. In fact, Activity 9.1 which is carried out throughout both this and section 9.1.2 starts with the sales budget. In order to most effectively convey a scaled-down miniature version of the entire budgeting process, a highly simplified budget building model is adopted throughout Activity 9.1 based on the assumption of single-product manufacture. In the real business world, of course, organisations will nearly always be concerned with preparing budgets for a massive range of products and/or services, and the required budget data will necessarily be far more complex and detailed than in Activity 9.1. However, we shall, by keeping the level of detail down to an absolute minimum, concentrate upon establishing a set of underlying principles which, though generalised, could then be applied to any budget preparation process that might be carried out in practice, irrespective of its degree of complexity. Providing excessive amounts of detail would in any case perhaps only blur rather than sharp focus the fundamental budgetary principles involved in applying the management technique of budget building.

ACTIVITY 9.1

Operating from rented premises comprising factory, office and sales distribution facilities, K. W. Chalky & Sons is a small family business. Raw material is purchased at a 'bought-in' price of £0.80p per kilogramme. The material is converted (at 2 kg per unit) through a unique transformation process known only to the firm's family members, resulting in a finished product which is subsequently sold to retail outlets throughout the British Isles at a standard price of £8 per unit. The firm's managers are currently planning business operations for the coming budget period and have the following expectations:

▶ raw material stocks will be increased from 2,000 kg to a closing stock of 2,400 kg, with both supplier's price of 80p and usage rate of 2 kg per finished unit remaining constant;

▶ finished goods stock (valued at £6 per unit) will be increased from 400 units to 800 units of closing stock, with £2,000 worth of work-in-progress (W-I-P) remaining constant;

▶ direct production labour is paid at a wage rate of £4.80 per hour and each unit requires half an hour of work time;

▶ variable production overheads (power, machine hour depreciation etc.) will be incurred at £1.20 per unit, while fixed production overhead (rents, insurances, straight-line depreciation etc.) will amount to £18,240 per period. (The variable depreciation rate is 20p/unit whilst fixed, straight-line depreciation will be charged at £1,040 for the period);

▶ general overhead expenses will be entirely fixed, costing: £17,280 administration, £1,120 finance charges, £26,000 selling and distribution;

▶ capital expenditures on new fixed assets will amount to £10,000;

▶ all material, labour, overhead and capital expenditures will be paid for in the period with the exception that creditors for raw materials will, through stricter credit control measures, rise by £1,480;

▶ unit sales of the finished product throughout Great Britain will comprise: England – 6,400; Ireland – 4,000; Scotland – 6,000; and Wales – 6,000;

▶ owing to this level of sales representing a significant increase on previous levels, outstanding debtors will rise by a factor of $12\frac{1}{2}\%$.

Required: Given the following opening balance sheet at the start of the coming budget period, carry out the budget building process for the period initially preparing all the necessary functional/subsidiary budgets which finally generate the master/summary budgets for K. W. Chalky & Sons.

OPENING BALANCE SHEET

	(£)	(£)	(£)
Fixed assets			29,600
Current assets			
Stocks: Raw materials (2,000 k. @ 80p/k.)	1,600		
W-I-P	2,000		
Finished goods (400 units @ £6)	2,400	6,000	
Debtors		7,680	
Cash at bank		5,200	
		18,880	
less Current liabilities			
Creditors		4,480	14,400
Net total assets			44,000
Capital		42,000	
Profit and loss account (balance b/f)		2,000	
Ownership funds/equity			44,000

Sales budget

We assume the first few bricks in our budget building exercise to be the sales figures. Underlying this assumption is that Chalky & Sons' business operations are limited primarily by how much they can sell (i.e. sales volume) at the

table 9.1

Sales budget

England (units)	Ireland (units)	Scotland (units)	Wales (units)	Total (units)
6,400	4,000	6,000	6,000	22,400
		Standard selling price (per unit):		£8
		Budgeted sales:		£179,200

standard price of £8. (Various pricing strategies used to determine suitable selling prices were discussed in detail in Chapter 7 which would have given rise to establishing Chalky's standard product selling price of £8 per unit). Here in effect we have identified sales demand as assuming the role of 'principal budget factor' and the *sales* budget is therefore the first one of the functional budgets to be prepared in Table 9.1.

Unit production and labour cost budgets

Production needs to be geared up not only to what level of sales is indicated by the sales budget (Table 9.1) but also in the light of any stockpiling or stock run-down that the business may be planning. As Chalky's management expect to increase the stock of finished goods from 400 to 800 units, the budgeted sales figure of 22,400 units needs to be adjusted for finished stock requirements. The adjusted figure then will provide the unit production level needed from which, given the direct labour data, budgeted labour cost can also be derived. The consolidation of both *unit production* volume and *labour cost* appears in Table 9.2.

Materials cost and purchases budgets

Note carefully that we have *two* operational volume levels – sales volume (of 22,400 units) and production volume (of 22,800 units). We must ensure that all pro-duction budgets, as with labour cost below, comply with the relevant *production* level (not until the production cost of sales budget later will we relate again to the sales level of 22,400 units). Once more a suitable stock adjustment needs to be effected, on this occasion to raw material stocks, consistent with stock-piling or stock run-down policy. Again, Chalky's management plan on increasing stocks of raw material (from 2,000 kg to 2,400 kg) and the consequence of this policy

table 9.2

Unit production and labour cost budget

Sales turnover (units)	add Closing stock (units)	(less) Opening stock (units)	Budgeted production (units)
22,400	800	(400)	22,800
	Standard labour hours (per unit):		$\frac{1}{2}$
	Budgeted labour hours:		11,400
	Standard wage rate (per hour):		£4.80
	Budgeted labour cost:		£54,720

table 9.3
Materials cost budget

Production (units)	Kilograms (per unit)	Total materials usage (kilograms)
22,800	2	45,600
	Standard purchase price (per kilo):	£0.80
	Budgeted materials cost:	£36,480

table 9.4
Material purchases budget

Materials usage (kg)	add Closing stock (kg)	(less) Opening stock (kg)	Materials requirement (kg)
45,600	2,400	(2,000)	46,000
	Standard purchase price (per kilo):		£0.80
	Budgeted purchases:		£36,800

is that purchases will have to be made not solely to fuel production requirements but also to build up the required stock level as well. First, a raw *materials cost* budget based on the data given and related to the production level of 22,800 units is needed (Table 9.3) which is then adjusted, in Table 9.4, for the necessary raw material stock-piling in order to budget the *material purchases* requirement.

Production overhead cost budget

Overhead costs of production are differentiated as to their underlying behaviour pattern (see Chapter 3) as being either fixed or variable. Note here that depreciation costs in production can be identified as being either unit-based (variable) *user* cost, i.e. incurred according to the degree of usage of manufacturing assets (for example, the running hours that machinery is used in producing units) or a time-based (fixed) *period* cost charged against production assets on, say, a quarterly or annual basis and incurred irrespective of fixed asset usage (e.g. straight-line/reducing balance methods of depreciation). Given Chalky's management expectations, budgeted *production overhead cost* is shown in Table 9.5.

table 9.5
Production overhead cost budget

Unit variable overhead	Production units	Budgeted variable overhead
£1.20	22,800	£27,360
	Budgeted fixed overhead (per period):	£18,240
	Budgeted production overhead cost:	£45,600

Note: Depreciation cost: variable (machine hour rate @ 20p/unit) £4,560 + fixed (straight-line) £1,040 = £5,600.

table 9.6

**Production cost of
sales budget**

	Material (2kg @ 80p)	Labour ($\frac{1}{2}$ hr. @ £4.80)	Variable O/H rate	Fixed O/H rate	Production cost
Production cost:	(£)	(£)	(£)	(£)	(£)
Per unit	1.60	2.40	1.20	0.80	6.00
In total (x 22,800 units)	36,480	54,720	27,360	18,240	136,800
Add opening stock (400 units @ £6/per unit):					2,400
Less closing stock (800 units @ £6/per unit):					4,800
Budgeted production cost of sales (22,400 units @ £6/per unit):					£134,400

Production cost of sales budget

By taking the costs from the previous budgets relating to production volume of 22,800 units and readjusting back to the sales level of 22,400 units we can compile the final production budget in Table 9.6. showing the *production cost of sales*.

It is important to realise that the production cost of sales budget and moreover the £6 per unit valuation of the finished product both result from an application of the absorption costing technique (see Chapter 2); all costs both fixed *and* variable are absorbed in ascertaining the 'full' production cost (of £6) per cost unit. With any changes from the planned production volume of 22,800 units (e.g. in future periods beyond this budget period) only the total variable costs would rise or fall in accordance with any increase or decrease in activity level respectively. The total fixed overhead costs of £18,240 per period would remain, in the short-term at least, unaffected by activity level (volume) changes. This holds important implications for both flexible budgeting in section 9.2 and overhead variance analysis in Chapter 10. An alternative cost treatment would be to apply the marginal costing technique (see Chapter 4) providing a variable production cost unit valuation of £5.20, not taking into account fixed overheads which would be written off as a 'lump-sum' figure of £18,240 against the relevant period's total *contribution*, i.e. £2.80 (selling price of £8 *less* £5.20 variable cost) per unit multiplied by whatever unit volume pertains in the coming relevant period.

General overhead and capital expenditure budget

In practice and more complex 'real world' situations, these two budgets will always be prepared separately, but because of the relative simplicity of the Chalky & Sons data here we will combine *general overhead* expenses and *capital expenditures* into a single budget. Note that although Chalky's managers anticipate all general overhead to comprise fixed costs, in reality there will almost always be some element of variable overheads, for instance, sales commissions payable to sales representatives and agents that will vary according to the level of sales achieved. The budget in Table 9.7 is the last of the functional/subsidiary budgets to be prepared.

table 9.7
General overhead and capital expenditure budget

Administration cost	Selling and distribution expenses	Finance charges	Budgeted general overhead
(£)	(£)	(£)	(£)
17,280	26,000	1,120	44,400

Budgeted capital expenditures:	10,000
Budgeted general overheads and capital expenditure:	£54,400

9.1.2 Summary/master budgets

No further fresh budgeted data needs to be prepared as all the budget detail necessary for the *summary* budgets is available in the building of the functional budgets we have already achieved in 9.1.1. The relevant figures can simply be extracted from these subsidiary budgets and summarised into a master plan for the organisation, that is its master budget. The budgets comprising the firm's master plan are the same central accounting statements that are required to be provided by the financial accountant for external reporting purposes, i.e. cash-flow statement, profit and loss account and balance sheet. In management accounting the budgeted versions of these important financial statements are obviously solely *internal* information requirements and almost certainly would not be made available for public consumption (remember Chapter 1's contrast of financial versus management accounting which was your first encounter with the two very different contexts within which accounting information is provided and used.). K. W. Chalky & Sons summary/master budget therefore involves finally the building of:

▶ A cash-flow budget.
▶ A budgeted income statement, i.e. profit and loss account.
▶ A budgeted balance sheet.

Because the following master budgets comprise little more than summary extracts of all the previous subsidiary/functional budgets presented in a pre-scribed conventional format, the body of each budget will contain a cross-reference column citing the relevant table from which the budgeted infor-mation is drawn.

Cash-flow budget

You may (or may not) have encountered in your financial accounting studies more than one way in which cash-flow statements are expressed. For instance, there is a (rather complex) format, often referred to as the 'indirect' method, which involves starting with the operating profit figure and working backwards to derive the cash situation by adding back in depreciation and non-cash items /movements, etc. We will avoid that rather more difficult approach here and instead adopt probably the simplest, most 'direct' mode of expression of cash flows in the following summary budget format:

K. W. CHALKY & SONS: CASH-FLOW BUDGET

	Table reference	(£)	(£)	(£)
Cash Inflow Sales	9.1			179,200
(less) Debtors increasea				(960)
				———
Cash Outflow				178,240
Production labour payments	9.2		54,720	
Raw material purchases	9.4	36,800		
(less) Creditors increasea		(1,480)	35,320	
		———		
Production overheads	9.5	45,600		
(less) Depreciationb		(5,600)	40,000	
		———		
General overheads	9.7		44,400	
Capital expenditure	9.7		10,000	184,440
				———
Cash Surplus/(Deficit)				(6,200)
Opening Balance	B.S.			5,200
				———
Budgeted Closing Balance/(Bank Overdraft)				(1,000)

Key: B.S. indicates a reference to the opening balance sheet at start of budget period.

Notes: aCreditors are expected to rise by £1,480 (given) while debtors are expected to increase from opening figure of £7,680 by $12\frac{1}{2}$ per cent (given), i.e. a rise of £960 (0.125 × £7,680). An increase in debtors/creditors levels of credit will result in *less* cash flowing, and vice-versa. Assuming all opening debtor/creditor balances outstanding at the beginning of the budget period are received/paid during the budget period, then an alternative view of these cash flows is as follows:

	Debtors (£)	Creditors (£)
Sales/purchases	179,200	36,800
add Opening balances received/paid (1)	7,680	4,480
less Closing balances outstanding	8,640 ((1) × 1.125)	5,960 ((1) + £1,480)
	———	———
Cash inflow/outflow	178,240	35,320

bYou should always remember that because depreciation expense is purely a book-keeping entry in the accounts (i.e. it is a non-cash item) involving no actual outflow of cash, then a suitable adjustment must always be made in a cash-flow statement/budget. Here the depreciation adjustment comprises the fixed straight-line charge of £1,040 (given) *plus* the variable machine hour rate of 20p per unit (given) multiplied by the production volume of 22,800 units (= £4,560), totalling thus:

	(£)
Fixed depreciation charge	1,040
Variable depreciation rate	4,560
	———
Total depreciation cost	5,600

Budgeted profit and loss account

In the US this summary budget statement is usually referred to as the business' *budgeted income statement*. The terms *profit and loss account* and *income statement* are entirely interchangeable. The former reference tends to be the term most widely favoured in the United Kingdom as well as those countries influenced by UK convention and practice.

K. W. CHALKY & SONS: BUDGETED PROFIT AND LOSS ACCOUNT

	Table reference	(£)
Sales	9.1	179,200
Product cost of sales	9.6	134,400
Production profit		44,800
General overhead expenses	9.7	44,400
Budgeted profit		400

Before proceeding to build the final summary budget (i.e. the budgeted balance sheet), the preparation of a summary schedule of fixed assets (SOFA) is necessary which will effectively act as an appendaged/supplementary piece of budget information supporting the balance sheet. The SOFA summarises the period's budgeted additions (i.e. items of capital expenditure) to, and depreciation of, the business' fixed assets in order to determine the budgeted net book value (NBV)/written down value (WDV) as at the end of the budget period.

SCHEDULE OF FIXED ASSETS (SOFA) SUMMARY

	Table reference	(£)	(£)
Opening fixed assets	B.S.		29,600
add Capital expenditure items budgeted	9.7	10,000	
less Depreciation budgeted	9.5	(5,600)	4,400
Budgeted closing fixed assets NBV/WDV:			34,000

Budgeted balance sheet

The budgeted balance sheet can be, rather vividly, described as a 'snapshot' of the expected financial state of affairs of the business as it will appear at a given moment in time, i.e. at the end of the budget period. This contrasts with both the budgeted cash flows and profit (or loss) statements which relate to the whole period of time rather than just a single, unique point in time. The budgeted balance sheet is the final 'brick' in the entire budget building process which is now at an end for K. W. Chalky & Sons.

K. W. CHALKY & SONS: BUDGETED BALANCE SHEET

	Table reference	(£)	(£)	(£)
Fixed assets	SOFA			34,000
Current assets				
Stocks: Raw materials				
(2,400 k. @ 80p/k.)	9.4	1,920		
W-I-P:	B.S.	2,000		
Finished goods				
(800 units @ £6)	9.2	4,800	8,720	
Debtors[a]	B.S.		8,640	
			17,360	
less Current liabilities				
Creditors[a]	B.S.	5,960		
Bank overdraft	C.F.	1,000	6,960	10,400
Net total assets				44,400
Capital	B.S.		42,000	
Profit and loss account				
Opening balance	B.S.	2,000		
Profit for budget period	P.L.	400	2,400	
Ownership funds/equity				44,400

Key: C.F. indicates a reference to the cash-flow budget.

P.L. indicates a reference to the budgeted profit and loss account.

Note: [a]See the first explanatory note directly after the cash-flow budget for detail relating to debtors and creditors figures.

Summary

Let us in conclusion sound a warning note – applicable to your studies of both financial accounting as well as management accounting! Never, repeat never, equate surpluses of cash to profits and deficits of cash to losses. There are frequently enormous differences between the cash-flow position and the profit/loss situation. The main reason lies with the *matching concept* in accounting which incorporates into profit/loss calculations certain items largely unconnected with physical flows of cash such as accruals, depreciation and profit on the sale of assets. In Activity 9.1 for instance, Chalky & Sons budget a profit of £400 whilst simultaneously expecting to suffer a cash deficit of £6,200, which transforms an opening cash balance of £5,200 to a closing bank overdraft of £1,000!

9.2 Flexible budgeting
·····················

It is entirely in the nature of planning, i.e. budgeting, that the actual outcome of events will not exactly coincide with what was planned and budgeted. 'Nothing ever works out to plan' is an often heard plaintive cry from individuals in private life as well as managers in business life! If, for instance, you were planning a journey from the north of England to, say, Lands End at the southernmost tip of the country, you might estimate a (budgeted) time of seven hours. The actual journey time is almost bound to be different, perhaps only by a few minutes if the plan (budget) was a good estimate. However, in reality, it is far more likely to be significantly more of a variation than just a few minutes. The underlying premise we shall adopt is perhaps now obvious. We shall safely assume that, practically speaking, there is going to be a difference between actual events/results and the planned/budgeted outcome. If, maybe through purely chance coincidence, budget agreed exactly with actual, then there would be no real need for the analysis that follows for the rest of this chapter and indeed the whole of the next – but we will assume differently.

Fixed budgets

At the outset managers need to lay their plans for what they expect future operations to be in the form of budgets. For management planning and budgetary control purposes there is a requirement to fix in place a budget (to use as a control device) well before managers eventually discover real outcomes in the shape of business results such as actual sales prices, revenues and expenditures. This original budget that management set is unsurprisingly called a *fixed budget*. A fixed budget is an *a priori* view of planned events and is based on the level of business activity originally forecast or expected.

DID YOU KNOW ...?
*that the term **a priori** is taken from the Latin; its literal meaning is 'from beforehand'. Not confined just to accounting it is often heard, for example, in the case of someone making an **a priori** judgement about a crime before having the benefit of hindsight that is provided by evidence and facts which come to light about the incident at a later stage.*

It would, however, be wholly inappropriate and potentially seriously misleading for management to compare original budgeted figures for a particular fixed level of activity with actual results achieved at what might be a radically different activity level. This very real problem is addressed and solved by a budgeting technique known as *flexible budgetary control*.

9.2.1 Flexible budgetary control

An allowance, frequently referred to as a 'budget cost allowance', needs to be made for the inevitable difference between the level of business activity budgeted and the actual activity level that transpires. *Flexible budgets* are the vehicle by which the original fixed budget is adjusted, up or down as necessary, to the actual level of activity. This is in order that the actual results can then be compared fairly with what *would* have been budgeted for the relevant activity level that has actually transpired. In short, flexible budgeting's fundamental aim and purpose lie in an attempt to compare 'like with like'.

We have already seen, in section 9.1, an example of a fixed budget being prepared. When you saw the subsidiary budgets of K. W. Chalky & Sons coming together to form the summary/master budget in Activity 9.1 you experienced a case of an original *a priori* fixed budget taking shape. Despite the fact that in that budget building exercise Chalky's budgeted sales were different from the budgeted production level, that particular difference arose simply because the stock level of finished units was required by management to be adjusted for an increase of 400 (from 400 up to 800) units in finished goods stock, i.e. merely a stock level, as opposed to an activity level, adjustment.

It was not even considered that the sales level could be anything other than that planned in the sales budget (i.e. 22,400 units) or that production output could be any different from the 22,800 units budgeted for in the production budget. As we have already said, it is highly unlikely that actual sales turnover subsequently achieved in the coming budget period will be precisely 22,400 units and actual volume of output exactly 22,800 units. If, for example, Chalky's resultant production level fluctuated below the budgeted level of 22,800 units by, say, 2,280 units (down to 20,520 units) then actual activity would be said to be 10 per cent below the fixed budget level. Consequently if all budgeted costs were recalculated to reflect a scaled-down activity level of 90 per cent of the original fixed budget, then truer and fairer, like with like, comparisons could be drawn between actual costs incurred and costs in the newly reworked 'flexed' budget. Herein lies the real value of flexible budgeting in that it provides *more meaningful* information resulting from a more equitable comparison (i.e. monitoring) of budget with reality.

However, intrinsically bound up with this suggestion of a 'reworking' (via a scaling down, or indeed up, if appropriate) of costs from the original fixed budget lies the vitally important consideration that costs display different patterns of cost behaviour. In Chapter 3 we specifically established various patterns of how costs behave in relation to fluctuations in volume, determining that any scaling down or up of budgeted costs would affect only the variable costs involved because only they are sensitive to changes in activity. Fixed costs, on the other hand, by definition would remain unaffected by any activity level change. In short, whereas an allowance needs to be made for the flexing of variable costs, budgeted fixed (i.e. period) costs in a flexed budget would simply stay the same as they were in the original fixed budget.

9.2.2 Application of the technique

Widely encountered in Chapter 3 (as well as others, for example, Chapter 6) was the familiar simple two-variable regression/cost equation:

$$y = a + bx$$

where: 'y' is total cost; 'a' is fixed cost per period; 'b' is variable cost per unit; and 'x' is volume (i.e. the level of activity in units).

This linear algebraic formula's application hinged entirely on its essential separation of total cost 'y' into the two distinct cost behaviour patterns of fixed cost 'a' and variable cost 'b' related to whatever relevant level of activity 'x' happens to apply in a given situation. Both the theory and practice underpinning the use of the flexible budgeting technique also hinges upon this principle of a two-way split of cost – once more based on identifying how costs behave, i.e. are they sensitive to changes in activity levels or are they not?

In a flexible (or *flexed*) budget:

▶ fixed cost is determined by dividing total fixed overhead costs budgeted originally by the number of budgetary control periods involved. This reflects the nature of fixed overhead as a period cost not in any way related to the level of activity but time-based. For instance, if the yearly budget is disaggregated into shorter quarterly periods for budgetary control purposes, then the budgeted fixed cost for a quarter will simply be the annual fixed overhead budgeted in total divided by a factor of four;

▶ variable cost is calculated very straightforwardly by multiplying the number of units at the relevant flexed level of activity by the budgeted variable cost per unit.

A minor problem arises with budgeted semi-variable costs however (see section 3.1.3). As previously explained these sorts of cost contain elements of both fixed *and* variable cost. It is therefore necessary to adopt a suitable cost estimation technique – several were discussed and exemplified in Chapter 3 – in order to determine the breakdown of the variable and fixed components of semi-variable cost. (In addition to variable, fixed and semi-variable a fourth pattern of cost behaviour, known as 'step' cost, was identified in Chapter 3. This poses no real problem, however, as both step-fixed and step-variable costs will be for all practical purposes treated as fixed and variable cost respectively – see section 3.1.3 again for further explanation if required.)

For practice in applying the flexible budgeting technique, both now and also shortly in Activity 9.2, take the case of Willbat Limited, producing a single product cost unit and expecting, in addition to its variable (£1 per unit) and semi-variable costs, to incur £640,000 per annum fixed cost commitments. Willbat's annual budget is for control purposes broken down into individual quarterly periods and, for the next three-month control period under review, to which Table 9.8's flexed data apply, business activity is budgeted at a level of 440,000 units. This represents the expected 100 per cent activity level as fixed in Willbat's original budget.

No problem is presented by the £640,000 fixed cost allocated evenly over the four three-month periods (at £160,000 per quarter) or the £1 unit variable cost, but Table 9.8's semi-variable costs require disaggregating into their fixed and variable cost component parts. For this purpose we adopt the 'high-low'

table 9.8
Fixed (100%) and flexed (all other %s) budget data

Level of activity							
In percentages	70%	80%	90%	100%	110%	120%	130%
In units (000s)	308	352	396	440	484	528	572
Costs	(£000)	(£000)	(£000)	(£000)	(£000)	(£000)	(£000)
Fixed	160	160	160	160	160	160	160
Variable (£1 per unit)	308	352	396	440	484	528	572
Semi-variable	194	216	238	260	282	304	326
Total	662	728	794	860	926	992	1,058

technique of cost estimation (see section 3.2.1) using the regression/cost equation ($y = a + bx$) featured at the beginning of this section. A pair of simultaneous equations can be solved, having taken the highest and lowest values from Table 9.8's data and inserted them into $y = a + bx$, thus:

Highest	$326 = a + 572b$ (1)
Lowest	$194 = a + 308b$ (2)
Deduct (2) from (1)	$132 = 264b$

$$\therefore b = \frac{132}{264} = 0.5 \text{ (i.e. 50p per unit)}$$

Thus the variable cost element of £0.05/unit is found. Then, by substituting this value for 'b' into the second simultaneous equation (it is immaterial whether this or equation (1) is used), the value of 'a' can be determined, as follows:

$$194 = a + (308)(0.5)$$
$$\therefore 194 = a + 154$$
$$\therefore a = 40$$

As our scaling factor is in £000s, then fixed cost per period represented by 'a' equals £40,000 per quarter. Having derived values for both 'a' and 'b', the semi-variable cost function is:

$$y = £40,000 + £0.5x$$

Check, for example, using the 100 per cent fixed budget activity level from Table 9.8., thus:

$$y = £40,000 + (£0.5)(440,000 \text{ units})$$
$$= £40,000 + £220,000 = \underline{£260,000} \text{ (semi-variable cost)}$$

As we know fully variable cost to be £1 per unit and fully fixed cost is £160,000 per quarter, Willbat's total cost function can be written as:

$$y = £200,000 + £1.5x$$

Check, again for example, using 100 per cent activity, thus:

$$y = £200,000 + (£1.5)(440,000 \text{ units})$$
$$= £200,000 + £660,000 = \underline{£860,000} \text{ (total cost)}$$

Still using the data from Table 9.8 for further practice consider the questions posed by Activity 9.2.

ACTIVITY 9.2

Required: Through application of the flexible budgetary control technique and in the context of the data for Willbat Limited already given (in Table 9.8.) provide answers to the following.

▶ What would total budgeted costs be for Willbat at flexed activity levels of 75 per cent and 125 per cent?

▶ Assuming a standard sales price of £2 per unit, what would have been Willbat's original budgeted amounts of contribution and profit in its fixed budget (i.e. at 100 per cent activity level)?

▶ Re-work both contribution and profit for Willbat, given the standard selling price of £2 per unit, at the flexed activity levels of 75 per cent and 125 per cent.

▶ At what budgeted activity level would Willbat's business operations just break even?

The first question may be answered either in the form of a cost statement presentation or (perhaps more succinctly) using the total cost formula/function; firstly work through the figures in the following disaggregated statement:

	Fully fixed cost (£000)	Semi-variable costs		Fully variable cost (£000)	Budgeted total cost (£000)
		Fixed element (£000)	Variable element (£000)		
At 75% activity (i.e. 330,000 units)	160	40	165[a]	330	695
At 125% activity (i.e. 550,000 units)	160	40	275[b]	550	1,025

Notes: [a]330,000 units multiplied by 50p/unit variable cost component = £165,000.
         [b]550,000 units multiplied by 50p/unit variable cost component = £275,000.
Fully variable costs are simply incurred at the rate of £1 per unit.

Alternatively, just apply the cost formula given by the total cost function in the form of the equation: $y = £200,000 + £1.5x$:

75% activity: £200,000 + (£1.5)(330,000 units) = £200,000 + £495,000
              = £695,000

125% activity: £200,000 + (£1.5)(550,000 units) = £200,000 + £825,000
               = £1,025,000

A suitable means of answering the second question would be to adopt the style of a marginal costing profit statement that you have already encountered (in Chapter 4):

WILLBAT LTD.: BUDGETED PROFIT STATEMENT (AT ORIGINAL 100% ACTIVITY LEVEL)

	(£000)	(£000)
Sales revenues: 440,000 units @ £2/unit		880
(*less*) Variable costs:		
Semi (440,000 units @ £0.50/unit)	(220)	
Fully (440,000 units @ £1/unit)	(440)	(660)
Budgeted contribution (440,000 units @ £0.50/unit)		220
(*less*) Fixed costs Semi	(40)	
Fully	(160)	(200)
Budgeted profit (at fixed budget activity level)		20

Note: Budgeted unit contribution is £2 selling price minus £1.50 variable (semi+fully) cost.

The answer to the third of the questions can most appropriately be presented, once again using a marginal costing/contribution layout, in the shape of the following flexed profit (or loss) budget statements:

WILLBAT LTD.: BUDGETED PROFIT AND LOSS STATEMENTS (FLEXED)

	@ 75% activity			@ 125% activity		
	(Units)	(Per unit)	(£000)	(Units)	(Per unit)	(£000)
Sales revenues	330,000	£2	660	550,000	£2	1100
(*less*) Variable costs	330,000	£1.50	(495)	550,000	£1.50	(825)
Contribution	330,000	£0.50	165	550,000	£0.50	275
(*less*) Fixed costs			(200)			(200)
Profit/(loss) at flexed budget activity levels			(35)			75

In the above results lies a simple clue for solving the requirement of the fourth and final question. What is it? The requirement is to determine the budgeted break-even point for Willbat's operations and the clue is that it must lie somewhere between the loss-making 75 per cent and the profit-making 125 per cent levels of activity. There are in fact several ways and means of arriving at the exact break-even activity level. One possible solution is to focus on the loss of £35,000 made at 75 per cent activity, and apply the notion of *contribution* towards covering the loss. At a unit contribution of 50p how many more units above 330,000 would Willbat require in order to generate £35,000 worth of contribution? Simple division provides the answer, *viz*:

$$\frac{£35,000}{£0.50 \text{ per unit}} = 70,000 \text{ extra units to break even}$$

Therefore the break-even point lies at 330,000 + 70,000 = <u>400,000</u> units.

Using a similar break-even concept, consider the answer to the second question, and think of the fixed budget profit at 100 per cent activity as being Willbat's *margin of safety* (remember this idea from Chapter 6, section 6.2.2?). With a £20,000 budgeted profit at a planned 440,000 unit activity level what safety margin exists to 'cushion' possible unit losses (i.e. lost contribution) before Willbat would just break even? Again, simple division (£20,000 ÷ £0.50) indicates that to lose 40,000 units would reduce Willbat to only breaking even. As the original profit of £20,000 is based on a fixed budget of 440,000 units, then the flexed budget (unit) break-even level is 440,000 – 40,000 (i.e. <u>400,000</u> units).

A final suggested means of solution would be for you to apply one of the break-even point formulae you encountered in section 6.2.1 of Chapter 6. By inserting Willbat's data into the following suitable formula, the budgeted break-even point is determined as:

$$\frac{\text{Fixed costs}}{\text{Unit contribution}} = \frac{£200,000}{£0.50} = \underline{400,000 \text{ units}}$$

Finally, this break-even point can be translated into either sales value (400,000 × £2) of £800,000 or a flexed budget percentage activity level of 91 per cent (rounded to the nearest percentage point) calculated thus:

$$\frac{400,000 \text{ units}}{440,000 \text{ units}} \times 100 = 90.90 \text{ (recurring)}$$

Self-check questions

9.1 R Limited manufactures three products: A, B and C.
   You are required:
   (a) Using the information given below, to prepare budgets for the month of January for:
      (i)   sales in quantity and value, including total value;
      (ii) production quantities;
      (iii) material usage in quantities;
      (iv) material purchases in quantity and value, including total value;
      (*Note:* Particular attention should be paid to your layout of the budgets.)
   (b) To explain the term principal budget factor and state what it was assumed to be in (a) of this question.

Data for preparation of January budgets

Sales:

Product	Quantity	Price each £
A	1,000	100
B	2,000	120
C	1,500	140

Materials used in the company's products are:

Material	M1	M2	M3
Unit cost	£4	£6	£9

Quantities used in:	units	units	units
Product: A	4	2	–
B	3	3	2
C	2	1	1

Finished stocks:

Product	A	B	C
Quantities			
1st January	1,000	1,500	500
31st January	1,100	1,650	550
Material stocks:	M1	M2	M3
	units	units	units
1st January	26,000	20,000	12,000
31st January	31,200	24,000	14,400

(Chartered Institute of Management Accountants)

9.2 The accounts of Squire plc show the following balance sheet as at January 1st 19X4:

	(£000)	(£000)		(£000)	(£000)
Share capital and reserves		340	Fixed assets		300
Current liabilities:			Current assets:		
Corporation tax	30		Stock	65	
Dividend	40		Debtors	50	
Creditors	40	110	Cash at bank	35	150
		£450			£450

Budgeted summary profit statements for the four quarters to December 31 19X4 are as follows:

	First quarter		Second quarter		Third quarter		Fourth quarter	
	(£000)	(£000)	(£000)	(£000)	(£000)	(£000)	(£000)	(£000)
Sales		150		135		165		150
Production cost of sales	102		94		110		102	
Administration and marketing expenses	23	125	21	115	25	135	23	125
Budgeted profit		25		20		30		25

Budgeted balances for debtors and creditors at end of each quarter are:

	31.3.X4	30.6.X4	30.9.X4	31.12.X4
	(£000)	(£000)	(£000)	(£000)
Debtors	60	45	65	55
Creditors	50	40	55	48

Note: Administration and marketing expense creditors are paid in month of purchase.

The management accountant of Squire provides further budget details for 19X4, which include:

(i) Dividend payment is planned for the first quarter, and corporation tax liability will be settled during the third quarter.

(ii) Heavy capital expenditure amounting to £128,000 is expected to be incurred and paid in the fourth quarter.

(iii) In order to partially finance the above capital payments, it is planned to issue further share capital of £25,000 and sell £5,000 of old (fully depreciated) plant and machinery. Both sets of proceeds are expected to be received in the quarter preceding the capital outlay.

(iv) Budgeted production cost of sales includes a charge for depreciation of £5,000 in each quarter.

Required:

(a) Prepare Squire's cash budget for each of the four quarters in 19X4.

(b) Comment (briefly) on the year-end cash position at the bank in the light of Squire's cash budget.

(c) 'The cash budget is a summary budget'. Briefly describe *two* other types of summary budget, and also explain what is meant by functional budgets. Give *four* examples of functional budgets together with a brief description of each.

(Accounting Degree)

9.3 (a) Exe plc manufactures one standard product and in common with other companies in the industry is suffering from the current depression in the market. Currently it is operating at a normal level of activity of 70 per cent which represents an output of 6,300 units, but the sales director believes that a realistic forecast for the next budget period would be a level of activity of 50 per cent.

	Level of activity		
	60%	70%	80%
	£	£	£
Direct materials	37,800	44,100	50,400
Direct wages	16,200	18,900	21,600
Production overhead	37,600	41,200	44,800
Administration overhead	31,500	31,500	31,500
Selling and distribution overhead	42,300	44,100	45,900
Total cost	165,400	179,800	194,200

Profit is 20 per cent of selling price.

You are required, from the data given in the current flexible budget above, to prepare a budget based on a level of activity of 50 per cent, which should show clearly the contribution which could be expected.

(b) Discuss briefly *three* problems which may arise from such a change in level of activity.

(Chartered Institute of Management Accountants)

9.4 (a) A company manufactures three products, chairs, tables and benches. From the following information you are to produce:

(i)   A Production Budget showing quantities to be manufactured and factory unit costs of each product;

(ii) A Purchasing Budget detailing quantities to be purchased and the total cost of materials;

(iii) A Direct Wages Budget showing hours to be worked in total and gross wages to be paid.

	Chairs	Tables	Benches
Sales in the next trading period, in units	4,000	1,000	500
Material requirements			
Timber (per unit)	0.5 ft³	1.2 ft³	2.5 ft³
Price of Timber £8 ft³			
Upholstery	0.2 yd²	–	–
Price of upholstery £4 yd²			
Fixing and Finishing material costs 5% of total material cost.			
Labour requirements			
Carpenters, hours per unit	0.75	0.8	1.3
Fixers and Finishers, hours per unit	0.25	0.3	1.0
Carpenters rate per hour £6			
Fixers and Finishers rate per hour £4.80			

Fixed factory overheads are estimated at £6,253 for the trading period and these are recovered on the basis of labour hours.

	Chairs	Tables	Benches
Finished stocks at beginning of period	200	300	40
Finished stocks at end of period	400	100	50
Material stocks at beginning of			
period – Timber	600 ft³	Upholstery	400 yd²
Material stocks at end of			
period – Timber	650 ft³	Upholstery	260 yd²

(b) The trading period to which this budget relates is of four weeks duration. The labour force is expected to perform as follows:

	Carpenters	Fixers
Normal hours per week, per person	40	40
Absenteeism and lateness	10%	15%

Calculate how many Carpenters and Fixers should be employed?

(c) From the information in (a) above, which is considered the 100 per cent level of activity, show a Production Budget flexed to output levels of 80 per cent, 90 per cent and 110 per cent of the target Production Budget. (All calculations to nearest £1.)

(Association of Accounting Technicians)

Further study

Drury, C. (1992) *Management and cost accounting*, 3rd edn, London: Chapman and Hall.

Emmanual, C., Otley, D. and Merchant, K. (1990) *Accounting for management control*, 2nd edn, London: Chapman and Hall.

Hopwood, A. (1974) *Accounting and human behaviour*, 1st edn, Hemel Hempstead: Prentice-Hall.

Layne, A. (1984) *Cost accounting – analysis and control*, 1st edn, Basingstoke: Macmillan.

Pizzey, A. (1989) *Cost and management accounting*, 3rd edn, London: Paul Chapman Publishing.

Pogue, G.A. (1984) 'Budgeting and management', in *Management Accounting*, March, Chartered Institute of Management Accountants.

Sizer, J. (1989) *An insight into management accounting*, 3rd edn, London: Penguin.

Wheldon, H. (1984) *Cost accounting*, 15th edn, London: Macdonald and Evans.

Wright, D. (1994) *A practical foundation in costing*, 1st edn, London: Routledge.

CHAPTER 10

Control accounting through standard costing/variance analysis

Objectives
· · · · · · · · · · · · · ·

By the end of this chapter you should be able to:

▶ Describe how control accounting operates through the technique of standard costing/variance analysis.

▶ Compute a full range of sales, profit, contribution and cost variances.

▶ Analyse and interpret the variances from an investigative management viewpoint.

▶ Understand the role of 'feedback' not only as it relates to standard costing/variance analysis but also in the context of the managerial planning, decision-making and control process established at the beginning of the book in Chapter 1.

Section 9.2 began with a suitable budgeting analogy, likening the nature of budgetary control informally to that of a traveller planning a journey to Lands End from the north of England and estimating a seven-hour journey time. A brief reiteration of this analogy also provides a convenient, introduction to this chapter's topic of control accounting through standard costing/variance analysis. To quote from section 9.2's opening paragraph: 'The actual journey time is almost bound to be different, perhaps only by a few minutes if the plan (budget) was a good estimate. However, in reality, it is far more likely to be significantly more of a variation than just a few minutes'. The word 'variation' holds the key to the door of control accounting techniques. However, precise standard costing terminology instead of using the everyday English language expression 'variation' adopts the more technical term *variance*. The specific costing sense that this term embodies is that of *actual* result or outcome showing a variance from *budget or standard*. (At this early juncture you are strongly advised to quickly re-read the short feature near the start of Chapter 9 addressing the question 'standards or budgets?' with the recommendation that, for all practical purposes, you treat standards/budgets as having identical uses in control accounting.)

Another important word in that quote from Chapter 9 is 'significantly'. An hour or two's difference from the seven hours planned in that earlier analogy might well be considered by the traveller a *significant* variation compared with, say, just a few minutes. If deemed significant, the traveller might want to find out the reason(s) why there is the variance – but, given our analogy, the reason(s) would no doubt be immediately obvious to the traveller (delays perhaps due to roadworks or an accident, longer stop for a break than planned etc.). In business situations, however, reasons for variances are likely not to be so patently obvious, making it far more important that relevant questions are asked and research/investigations carried out as to their cause. The issue of significance is a vital one as are two other questions, relating to *responsibility* for, and potential *inter-relationships* between, variances.

▶ Significance? It would simply not be feasible to research the reasons for every single variance from standard that arises. Only where the amounts involved are significantly different from expected should the reasons be investigated further. Moreover, this sensible approach to problem solving is entirely consistent with another well-established business principle, i.e. 'management by exception';

▶ Responsibility? In the process of investigating a significant variance, part of the research will involve the question of who is responsible for the variance arising. In its role as a planning and control device, standard costing/ variance analysis (as with budgetary control in the previous chapter) should help to indicate areas of individual responsibility clearly within the boundaries of what, in divisional performance analysis, are known as *responsibility centres;* these are dealt with in detail in Chapter 11. Where clear lines of responsibility are defined this should encourage and positively motivate individual managers, staff and employees in general to meet their responsibilities through efficient job performance. On the other hand, demotivation is a real danger if blurred lines of responsibility only result in blame for 'below par' performance being misplaced.

▶ Inter-relationships? As you will see later in the chapter, it is important not to view variances in isolation from each other – there may exist causal/interdependent relationships between variances. For example, buying cheap materials at a price below standard (which would represent a favourable variance on price – see section 10.1.1) might well result in inef- ficiencies with more materials being required in production than expected (perhaps because of their inferior quality) representing above standard usage which would in turn be reflected by an adverse efficiency variance (again see section 10.1.1).

figure 10.1
Extract (phases V & VI) from Figure 1.1's 'Structure of the management decision-making, planning and control process'

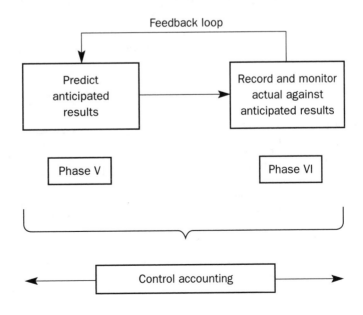

Control accounting using budgets/standards

Briefly refer back to Figure 1.1, p. 7, and it will remind you of the general structural framework underlying this book. Now you need to focus sharply on the last two phases of that flow diagram – phases V and VI. If you remember, section 1.2.5's description of phase V referred to it as both an end and a beginning – the end of decision accounting and the start of control accounting. Because Part 2 of the book has already dealt with decision accounting techniques in detail, eliminate the word 'choose' from phase V. The rest of the wording in the phase V box indicates the beginning of the control accounting segment of the overall framework, and is reproduced as an extract in Figure 10.1 for ease of reference.

For the purposes of this chapter, Figure 10.1 needs to be expanded a little; its development, with the necessary further detail, appears in Figure 10.2.

Taking the flow in Figure 10.2 from left to right, consider stage by stage the ingredients in the expanded control accounting sequence.

▶ *Prepare the plan.* The wording in Figure 10.1's phase V 'predict anticipated results' is tantamount to Figure 10.2's box (1). Preparation of the organisation's plan consists of the budget building process which you experienced through Activity 9.1. This process results in generating the business' *fixed* budget (remember K. W. Chalky & Sons from Chapter 9?).

▶ *Record actual results.* This exercise is represented by the first, fourth and seventh words of Figure 10.1's phase VI. At this stage you need to again read carefully the opening paragraph of section 2.1 in Chapter 2. From virtually the outset of the book it was made clear that the book-keeping exercise of *recording* costs and revenues will not be a feature of our studies. At the end of section 2.1.'s opening paragraph, the first bullet-point represents the actual results recorded in the form of past costs (from the historic cost records). The second bullet-point reflects the type of costs/revenues focused upon in this and the previous chapter, i.e. budgeted/standard costs and revenues.

▶ *Flex the fixed budget.* This is a vital exercise to put in place the means by which a true 'like-with-like' comparison (i.e. variance analysis) can be carried out in the next and final stage, box (4). For this stage it must be assumed of you that you are conversant with the flexible budgetary control

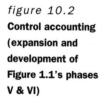

figure 10.2
**Control accounting
(expansion and
development of
Figure 1.1's phases
V & VI)**

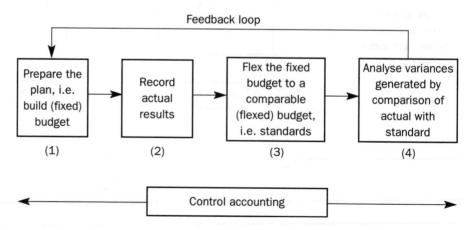

technique that we demonstrated in detail throughout section 9.2 of the previous chapter (remember Willbat Limited?). Flexing the original, fixed budget data to the level of activity that actually pertained provides us with the *standards* from which subsequent variance analyses can be performed. For our purposes throughout this chapter you are provided with box (3)'s relevant data in the form of Table 10.1.

▶ *Analyse variances.* This is the entire reason why this chapter exists. Box (4) represents the all-important process known as *monitoring* and is the end, i.e. final purpose, of control accounting. This last stage in Figure 10.2. is tantamount to Figure 10.1.'s phase VI: 'monitor actual against anticipated results'. In fact it would assist greatly in appreciating this end to the control sequence of the whole managerial decision-making, planning and control process, illustrated in Figure 1.1, if you were to re-read the phase VI paragraph in Chapter 1, section 1.2.6.

table 10.1

Variance analysis data: fixed and flexed budgets

Unit standard data	Unit value (£)		Fixed budget (original) (£)		Flex – to 80% actual (= –20% allowance) (£)	Flexed budget (standard) (£)	
		Sales:					
1u @ £70	70.00	Units (u) Price (£)	6,250u @ £70	437,500	–87,500 (A)	5,000u @ £70	350,000
		Raw materials:					
0.03t @ £840	25.20	Tonnes (t) Price (£)	187.5t @ £840	157,500	–31,500 (F)	150t @ £840	126,000
		Production labour:					
2h @ £7	14.00	Hours (h) Rate (£)	12,500h @ £7	87,500	–17,500 (F)	10,000h @ £7	70,000
		Variable overhead:					
2h @ £5	10.00	Hours (h) Rate (£)	12,500h @ £5	62,500	–12,500 (F)	10,000h @ £5	50,000
		Contribution:					
1 u @ £20.80	20.80	Units (u) Rate (£)	6,250u @ £20.80	130,000	–26,000 (A)	5,000u @ £20.80	104,000
		Fixed overhead:					
2h @ £4	8.00	Hours (h) Rate (£)	12,500h @ £4	50,000	Do not flex		50,000
		Profit:					
1u @ £12.80	12.80	Units (u) Rate (£)	6,250u @ £12.80	80,000	–26,000 (A)		54,000

Notes:
1 The overhead absorption rates in the original, fixed budget are based on direct (production) labour hours. Other bases are, however, possible – see Chapter 2 (section 2.2) on the absorption costing technique which indicates several alternative absorption rates/bases.
2 See Table 10.2 for the actual data (which relates to an actual 80% activity level of 5,000 units) and the important note on adverse (A) and/or favourable (F) variances which is directly prior to the start of section 10.1 on the next page.

A final word concerns the feedback loop in Figure 10.2 (equivalent to its counterpart in Figure 10.1). Feedback is the central feature of monitoring and control and can be briefly described through the use of another analogous device, the operation of a central heating system. The heat level required is the planned (budgeted/standard) temperature, and the monitoring is done by a comparator mechanism which compares actual temperature achieved (actual results) with the planned temperature. This monitoring (i.e. comparison of actual with standard temperatures) will reveal a *variance* which is acted upon through the thermostatic control in the system. The thermostat is equivalent to both the 'controller' and management 'action' in business. If more heat is required the thermostat will stay open to allow heat to increase until the planned temperature (i.e. budget/standard) is achieved. A thermostat may be reset from time to time and this represents the periodic adjustments in budgetary control systems which would lead to new fixed budgets being established and built, and allows the control accounting sequence or process to continue its cycle.

Can you think ...? of another typical control example of anything, in addition to a central heating system, that is reflective of a feedback process in operation.

Answer

The 'automatic pilot' control system in an aeroplane.

For the budgetary control period under review, the unit standard data and budgeted figures are already provided in Table 10.1 while the actual results recorded in the period are given in Table 10.2 (alongside the flexed budget/standard data which is shown again for ease of comparison).

The final column in Table 10.2 is the result of the comparison exercise between standard and actual (i.e. the comparator mechanism in our central heating system analogy above) which generates the variances. Detailed analysis of the variances is carried out now throughout the Activities in sections 10.1 and 10.2. (Note: A variance must always be qualified as to whether it is 'Adverse' (A) or 'Favourable' (F). With cost variances, when actual is greater than standard = (A) and vice-versa = (F); with sales, contribution and profit variances, when actual is greater than standard = (F) and vice-versa = (A). This assumes that contribution is positive, i.e. sales are higher than variable cost).

10.1 Analysis of variable cost variances

Often described as 'marginal' cost, variable cost comprises prime costs plus variable overhead (see Chapter 4). Moreover, prime cost is in turn made up of all forms of direct cost, i.e. raw materials, production labour and any direct expenses if they arise (see Chapter 2). As is usually the case in variance accounting, we assume the absence of direct expenses (they are very rare in practice as Chapter 2's section 2.1.4 explained). Because all types of variable cost are, by

table 10.2
Variance analysis data: standard (flexed budget) and actual

	Standard	(£)	Actual	(£)	Variance (£)
Sales					
Units (u)	5,000u		5,000u		
Price (£)	@ £70	350,000	@ £72	360,000	10,000 (F)
Raw materials					
Tonnes (t)	150t		137.5t		
price (£)	@ £840	126,000	@ £920	126,500	500 (A)
Production labour					
Hours (h)	10,000h		11,250h		
Rate (£)	@ £7	70,000	@ £7.20	81,000	11,000 (A)
Variable overhead					
Hours (h)	10,000h		11,250h		
Rate (£)	@ £5	50,000	@ £4.40	49,500	500 (F)
Contribution					
Units (u)	5,000u		5,000u		
Rate (£)	@ £20.80	104,000	@ £20.60	103,000	1,000 (A)
Fixed overhead		50,000		48,000	2,000 (F)
Profit		54,000		55,000	1,000 (F)

Notes:

1 Actual contribution per unit comprises:

	(£)
Sales: £360,000 ÷ 5,000u	= 72.00
Variable costs:	
Raw materials: £126,500 ÷ 5,000u	= 25.30
Direct labour: £81,000 ÷ 5,000u	= 16.20
Variable overhead: £49,500 ÷ 5,000u	= 9.90
Contribution: £103,000 ÷ 5,000u	= £20.60

2 See Table 10.1 for budgeted/standard unit contribution specification of £20.80.

definition, sensitive to changes in activity level (see Chapter 3) all cost items in this classification category flex, as is apparent from the data in Table 10.1. In addition, sales revenue is a variable and also flexes – the analysis of sales variances is dealt with later in section 10.2 along with fixed overheads (which, remember, do *not* flex). For the purposes of this section, we restrict our attention solely to costs as we analyse raw material, production labour and variable overhead variances.

All variable cost variances contain two fundamental aspects or dimensions – an *expenditure* aspect and an *efficiency* dimension. Excluding fixed overhead, the variance column in Table 10.2 comprises only *total* cost variances which need to be analysed into these two aspects or dimensions. Two key generic formulae underlie the calculation of both these aspects/dimensions, as follows:

$$\text{Expenditure: } (AP - SP) \times AQ$$

where: AP is the actual price; SP is the standard price; and AQ is the actual quantity.

$$\text{Efficiency: } (AQ - SQ) \times SP$$

where: SQ is the standard quantity; and other acronyms are as above.

It is established cost accounting convention that expenditure variances are evaluated on the basis of *actual* quantities (rather than standard) and that efficiency variances are determined using *standard* prices (as opposed to actual). We shall adopt the convention as it is universally applied in practice. If you are interested in seeing a possible alternative treatment, however, you might refer to some suitable text that goes beyond the conventional approach.[1]

Another convention in management accounting is that, although the fundamental nature of the division into expenditure/efficiency applies throughout the analysis of variable cost variances, by tradition both the sub-divisions of raw material and one of direct labour (into their relevant aspects/dimensions) go by other different descriptions, *viz*:

▶ material expenditure is conventionally referred to as a *price* variance;
▶ material efficiency is conventionally referred to as a *usage* variance;
▶ labour expenditure is conventionally referred to as a *rate* variance.

However, you need to be aware that it is purely a 'name' difference. The basic underlying sense behind the different names remains exactly the same, for example, 'price' is 'expenditure' and vice-versa. Until an added third dimension called *volume* appears in section 10.2, you are advised here to concentrate exclusively upon just the two essential aspects of expenditure and efficiency, maybe thinking of them as the two sides of a coin which together make up the whole (i.e. total) coin.

You may like to perform your variance calculations using the key generic formulae just indicated (indeed the Activities in this section do require this of you). However, an alternative approach is also available via the use of a structured layout or *framework*. Personally, I prefer the latter rather than formulae, and the framework approach will be adopted for my calculations throughout the Activities. Having set the framework up the relevant variances automatically emerge by, in effect, falling out of the framework's very structure! Nevertheless either approach, framework *or* formulae, can be used – perhaps utilising one method to cross-check with the other (though this is likely to be unfeasible given the time constraints and pressure of examinations). However, when you study them together you should find that mastery of one approach will effectively also contribute to your understanding of the other.

10.1.1 Material and labour cost variance analysis

We shall begin our variance analysis with the direct cost elements of variable cost, i.e. raw materials and production labour (often referred to as direct material and direct labour). Throughout the ensuing analysis using the framework approach, total variances (remember, Table 10.2's 'variance' column amounts) are given by simply comparing the opposite extremes of the framework, bottom level with top level, i.e. *standard at standard* compared with *actual at actual*. A total variance subdivides into the expenditure/efficiency dimensions described so far. This will perhaps make more sense now as you attempt Activity 10.1.

Base your variance calculations and relevant observations upon the data provided for you in Table 10.2.

 Required: Apply both framework and formulaic approaches in order to analyse the total variance for raw materials into its component parts of expenditure (i.e. materials *price* variance) and efficiency (i.e. materials *usage* variance).

Consider first my preferred framework approach to analysing the variances required in Activity 10.1:

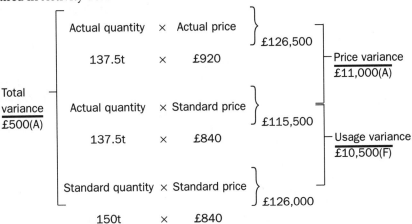

To verify the variance subdivisions on the right hand side in the above framework, you need now to insert your figures into the equations below, applying the earlier key formulae for expenditure (price) and efficiency (usage) – not forgetting, of course, to qualify each variance in the end bracket as (A) or (F):

 Expenditure: (AP – SP) x AQ
 Price variance = (£920 – £840) x 137.5 = £11,000(A)

 Efficiency: (AQ – SQ) x SP
 Usage variance = (137.5 – 150) x £840 = £10,500(F)

The raw materials total variance reflects the combined effect of its subdivisions into price and usage. In total it is £500(A) because the raw material required to meet actual production of 5,000 units was expected to be at a cost of £126,000 (standard at standard) but actually cost more, i.e. £126,500 (actual at actual).

Material price and usage variances

In Activity 10.1 it is assumed that the amount of raw materials purchased is the same as the quantity issued and used to produce output. In practice there will almost always be a delay between buying the material and it being used, i.e. issued to production, and price variances may be extracted at either point in time. However, it is a preference of convention that a price variance will be accounted for at the earliest possible opportunity, that is at the time of purchase rather than waiting for material to be issued/used. If the problem of choosing between the two arises in an examination because the question does not indicate to you the appropriate basis for the 'actual quantity' figure, then adopt the preferred practice of calculating price variances *at the point of purchase*.

Can you calculate ... using the following data (unconnected with that in Tables 10.1 and 10.2) the material price variance on the basis of:

(i)　the point of purchase of the materials;
(ii)　the stage of issue to/use in production.

Data:

Standard materials unit requirement	30 kilograms @ £0.20 per kg.
Actual material purchases	4,000 kilograms costing £760.
Material stocks – opening	1,000 kilograms.
– closing	1,700 kilograms.
Unit production/output	100 units.

Answer

(i)　(£0.19 – £0.20) × 4,000 kg = £40 (F)

(ii)　(£0.19 – £0.20) × 3,300 kg = £33 (F)

Notes: Actual price of 19p/kg calculated thus:

$$\frac{\text{Cost of materials purchased}}{\text{Quantity of kilograms}} = \frac{£760}{4,000\text{kg}} = £0.19/\text{kg}$$

Issue to/usage in production calculated thus:

		(kg.)
	Opening stock	1,000
add	Purchases	4,000
		5,000
(less)	Closing stock	(1,700)
	Quantity issued/used	3,300

For information, the materials usage variance (obviously based on issues) is as follows:

(3,300 kg – 3,000 kg) x £0.20 = £60 (A)

Now back to Tables 10.1 and 10.2. The 'standard quantity' figure of 150 tonnes represents the amount of material that should have been used to produce 5,000 units, but as less actual quantity was needed (i.e. 137.5 tonnes) the (F) variance indicates efficiency in usage. The *prima facie* implication is that the production process has been efficient in its operations and that the production department deserves credit. However, it may be dangerous to jump to what might prove to be a premature conclusion. The whole point of variance analysis is to investigate reasons for the variances, but only in this case if the material variances are deemed significant in amount (do you remember the three vital questions near the start of the chapter, i.e. significance, responsibility and inter-relationships?). Ostensibly the production department has fulfilled its responsibilities admirably, but upon further investigation it may be found that there exists a causal relationship between the usage and price variances. For instance, the purchasing department through astute buying practice may have managed to acquire superior quality raw materials (which, moreover, may be scarce and subject to strong competition) at a price above standard. The result has perhaps been more efficient usage as the better quality material has spun out further. So although the (maybe superficial) conclusion is that the purchasing manager is underperforming by paying too much, there may in reality be a case for congratulating the buyer/buying office on the (A) variance – for exhibiting clever business acumen and initiative in carrying out the responsibility of effective materials acquisition! On the other hand the purchasing department may be slack and irresponsible by simply paying too high a price (£920/t compared with £840/t for standard quality materials – an investigation would doubtlessly reveal the true reason.

Labour rate and efficiency variances

Let us continue our analysis, this time of the *labour* total cost variance into its subdivision dimensions of rate and efficiency, through your participation in Activity 10.2. First, however, be aware that when using the generic formulae approach, the notation changes slightly. The 'P' and the 'Q' that represented price and quantity earlier now change to 'R' and 'H':

▸ Expenditure: $(AR - SR) \times AH$, where: AR is actual wage rate; SR is standard wage rate; and AH is actual hours worked. The wage rate is the *price* of labour.
▸ Efficiency: $(AH - SH) \times SR$, where: SH is the standard number (i.e. *quantity*) of hours that should have been worked; and other acronyms are as above.

ACTIVITY **10.2**

Again base your variance calculations and subsequent observations on the data you are provided with in Table 10.2.

Required: Apply firstly framework and then, secondly, formulaic approaches in your analysis of the total variance for production labour subdivided into expenditure, i.e. the labour *rate* variance, and its other subdivision, the labour *efficiency* variance.

Construction of the framework for analysis of the variances required in Activity 10.2 is thus:

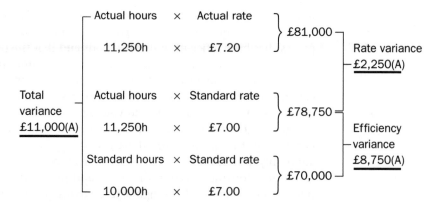

To check the sub-variances on the right-hand side of the framework that combine in the total labour cost variance, again put your data into the equations below, using the earlier formulae for expenditure (rate) and efficiency:

Expenditure: (AR − SR) × AH
Rate variance = (£7.20 − £7) × 11,250 = £2,250(A)

Efficiency: (AH − SH) × SR
Efficiency variance = (11,250 − 10,000) × £7 = £8,750(A)

Two adverse variances make up the total labour cost variance of £11,000(A) which, as with all total variances, can be determined by a simple comparison of 'standard at standard' (i.e. the bottom tier of the framework) − £70,000 with 'actual at actual' (top tier) of £81,000.

Sometimes referred to as the *wages* rate variance, our labour rate reveals an (A) variance owing to 20p more (£7.20/h − £7/h) actually being paid to the workforce than planned. Again this may be worthy of investigation, particularly when you consider that workers paid above a standard wage rate have performed below the standard expected − this is indicated by the need to have actually worked more hours (11,250h) than should have been required for production of 5,000 units (i.e. 10,000h). This substandard labour performance is reflected clearly in the (A) efficiency variance.

So, at least on the surface, management have paid too high a price to an inefficient workforce. However, this may have been due, for example, to particularly strong wage negotiations being carried out by a powerful trade union on behalf of its members and securing agreement to a higher wage settlement than originally anticipated by management. Furthermore, on the labour performance issue it may simply be a case of standards of worker efficiency being set too high in the first place, there was poor standard setting rather than weak performance by the workers. In short, further investigations once more may often reveal causes not immediately apparent or indeed consistent with first (premature?) impressions or conclusions.

10.1.2 Variable overhead cost variance analysis

Although here we concentrate purely on *variable* overheads, the following short discussion regarding overhead absorption rates is equally applicable to the opening step in the analysis of fixed overhead cost variances. The first step in analysing overhead (i.e. indirect cost) variances is to calculate the budgeted or standard 'overhead absorption rate' (OR). This opening step may not always be necessary as occasionally in examinations the OR(s) will already be provided for you in the question itself. This is also the case in Table 10.1 where you were presented with the ORs as part of the variance analysis data (£5/h variable and £4/h fixed). If required to make the calculation, however, simply divide original budgeted overhead by the relevant absorption base, in our case *production labour hours*, but remember there are other possible bases available too for overhead absorption (e.g. machine hours, see section 2.2 of Chapter 2). If Table 10.1 had not readily made the ORs available to you, then first the general calculation followed by the individual computations (using our data) for the variable overhead rate (VOR) and, for later reference in section 10.2, the fixed overhead absorption rate (FOR) are as follows:

$$\text{General} \qquad \frac{\text{Budgeted overheads}}{\text{Budgeted hours}} \qquad = \text{OR per hour}$$

$$\text{Variable} \qquad \frac{\pounds 62{,}500}{12{,}500\text{h}} \qquad = \pounds 5/\text{h VOR}$$

$$\text{Fixed} \qquad \frac{\pounds 50{,}000}{12{,}500\text{h}} \qquad = \pounds 4/\text{h FOR}$$

Before embarking on Activity 10.3 note that, when adopting the formulaic approach to variable overhead analysis, the notation is the same as for labour variances except that now:

▶ instead of actual wage rate AR denotes actual overhead rate; and
▶ instead of standard wage rate SR denotes standard VOR.

Once more base your variance calculations and suitable observations on the data provided for you in Table 10.2.

Required: Apply both framework as well as formulaic approaches to analyse the total variance for variable overhead cost into its dimensions of expenditure and efficiency.

The framework analysis of the variances required in Activity 10.3 is as follows:

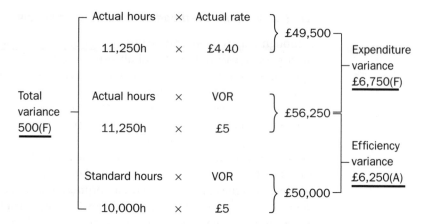

In order to cross-check the total variance's dimensions on the right-hand side of the above framework, once again insert your data into the generic formulae for expenditure and efficiency variances:

Expenditure: $(AR - SR) \times AH$
Variance = $(£4.40 - £5) \times 11{,}250 = £6{,}750(F)$

Efficiency: $(AH - SH) \times SR$
Variance = $(11{,}250 - 10{,}000) \times £5 = 6{,}250(A)$

In the case of overheads (applicable to fixed as well as variable) you need to be crystal clear that comparison of the framework's top level with its bottom tier is tantamount to comparing overhead actually *incurred* with overhead *absorbed*. Actual variable overhead expenditure (of £49,500, i.e. variable overhead incurred) is less than the variable overhead recovered by the 10,000 standard hours which have been produced at a VOR of £5/h (£50,000, i.e. variable overhead absorbed). What results here is an (F) total variance of £500 which, put most simply, is the 'over-absorption' of variable overhead. Indeed, the general rule for overhead variance analysis (again applying equally to fixed overhead cost) is that:

▶ *over*-absorptions are reflected by *favourable* variances; while
▶ *under*-absorptions are reflected by *adverse* variances.

Your final observation would be to realise that where labour hours are used for variable overhead absorption then, in variance analysis, because the absorption rate is a 'labour-hour' based one, the variable overhead efficiency variance will always be consistent with the labour efficiency variance in terms of either (F) or (A).

Contribution variance
You will recall from earlier studies (Chapter 4 in particular on the marginal costing technique) that variable costs deducted from sales value results in the important management accounting concept/notion of *contribution* towards fixed overhead and profit. As we have now just finished analysing all the vari-

able cost variances, this is the most suitable point in the text to introduce the *contribution variance*. To give it its technically more accurate and complete title, it is referred to as the 'sales volume contribution variance'. This expanded title makes clear reference to the final couple of elements involved in variance analysis which we deal with next in section 10.2, i.e. *sales* variances and the further, third dimension of analysis called *volume*.

Referring once more to Table 10.1, the contribution 'sub-total' level is the stage at which all variable costs have been deducted from sales. At both this level and the 'bottom-line' profit level as well, the total figure of £26,000 (A) is pre-fixed by a minus sign. This indicates *loss* of contribution between the original fixed budget and the flexed-down (standards) budget which relates to the actual 5,000 unit sales activity level achieved. Budgeted/standard contribution is £20.80 per unit, i.e. variable costs of material (£25.20), labour (£14) and variable overhead (£10) totalling £49.20 deducted from sales price of £70. Because 1,250 units less than that originally planned (fixed budget of 6250u *less* flexed budget of 5000u actual sales) is representative of the actual level of activity, then 1,250 'lots' of £20.80 contribution have actually been lost. This is viewed as a bad result and therefore is reflected in an adverse contribution variance – meaning there is £26,000 less money available (compared with the original plan/expectation) to contribute towards fixed overhead costs and profit, which itself is reduced from the original budgeted £80,000 to a lower flexed profit of £54,000.

At this conclusion of section 10.1 you might fruitfully imagine both Tables 10.1 and 10.2 merged together. Such a merger would produce a detailed variance analysis operating statement compiled according to the *marginal costing* technique. You ought to remember that under marginal costing, fixed overheads are not afforded detailed treatment, they are not subjected to the absorption process, but are merely treated as a lump sum amount ('period' cost) and written off in total against the contribution for the relevant period. Similarly at this point in variance analysis, the fixed overhead originally budgeted (£50,000) would simply be compared with the amount actually incurred (£48,000) and written off as a single expenditure variance of 2,000(F) against contribution.

Under the absorption costing technique however, as you would expect, fixed overhead cost is afforded a greater degree of detailed analysis (as we shall see in the next section). Indeed the chapter concludes at the end of section 10.2 with a complete variance analysis operating statement based on an *absorption costing* presentation of the data. However, it is recognised in management accounting, as Part 2 of the book largely testified, that for managerial decision-making purposes marginal costing as a technique (also see Chapter 4) is a more suitable approach to providing decision information than is absorption costing. In examinations you need to keep a keen eye on the requirement of the question. Generally a full absorption costing approach will be asked for in examinations, but be aware that the 'alternative' marginal cost treatment may constitute the more suitable vehicle for management information purposes in certain circumstances.

As the variance analysis in section 10.2 is conducted in terms of absorption costing, then the aforementioned sales volume *contribution* variance (which is a marginal costing variance) needs to be more appropriately broken down into its two more detailed (absorption costing) 'volume' dimensions of:

▶ a sales volume *profit* variance; and
▶ an *overall* fixed overhead volume variance.

10.2 Analysis of fixed overhead and sales variances

As we mentioned earlier (see the second paragraph of section 10.1) our variance analysis data base in Table 10.2 contains in the end 'variance' column only total cost variances, with the exception of fixed overhead, which we now analyse in detail. The fixed overhead variance of £2,000(F) is not a total variance – it is only the *expenditure* aspect of fixed cost, as is the sales variance of £10,000(F) which reflects only the selling *price* dimension of revenue. In fact, it is important at this stage that you are fully aware that *all* the expenditure (or 'price' in the case of sales) and efficiency variance aspects of our analysis appear in that final variance column. As you know through your experience of Activities 10.1 to 10.3, the total variable cost variances have already been sub-divided into their expenditure and efficiency component parts in section 10.1. In addition to (and including) the price/expenditure dimensions of sales/fixed overhead variances respectively shown in the variance column, we now need to look further at the detail of the extra dimension in both sales and fixed overhead analysis known as *volume*. It is also worth noting at this point that the total at the foot of the variance column of £1,000(F) is the sum-total of all expenditure (or price as regards sales) and efficiency variances. This (F) variance explains the difference between a standard, expected profit of £54,000 (shown at the foot of the 'flexed budget' column) and an actual profit of £55,000 that has resulted in reality (at the bottom of the 'actual' column). First consider analysis of the sales variances.

10.2.1 Sales variance analysis

You might recall a brief analogy earlier with cost variances relating expenditure to one side of a coin and efficiency to the other – the two variance aspects together comprising the whole coin, i.e. the total variance. With sales variances, selling price replaces expenditure on the one side and sales volume substitutes for efficiency on the other, but again both sides together make up the whole/total sales variance. Essentially, a total sales variance arises because of two differences existing between actual and standard/budgeted data, namely:

▶ the standard sales price not actually being charged; and
▶ the original, fixed budget level of sales activity (planned sales volume) not actually occurring – remember, the sales volume that actually occurs forms the basis of the flexed budget activity level (and provides the relevant standards for analysing all *non-volume* aspects of variances).

Analysis of the first difference (due to sales price) employs identical logic to that used for materials price variance calculation in section 10.1.1. In fact, the same formula can be adopted with only minor changes to the notation, *viz*:

Price: (AP – SP) × AQ, where: 'P' now denotes selling price and 'Q' represents sales volume.

Indeed, *only* the formulaic approach to variance analysis can be used for sales variances as the basis for evaluating the second difference (due to sales volume) is not simply standard price (as, for example, is the base for materials efficiency/usage variance calculation (see section 10.1.1). The basis for computing the sales volume variance is the budgeted profit (BP) margin per unit, whilst it is the budgeted volume (BQ) that is compared with actual – so even the formulaic notation is quite unfamiliar, as:

$$\text{Volume: (AQ} - \text{BQ)} \times \text{BP}$$

It is the application of a budgeted profit *margin* rather than a standard *price* that renders use of the framework approach to variance analysis unsuitable. This description will become more apparent as you undertake Activity 10.4.

ACTIVITY 10.4

Base your variance calculations and any observations upon the data you are provided with in *both* Tables 10.1 and 10.2.

Required: Apply only the formulaic approach in order to analyse the sales variances into the dimensions of sales price (i.e. the selling price variance) and volume (i.e. the sales volume profit variance).

Insert your figures into the relevant formulae/equations required by Activity 10.4 thus:

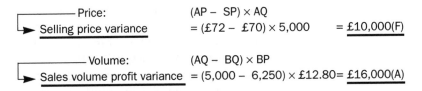

Price:
Selling price variance

$$(\text{AP} - \text{SP)} \times \text{AQ}$$
$$= (\pounds72 - \pounds70) \times 5{,}000 \quad = \underline{\underline{\pounds10{,}000\text{(F)}}}$$

Volume:
Sales volume profit variance

$$(\text{AQ} - \text{BQ)} \times \text{BP}$$
$$= (5{,}000 - 6{,}250) \times \pounds12.80 = \underline{\underline{\pounds16{,}000\text{(A)}}}$$

Remember that with *cost* variance analysis a higher actual cost price than standard results in an adverse variance (i.e. more actual cost than planned). However, you can plainly see here that with *sales* variances a higher actual selling price compared to standard generates a favourable variance, because more sales revenue than standard results. Although, on the other hand, the fall in volume (causing lower profit) more than adversely outweighs the favourable benefit of a higher price. You should note that this instance is a perfect example of classic economic theory in action; the higher the sales price, the lower the sales demand. The £16,000(A) sales volume profit variance is one of two ingredients of the sales volume contribution variance discussed at the end of section 10.1. The other, second ingredient is the 'overall' fixed overhead volume variance. So now we turn to analysing fixed overhead variances.

10.2.2 Fixed overhead variance analysis

You are already familiar with the new dimension of 'volume' because it has just appeared in the context of sales variances. However, with the analysis of sales it was simply one side of the coin (replacing efficiency) – if you permit me to continue use of the coin analogy, with fixed overheads we would need a three-sided coin! This is because volume now is *additional* to (not a replacement for) the aspects of expenditure and efficiency which have featured throughout almost all of the analysis. The added dimension arises here because fixed overhead, unlike all the other cost components, does not change with fluctuations in the level or volume of activity. Hence, there is also now a volume reason for actual results varying from budget/standard, and it needs accounting for along with the expenditure and efficiency variances encountered so far.

At the start of section 10.1.2, dealing with variable overheads, it was stated that the first step in overhead variance analysis was to determine the budgeted overhead absorption rate. This was done for fixed overheads as well as variable at the end of that section's opening paragraph, ascertaining the fixed overhead rate (FOR) of £4 per hour. As in Activity 10.5 we also aggregate fixed *plus* variable overhead in a final analysis of 'total' overhead variances, then we need to determine a total overhead rate (TOR). This can be achieved simply by adding together the fixed and variable hourly rates already ascertained (i.e. fixed of £4 + variable of £5 = TOR of £9 per hour) or by taking total budgeted overhead and dividing it by budgeted labour hours, thus:

$$\frac{\text{Budgeted total (fixed + variable) overhead}}{\text{Budgeted hours}} = \frac{£50,000 + £62,500}{12,500\text{h}} = £9/\text{h TOR}$$

We now also depart here from using the key generic formulae applied throughout the variance analysis so far. Assuming you are now completely familiar with the formulaic approach through your regular insertion of the relevant data into the earlier formulae in Activities 10.1 to10.4, we now turn to a purely framework approach for fixed (and total) overheads for which the formulae would be rather more complex, and perhaps a little too unwieldy to handle, as we now incorporate the added, third dimension of volume into our overhead analysis. To accommodate the additional dimension, our three-level framework used previously now needs to become a four-tier construct. The extra level is inserted at the second-tier stage (down from framework top), and is described as 'budgeted expenditure' – containing the relevant overhead detail from the fixed, original budget column in Table 10.1.

ACTIVITY **10.5**

Base your variance calculations and related observations upon the data provided for you in *both* Tables 10.1 and 10.2.

Required: Apply only the framework approach in your analysis of fixed overhead and total overhead into their three dimensions of expenditure, volume and efficiency.

Consider first in your response to Activity 10.5 *fixed* overhead in the newly required four-level framework construction as follows:

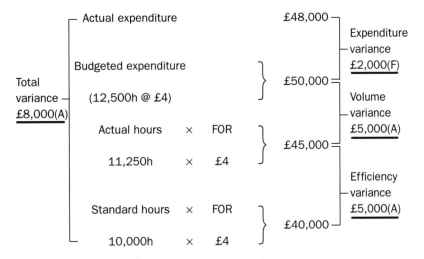

Second, insert the relevant figures for *total* (fixed + variable) overhead into the four-level framework construct, thus:

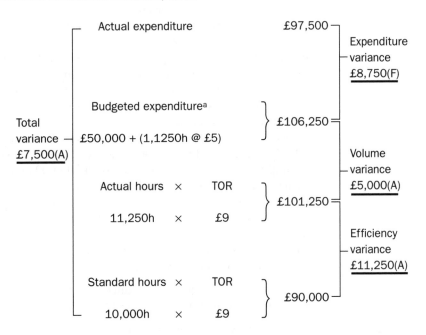

Note: [a]Original budgeted fixed overhead (£50,000) does not flex while variable overhead (@ VOR of £5) flexes in accordance with actual hours/activity.

The analysis of total overheads is really only provided for completeness, but you should observe how it is simply a consolidation of the variable overhead cost variances analysed earlier in Activity 10.3 (section 10.1.2) blended with the fixed overhead variance analysis carried out first in Activity 10.5. We now focus further comments purely on the analysis of fixed overheads.

As you experienced earlier (with variable overheads) comparing the framework's top level with bottom level is in fact the very exercise of working out whether there has been an under- or over-absorption of fixed overhead. This involves comparing fixed overhead actually incurred (top level-actual expenditure) with bottom level-fixed overhead absorbed. The total variance reflects the under-/over-absorption of fixed overhead. As actual overhead incurred (£48,000) is greater than the fixed overhead absorbed by the 10,000 standard hours recovering overhead at an absorption rate of £4/h (£40,000) then there has been an under-recovery of overhead (of £8,000). Such an under-absorption is a bad (adverse) result. Recall here the general rule (from section 10.1.2) that over-absorptions are reflected in (F) variances whilst under-absorptions are manifested in (A) variances. You would find it particularly beneficial here to quickly re-read section 2.2.1 of Chapter 2 (particularly the second half) which first discussed in some detail under/over-absorptions of overhead.

The fixed overhead *expenditure* variance is fairly self-explanatory as £2,000(F) simply means less money has actually been spent on fixed overheads than originally budgeted. More detailed observations are perhaps called for in order to appreciate more fully the features of the fixed overhead *volume* and *efficiency* variances. Unlike efficiency, volume variances arise with respect to fixed overheads only (efficiency applies to both fixed *and* variable).

A volume variance often is referred to by other descriptions such as 'capacity usage' or just simply 'capacity'. I prefer the double-barrelled composite description of 'volume-capacity' or even more preferably (being superior in descriptive quality and accuracy) the term 'pure' volume variance. As implied by the very names themselves (volume or capacity), this variance reflects the difference between planned or budgeted capacity and the actual capacity level achieved, that is the number of hours actually worked. Lower actual usage (11,250h) compared with the budgeted usage of capacity (12,500h) is here highlighted by the (A) variance between £45,000 and £50,000. 'Pure' *volume-capacity* variances are inevitably the automatic outcome of over-/underutilisation of planned capacity and can always be calculated simply by evaluating such over-/underusage at the FOR – in this case underused capacity of 1,250h (12,500 budgeted less 11,250 actual) at a £4 FOR = £5,000(A). Over-/ under-capacity usages can conveniently be paralleled with over-/under-absorptions in that a further general rule emerges, namely:

▶ over-capacity usage always results in (F) variances; while
▶ under-capacity usage always results in (A) variances

An efficiency variance with fixed overhead is based on exactly the same principles as with variable overhead cost (see section 10.1.2). Here it is reflected in the inefficient working of 1,250h more than standard, evaluated at FOR of £4 = £5,000 (A), coincidentally the same as volume. It is sometimes called a 'productivity' or, perhaps more frequently, a *volume-efficiency* variance (not to be confused with the 'pure' volume-capacity variance). You might notice that, to avoid any such confusion, it is the latter more common name for the efficiency variance which in fact indicates the reason why, in the previous paragraph, the volume variance was said to be more accurately referred to as the 'pure' volume variance. The alternative term 'volume-efficiency' comes about because convention, on occasions, teams up efficiency with volume-capacity to create a combined *overall* volume variance. Though not shown explicitly in Activity 10.5, this 'overall' volume variance in terms of fixed overhead would be £10,000(A), resulting from the efficiency variance of £5,000(A) *plus* the 'pure' volume variance of £5,000(A). 'Pure' volume clearly and simply measures over-/underusage of capacity and excludes any efficiency aspect. In examination questions you may be called upon to perform a volume variance calculation. As a general guide, if only overhead expenditure is asked for in addition to volume, then provide the combined 'overall' volume variance (perhaps with a note of its further breakdown into volume-capacity and efficiency for the examiner's added information). However, if both overhead expenditure and efficiency/productivity variances are specifically called for as well as volume then give the 'pure' volume variance.

Immediately after Activity 10.5 it was mentioned that the *total* overhead variance analysis was provided purely for completeness. In order to give you the complete picture, the combined 'overall' total volume variance for overheads is given directly below, followed by the closing description of the *profit variance* which ends with a summary operating statement of all variances analysed in this chapter. First, the 'overall' total overhead (fixed + variable) volume variance comprises:

'Pure' volume-capacity	£5,000(A)	
		£16,250(A)
Volume-efficiency/productivity	£11,250(A)	

Profit variance

There is nothing mystical or difficult to comprehend about the profit variance! It is in fact probably the simplest of all the variances to understand as it is merely the sum-total of all variances (sales and cost) put together. Another way of viewing it is that it provides the reconciliation between the original planned profit (i.e. fixed budget profit of £80,000) and the actual profit resulting in reality (i.e. £55,000). If you look again at the 'bottom-line' profit level in Tables 10.1 and 10.2 you can clearly see the comparison in the figures at the foot of those tables. So the profit variance amounts to £25,000(A) – profit expectation of £80,000 less actual realisation of £55,000.

Rather than looking to every single variance for the composition of the profit variance (this is done for you anyway at the end of the chapter, in the variance analysis operating statement reconciling original budget with actual profits) you might finally consider it in the shape of its much briefer 'two-fold' make up. The opening paragraph of section 10.2 focused upon the total £1,000(F) figure at the foot of the 'variance' column in Table 10.2 representing the difference between standard (£54,000) and actual (£55,000) profits. There it was asserted that this column total is reflective of all sales price, expenditure and efficiency variances rolled into one! That is one 'fold' in the profit variance's two-fold build-up. The other 'fold' is embodied in the (adverse) contribution variance which we discussed in detail at the end of section 10.1. The contribution variance is a single, compact reflection of the effect of the third dimensional feature of variance analysis, i.e. volume. This aspect of the analysis links the original activity level planned (6,250 units) with the actual level achieved (5,000 units). In short, the volume difference is highlighted by the vitally important exercise of *flexing*, transforming the original fixed budget into the more realistic (for comparison purposes) flexed budget which provides the standards to measure against actual. As we saw earlier (at the end of section 10.1) the contribution variance is £26,000(A) and this is the total of the 'flex allowance' column in Table 10.1. If you put this together with the 'variance' column total you can see clearly the two-fold composition of the profit variance, thus:

	(£)
'Variance' column total (i.e. sales price/expenditure and efficiency)	1,000(F)
'Flex allowance' column total (i.e. volume)	26,000(A)
Profit variance	25,000(A)

In turn the contribution variance can be seen in its disaggregated volume variance form of:

	(£)
Sales volume profit variance	16,000(A)
'Overall' fixed overhead volume variance	10,000(A)
Fixed budget-flexed budget volume adjustment/allowance	26,000(A)

Containing this disaggregation of the volume effect, the complete variance analysis operating statement appears summarised below. It is based on an *absorption costing* presentation of the data (therefore excluding contribution variance which is now in the form of the above breakdown). However, remember that for purposes of management decision information a 'contribution/ marginal costing' format would be preferable.

Can you redraft ...? the Variance Analysis Operating Statement below into a summary marginal costing format, clearly showing the (sales volume) contribution variance for management's decision information purposes linking budgeted with actual contribution.

VARIANCE ANALYSIS OPERATING STATEMENT
(ABSORPTION COSTING)

	(£)	(£)	(£)
Budgeted profit			80,000
Variances			
Sales			
Selling price variance	10,000(F)		
Sales volume profit variance	16,000(A)		
Total variance		6,000(A)	
Raw materials			
Price variance	11,000(A)		
Usage variance	10,500(F)		
Total variance		500(A)	

	(£)	(£)	(£)
Production labour			
Rate variance	2,250(A)		
Efficiency variance	8,750(A)		
Total variance		11,000(A)	
Variable overheads			
Expenditure variance	6,750(F)		
Efficiency variance	6,250(A)		
Total variance		500(F)	
Fixed overheads			
Expenditure variance	2,000(F)		
Volume variance	10,000(A)		
Total variance		8,000(A)	
Profit variance			25,000(A)
Actual profit			55,000

Answer

Variance analysis operating statement (Marginal Costing)

	(£)	(£)
Budgeted contribution (see Table 10.1)		130,000
Marginal cost variances		
Sales price variance	10,000 (F)	
Variable costs		
Raw materials	500 (A)	
Production labour	11,000 (A)	
Variable overheads	500 (F)	1,000 (A)
		129,000
Sales volume contribution variance		26,000 (A)
Actual contribution (see Table 10.2)		103,000
(*less* actual) Fixed overhead costs		48,000
Actual profit		55,000

		(£)
	*Budgeted profit	80,000
add	Budgeted fixed overheads	50,000
	Budgeted contribution	130,000

Self-check questions

10.1 Shown below is the standard prime cost of a tube of industrial adhesive, which is the only product manufactured in one department of Gum plc.

Industrial adhesive

	£ per tube	£ per tube
Materials: Powder	1.50	
Chemicals	0.60	
Tube	0.30	2.40
Labour – Mixing and pouring		1.80
Total Standard Prime Cost		£4.20

The standard material allowance for each tube of adhesive is 2 lbs of powder, $\frac{1}{4}$ litre of chemical and one tube. The standard wage rate for mixing and pouring is £4.50 per hour.

During the previous month 4,500 tubes of adhesive were produced, there were no work-in-progress stocks at the beginning or end of the month, and the receipts and issues of materials during the month are shown below:

	Powder	Chemicals	Tubes
Opening stock:	1,500 lbs	200 litres	100 tubes
Purchases:	10,000 lbs at 70p per lb	600 litres at £2.30 per litre	200 tubes at 40p each
		600 litres at £2.50 per litre	5,000 tubes at 30p each
Issues:	9,800 lbs	1,050 litres	4,520 tubes

The above materials are used exclusively in the production of the adhesive and it is the policy of the company to calculate any price variance when the materials are purchased.

The direct employees operating the mixing and pouring plant worked a total of 2,050 hours during the previous month and earned gross wages of £8,910.

Required:

(a) Calculate for the previous month the following variances from standard cost:
   (i) Materials price variance, analysed as you consider appropriate.
   (ii) Materials usage variance, analysed as you consider appropriate.
   (iii) Direct labour efficiency variance.
   (iv) Direct wages rate variance.
(b) Discuss the possible causes of the material variances and the direct labour efficiency variance.

(Chartered Association of Certified Accountants)

10.2 The following standard costs apply to a product which normally sells for £45 each.

	£
Direct raw materials 15 kg at 60p kg	9.00
Fixing items 6 at 3p each	0.18
Direct Wages 6 hours at £2.00 hr.	12.00
Overheads (recovered on direct labour hour basis)	18.00
Total standard cost of production	£39.18

Last month's results were:

3,400 units were produced; sales were 4,500 units; Income £198,000.

54,000 kilos of raw material were used at a total cost of £31,860.

21,000 fixing items were used at 2.95p each.

Direct wages – £40,000 paid for 20,550 hours worked.

Actual overhead incurred was £61,000.

Stock at beginning of month was 2,000 units valued at standard cost.

Required:

(a) Calculate the appropriate variances from standard for:
  (i)   raw materials;
  (ii) fixing items;
  (iii) direct wages;
  (iv) overheads;
  (v)   sales.

(b) Briefly comment on the likely causes of the direct wages variances.

(Association of Accounting Technicians)

10.3 The following statement has been produced for presentation to the general manager of Department X.

	Month ended 31 October		
	Original budget £	Actual result £	Variance £
Sales	600,000	550,000	(50,000)
Direct materials	150,000	130,000	20,000
Direct labour	200,000	189,000	11,000
Production overhead:			
Variable with direct labour	50,000	46,000	4,000
Fixed	25,000	29,000	(4,000)
Variable selling overhead	75,000	72,000	3,000
Fixed selling overhead	50,000	46,000	4,000
Total costs	550,000	512,000	38,000
Profit	50,000	38,000	(12,000)
Direct labour hours	50,000	47,500	
Sales and production units	5,000	4,500	

Note: There are no opening and closing stocks.

The general manager says that this type of statement does not provide much relevant information for him. He also thought that the profit for the month would be well up to budget and was surprised to see a large adverse profit variance.

Required:

(a) Redraft the above statement in a form which would be more relevant for the general manager.

(b) Calculate all sales, material, labour and overhead variances and reconcile to the statement produced in (a).

(c) Produce a short report explaining the principle upon which your redrafted statement is based and what information it provides.

(Chartered Institute of Management Accountants)

10.4 BS Limited manufactures one standard product and operates a system of variance accounting using a fixed budget. As assistant management accountant you are responsible for preparing the monthly operating statements. Data from the budget, the standard product cost and actuals for the month ended 31 October 19X2 are given below.

Required:

Using the data given prepare the operating statement for the month ended 31 October 19X2 to show the budgeted profit; the variances for direct materials, direct wages, overhead and sales, each analysed into causes; and actual profit.

BUDGETED AND STANDARD COST DATA:

Budgeted sales and production for the month: 10,000 units
Standard cost for each unit of product:

Direct material:	X	10 kilograms @ £1 per kilogram
	Y	5 kilograms @ £5 per kilogram
Direct wages		5 hours @ £3 per hour

Fixed production overhead is obsorbed @ 200 per cent of direct wages

Budgeted sales price has been calculated to give a profit of 20 per cent of sales price.

ACTUAL DATA FOR MONTH ENDED 31 OCTOBER:

Production, 9,500 units sold at a price of 10 per cent higher than that budgeted.

Direct materials consumed:

| X | 96,000 kilograms @ £1.20 per kilogram |
| Y | 48,000 kilograms @ £4.70 per kilogram |

Direct wages incurred 46,000 hours @ £3.20 per hour
Fixed production overhead incurred £290,000

(Chartered Institute of Management Accountants)

Further study
••••••••••••••••

Arnold, J., Carsberg, B. and Scapens, R.W. (1980) *Topics in management accounting*, 1st edn, Philip Allan.

Arnold, J. and Hope, T. (1990) *Accounting for management decisions*, 2nd edn, Hemel Hempstead: Prentice-Hall.

Drury, C. (1992) *Management and cost accounting*, 3rd edn, London: Chapman and Hall.

Edwards, E. (1986) 'Installing and operating a standard costing system', in *Management Accounting*, December, Chartered Institute of Management Accountants.

Glautier, M. and Underdown, B. (1994) *Accounting theory and practice*, 5th edn, London: Pitman.

Horngren, C.T., Foster, G. and Datar, S. (1994) *Cost accounting – a managerial emphasis*, 8th edn, Hemel Hempstead: Prentice-Hall.

Layne, A. (1984) *Cost accounting – analysis and control*, 1st edn, London: Macmillan.

Pizzey, A. (1989) *Cost and management accounting*, 3rd edn, Paul Chapman Publishing.

Sizer, J. and Coulthurst, N. (1984) *A casebook of British management accounting*, 1st edn, Institute of Chartered Accountants in England and Wales.

Walker, J. (1989) 'The analysis of production overhead variances', in *Management Accounting*, June, Chartered Institute of Management Accountants.

Wheldon H. (1984) *Cost accounting*, 15th edn, London: Macdonald and Evans.

Wright, D. (1994) *A practical foundation in costing*, 1st edn, London: Routledge.

CHAPTER 11

Control of divisional management performance

Objectives
· · · · · · · · · · · · ·

By the end of this chapter you should be able to:

▶ Understand the nature of divisionalisation – its aim, benefits and problems within organisations.

▶ Describe responsibility accounting in the context of its structure based around control areas designated as responsibility centres.

▶ Apply suitable control techniques for appraising divisional managerial performance.

▶ Recognise and reconcile the inherent potential conflict between divisional managers' own vested interests and those of the divisionalised organisation.

Many organisations, usually larger groups of companies, carry out their activities through divisionalised structures. Not many years ago, for example, Ford Motor Company which had never in its long history produced luxury cars, acquired the British car manufacturing interests of Jaguar, thus forming a new luxury car division within the firm. However, managerial control of divisionalised organisations brings with it its own particular and, in some respects, unique problems. This chapter addresses such problematic issues through an introduction to a management appraisal system known as 'responsibility accounting', and furthermore through the (divisional) managerial performance control measures of 'return on investment' and 'net residual income'. Prior to your study of these specific control issues, however, the general nature of *divisionalisation* is first of all described

11.1 Divisionalisation and responsibility accounting
· ·

The overall aim of divisionalisation lies in the improvement of group operational efficiency with respect to increasing corporate profitability and attaining organisational objectives (recall phase I of the managerial planning, decision-making and control process/framework established at the very outset of the book in section 1.2). Achievement of this general aim, largely through delegation of managerial authority, may also help organisations to realise certain subsidiary aims which, in turn, may lead to the following principal benefits being derived from a policy of divisionalisation:

▶ *Specialised local knowledge* as divisional managers have 'on the spot' contact with prevailing local conditions, and are therefore more able to make faster, controlled and well-informed plans and decisions.

▶ *Motivation* of divisional managers to achieve higher performance levels is improved through delegation of central authority giving greater freedom, responsibility and independence in planning, control and decision-making.

▶ *A suitable training ground* is provided for non-senior management from which to develop and progress to higher levels of managerial responsibility.

▶ *Top management* is allowed to concentrate upon major corporate objectives, devoting more (or all) of its time to strategic longer-term planning for the organisation as a whole.

▶ *Communications* are improved through shorter and speedier local lines of communication together with a reduced need for head-office contact, thereby cutting down the possibility of errors and/or delays in communication.

▶ *Diversification* through the 'portfolio effect' of investing in a variety of operational areas/activities helps to reduce, and ultimately minimise, the organisation's general level of risk.

In contrast to the above advantages attributed to divisionalised structures, you need to be aware of the serious disadvantage that exists mainly in regard to the control problem of *sub-optimisation*. Sub-optimal plans and decisions may occur when individual divisional managers are tempted to take action that is optimal in terms of their own particular divisional best interests, but which causes the organisation as a whole to incur extra costs/loss of benefits that outweigh the corresponding gains realised. This problem area is dealt with more fully later on (in section 11.2.2).

11.1.1 Responsibility accounting

Responsibility accounting can be defined as a system of accounting which separates costs and revenues into spheres of managerial responsibility in order to appraise the performance achieved by those managers to whom authority has been delegated. The system is an important control concept and is particularly appropriate where organisations operate on a divisionalised basis. Individual managers in organisations where responsibility accounting is practised are held responsible for controlling different elements of operations which ultimately reflect efficient or inefficient performance. Such performance may be in terms of such things as effective cost control, levels of profitability attained, and economical/optimal use of capital resources.

A principal feature of divisionalisation is *delegation of authority* to managers to make plans and control decisions. In a responsibility accounting system, individuals (from divisional managers down to shop-floor forepersons) are held responsible for their specific managerial activities which necessarily involve the making of operating plans/decisions. These individual managers are then further responsible for the costs and benefits that flow from such control activities. However, it is vitally important that these systems are suitably designed to ensure that the degree of responsibility demanded of a manager is equalled by a commensurate amount of delegated authority of a level sufficient to carry out the assigned duties.

The routine operation of a responsibility accounting system needs to be based on an organised framework. Such a framework comprises areas of control activity known as *responsibility centres*.

11.1.2 Responsibility centres

From a hierarchical standpoint you might consider responsibility centres as capable of being classified on three distinctly separate levels, thus:

▶ Level (1): Cost centre.
▶ Level (2): Profit centre.
▶ Level (3): Investment centre.

You can conveniently view the above sequence as a progression, moving upwards from (1) to (3), and relating to increasingly higher levels of managerial authority and responsibility. The nature of this hierarchical structure is presented for you in Table 11.1.

Cost centre

A *cost centre* is an area of responsibility to which costs are attributed for purposes of cost collection and control. It may be a particular department or section; a machine group or an individual machine; a group of people (e.g. salespersons) or even an individual salesperson. You encountered many such examples very early on in the book when the role of cost centres was discussed in Chapter 2 (section 2.1.2), and you would benefit here from a quick re-read of that particular section.

Establishment of cost centres is fundamental to management planning and control because often they play a sort of 'dual' role in so far as they can also serve as *budget centres,* thus facilitating cost control by providing a base for comparison of budgeted costs with actual. Again you have experienced this planning and control aspect previously (in both Chapters 9 and 10). For purposes of responsibility accounting, cost centre costs should be clearly identified as to whether they are *controllable* or *non-controllable*. It is vitally important that

table 11.1

Responsibility centre hierarchy

Responsibility centre	Areas of responsibility			
Investment centre	Profit on investment	Revenue less (costs) $\Big\}$	=	Profit
Profit centre		Revenue less (costs) $\Big\}$	=	Profit
Cost centre		Costs		

cost centre managers should not be held responsible for costs incurred due to factors outside of their control. Furthermore, management appraisal of their performance in terms of cost control should be based only on the 'controllable' elements of cost. We return to this issue again later in section 11.2.2.

Profit centre

A *profit centre* is an area of responsibility to which both costs *and* revenues are attributed for purposes of assessing profit performance. Profit centres extend the cost centre principle to include managerial responsibility for ensuring that departments, processes, sections of businesses as well as whole divisions themselves operate as profitable concerns. Divisionalisation within organisations in particular requires that profit centres be established, and furthermore that divisional managers be held responsible for both the costs and benefits resulting from their planning and control activities.

Investment centre

An *investment centre* is an area of responsibility in which a divisional manager is held responsible not solely for profits, but also for the extent to which they reflect the efficient use of *capital* invested in that manager's division. Investment centres represent the furthest stage in the devolution of managerial control/ planning authority and responsibility within divisionalised organisations.

Although delegated authority and responsibility is for divisional profit relative to divisional investment, you should note that often major capital investment decisions (see Chapter 8) are normally effected outside individual divisions by central (i.e. head-office) rather than divisional management. Divisional managerial performance appraisal within investment centres is therefore based upon two elements – *profit* and *investment*. Consequently a technique most commonly used for measuring divisional performance is the return (i.e. profit) on investment (ROI) criterion. You may already be familiar with the ROI technique from your financial accounting studies where it would (probably) have been referred to by its alternative name of 'return on capital employed' (ROCE). Widely used in ratio analysis, being the *primary* financial ratio, you can regard the ROCE measure for all practical purposes as identical to ROI.

11.2 Measurement of divisional performance
....

In this section we shall consider appraisal of divisional management performance with respect to the two most relevant forms of accounting measure, *viz*:

▶ Return on investment (ROI) technique.
▶ Net residual income (NRI) technique.

11.2.1 Return on investment

The ROI statistic is a *relative* measure expressed in a single percentage ratio figure. As a measurement technique it can be used in a twofold application sense, both to:

- ▶ compare divisional performances within an organisation (in this way it serves as an internal *control* technique); and
- ▶ decide upon the acceptance or rejection of investment opportunities that become available to the organisation (in this sense serving as a *planning* decision technique).

ROI can be calculated on both a primary and a secondary level:

(1) *Primary level:* ROI $= \dfrac{\text{Net profit}}{\text{Net investment in assets}} \times 100 = \%$

where: 'net profit' is the level of return; and 'net investment in assets' is one of several possible bases for measuring the level of capital employed in an organisation/division.

The above primary ratio in (1) can be disaggregated into two subsidiary or secondary measures of divisional performance: (i) profit margin on sales; and (ii) asset turnover. The formula for the ROI statistic at this subsidiary level is as follows:

(2) *Secondary level:* ROI $= \left[\dfrac{\text{Net profit}}{\text{Sales}} \times \dfrac{\text{Sales}}{\text{Net assets}} \right] \times 100 = \%$

Can you calculate ...? the ROI on both (i) primary level and (ii) secondary level, given the following data:

Level of return (i.e. profit): £180,000
Level of asset investment (i.e. capital employed): £1.5 million
Level of sales (i.e. turnover): £2.25 million

Answer

(i)   Primary level

$$\text{ROI} = \frac{\text{Net profit}}{\text{Net investment}} = \frac{£180,000}{£1,500,000} \times 100 = \underline{12\%}$$

(ii)   Secondary level

$$\text{ROI} = \left[\frac{\text{Net profit}}{\text{Sales}} \times \frac{\text{Sales}}{\text{Net assets}} \right] \times 100$$

$$= \left[\frac{£180,000}{£2,250,000} \times \frac{£2,250,000}{£1,500,000} \right] \times 100$$

$$= [0.08 \times 1.5] \times 100 = 12\%$$

Profit margin on sales = 8%; Asset turnover = 1.5 times.

table 11.2
**ROI improvement
through divisional
management action**

Management action		Effect on ROI
Reduce level of costs	} =	Improvement in *profit* element
Increase profit mark-up on sales		
Reduce net assets employed	} =	Improvement in *asset utilisation* element
Increase level of sales		

The breakdown in (2) above emphasises that the ROI statistic is not only a function of *profitability* but is also a result of *asset utilisation*. Divisional performance can be improved in terms of ROI by management action involving either, or both, of these elements, summarised for you in Table 11.2.

When ROI is used for purposes of comparative divisional performance care needs to be exercised to ensure that, as far as possible, the bases for both net profit and net investment figures are determined by the use of 'uniform' accounting principles and procedures. Uniform accounting systems would, for example, adopt only one of the various possible bases that reflect capital employed as standard. In our illustration above we used net investment in assets as the base as opposed to, for instance, the level of shareholders' equity – others are possible. But consistency in the adoption of one as a standard base is crucial if meaningful comparisons are to be drawn between divisions and their relative efficiency in the use of capital.

For purposes of appraising a divisional manager's performance you need to clearly differentiate between cost and investment items which are within the control of divisional managerial authority and those items that lie outside the manager's control. Here you might recall our earlier comments about this important criterion of responsibility accounting systems that a manager should only be held accountable for (and hence managerial performance appraisal based upon) those cost and investment items that lie within the manager's sphere of control. To reinforce this fundamental principle further consider Table 11.3, which presents a typical divisional income (i.e. profit) statement suitable for control and appraisal purposes. Read the table in conjunction with the discussion in the following couple of paragraphs.

Variable cost of sales items, which are controllable on a divisional basis, when deducted from divisional sales (both internal and external) will give a *divisional contribution* figure. This amount then contributes towards covering controllable divisional fixed costs, which are inclusive of depreciation charged against the division's controllable investment in fixed assets.

The resulting *controllable operating income* represents the profit measure upon which the divisional manager's performance appraisal should be based. Subsequent accounting for 'non-controllable' items is then necessary to further determine *divisional net income*. This final net figure represents profit after considering all non-controllable items that would include any arbitrary allocations or apportionments of central costs by way of charges for head-office administration and services (such as group computer facilities, training and premises). In short, the key level for managerial appraisal purposes is that of divisional 'controllable' profit.

table 11.3

Measurement of divisional profit centre performance

Divisional income statement		
	(£)	(£)
Revenue (from sales)		
Inter-divisional transfers	XX	
External sales	XX	
Divisional sales revenue		XXX
Variable costs (controllable)		
Direct cost of sales	(XX)	
Variable divisional overhead	(XX)	(XXX)
Divisional contribution		XXX
Fixed costs		
Controllable fixed divisional overhead	(XX)	
Depreciation on controllable fixed asset investment:	(XX)	(XXX)
Controllable operating income		XXX
Non-controllable costs		
Non-controllable divisional overhead	(XX)	
Depreciation on non-controllable fixed asset investment	(XX)	
Allocated/apportioned central charges	(XX)	(XXX)
Divisional net income		£XX

The limitations of ROI

The principal drawback connected with the use of the ROI measure is that it can allow *sub-optimal* planning decisions to be taken by divisional managers. A manager whose performance is appraised on the basis of ROI will be unwilling to accept projects and opportunities which do not realise a rate of return at least equal to the current ROI being earned by that division. In order to maintain divisional performance levels, managers will reject investment opportunities that fall short of the required ROI because the effect of their acceptance would be to dilute or reduce the divisional manager's overall ROI. Activity 11.1 will help illustrate this control problem.

ACTIVITY 11.1

Mick Baxter is one of the divisional managers in Cavy plc. The current level of asset investment in his division stands at £4 million with a current return of £800,000 profit. A new project opportunity is available which would involve additional investment of £1.6 million with an estimated £240,000 of income being generated as return on the new investment amount. Mick's divisional performance is appraised on the basis of the ROI technique.

Required: Guided by the ROI investment criterion would Mick be willing to undertake the new project opportunity? Show relevant calculations.

Your relevant calculations should take the form of the workings in the following summary exhibit:

	Current position	New project	New position
Investment level (£000)	4,000	1,600	5,600
Income from investment (£000)	800	240	1,040
ROI:	20%	15%	18.6%

In the light of these calculations, you can see that the ROI investment measurement technique would lead Mick to reject the new investment opportunity because it would lower the *overall* ROI earned by the division from its current requirement of 20 per cent to a diluted return of 18.6 per cent. Mick's investment planning decision here to reject the project opportunity, however, may be sub-optimal in terms of Cavy plc as a whole. If, for example, Cavy's organisational cost of capital (i.e. its minimum required corporate rate of return) is 10% then any projects yielding a return in excess of 10 per cent would contribute towards the overall wealth of the Cavy organisation. As the new project opportunity generates a 15 per cent ROI (less than the current ROI, but above Cavy's minimum requirement of 10 per cent) Mick should consider accepting the new investment.

Rejection by divisional managers of such opportunities (as in Activity 11.1) would represent sub-optimal planning for the organisation as a whole. It was to avoid such sub-optimisation problems that an alternative divisional performance measurement method to ROI was developed which became known as the *net residual income* (NRI) technique.

11.2.2 *Net residual income*

By way of stark contrast to ROI's relative measure, the NRI technique is an *absolute* income measure. Its basic decision rule is that all new investment opportunities which generate a positive return in excess of the organisation's cost of capital should be accepted by divisions within that organisation. Effectively, the NRI technique works by charging divisions with an imputed (i.e. notional) interest charge, equal to the organisation's cost of capital, for their use of capital. Thus any new projects realising a surplus of income *after* being charged interest should be accepted for the financial benefit of the organisation as a whole. In Activity 11.2 we return to Mick Baxter's planning decision in Activity 11.1, but this time the problem is tackled from the viewpoint of applying the NRI (rather than the ROI) technique.

Required: Using the same Cavy plc data as in Activity 11.1, how would Mick's willingness (or otherwise) to undertake the new project opportunity on behalf of his division be affected if he were now to be guided by the NRI investment criterion instead of the ROI technique? Show relevant calculations.

Adopting a similar summary exhibit to that used in Activity 11.1, your relevant calculations should take the following worked format:

	Current position (£000)	New project (£000)	New position (£000)
Investment level	4,000	1,600	5,600
Income from investment	800	240	1,040
(less) Interest charged on the investment @ 10%	(400)	(160)	(560)
NRI.:	400	80	480

DID YOU KNOW ...?

that originally it was to counteract its divisional managers' sub-optimal behaviour that top management of the General Electric Corporation in the United States in the 1960s initiated the NRI approach to making divisional investment plans and decisions in order that managers of divisions should act in the best interests of the organisation as a whole. Such alignment of individual manager's own vested interests with those of the corporate entity in general is the desirable motivational condition known as **goal congruence.**

On the basis of the NRI investment measurement technique, you can see that Mick would now decide to accept the new investment opportunity. This is because in absolute terms *both* his division's and Cavy's residual income is increased after applying the 10 per cent cost of capital charged by Cavy to its divisions as a measure of its minimum required return on capital invested in those divisions.

In arriving at a figure for NRI you need to remember that precisely the same requirements with respect to 'controllability' apply. We discussed this issue of controllable (*vis-á-vis* non-controllable) cost and investment items previously with regard to responsibility accounting systems in section 11.1, and more specifically in connection with ROI and the divisional income statement in Table 11.3 of section 11.2.1. A similar form of statement to that appearing in Table 11.3, but now with the accent on *residual income*, is given in Table 11.4.

You need to notice from Table 11.4. that NRI statements also should clearly differentiate between controllable and non-controllable items if they are to be used for purposes of appraising the performance of divisional managers. A slight shift of emphasis, however, occurs in Table 11.4 in so far as the key level for managerial appraisal now is to focus upon *controllable residual income* (rather than *controllable operating income* as was the case in Table 11.3).

A brief but relevant concluding note is to point out the striking similarity between the two divisional measurement techniques dealt with in section 11.2

table 11.4

Measurement of divisional investment centre performance

Divisional residual income statement		
	(£)	(£)
Revenue (from sales):		
Inter-divisional transfers	XX	
External sales	XX	
Divisional sales revenue		XXX
Controllable costs		
Variable costs controlled by division		(XXX)
Divisional contribution		XXX
Fixed costs controlled by division		(XXX)
Controllable operating income		XXX
Interest (imputed charge) on		
controllable investment		(XXX)
Controllable residual income		XXX
Non-controllable costs		
Non-controllable divisional overhead	(XX)	
Depreciation on non-controllable fixed		
assets	(XX)	
Allocated/apportioned central charges		
(excluding imputed interest)	(XX)	
Interest (imputed charge) on		
non-controllable investment	(XX)	(XXX)
Divisional net residual income		£XX

and the capital investment decision/appraisal techniques of *net present value* (NPV) and *internal rate of return* (IRR) covered in detail in Chapter 8 of the book. The basic similarities are that:

▶ ROI adopts the same 'relative' approach to controlling divisional investment plans and decisions as IRR by appraising investment projects according to whether they satisfy a particular percentage rate of return on investment.

▶ NRI adopts the same 'absolute' approach to controlling divisional investment plans and decisions as NPV by recommending acceptance of all projects which realise a surplus of income after *discounting* the project at the organisation's relevant cost of capital.

Self-check questions
••••••••••••••••••••••••

11.1 At a recent meeting of the board of the Alpha Omega Group, the group finance director proposed that all properties owned by operating companies should be transferred to a newly formed group property company and that the properties should be leased back to the operating companies at a rental of 10 per cent of their value assessed by professional valuers.

AB Ltd, one of the operating companies, currently owns a factory that was valued at £150,000 ten years ago when the company was acquired by the Alpha Omega Group. The company expects the factory to be valued at £300,000 now.

In calculating its profits hitherto, it has been charging depreciation on a straight-line basis of $1\frac{1}{2}$ per cent per annum on the value ten years ago of this factory.

In the year just ended, AB Ltd's sales were £1,100,000, its profits were £91,000, and its return on capital employed (ROCE) was 26 per cent.

You are required to:

(a) Calculate the change in AB Ltd's ROCE that would result from acceptance of the Group's proposal if all other relevant factors did not change.

(b) Discuss briefly the extent to which the results of the above proposed transaction cast doubt on the validity of the use of ROCE as a means of measuring company performance within the Group.

(Chartered Association of Certified Accountants)

11.2 Hawlit Ltd, a transport company, is planning its future investment strategy. Hawlit's best projections of profit outcome are dependent upon the cost of diesel fuel.

	Annual net income at following costs (£) per gallon:				
Annual investment level	1.20	1.25	1.30	1.40	1.50
£000	£000	£000	£000	£000	£000
350	55	52	46	40	30
400	60	58	52	46	35
450	68	63	55	47	35
500	72	68	58	49	34
550	74	67	56	43	30
600	75	64	53	40	25
Estimated probability of outcome	0.1	0.1	0.4	0.3	0.1

The company's minimum required rate of return is 10 per cent pa.

You are required to:

(a) Compute, for each level of investment, the return on investment (ROI) and the residual income.

(b) Calculate the optimal investment level, stating your reasons.

(c) Evaluate the merits of residual income and return on investment as measures of performance.

(Chartered Association of Certified Accountants)

11.3 You have recently been appointed as management accountant attached to the headquarters of the Alphabet Group plc, with special responsibility for monitoring the performances of the companies within the group. Each company is treated as an investment centre and every month it produces an operating statement for the group headquarters. Summaries of the statements for

companies X and Y, which make similar products selling at similar prices, for
the last month showed a typical situation:

EXTRACT FROM COMPANY MONTHLY OPERATING STATEMENTS

		X	Y
		£000	£000
	Sales	600	370
less	Variable costs	229	208
	= Contribution	371	162
less	Controllable fixed overheads		
	(including depreciation on company assets)	65	28
	= Controllable profit	306	134
less	Apportioned group costs	226	119
	= Net profit	80	15
	Company assets	£6.4m	£0.9m
	Estimated return on capital employed		
	(on annual basis)	15%	20%

Although both companies are earning more than the target return on capital
of 12 per cent, there is pressure on interest rates which means that this rate
must be increased soon and the board is concerned at the relatively low return
achieved by X.

You are required to:

(a) Compare and discuss the relative performance of the two companies as
shown in the summarised operating statements.

(b) Redraft the operating statements using an alternative performance
measurement to return on capital employed and interpret them against a
background of rising interest rates.

(c) Critically compare the use of return on capital employed and the
alternative performance measure used in (b) to assess the performance
of investment centres.

(Chartered Institute of Management Accountants)

11.4 The Solo Division of Chart Products Ltd sells only one standard product. The
budgets for 19X2 show the following information:

	£
Selling price per unit	40
Variable costs per unit	24
Total fixed costs	200,000
Investment	800,000
Sales units	30,000

You are required to answer the following questions, considering each one quite independently from the others, and supporting your answers with appropriate calculations:

(a) What is the budgeted ROI (return on investment) for the division for 19X2?

(b) The minimum desired ROI for the company is 20 per cent and the divisional manager wishes to maximise RI (residual income). A new customer can be obtained who will buy 10,000 units at £32 each. These units would be in addition to those in the budget, but acceptance of the order would involve an increase in divisional fixed costs of £40,000 and an investment in additional assets of £140,000. Should the order be accepted?

(c) The minimum desired ROI for the company is 20 per cent and the divisional manager wishes to maximise RI. The division manufactures components for its product at a variable cost of £4 per component. An outside supplier has offered to supply the 30,000 components needed at a cost of £5 each. The components that the supplier would provide are equivalent to those now being made and the supplier is reliable. If the component is purchased, fixed costs will be reduced by £20,000 pa and assets with a book value of £60,000 will be sold at book value. Should the component be bought already made or be manufactured?

(d) Again, the minimum desired ROI is 20 per cent and the divisional goal is maximisation of RI. The manager is considering the introduction of a new product. It will sell for £20, variable costs are £12, fixed costs will increase by £80,000 and sales are expected to be 15,000 units pa. These sales would be in addition to, and would not affect, the 30,000 units of sales in the budget. What is the most additional investment in assets that can be made without reducing RI?

(e) Assuming the same facts as in (d) above, except that investment in the new product is to be fixed at £400,000 and that the introduction of the new product will stimulate sales of the existing product, what is the total number of units of the existing product which must be sold in 19X2 to justify the introduction of the new product?

(f) Briefly discuss the problem in a divisional organisation structure of having multiple goals, in particular those of ROI and RI. Use the calculations in (a) to (e) to illustrate your answer.

(Chartered Association of Certified Accountants)

Further study
· · · · · · · · · · · · · · · · ·

Arnold, J., Carsberg, B. and Scapens, R.W. (1980) *Topics in management accounting*, 1st edn, Philip Allan.

Arnold, J. and Hope, T. (1990) *Accounting for management decisions*, 2nd edn, Hemel Hempstead: Prentice-Hall.

Drury, C. (1992) *Management and cost accounting*, 3rd edn, London: Chapman and Hall.

Emmanual, C., Otley, D. and Merchant, K. (1990) *Accounting for management control*, 3rd edn, London: Chapman and Hall.

Lucey, T. (1992) *Management accounting*, 3rd edn, D.P. Publications.

Pogue G. A. (1984) 'Divisional performance measurement', in *Management Accounting*, December, Chartered Institute of Management Accountants.

CHAPTER 12

Further management planning techniques/developments

Objectives
· · · · · · · · · · · · ·

By the end of this chapter you should be able to:

▶ Describe a range of relatively recent (technological) developments within modern management planning environments.

▶ Apply the specific quantitative (operational research) technique for optimal resource allocation referred to as linear programming.

▶ Appreciate the use of the materials requirements planning approach in advanced/automated manufacturing industries and technologies.

▶ Understand the principle of just-in-time systems and the philosophy behind their application in the sphere of today's management planning and production techniques.

Qualified management accountants, as well as students of management accounting, should be aware of the different operational research/quantitative techniques that are available for resolution of problems regarding management's basic functions of planning and control. Such operational management techniques include, for example, statistical forecasting/estimation. In the context of total cost estimation, we described this statistical technique at some length in Chapter 3 (section 3.2.3) where we dealt with the problem of cost forecasting, employing methods such as correlation and regression analysis techniques. Initially our focus in this chapter is upon the quantitative management planning technique of *linear programming*, aimed at achieving solutions to problems of optimal allocation of scarce resources.

12.1 Linear programming (LP)
· ·

Scarce resource allocation problems should not be new to you as they appeared in the guise of the 'limiting factor' at the end of Chapter 4 in discussion of the marginal costing technique. In the summary concluding that chapter it was said that marginal costing was 'only able to cope with situations where a *single* binding constraint limits operations'. We went on to state that 'where linearity is valid as a reasonable assumption, then a more sophisticated aid . . . is offered by the operational research technique known as "linear programming" (LP).' Although in Chapter 4 the terms 'limiting factor' and 'scarce resource' were used entirely interchangeably, throughout this section they will simply be referred to as *constraints* in an LP solution to an optimal resource allocation problem.

12.1.1 Formulation of LP problems

Several examples of types of 'constraints' were provided at the start of section 4.3, and you would benefit now from re-reading that section's opening paragraph. Constraints set the body of the framework for formulating LP problems, but the standard layout (i.e. formulation) for the entire problem begins with the object of the exercise at its head – thus the first line of any LP formulation is what is technically termed the *objective function*. In management accounting situations the objective function will always be to optimise/maximise product 'contribution'. You might remember from Activity 4.2 in section 4.3 that maximisation of product contribution was the aim there, too, but only in the context of a single constraint applying. Our LP formulations here will contain several constraints applying concurrently in 'binding' the optimal solution. The optimal LP solution will indicate to management the *best mix* of products to plan in order to achieve the objective of an optimum/maximum contribution towards the organisation's fixed costs initially and, thereafter, profit (which in turn will be optimal). In short, a standard LP formulation will appear thus:

Objective function: Maximisation of product contribution (often expressed as Max C or Z).

Subject to:
Constraints (one per line of the formulation, e.g.)
(1) Skilled labour hours $\leq$ xxx
(2) Machine hour capacity $\leq$ xxx
(3) Contractual commitment $\geq$ xxx
(4) Storage space capacity $\leq$ xxx
(5) Non-negativity requirement ≥ 0
Key: xxx = numerical value of constraint (e.g. limited number of available hours, cubic metres, units required etc.)
$\leq$ = less than or equal to
$\geq$ = greater than or equal to.

In the above formulation:

▸ a contractual commitment may take the form of, for example, a legally binding agreement to supply a customer with an order for a minimum number of product units;
▸ the non-negativity constraint is a technical requirement to ensure against negative production quantities appearing in the optimal product mix plan; when using an LP computer software package this constraint will often be an inbuilt programme specification (i.e. effected automatically and not in need of specifying formally as in constraint (5) above).

To give you a practical sense of how to formulate (and solve) LP problems in the above manner, a worked illustration (CD Limited) is provided in the next section.

12.1.2 Solution of LP problems

Where you are faced with only two products from which to find the optimal mix, then use of a graphical approach is recommended because of its relative simplicity compared with other, mathematical methods. This is indeed the case with CD Limited. When more than two products are present in the problem, then mathematical means such as the 'simplex' technique (which lies outside the scope of this introductory accounting text) need to be used. Often such solutions in practice make use of computer facilities because the addition of extra product variables greatly increases the complexity of the problem. LP computer software packages are relatively commonplace nowadays.

Nevertheless, simpler mathematical devices like the application of simultaneous equations will be used next in support of the graphical solution to CD Limited's product mix problem. CD Limited produces and sells two products, C and D. Relevant data from which CD's management team require a 'best product mix' solution to generate an optimal contribution towards covering the firm's fixed overheads and making maximum profit are thus:

	Product C	Product D
Selling prices	£20	£16
Variable costs	£10	£12
Production hours required per product	4 hours	1 hour

▶ Fixed overhead costs in total comprise £400,000;
▶ Production hours in total available are 400,000;
▶ Storage capacity in the warehouse is limited to a maximum number of 300,000 units of product D (there is no constraint on the number of product C that can be stored).

Solution of CD Limited's product mix problem
If not explicitly provided in a question's data, you may be called upon to compute the product contribution. This is very straightforward, as follows:

Product C: Sales price (£20) *less* Variable cost (£10) = £10 contribution;
Product D: Sales price (£16) *less* Variable cost (£12) = £4 contribution.

The next stage of the solution is to formulate the LP problem as outlined in section 12.1.1. Questions will normally, if for no other reason than technical completeness, require you to lay out the problem in the prescribed standard format (where here 'C' and 'D' represent the products), thus:

Objective function:	Max Z = 10 C + 4 D	
Subject to:	4 C + D ≤ 400,000	(Production hours)
	D ≤ 300,000	(Storage capacity)
	C, D ≥ 0	(Non-negativity)

Having formulated the problem it remains for you to solve it, suitably by graphical means (see Figure 12.1) as only two product variables are involved. The solution process is as follows:

▶ construct axes for each product variable (unlike in C-V-P analysis and cost estimation, for example, it is not important which variable goes on which axis);

▶ plot the constraint lines on the graph (this is not difficult for the storage constraint as it only affects D and, therefore, is a straight line drawn parallel to the C axis, intersecting the D axis at the storage capacity limit, i.e. 300,000);

▶ where a constraint applies to both product variables it is necessary to determine the maximum number of each product that the constraint will allow. As available production hours of 400,000 affects both C and D you need to consider the constraint *equation* (i.e. the constraint line represents 'full' utilisation of the resource – 400,000 hours – not 'less than' and is therefore an equality) thus:

$$4\,C + D = 400,000$$

(i)   when C is zero, D = 400,000: plot this coordinate on the D axis;
(ii)   when D is zero, C = 100,000: plot this coordinate on the C axis;

▶ identify the feasible region on the graph (Figure 12.1's shaded area/ polygon oabc): this is the area within which *both* product variables' production is possible, that is where no product mix of C and D violates any of the constraints as the area lies within *all* of the binding constraints;

▶ the optimal solution (best product mix) will lie at one of the corners of the feasible region, so you take readings from the graph as follows:

@ point a: 100,000 C = (100,000)(£10) = £1,000,000
@ point b: 25,000 C + 300,000 D = (25,000)(£10) + (300,000)(£4) = £1,450,000
@ point c: 300,000 D = (300,000)(£4) = £1,200,000

Maximum contribution is generated by point b's optimal product mix of 25,000 units of C plus 300,000 units of D giving:

		£
	Optimal contribution	1,450,000
less	Fixed overhead costs	400,000
	Optimal profit	£1,050,000

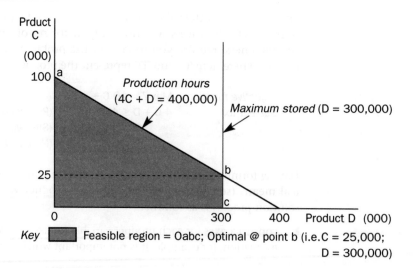

figure 12.1
Linear programming graphical solution

Key — Feasible region = Oabc; Optimal @ point b (i.e. C = 25,000; D = 300,000)

You can cross-check this optimum by carrying out a simple simultaneous equations calculation, mathematically representative of where the constraint equations intersect at point b, thus:

(1) $4C + D = 400,000$
(2) $ D = 300,000$
_____
(3) $4C = 100,000$ [Subtract (2) from (1) to get (3)]

∴ $C = 100,000 \div 4 = \underline{25,000}$

Finally, substitute this value for C into equation (1):

(4) $(25,000) + D = 400,000$
∴ $100,000 + D = 400,000$
∴ $D = 400,000 - 100,000 = \underline{300,000}$

12.2 Developments in management planning

Just as many quantitative planning techniques, like the linear programming discussed in the previous section, often employ computer facilities, most modern production environments (known as advanced or automated manufacturing technologies) rely heavily on computerised means as an aid to manufacture. Widespread use of computers is to be found in robotics technology, for example, where robots are programmed to carry out tasks such as assembly that previously in traditional environments were manually intensive and labour dominated. One such area progressively developing since the 1960s is a management technique referred to as *materials requirements planning* (MRP).

12.2.1 *Materials requirements planning (MRP)*

MRP began its development early in the 1960s being a computerised way of synchronising, integrating and combining the needs of a materials procurement programme with those of production planning through to completed stock/finished goods stage.

MRP comprises an efficient logistics process of ordering raw material, components and sub-assemblies (either 'bought-in' or produced 'in-house' parts) to be available immediately prior to each subsequent stage in manufacture, thereby sustaining the flow of production towards the end-product (i.e. the finished stock item). MRP can therefore be said to underpin both production planning/scheduling requirements as well as satisfying material parts/sub-components purchasing and procurement needs.

You should be aware that, using computers, MRP works via a two-step development process:

▶ Step 1: customer demand for finished products defined in terms of required quantity and required delivery date/time provide the specifications for a *master production schedule* (MPS).

▶ Step 2: this MPS (from step 1) subsequently provides the basis for determining the raw material, component and sub-assembly requirements related to each previous stage of product manufacture using *back-scheduling* consistent with the relevant, given lead times and quantities.

Back-scheduling involves working backwards from an end-requirement (i.e. the finished goods stock needed to satisfy customer demand) and 'time-adjusting' the ordering events necessary prior to product completion to ensure all required material parts and sub-components are available for production at each stage of manufacture, having taken into account quantity deliveries, lead times on parts and components etc. In short, the starting point for an MRP's systems operation depends on information and data contained in the MPS relating to *expected* (i.e. estimated) as well as *existing* customer demand (i.e. known orders).

In general, as with all computerised data systems, MRP's defining elements are four-fold: (i) pre-requisite data; (ii) systems data input; (iii) systems data processing; (iv) systems data output.

(i) *Pre-requisite data* comprises both known existing and estimated (unknown) customer orders/demand (embodied in the MPS); bill of materials structures, i.e. product material specifications (including any design up-dating/changes to product specs.); current and planned stock levels/receipts.
(ii) *Systems data input* consists of MPS, bill of materials (BOM) and stock records files.
(iii) *Systems data processing* is carried out by the MRP computer programme.
(iv) *Systems data output* provides a time-phased schedule of planned order releases (this is the whole object of the MRP operation, i.e. the materials requirements plan itself!). In addition, other output will include a status report for stock planning and control purposes.

Taken together with Figure 12.2, which illustrates for you the overall structure of an MRP system, the following elaboration upon the role of each computer file involved completes our description of MRP:

▶ The MPS file contains the planned production of finished goods expressed (normally) in weekly time frames. Because the plan is partly based on expected or estimated demand it is referred to as a 'push' system (that is pushing manufacture through to meet both actual as well as forecast demand for finished goods). This contrasts with the 'pull' nature of, for example, just-in-time (JIT) systems (described in the next section) which are based only on known customer demand and do not therefore involve estimates or forecasts.
▶ The BOM file, given the MPS requirement, holds the information relating to how finished goods production is to be achieved. BOM structures detail (component by component, sub-assembly by sub-assembly, raw material by raw material) all the ingredients of product manufacture stage by stage. Their nature is that of a 'multi-layered' breakdown or disaggregation of the total product specification.
▶ The stock records file details existing stocks and stock movements on component parts, sub-assemblies, raw materials and finished goods.

figure 12.2
**Overall structure
of an MRP
system**

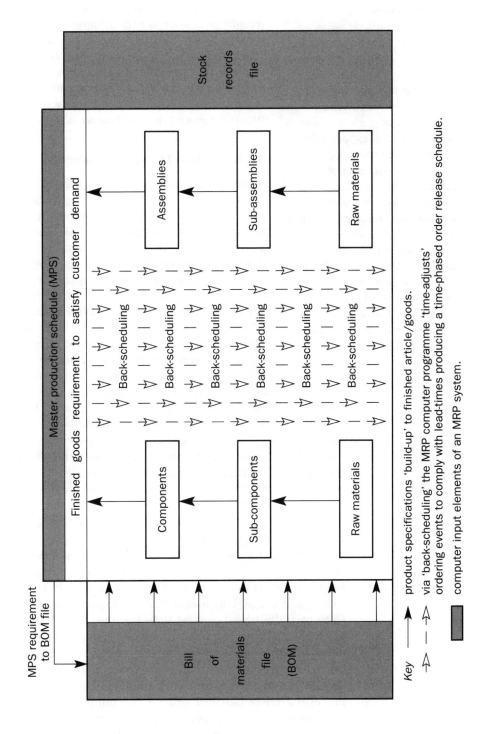

Master production schedule (MPS)

Finished goods requirement to satisfy customer demand

Stock records file

Assemblies

Sub-assemblies

Raw materials

Back-scheduling

Back-scheduling

Back-scheduling

Back-scheduling

Back-scheduling

Back-scheduling

Components

Sub-components

Raw materials

MPS requirement to BOM file

Bill of materials file (BOM)

Key ——▶ product specifications 'build-up' to finished article/goods.

– –⇢ via 'back-scheduling' the MRP computer programme 'time-adjusts'
⇢ ordering events to comply with lead-times producing a time-phased order release schedule.

▮ computer input elements of an MRP system.

Knowing 'what' (MPS), 'how' (BOM) and 'with what' (stock records) production is to be achieved, the MRP programme synthesises the data to identify 'when' events will be required to happen. This is manifested in the output of the *time-phased order release schedule*. This schedule of orders recognises lead time constraints and, by working backwards from product completion date, blends and fits material requirements precisely with those of manufacture (this is the process described earlier as back-scheduling).

12.2.2 Just-in-Time (JIT) production and purchasing

A suitable description of *just-in-time* (JIT) is that it is a management technique aimed at planning to keep levels of stock and wastage down to an absolute minimum, through arrangement of the flow of work enabling flexible manufacturing systems to operate swiftly but to high standards of output quality. This description clearly reflects its role in progressive production environments. The concept of JIT is part of an important range of techniques (such as computer-aided design and manufacturing systems, CAD/CAM) which have evolved in parallel with the advance of production technologies in the age of automation and industrial efficiency up to recently dominated by Japan. Certain traditional areas of manufacturing activity are non-value generating in nature. Examples include the waiting, storing, inspecting and handling phases of manufacture. It is precisely these elements that JIT systems aim to eliminate completely or, at least, reduce to a bare minimum.

JIT production is in essence a system primarily driven by demand for finished products. In this sense you need to recognise why it is thus described as a 'demand-pull' system, contrasting sharply with the 'demand-push' nature of the MRP management planning technique detailed in section 12.2.1. Product components on, for instance, an assembly line are only manufactured as and when needed for the next phase of production. Beneath this wider umbrella of JIT production systems in general falls the specific development of JIT purchasing procedures in particular.

JIT purchasing involves maintaining raw material stocks at as close to zero amounts as possible. You should appreciate that this requirement involves 'fine tuning' in so far as raw material receipts are closely synchronised with their subsequent usage. This means that the logistics and timings involved need to be carefully honed to meet tight schedules which equate the receiving of materials with their almost instant use. The principle necessitates ultimate dependence on supremely reliable sources of material supply. In response to the purchaser agreeing long-term contractual commitments with a select few of dependable suppliers (which itself results in cost savings through placing and processing fewer purchase orders) the supplier guarantees timely delivery together with quality inspection checks of materials *before* they leave the suppliers' own premises. This leads to cost efficiencies in reducing the need for the purchasing factory to carry out its own 'in-house' tests on material quality.

Delivery of materials is directly to the factory shop-floor and takes place immediately prior to their use in production. Factory jobs and processes therefore do not draw their material requirements from stores. The consequence of this is a dramatic reduction, or even avoidance entirely, of the operating and investment costs associated with handling, storing and waiting for materials. Organisations, however, will often adopt a combination of JIT and 'conventional' purchasing systems to suit different aspects of manufacture, and therefore JIT purchasing may be seen to play a part along with other more traditional purchasing procedures within varied spheres of production activity.

Inevitably there are dangers inherent in the JIT concept as it is applied to purchasing because of its focus on meeting critical time and quality constraints. There is little or no room for error or shortcomings on the part of the suppliers. Purchase contracts with suppliers need to provide for the potentially serious legal, financial and operational repercussions likely to arise from disruptions to production schedules planned to comply with the most demanding 'knife-edge' requirements of quality and timing.

Further study

Arnold, J. and Hope, T. (1990) *Accounting for management decisions*, 2nd edn, Hemel Hempstead: Prentice-Hall.

Ashton, D., Hopper, T. and Scapens, R.W. (1995) *Issues in management accounting*, 2nd edn, London: Macmillan.

Bromwich, M. and Bhimani, A. (1994) *Management accounting: pathways to progress*, 1st edn, London: Chartered Institute of Management Accountants.

Clarke, P.J. (1995) 'The Old and the New in Management Accounting', *Management Accounting*, June, Chartered Institute of Management Accountants.

Cobb, I. (1992) 'JIT and the management accountant', in *Management Accounting*, February, Chartered Institute of Management Accountants.

Drury, C. (1992) *Management and cost accounting*, 3rd edn, London: Chapman and Hall.

Johnson, H.T. and Kaplan, R.S. (1987) *Relevance lost – the rise and fall of management accounting*, Boston: Harvard Business School.

Harper, W. (1995) *Cost and management accounting*, 1st edn, London: Macdonald and Evans.

Horngren, C.T., Foster, G. and Datar, S. (1994) *Cost accounting – a managerial emphasis*, 8th edn, Hemel Hempstead: Prentice-Hall.

Maskell, B. (1993) 'Why MRP2 hasn't created world-class manufacturing . . . where do we go from here?', in *Management Accounting*, November, Chartered Institute of Management Accountants.

Ryan, B. and Hobson, J. (1985) *Management accounting – a contemporary approach*, 1st edn, London: Pitman.

Scapens, R.W. (1991) *Management accounting – a review of recent developments*, 1st edn, London: Macmillan.

Wright, D. (1994) *A practical foundation in costing*, 1st edn, London: Routledge.

Appendix 1a

Present value of £1 (Notation: V_{n7})

Year	5%	6%	7%	8%	9%	10%	11%	12%	13%	14%	15%	16%	17%	18%	19%	20%	21%	22%	23%	24%	25%	26%	27%	28%	29%	30%	35%	40%
0	1.000	1.000	1.000	1.000	1.000	1.000	1.000	1.000	1.000	1.000	1.000	1.000	1.000	1.000	1.000	1.000	1.000	1.000	1.000	1.000	1.000	1.000	1.000	1.000	1.000	1.000	1.000	1.000
1	.952	.943	.935	.926	.917	.909	.901	.893	.885	.877	.870	.862	.855	.847	.840	.833	.826	.820	.813	.807	.800	.794	.787	.781	.775	.769	.741	.714
2	.907	.890	.873	.857	.842	.826	.812	.797	.783	.769	.756	.743	.731	.718	.706	.694	.683	.672	.661	.650	.640	.630	.620	.610	.601	.592	.549	.510
3	.864	.840	.816	.794	.772	.751	.731	.712	.693	.675	.658	.641	.624	.609	.593	.579	.564	.551	.537	.524	.512	.500	.488	.477	.466	.455	.406	.364
4	.823	.792	.763	.735	.708	.683	.659	.636	.613	.592	.572	.552	.534	.516	.499	.482	.467	.451	.437	.423	.410	.397	.384	.373	.361	.350	.301	.260
5	.784	.747	.713	.681	.650	.621	.593	.567	.543	.519	.497	.476	.456	.437	.419	.402	.386	.370	.355	.341	.328	.315	.303	.291	.280	.269	.223	.186
6	.746	.705	.666	.630	.596	.564	.535	.507	.480	.456	.432	.410	.390	.370	.352	.335	.319	.303	.289	.275	.262	.250	.238	.227	.217	.207	.165	.133
7	.711	.665	.623	.583	.547	.513	.482	.452	.425	.400	.376	.354	.333	.314	.296	.279	.263	.249	.235	.222	.210	.198	.188	.178	.168	.159	.122	.095
8	.677	.627	.582	.540	.502	.467	.434	.404	.376	.351	.327	.305	.285	.266	.249	.233	.218	.204	.191	.179	.168	.157	.148	.139	.130	.123	.091	.068
9	.645	.592	.544	.500	.460	.424	.391	.361	.333	.308	.284	.263	.243	.225	.209	.194	.180	.167	.155	.144	.134	.125	.116	.108	.101	.094	.067	.048
10	.614	.558	.508	.463	.422	.386	.352	.322	.295	.270	.247	.227	.208	.191	.176	.162	.149	.137	.126	.116	.107	.099	.092	.085	.078	.073	.050	.035
11	.585	.527	.475	.429	.388	.350	.317	.287	.261	.237	.215	.195	.178	.162	.148	.135	.123	.112	.103	.094	.086	.079	.072	.066	.061	.056	.037	.025
12	.557	.497	.444	.397	.356	.319	.286	.257	.231	.208	.187	.168	.152	.137	.124	.112	.102	.092	.083	.076	.069	.062	.057	.052	.047	.043	.027	.018
13	.530	.469	.415	.368	.326	.290	.258	.229	.204	.182	.163	.145	.130	.116	.104	.093	.084	.075	.068	.061	.055	.050	.045	.040	.037	.033	.020	.013
14	.505	.442	.388	.340	.299	.263	.232	.205	.181	.160	.141	.125	.111	.099	.088	.078	.069	.062	.055	.049	.044	.039	.035	.032	.028	.025	.015	.009
15	.481	.417	.362	.315	.275	.239	.209	.183	.160	.140	.123	.108	.095	.084	.074	.065	.057	.051	.045	.040	.035	.031	.028	.025	.022	.020	.011	.006
16	.458	.394	.339	.292	.252	.218	.188	.163	.141	.123	.107	.093	.081	.071	.062	.054	.047	.042	.036	.032	.028	.025	.022	.019	.017	.015	.008	.005
17	.436	.371	.317	.270	.231	.198	.170	.146	.125	.108	.093	.080	.069	.060	.052	.045	.039	.034	.030	.026	.023	.020	.017	.015	.013	.012	.006	.003
18	.416	.350	.296	.250	.212	.180	.153	.130	.111	.095	.081	.069	.059	.051	.044	.038	.032	.028	.024	.021	.018	.016	.014	.012	.010	.009	.005	.002
19	.396	.331	.277	.232	.194	.164	.138	.116	.098	.083	.070	.060	.051	.043	.037	.031	.027	.023	.020	.017	.014	.012	.011	.009	.008	.007	.003	.002
20	.377	.312	.258	.215	.178	.149	.124	.104	.087	.073	.061	.051	.043	.037	.031	.026	.022	.019	.016	.014	.012	.010	.008	.007	.006	.005	.002	.001
25	.295	.233	.184	.146	.116	.092	.074	.059	.047	.038	.030	.025	.020	.016	.013	.011	.009	.007	.006	.005	.004	.003	.003	.002	.002	.001	.001	.000
30	.231	.174	.131	.099	.075	.057	.044	.033	.026	.020	.015	.012	.009	.007	.005	.004	.003	.003	.002	.002	.001	.001	.001	.001	.000	.000	.000	.000
35	.181	.130	.094	.068	.049	.036	.026	.019	.014	.010	.008	.006	.004	.003	.002	.002	.001	.001	.001	.001	.000	.000	.000	.000	.000	.000	.000	.000
40	.142	.097	.067	.046	.032	.022	.015	.011	.008	.005	.004	.003	.002	.001	.001	.001	.000	.000	.000	.000	.000	.000	.000	.000	.000	.000	.000	.000
45	.111	.073	.048	.031	.021	.014	.009	.006	.004	.003	.002	.001	.001	.001	.000	.000	.000	.000	.000	.000	.000	.000	.000	.000	.000	.000	.000	.000
50	.087	.054	.034	.021	.013	.009	.005	.003	.002	.001	.001	.000	.000	.000	.000	.000	.000	.000	.000	.000	.000	.000	.000	.000	.000	.000	.000	.000

Note: The above present value factors are based on year-end interest calculations.

Appendix 1b

Cumulative present value of £1 per annum (I.e. present value of an Annuity of £1) (Notation: $A_{n\rceil}$)

Year	5%	6%	7%	8%	9%	10%	11%	12%	13%	14%	15%	16%	17%	18%	19%	20%	21%	22%	23%	24%	25%	26%	27%	28%	29%	30%	35%	40%
1	.952	.943	.935	.926	.917	.909	.901	.893	.885	.877	.870	.862	.855	.847	.840	.833	.826	.820	.813	.807	.800	.794	.787	.781	.775	.769	.741	.714
2	1.859	1.833	1.808	1.783	1.759	1.736	1.713	1.690	1.668	1.647	1.626	1.605	1.585	1.566	1.546	1.528	1.510	1.492	1.474	1.457	1.440	1.424	1.407	1.392	1.376	1.361	1.289	1.224
3	2.723	2.673	2.624	2.577	2.531	2.487	2.444	2.402	2.361	2.322	2.283	2.246	2.210	2.174	2.140	2.106	2.074	2.042	2.011	1.981	1.952	1.923	1.896	1.868	1.842	1.816	1.696	1.589
4	3.546	3.465	3.387	3.312	3.240	3.170	3.102	3.037	2.974	2.914	2.855	2.978	2.743	2.690	2.639	2.589	2.540	2.494	2.448	2.404	2.362	2.320	2.280	2.241	2.203	2.166	1.997	1.849
5	4.329	4.212	4.100	3.993	3.890	3.791	3.696	3.605	3.517	3.433	3.352	3.274	3.199	3.127	3.058	2.991	2.926	2.864	2.804	2.745	2.689	2.635	2.583	2.532	2.483	2.436	2.220	2.035
6	5.076	4.917	4.767	4.623	4.486	4.355	4.231	4.111	3.998	3.889	3.784	3.685	3.589	3.498	3.410	3.326	3.245	3.167	3.092	3.021	2.951	2.885	2.821	2.759	2.700	2.643	2.385	2.168
7	5.786	5.582	5.389	5.206	5.033	4.868	4.712	4.564	4.423	4.288	4.160	4.039	3.922	3.812	3.706	3.605	3.508	3.416	3.327	3.242	3.161	3.083	3.009	2.937	2.868	2.802	2.508	2.263
8	6.463	6.210	5.971	5.747	5.535	5.335	5.146	4.968	4.799	4.639	4.487	4.344	4.207	4.078	3.954	3.837	3.726	3.619	3.518	3.421	3.329	3.241	3.156	3.076	2.999	2.925	2.598	2.331
9	7.108	6.802	6.515	6.247	5.995	5.759	5.537	5.328	5.132	4.946	4.772	4.607	4.451	4.303	4.163	4.031	3.905	3.786	3.673	3.566	3.463	3.366	3.273	3.184	3.100	3.019	2.665	2.379
10	7.722	7.360	7.024	6.710	6.418	6.145	5.889	5.650	5.426	5.216	5.019	4.833	4.659	4.494	4.339	4.192	4.054	3.923	3.799	3.682	3.571	3.465	3.366	3.269	3.178	3.092	2.715	2.414
11	8.306	7.887	7.499	7.139	6.805	6.495	6.207	5.938	5.687	5.453	5.234	5.029	4.836	4.656	4.486	4.327	4.177	4.035	3.902	3.776	3.656	3.544	3.437	3.335	3.239	3.147	2.752	2.438
12	8.863	8.384	7.943	7.536	7.161	6.814	6.492	6.194	5.918	5.660	5.421	5.197	4.988	4.793	4.610	4.439	4.278	4.127	3.985	3.851	3.725	3.606	3.493	3.387	3.286	3.190	2.779	2.456
13	9.394	8.853	8.358	7.904	7.487	7.103	6.750	6.424	6.122	5.842	5.583	5.342	5.118	4.910	4.715	4.533	4.362	4.203	4.053	3.912	3.780	3.656	3.538	3.427	3.322	3.223	2.799	2.469
14	9.899	9.295	8.745	8.244	7.786	7.367	6.982	6.628	6.302	6.002	5.724	5.468	5.229	5.008	4.802	4.611	4.432	4.265	4.108	3.962	3.824	3.695	3.573	3.459	3.351	3.249	2.814	2.478
15	10.380	9.712	9.108	8.559	8.061	7.606	7.191	6.811	6.462	6.142	5.847	5.575	5.324	5.092	4.876	4.675	4.490	4.315	4.153	4.001	3.859	3.726	3.601	3.483	3.373	3.268	2.825	2.484
16	10.838	10.106	9.447	8.851	8.313	7.824	7.379	6.974	6.604	6.265	5.954	5.669	5.405	5.162	4.938	4.730	4.536	4.357	4.190	4.033	3.887	3.751	3.623	3.503	3.390	3.283	2.834	2.489
17	11.274	10.477	9.763	9.122	8.544	8.022	7.549	7.120	6.729	6.373	6.047	5.749	5.475	5.222	4.990	4.775	4.576	4.391	4.219	4.059	3.910	3.771	3.640	3.518	3.403	3.295	2.840	2.492
18	11.690	10.828	10.059	9.372	8.756	8.201	7.702	7.250	6.840	6.467	6.128	5.818	5.534	5.273	5.033	4.812	4.608	4.419	4.243	4.080	3.928	3.786	3.654	3.529	3.413	3.304	2.844	2.494
19	12.085	11.158	10.336	9.604	8.950	8.365	7.839	7.366	6.938	6.550	6.198	5.877	5.584	5.316	5.070	4.844	4.635	4.442	4.263	4.097	3.942	3.799	3.666	3.539	3.421	3.311	2.848	2.496
20	12.462	11.470	10.594	9.818	9.129	8.514	7.963	7.469	7.025	6.623	6.259	5.929	5.628	5.353	5.101	4.870	4.657	4.460	4.279	4.110	3.954	3.808	3.673	3.546	3.427	3.316	2.850	2.497
25	14.094	12.783	11.654	10.675	9.823	9.077	8.422	7.843	7.330	6.873	6.464	6.097	5.766	5.467	5.195	4.948	4.721	4.514	4.323	4.147	3.985	3.834	3.694	3.564	3.442	3.329	2.856	2.499
30	15.372	13.765	12.409	11.258	10.274	9.427	8.694	8.055	7.496	7.003	6.566	6.177	5.829	5.517	5.235	4.979	4.746	4.534	4.339	4.160	3.995	3.842	3.701	3.569	3.447	3.332	2.857	2.500
35	16.374	14.498	12.948	11.655	10.567	9.644	8.855	8.176	7.586	7.070	6.617	6.215	5.858	5.539	5.251	4.992	4.756	4.541	4.345	4.164	3.998	3.845	3.703	3.571	3.448	3.333	2.857	2.500
40	17.159	15.046	13.332	11.925	10.757	9.779	8.951	8.244	7.634	7.105	6.642	6.234	5.871	5.548	5.258	4.997	4.760	4.544	4.347	4.166	3.999	3.846	3.703	3.571	3.448	3.333	2.857	2.500
45	17.774	15.456	13.606	12.108	10.881	9.863	9.008	8.283	7.661	7.123	6.654	6.242	5.877	5.552	5.261	4.999	4.761	4.545	4.347	4.166	4.000	3.846	3.704	3.571	3.448	3.333	2.857	2.500
50	18.256	15.762	13.801	12.234	10.962	9.915	9.042	8.305	7.675	7.133	6.661	6.246	5.880	5.554	5.262	5.000	4.762	4.545	4.348	4.167	4.000	3.846	3.704	3.571	3.448	3.333	2.857	2.500

Note: The above present value factors are based on year-end interest calculations.

Solutions to the self-check questions

Question 2.1

(a) Calculation of direct labour hour overhead absorption rate:

$$\frac{\text{Budgeted overheads}}{\text{Budgeted direct labour hours}} = \frac{£52,000}{3,760} = \underline{\underline{£13.83 \text{ per hour}}}$$

	B	A	Z
Prime cost	34	35	22
Production overhead	110.6	82.98	55.32
(£13.83) (× 8)	—— (× 6)	—— (× 4)	——
Unit production cost	144.6	117.98	77.32

(b)

Cost	£	Driver	Number	Rate
Assembly dept	20,860	Labour hours	3,760	£5.55
Set-up	10,500	Production runs	15	£700
Storage	7,200	Requisitions	60	£120
Quality	4,200	Production runs	15	£280
Handling	9,240	Orders	30	£308

	B	A	Z
Output in units	240	200	160
	£	£	£
Prime cost	8,160	7,000	3,520
Assembly dept	10,656	6,660	3,552
Set-up	4,200	3,500	2,800
Storage	2,400	2,400	2,400
Quality	1,680	1,400	1,120
Handling	3,696	3,080	2,464
	30,792	24,040	15,856
Unit production cost	£128.3	£120.2	£99.1

(c) The conventional approach usually absorbs overhead costs on the basis of direct labour hours. As direct labour as a proportion of total production cost continues to fall this leads to more distortion. ABC is based on the principle that activities cause costs and therefore the use of activities should be the basis of attributing costs to cost units. Costs are identified with particular activities and the performance of those activities is linked with products. The activity is known as the cost driver and the costs associated with that activity are then attributed to cost units using a cost driver rate. This more accurately reflects the usage of the activity by the product.

Question 2.2

	Production departments			Service departments	
	Manufacturing £	Assembly £	Finishing £	Power £	Administration £
Primary attribution	24,000	21,000	18,000	3,000	5,000
Secondary apportionment					
Power	1,200	750	450	(3,000)	600
Administration	1,960	1,680	1,120	840	(5,600)
Power	336	210	126	(840)	168
Administration	59	50	34	25	(168)
Power	10	6	4	(25)	5
Administration	2	2	1	–	(5)
	27,567	23,698	19,735	–	–

Note: The appropriate method used above is the repeated distribution/continuous apportionment method.

Question 2.3

Completed 7 × 4 Table

	Faculty			
	A	B	C	Total
Budgeted own overheads	8,000	11,000 (vii)	6,000	25,000 (xiv)
Budgeted share of service department overhead:	6,000	9,000 (ii)	12,000 (iii)	27,000 (i)
Total budgeted overheads	14,000 (iv)	20,000	18,000 (x)	52,000 (xv)
Budgeted labour hours	7,000 (v)	2,000	3,600 (xiii)	12,600 (xvi)
Overhead absorption rate	2	10 (viii)	5 (xii)	N/A
Actual labour hours	5,000	2,200 (ix)	3,800 (xi)	11,000
Over/(under) absorption	(4,000) (vi)	2,000	1,000	(1,000) (xvii)

- Total service department overhead $= 6{,}000 \div \frac{2}{9} \; (A(2)+B(3)+c(4)=\frac{9}{9}) = 27{,}000$ (i)
- B share of service department overhead $= 27{,}000 \times \frac{3}{9}$ $= 9{,}000$ (ii)
- C share of service department overhead $= 27{,}000 \times \frac{4}{9}$ $= 12{,}000$ (iii)
- Total overheads A $= 8{,}000 + 6{,}000$ $= 14{,}000$ (iv)
- Budgeted hours A $= 14{,}000 \div 2$ $= 7{,}000$ (v)
- Under absorbed A $= (7{,}000 - 5{,}000) \times 2$ $= (4{,}000)$ (vi)
- Own overheads B $= 20{,}000 - 9{,}000$ $= 11{,}000$ (vii)
- Overhead absorption rate B $= 20{,}000 \div 2{,}000$ $= 10$ (viii)
- Actual hours B $= 2{,}000 + (2{,}000 \div 10)$ $= 2{,}200$ (ix)
- Total overheads C $= 6{,}000 + 12{,}000$ $= 18{,}000$ (x)
- Actual hours C $= 11{,}000 - (5{,}000 + 2{,}200) = 3{,}800$ (xi)
- Overhead absorption rate C $= (18{,}000 + 1{,}000) \div 3{,}800 = 5$ (xii)
- Budgeted hours C $= 18{,}000 \div 5$ $= 3{,}600$ (xiii)
- Total budgeted own overheads $= 8{,}000 + 11{,}000 + 6{,}000 = 25{,}000$ (xiv)
- Total budgeted overheads $= 25{,}000 + 27{,}000$ $= 52{,}000$ (xv)
- Total budgeted labour hours $= 7{,}000 + 2{,}000 + 3{,}600 = 12{,}600$ (xvi)
- Total over/(under) absorption $= (4{,}000) + 2{,}000 + 1{,}000 = (1{,}000)$ (xvii)

Question 2.4

(a) Overhead (absorbed)

	Budgeted overhead (1)	Budgeted hours (2)	Absorption rate (1) ÷ (2)	×	Actual hours (3)	=	Overhead absorbed (4)
	£	(hrs)	(£/hr)		(hrs)		(£)
Filling	110,040	13,100	8.40		12,820		107,688
Sealing	53,300	10,250	5.20		10,075		52,390

Overhead (actually incurred) distribution statement

	Filling (£)	Sealing (£)	Maintenance (£)	Canteen (£)
Primary attribution	74,260	38,115	25,050	24,375
Secondary apportionment				
Canteen	14,625	7,800	1,950	(24,375)
Maintenance	18,900	7,290	(27,000)	810
Canteen	486	259	65	(810)
Maintenance	45	18	(65)	2
Canteen	1	1	–	(2)
	108,317	53,483	–	–

Under/over-absorption

	Overheads incurred *(see above statement)* (£)	Overheads absorbed *(see column (4) above)* (£)	(Under)/over-absorption (£)
Filling	108,317	107,688	(629)
Sealing	53,483	52,390	(1,093)

(b) The objectives of overhead apportionment and absorption (i.e. cost ascertainment in general) are two-fold:
  (i) Stock valuation – for consistency with SSAP9 absorption costing is required in valuing stocks of W-I-P and finished goods
  (ii) Income determination – the cost of goods sold figure (based on absorption costing) will directly affect the level of profit/loss. Arbitrary choice of absorption rate will have a critical impact on both (i) and (ii).

Question 2.5

(a) Overhead distribution/cost apportionment statement

	Basis	Service 1 (£)	Service 2 (£)	Production A (£)	Production B (£)	General factory (£)
Primary attribution	Allocation	93,800	38,600	182,800	124,800	210,000
Secondary apportionment						
General factory	Floor space	10,500	21,000	31,500	147,000	(210,000)
Service # 1	Personnel	(104,300)		91,262	13,038	
Service # 2	Hours usage		(59,600)	8,221	51,379	
				313,783	336,217	
Overhead absorption base						
Budgeted direct labour hours				120,000	20,000	
∴ *Overhead absorption rates* (revised)				£2.61	£16.81	

(b) Differences between overhead absorption rates

	Current overhead rate	Revised overhead rate	% Change in rate
Production cost centre A	£3.10	£2.61	16%
Production cost centre B	£11.00	£16.81	53%

Comment: Extent of change in rates – significant in A; highly significant in B.

Reasons likely to be because:

(i) Budgeted direct labour hours used as absorption base rather than regular/average labour activity which would tend to keep rates steadier from year to year – but what is 'regular/average labour activity?' Perhaps problematic to determine.

(ii) Production cost centre A direct labour hours have increased by 20 per cent.

(iii) Production cost centre B direct labour hours have decreased by 50 per cent.

(iv) Fixed overhead and variable overhead are not differentiated between, i.e. absorption rates are not broken down by behaviour of overhead cost.

(c) Overhead distribution/cost apportionment statement

	Basis	Service 1 (£)	Service 2 (£)	Production A (£)	Production B (£)	General factory (£)
Primary attribution	Allocation	93,800	38,600	182,800	124,800	210,000
Secondary apportionment						
General Factory	Floor space	10,500	21,000	31,500	147,000	(210,000)
Service # 1	Personnel	(104,300)	20,860	73,010	10,430	
Service # 2	Hours usage	2,682	(80,460)	10,728	67,050	
Service # 1	Personnel	(2,682)	536	1,878	268	
Service # 2	Hours usage	18	(536)	71	447	
Service # 1	Personnel	(18)	4	12	2	
Service # 2	Hours usage		(4)	1	3	
				300,000	350,000	

Overhead absorption base

				A	B	
Budgeted direct labour hours				120,000	20,000	

∴ *Overhead absorption rates* (recalculated)

				A	B	
				£2.50	£17.50	

(d) Comments in light of assumptions

(i) As production cost centre B is highly mechanised and (relative to A) non-labour intensive, a machine hour absorption rate would be an improvement on the direct labour hour rate currently applied.

(ii) Although overhead attribution procedures paying regard to reciprocal servicing arrangements (i.e. as in part (c)'s calculations) are to be preferred to procedures which simply ignore such reciprocations (i.e. as in part (a)'s calculations) both would be improved upon by recognising and effecting a breakdown of overhead into its fixed and variable cost component parts.

Question 3.1

(a) Two sketches depicting curvilinear variable cost and linear variable cost.

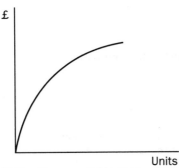

(i) Curvilinear variable cost

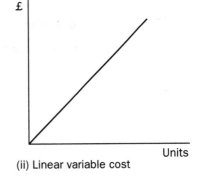

(ii) Linear variable cost

(b) (i) A semi-variable cost (sometimes called a semi-fixed/mixed cost) is a cost containing both fixed and variable elements and which is therefore partly affected by fluctuations in volume.

(b) (ii) A stepped fixed cost is one which is constant between wide ranges of activity, but nevertheless at certain discrete and rare intervals it does change to a different level of cost, and usually by a significant amount.

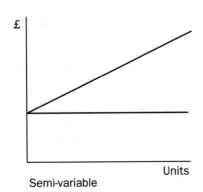

Semi-variable

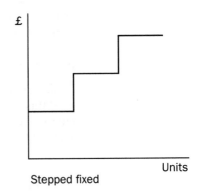

Stepped fixed

Example: Car/van hire (with no mileage allowance included in fixed rental, i.e. all miles charged at a unit rate).

Example: Supervisory labour.

(c) (i) Machine hour depreciation – which (if a single and constant depreciation rate per hour is used to write down the value of an asset) reflects perfect linear *variable* cost behaviour. Two common examples of assets which might be depreciated on a machine hour basis are: heavy earthmoving/digging machinery and equipment (machine hours worked); and aircraft (machine flight hours).

(ii) You ought *not* agree with the statement. Depreciation does nothing whatsoever to provide funds for the replacement of assets. The depreciation entries in the accounts merely write down (or write off) asset values thereby representing the cost and benefit of their use. Other means (e.g. sinking funds) need to be employed to ensure that funds/cash are available for replacing assets when their useful life is over.

Question 3.2

(a) Overhead cost items' behaviour patterns

Item ref.	Brief description	Graph ref.
1	Depreciation of equipment	C
2	Cost of service	F
3	Royalty	B
4	Supervision cost	H
5	Depreciation of equipment	E
6	Cost of a service	K
7	Storage/carriage service	G
8	Outside finishing service	D

(b) Examples of overhead cost items representing graphs (A and J) not referred to in answer (a) above:

Graph A: Vehicle hire cost, where hire charge/rental fee is fixed according to length of hire time, and also includes cost coverage for a certain allowed mileage without charge. However, beyond such a mileage allowance a 'per mile' charge comes into operation for additional travel by vehicle within hire time.

Graph J: Outside maintenance service cost, where outside maintenance engineers' time spent on service calls is costed at a rate which increases when certain activity level (i.e. time threshold) is reached. For instance, £12 per hour for first 4 hours, £14 per hour for next 4 hours, then £16 per hour for any extra time spent on a service call.

(c)

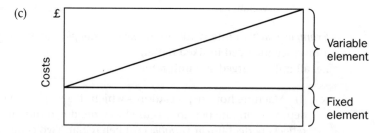

Example: Telephone/electricity charges.

Question 3.3

(a) At the two extremes, cost behaviour can be described as being either:

(i) *Fixed* – i.e. not affected by activity level fluctuations but time-related insofar as fixed costs may change with the passage of time; or

(ii) *Variable* – i.e. wholly affected by activity level fluctuations because variable costs vary in direct proportion to changes in the level of output, sales, hours worked, etc.

Other patterns of cost behaviour (semi- and step) can be identified as lying between the two above extremes.

(b) Calculation of total cost estimate for Period 5:

First, the preliminary step of time adjusting the cost data is needed so that cost increases can then be analysed as due purely to the effect of an increase in production units, i.e. eliminate the cost inflation bias:

Period	Cost index	Total cost	Time-adjustment of cost	Time-adjusted cost	Production units
		(£)		(£)	
1	100	2,600	$£2,600 \times \dfrac{100}{100} =$	2,600	1,500
2	110	3,256	$£3,256 \times \dfrac{100}{110} =$	2,960	1,800
3	120	4,560	$£4,560 \times \dfrac{100}{120} =$	3,800	2,500
4	125	5,800	$£5,800 \times \dfrac{100}{125} =$	4,640	3,200

Second, the high–low technique of cost estimation is applied to find values for the coefficients 'a' and 'b' (in the estimation formula: $y = a + bx$):

High–low	Period		$y = a + bx$
High	4	(1)	$4,640 = a + 3,200\ b$
Low	1	(2)	$2,600 = a + 1,500\ b$

Subtract (2) from (1): $2,040 = 1,700\ b$

$\therefore \text{'b'} = \dfrac{2,040}{1,700} = \underline{1.2}$

Substitute 'b' in (1): $4,640 = a + (3,200)(1.2)$

$= a + 3,840$

$\therefore \text{'a'} = 4,640 - 3,840 = \underline{800}$

Thus, using high–low means, the cost estimation formula is:

$$y = £800 + £1.20x$$

To determine a cost estimate for period 5, when 4,000 units are planned to be produced, simply plug in that activity level, i.e. variable 'x' value:

$$y = £800 + (£1.20)(4,000)$$
$$= £800 + £4,800$$

∴ *Total cost (high–low) estimate for period 5 =* £5,600

The third and final step is then to update this estimate of £5,600 by the expected period 5 index factor of 135, i.e. multiply by 1.35:

$$£5,600 × 1.35 = £7,560$$

This amount of £7,560 now represents the future value of total cost to be expected for a future period of time (period 5) based on a planned activity level of 4,000 production units.

Question 3.4

(a) (i) Delivery costs plotted on a scattergraph:

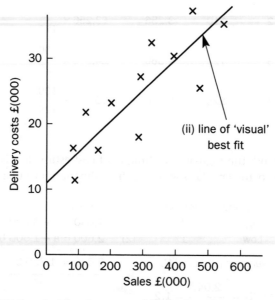

(iii) Level of fixed costs read from the 'y' axis at the intercept point 'a'
= £11,000 (approximately).

(b) Estimation formula which may be used to predicting future delivery costs for any level of sales:

$$y = a + bx$$

where: y = total delivery costs
              a = fixed delivery cost per period
              b = variable delivery cost per £ of sales
              x = sales level

Note: Sales level in this question is measured in value, i.e. £000, and the variable cost expressed in terms of sale '£'s – but it could equally well be gauged in volume, i.e. units of sale and the variable cost per sale unit.

The above formula is a simple two-variable (i.e. dependent 'y' and independent 'x') function which underpins all the linear cost estimation techniques dealt with in this chapter. By plugging in any given future level of activity (i.e. sales) the formula will generate/estimate a corresponding future level of cost (i.e. total delivery cost). This total cost comprises of a fixed element 'a' (intercept value of £11,000 in part (a) of this question) plus a variable element 'b' (not required to be calculated here).

Question 3.5

(a) (i) Algebraic cost function (including role of each term) 'which can be used to estimate the costs which the firm is likely to incur'.

$$y = a + bx$$

where: y = total cost of the firm
a = fixed costs in total
b = variable cost per unit
x = firm's activity level (in units)

(ii) Three methods of cost estimation which are based on the function/ formula, y = a + bx, above (others are possible e.g. analysis of accounts; industrial engineering estimates).

1 High–low (two point) method: based on the two extreme values in a set of observations of two variables. It may not, however, be representative of the data set as a whole. Simple to apply, easy to understand.

2 Scattergraph (visual fit/inspection) method: based on the graphing of all values in a series of observations. Takes account of all data available – but highly subjective with no statistical accuracy/validity.

3 Regression ('least-squares') analysis method: based on statistical approach to estimating, guaranteeing statistically 'best-fitting' function using all observed data. Appropriate for wide use of computer facilities. 'Scientific'/statistically sound approach to estimation problems.

(b) Cost behaviour understanding:

Example	Letter	Cost behaviour pattern
(a)	3	Fixed
(b)	4	Step-variable
(c)	8	Step-fixed
(d)	1	Semi-variable
(e)	6	Semi-variable
(f)	2	Variable
(g)	5	Semi-variable
(h)	3	Fixed
(i)	1	Semi-variable
(j)	3	Fixed
(k)	7	Variable

Year	Tons (x) (000)	Costs (y) (£000)	x^2 (million)	xy (£ million)
19X4	1.8	4.467	3.24	8.0406
19X5	2.0	4.522	4.00	9.0440
19X6	2.4	4.746	5.76	11.3904
19X7	2.1	4.410	4.41	9.2610
19X8	2.8	5.145	7.84	14.4060
	11.1	23.290	25.25	52.1420
	Σx	Σy	Σx^2	Σxy

Normal equations: $\Sigma y = na + b\Sigma x$

$\Sigma xy = a\Sigma x + b\Sigma x^2$

(1) 23.290 = 5a + 11.1b   Multiply (1) by 2.22
(2) 52.142 = 11.1a + 25.250b   to get equation (3)
(3) 51.704 = 11.1a + 24.642b ←──────┘

0.438 = 0.608b   Subtract (3) from (2)

$$\therefore b = \frac{.438}{.608} = 0.7204$$

Substitute in (1):   23.29 = 5a + (11.1)(.7204)

$\therefore$ 5a = 15.2936

$\therefore$ a = 3.0587

(i) Level of fixed costs: £3,059 per year (i.e. 19X9)

(ii) Variable cost per Fandango: £0.7204 (in 19X9)

Question 4.1

(a) Absorption (full-cost) and marginal (period) costing statements

	Absorption		Marginal	
	£000	£000	£000	£000
Sales (10,000 units @ £5/unit)		50		50
Cost of production (15,000 units)				
Direct materials (@ £1/unit)	15		15	
Direct labour (@ £2/unit)	30		30	
Variable overhead (@ £0.40/unit)	6		6	
Fixed overhead (@ £0.80/unit)	12		–	
	63		51	
(*less*) Closing stock (5,000 units)	(21)[1]		(17)[2]	
Cost of sales (10,000 units)		42		34
Contribution		–		16
Fixed overhead		–		12
Profit		8		4

Note: Closing stocks: [1]5,000 units @ full-cost: 5,000 x £4.20/unit = £21,000

[2]5,000 units @ marginal cost: 5,000 x £3.40/unit = £17,000

(b) No mistakes are made in either statement. Different results occur simply because different costing techniques are applied:

Absorption costing: when production is greater than sales this technique gives the higher profit because an element of fixed overhead cost is carried forward into next period's costing statement as part of stock valuation, i.e. £4,000 (5,000 units @ £0.80/unit) in this instance creating the higher profit figure. Argument for: complies with SSAP 9.

Marginal costing: in this example this technique generates the lower profit because all fixed overhead cost (i.e. £12,000) is written off in the period against the contribution (i.e. £16,000) for the period. On occasions where sales are greater than production levels this technique will give the higher profit. Argument for: particularly relevant for short-term operating decision purposes. Arguments against: marginal costing is unsuited to long-run situations, while absorption costing can provide dangerously misleading information for management decision-making activities.

Question 4.2

(a) Advice to management and assumptions:

	£
Price of component from Trigger plc	50
Marginal/variable cost of manufacture	34
Contribution generated by manufacturing in preference to purchase from Trigger plc	16

Management of Springer plc would be best advised to manufacture the component rather than buy it in.

Assumptions made:
(i)   Fixed overheads will not be affected by decision, i.e. no further fixed costs incurred by manufacture, nor any reduction in fixed overhead if component purchased.
(ii) All marginal costs of material, labour and overhead are 100 per cent variable.
(iii) Manufacture of component will not replace more lucrative work, particularly if scarcity of any resource involved (see (b) (ii) for instance). This may require some further investigation.

(b) Effect on advice under following two separate decision situations:
(i) While each component manufactured generates £16 contribution relative to purchase price from Trigger plc, incremental fixed costs of £56,000 now apply. If volume of manufacture exceeds incremental break-even point (BEP), then continued manufacture worthwhile:

$$\text{Incremental BEP} = \frac{£56,000}{£16} = \underline{3,500 \text{ components}}$$

Advice:
Up to BEP of 3,500 components continued manufacture is not worthwhile, therefore purchase. If annual output is greater than BEP of 3,500 components continued manufacture is worthwhile.

(ii) Existing product comparison with component manufacture:

	Price	Marginal cost	Contribution	Scarce resource – labour	Contribution per labour hour
	(£)	(£)	(£)	(hours)	(£)
Component manufacture	50	34	16	4	4
Existing product	90	50	40	8	5

Advice:
As the existing product offers a greater contribution per unit of scarce resource (i.e. labour hours) then it is more worthwhile to use labour on increasing production of existing product rather than manufacturing component which should now be purchased from Trigger plc at £50. Confirmation of this advice is thus: if four scarce hours were used manufacturing one component, this sacrifices £20 (4 × £5) of potential contribution from the existing product. This £20 lost contribution must be added to component marginal cost of £34 to get a £54 relevant cost which is greater than the purchase price of £50 from Trigger plc.

(c) A brief reply to Springer plc's production director:
The cost of special grinding equipment is a past 'sunk' cost and irrelevant to the production/purchase decision. Also irrelevant is the conventional writing-off of the written down book value of the asset – conventional depreciation is merely the allocation over time of an original 'sunk' cost.

Question 4.3

(a) Presentation of statements showing:
(i) *Profit for the current year*

	Potatoes	Turnips	Parsnips	Carrots	Total
Acres:	25	20	30	25	100
	(£)	(£)	(£)	(£)	(£)
Sales revenue	25,000	20,000	40,500	40,500	126,000
(less) Variable costs	(11,750)	(10,200)	(17,850)	(16,500)	(56,300)
Contribution	13,250	9,800	22,650	24,000	69,700
(less) Fixed overhead					(54,000)
Profit					15,700

Supporting calculations

	Potatoes	Turnips	Parsnips	Carrots
Tonne yield per acre	10	8	9	12
	(£)	(£)	(£)	(£)
Selling price per tonne	100	125	150	135
∴ Sales revenue per acre	1,000	1,000	1,350	1,620
(less) Variable costs per acre	(470)	(510)	(595)	(660)
∴ Contribution per acre	530	490	755	960

(ii) *Profit for the recommended production mix*

	PT area (45 acres)		PC area (55 acres)	
	Potatoes	Turnips	Parsnips	Carrots
Contribution per acre	£530	£490	£755	£960
Ranking via contribution per unit of limiting factor (i.e. per acre)	First	Second	Second	First
Minimum tonnes required	40	40	36	36
Minimum acres required	4	5	4	3
Remaining acres allocation	36	–	–	48
Recommended acre mix	40	5	4	51
∴ Contribution	£21,200	£2,450	£3,020	£48,960

	(£)
Contribution in total from recommended acre mix	75,630
(less) Fixed overhead	(54,000)
Profit for the recommended production mix	21,630

(b) (i) Advice as to which crop to concentrate production upon:
Concentration should be on production of carrots, because carrots generate highest contribution per unit of limiting factor/scarce resource (i.e. acres) giving £960 contribution for every acre of land.

(ii) Calculation of profit from optimal strategy

	(£)
Contribution (optimal) from carrot production using total 100 acres × £960/acre:	96,000
(less) Fixed overhead	(54,000)
Optimal profit	42,000

Question 4.4

(a) Determination of shop space module allocation to optimise profit

	Ranges				
	A	B	C	D	E
Contribution per module	(£)	(£)	(£)	(£)	(£)
1 module	1,350	1,400	1,200	1,600	1,000
(i) 2 modules	1,250	1,260	1,150	1,300	1,100
(Sales × contribution %)					
Total contribution:					
(ii) 1 module:	1,350	1,400	1,200	1,600	1,000
(iii) 2 modules:	2,500	2,520	2,300	2,600	2,200
((iii) = double (i))					
Contribution from the second module ((iii) − (ii))	1,150	1,120	1,100	1,000	1,200

Ranking order for allocation of modules (based on contribution per module)

(1) Range D: 1st module   (£1,600 per module)
(2) Range B: 1st module   (£1,400 per module)
(3) Range A: 1st module   (£1,350 per module)
(4) Range C: 1st module   (£1,200 per module)
(5) Range A: 2nd module   (£1,150 per module)
(6) Range B: 2nd module   (£1,120 per module)
(7) Range C: 2nd module   (£1,100 per module)

Note: Although range E's second module offers £1,200 contribution per module it does not feature in optimal allocation because the first E module is a necessary prerequisite but only offers £1,000 contribution/module.

(b) Calculation of profit for each range and for total shop:

	Range				
	A	B	C	D	Total
	(£)	(£)	(£)	(£)	(£)
Contribution	2,500	2,520	2,300	1,600	8,920
(*less*) Operating costs	(1,600)	(1,600)	(1,600)	(800)	(5,600)
(£5,600 ÷ 7 'pro-rata')					
Profit:	900	920	700	800	3,320

(c) Solution to this part requirement can be extracted from section 4.3 of Chapter 4.

Question 5.1

(a) Maximin criterion

Pay-off matrix (values in pence)

Magazines: Number demanded: stocked	10	12	14	16	18	20	22	Minimum pay-off
10	100	100	100	100	100	100	100	100
12	70	120	120	120	120	120	120	70
14	40	90	140	140	140	140	140	40
16	10	60	110	160	160	160	160	10
18	(20)	30	80	130	180	180	180	(20)
20	(50)	0	50	100	150	200	200	(50)
22	(80)	(30)	20	70	120	170	220	(80)

Applying the maximin criterion: as the highest minimum pay-off results from stocking ten magazines (i.e. £1.00) store management should decide on this optimal number.

(b) Expected values

Pay-off matrix (money values in pence)

Magazines: Number demanded:		10	12	14	16	18	20	22	Expected
stocked	Probability	.05	.1	.15	.3	.2	.15	.05	Value
10		5	10	15	30	20	15	5	100
12		3.5	12	18	36	24	18	6	117.5
14		2	9	21	42	28	21	7	130
16		0.5	6	16.5	48	32	24	8	135
18		(1)	3	12	39	36	27	9	125
20		(2.5)	0	7.5	30	30	30	10	105
22		(4)	(3)	3	21	24	25.5	11	77.5

Applying the EMV criterion: maximum EMV from stocking sixteen magazines (i.e. £1.35); therefore store management should decide on this optimal number. EMV is the more suitable criterion being superior to maximin and because the management action of stocking is repeated regularly (i.e. each week).

Question 5.2

Decision tree solution to British Aircraft Company strategy

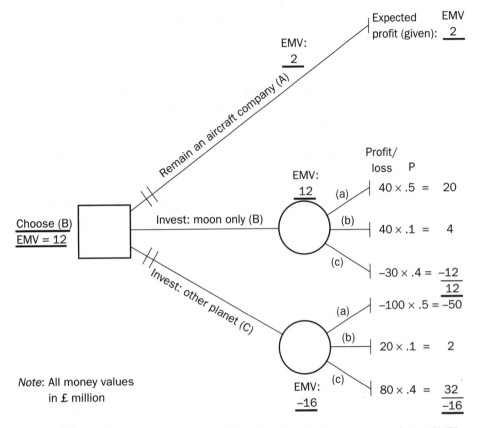

Recommendation to management of British Aircraft Company: applying EMV decision technique/criterion, choose decision strategy (B) – i.e. invest in building space craft capable only of reaching the moon.

Question 5.3

(a) Adjust 'gross pay-offs' by deducting cost of purchasing patent rights to arrive at 'net monetary values' (M) which are then substituted for 'M' in the subjective utility function: $U(M) = 2(10 + M)^{\frac{1}{2}}$. Finally, apply probabilities for SEU values.

'CORNIX'
Monetary values in £000s

Gross pay-off	Cost of patents	Net value	Utility function =	U(M)	Probability	SEU
7	1	6	$2(10 + 6)^{\frac{1}{2}}$	8	0.2	1.6
16	1	15	$2(10 + 15)^{\frac{1}{2}}$	10	0.5	5.0
27	1	26	$2(10 + 26)^{\frac{1}{2}}$	12	0.3	3.6
						10.2

'SOLITAIRE'

-5	1	-6	$2(10-6)^{\frac{1}{2}}$	4	0.2	0.8
0	1	-1	$2(10-1)^{\frac{1}{2}}$	6	0.5	3.0
40	1	39	$2(10+39)^{\frac{1}{2}}$	14	0.3	4.2
						8.0

On the basis of SEU model, advise Sanderone's management team to buy manufacturing and patent rights to 'CORNIX' which maximises (subjective expected) utility: 10.2 > 8.0 utiles.

(b) (i) The principal advantage of the SEU criterion over 'expected monetary values' (EMV) is that it incorporates 'risk attitudes'. The EMV approach is a purely 'risk neutral' model and is incapable of reflecting risk preferences (i.e. risk aggressiveness/risk aversion). The following diagrams of EMV and SEU functions illustrate the principal advantage of the SEU approach:

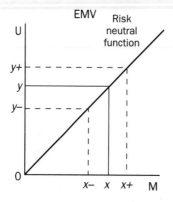

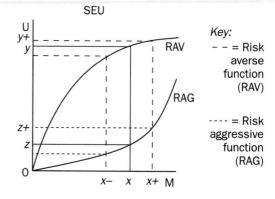

Note:
Money (M) changes (x+/x−) are reflected by *equal* changes (y+/y−) in utility (U)

Note:
Equal money (M) changes reflected by *differing* utility (U) changes.
Risk averse → proportionately less U from extra M (x+ and y+)
Risk aggressive → proportionately more U from extra M (x+ and z+)
[The opposite applies with decrease in M]

(ii) Although the SEU model does typify the approach of rational economic man, stringent and demanding assumptions are contained in the model:

Assumptions (any 3 from the following)

▶ Maximisation: maximum utility will always be sought by decision-maker.
▶ Omniscience: complete knowledge about all available alternatives.
▶ Consistency: decision-maker will be consistent in choices between alternatives.
▶ Human information processing: decision-maker has sufficient mental capacity to utilise 'total information set' in second assumption to evaluate alternatives.

(c) SEU and EMV approaches' main criticism is that they fail to recognise individuals' limited capacity as regards rational economic activity.

Individuals are limited by virtue of many factors, such as environment, education, mental capacity, society in general.

Bounded Rationality – (Herbert Simon) – pays recognition to such limiting/constraining factors.

Simon developed this approach to describe individual decision-making activity in terms of *satisficing* behaviour which implies:

▶ non-maximisation of utility/satisfaction.
▶ information 'overload' is avoided by rejection of information.
▶ search limitation – restriction on alternatives evaluated.

Question 5.4

Workings:
(i) *Contribution per unit*

	A	B	C
Sales price per unit	340	190	130
Variable cost per unit:	140	110	70
Contribution per unit:	200	80	60

(ii) *Fixed costs (£000)*

Rights	130	190	200
Manufacturing	120	20	20
Advertising	50	30	20
	300	240	240

(a)

Statement of EMV of each product (£000)

Product	Unit sales volume	Total contribution	Fixed cost	Profit	Probability	EMV
A	0	0	(300)	(300)	0.1	(30)
	2,500	500	(300)	200	0.4	80
	4,000	800	(300)	500	0.5	250
						300
B	3,000	240	(240)	0	0.1	0
	4,000	320	(240)	80	0.3	24
	6,000	480	(240)	240	0.3	72
	8,000	640	(240)	400	0.3	120
						216
C	7,000	420	(240)	180	0.8	144
	8,000	480	(240)	240	0.1	24
	9,000	540	(240)	300	0.1	30
						198

Therefore on EMV decision rule/criterion, select product A. *Note*: Also see the decision tree at end of solution.

(b) (i) Accuracy of:

1. Cost estimates
2. Revenue estimates
3. Probability estimates (Subjective?)
4. Sales volume estimates (Non-discrete levels?)

(ii) Risk attitudes: Management may be risk averse → EMV does not account for it! Product C always produces a profit – A could lose heavily; B may only break-even.

(iii) Dis-utility of a large loss (£300,000 on A) may be weighted more heavily than the positive utility of a greater gain (£500,000). Bankruptcy perhaps from 0.1 chance of £300,000 loss.

(c) *Calculate gross and net values* of the market research study:

The market research study (i.e. perfect information) 'ascertains with complete accuracy exactly' the specific sales level.

		Profit (£000)	Decision/ Action
When it indicates	0 sales volume	(300)	**Do not** proceed
	2,500 sales volume	200	Proceed
	4,000 sales volume	500	Proceed

Calculate EMV <u>with</u> study and compare with EMV <u>without</u> study

Sales indicated by study	Profit	Probability	EMV
2,500	200	.4	80
4,000	500	.5	250
∴ EMV *with* study			330
EMV *without* study			300
Gross value of study			30
less cost of study			20
Net value of study			£10

Alternatively

Sales	Profit (incl. study cost)	Probability	EMV
0	(20)	0.1	(2)
2,500	180	0.4	72
4,000	480	0.5	240
			310

(£000)

Revised EMV	= 310
Original EMV	= 300
Increase in EMV	= £10

Unit demand	Contribution	Fixed	(£000)	P	EMV (£000)
EMV: £300,000					
0	(£340 – £140) (0) –	£300,000 =	–300	× 0.1 =	–30
2,500	(£200) (2,500) –	£300,000 =	200	× 0.4 =	80
4,000	(£200) (4,000) –	£300,000 =	500	× 0.5 =	250 / 300
EMV: £216,000					
3,000	(£190 – £110) (3,000) –	£240,000 =	0	× 0.1 =	0
4,000	(£80) (4,000) –	£240,000 =	80	× 0.3 =	24
6,000	(£80) (6,000) –	£240,000 =	240	× 0.3 =	72
8,000	(£80) (8,000) –	£240,000 =	400	× 0.3 =	120 / 216
EMV: £198,000					
7,000	(£130 – £70) (7,000) –	£240,000 =	180	× 0.8 =	144
8,000	(£60) (8,000) –	£240,000 =	240	× 0.1 =	24
9,000	(£60) (9,000) –	£240,000 =	300	× 0.1 =	30 / 198

Choose A

A

B

C

EMV: £300,000

Question 6.1

(a) (i) Conventional break-even chart

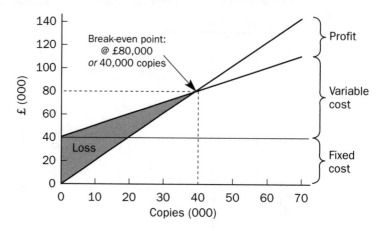

Break-even point:
@ £80,000
or 40,000 copies

Profit

Variable
cost

Loss

Fixed
cost

£ (000)

Copies (000)

(ii) *Verification of break-even point by calculation:*

$$(\text{Note: P/V ratio} = \frac{\text{Contribution}}{\text{Selling price}} = \frac{£1}{£2} = 50\% \text{ or } .5)$$

Use any of the following formulae:

1. $$\frac{\text{Fixed cost}}{\text{Contribution}} = \frac{£40,000}{£1} = \underline{40,000 \text{ copies}}$$

2. $px = a + bx$ (where p = price; a = fixed costs; b = variable cost)
    $\therefore 2x = 40,000 + 1x$
    $\therefore \quad x = \underline{40,000 \text{ copies}}$

3. $$\frac{\text{Fixed cost}}{\text{P/V ratio}} = \frac{£40,000}{.5} = \underline{£80,000}$$

(iii) *Margin of safety* @ 55,000 copies:

Margin of safety   =   Actual sales − Break-even point sales

∴ Margin of safety   =   55,000 − 40,000 = <u>15,000 copies</u>

or £110,000 − £80,000 = <u>£30,000</u>.

(b) The market trader's offer of £1,800 is *acceptable* if:

(i) it represents the highest possible offer available;
(ii) alternative use for redundant stocks (e.g. waste paper disposal proceeds)
     will not realise greater income.

Historical/'sunk' costs of the 10,000 copies are irrelevant to the decision.

If copies not yet 'bound and finished' (assuming same 20p per copy as PPII) → then *minimum offer acceptable* becomes (10,000 × 20p) = £2,000.

Other factors probably worth considering include:

1 Effect on 'goodwill' of regular outlets: usual stockists may not appreciate their current stocks of the publication being 'undercut' by market trader;
2 Perhaps offer surplus copies to regular customers at 'cut-price'.

Question 6.2

(a) Up to the 'crossover' point of total revenue (TR) and total costs (TC) at any point on the scale of volume a loss, for example, point (a), is made because cost 'outgoings' are greater than sales 'incomings'. After the crossover point of TR and TC the reverse applies – i.e. costs going out are now less than sales revenues coming in. Any point on the volume scale, for example, point (b), after this 'crossover' of TR and TC will show a profit. In accounting this crossover point is known as the 'break-even point'.
(b) Solution to this part requirement can be extracted from section 6.3 of Chapter 6 which critically identifies and examines certain C-V-P assumptions.

Question 6.3

(a) Costing terms defined and explained:
(i) *Break-even point* can be defined as the level of volume at which there is neither a profit nor loss. It may be expressed in terms of either units or value.

It can be calculated from formulae, e.g.

$$\frac{\text{Fixed costs}}{\text{Contribution/unit}} = \text{BEP in units}$$

$$Or: \frac{\text{Fixed cost} \times \text{sales value}}{\text{Total contribution}} = \text{BEP in value}$$

Alternatively, the BEP may be ascertained graphically by reading from a break-even chart.

(ii) *Margin of safety* can be defined as the excess of normal or actual sales over sales at breakeven point. As with the break-even point, it may be expressed either as a value or number of units. The margin of safety clearly indicates what reduction in the level of activity is possible before the organisation is just breaking even.
(iii) *Profit/volume (P/V or Contribution/sales) ratio* is an expression of the rate at which contribution is made towards covering fixed costs and then making profit. It is a useful tool in that it can be used to:

(a) calculate BEP; and

(b) measure the effect of changes in the activity level on profit.

It is given by the formula:

$$\frac{\text{Contribution per unit}}{\text{Selling price per unit}} \times 100 = \text{P/V ratio in percentage terms.}$$

When divided into fixed costs it gives the BEP in terms of value.

(iv) *Contribution breakeven chart* is a variation of the conventional or traditional break-even chart and is constructed by plotting the variable cost coordinates below the fixed cost coordinates (i.e. the opposite to a conventional chart). Its usefulness lies in its portrayal of the contribution towards fixed costs and, thereafter, profit. In so illustrating the contribution graphically, it serves to emphasise the importance of the contribution concept in marginal costing and C-V-P analysis.

(b) Profit-volume (P/V) chart

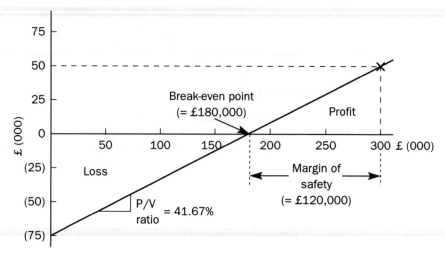

(c) Calculation of P/V (or C/S) ratio

Contribution = Sales – Variable/Marginal Cost

∴ Contribution = £300,000 – £175,000 = £125,000

$$\text{P/V ratio} = \frac{\text{Contribution}}{\text{Sales}} = \frac{£125,000}{£300,000} = 0.4167 \text{ or } 41.67\%$$

Verification (by calculation) of BEP derived from P/V chart in (b):

$$\text{BEP} = \frac{\text{Fixed costs}}{\text{P/V ratio}} = \frac{£75,000}{0.4167} = £180,000$$

(d) Solution to this part requirement can be extracted from section 6.3 of Chapter 6.

Question 6.4

(a) Graph showing Zed plc's results for six months ended 30th April

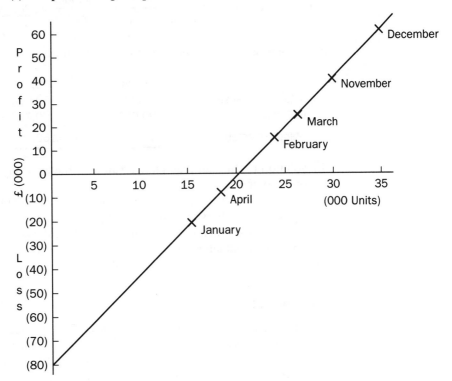

Determination/confirmation of above graphed C-V-P detail

(i) Every 1,000 increase/(decrease) in units results in £4,000 increase/(decrease) in profit

∴ Contribution per unit = £4

Taking any month, e.g. April	£
Total contribution (18,000 × £4)	72,000
Loss	8,000
∴ *Fixed costs*	£80,000

(ii)

Selling price per unit	£10
Contribution per unit	£4
Variable cost per unit	£6

(iii) $\dfrac{\text{Contribution per unit}}{\text{Selling price per unit}} = \dfrac{£4}{£10}$

$\therefore$ *P/V ratio* = <u>0.4 or 40%</u>

(iv) *Break-even point* $= \dfrac{\text{Fixed costs}}{\text{Contribution}} = \dfrac{£80,000}{£4} = \underline{\begin{array}{c}20,000\text{ units}\\(\text{or }£200,000)\end{array}}$

(v) Assuming actual/normal sales to be 35,000 units

	Units	£
Actual/normal sales	35,000	350,000
BEP sales	20,000	200,000
Margin of safety	15,000 units or	£150,000

(b) Solution to this part requirement can be extracted from section 6.3 of Chapter 6.

(c) The relevant range's essential use or nature is to restrict the scope of break-even analysis to within certain practical parameters. Only C-V-P relationships which reflect the normal and regular activity scale of business operations will fall within the sphere or span of the relevant range of analysis.

Question 7.1

(a)

Product		House		Horse		Hellefump	
Unit volume		10,000		5,000		8,000	
	Unit	Total	Unit	Total	Unit	Total	
Current year	(£)	(£000)	(£)	(£000)	(£)	(£000)	
Materials (M)	80		120		100		
Labour/overheads (1.5 × M)	120		180		150		
Total cost	200		300		250		
Profit/(loss)	20		(20)		10		
Selling price	220		280		260		
Next year							
Selling price (current + 5%)	231		294		273		

(i)

Variable costs	House	Horse	Hellefump
Materials (current + 10%)	88	132	110
Saw	25	25	25
Shape	10	10	10
Drill			30
Paint	20		20
Assemble	22	22	22
Total variable cost	165	189	217

(ii)	Contribution	66	660	105	525	56	448
(i)	*Fixed costs*						
	Saw		40		20		32
	Shape		60		30		48
	Drill						48
	Paint		200				160
	Assemble		80		40		64
	Total fixed cost	38	380	18	90	44	352
(iii)	Profit	28	280	87	435	12	96

(b) Traditional absorption rate (arbitrarily chosen) of percentage on direct materials cost is unsuitable for pricing decisions. The effect of change next year is to adopt a more appropriate 'operations/activities' based approach to costing and pricing. Change will have the effect of Horse being transformed from a loss-maker to the most profitable product in the range.

Question 7.2

(i) Solution to this part requirement can be extracted from section 7.2.3 of Chapter 7.

(ii) A tabulation is a suitable format, thus:

Selling price (£)	Marginal cost (£)	Unit contribution (£)	Sales demand (Units)	Gross contribution (£000)	Machine cost (£000)	Net contribution (£000)
40	20	20	2,000	40	8	32
38	20	18	2,400	43.2	10	33.2
36	20	16	3,000	48	12	36
34	20	14	3,800	53.2	16	37.2
32	20	12	4,800	57.6	20	37.6
30	20	10	6,000	60	24	36
28	20	8	7,500	60	30	30

Product should be sold at a price of £32 to realise an optimal/maximum net contribution of £37,600 with ten machines needing to be acquired to produce 4,800 units.

Question 7.3

(a)

(i) The break-even point (see above graph):
Will be the level of production at which total contribution = fixed costs

Contribution = £20 − (£8 + £7) = £5/unit
Fixed costs = 120,000 × £2 = £240,000
Break-even point = 240,000/5 = 48,000 units

(ii) If sales fall to 100,000, (see above graph), profit will be (100,000 × £5) −
£240,000 = £260,000

(iii) To generate profit of 20 per cent of sales:

20% × price = £4/unit
Total contribution: 5Q = 240,000 + 4Q
                       Q = 240,000 units (∴ production would have to double)

(b) The principal points to be covered here concern the assumptions that are
made about cost and revenue behaviour. The basic accounting break-even
analysis makes different assumptions from those implied in a more economics
based model. Limiting assumptions may be acceptable within restricted
ranges. Linear relationships may be unrealistic. Other factors (e.g. risk,
interdependencies) are ignored. See section 6.3 of Chapter 6 for further details.

(c) Optimal production level, assuming profit maximisation objective, will be
where marginal cost = marginal revenue

Marginal cost = variable cost = 8 + 7 = 15

From market research information, price (P)/demand (Q) relationship
suggests price = 28 − Q/15

$$\text{Total revenue} = P \times Q = 28Q - 2Q/15$$

Marginal revenue = (differentiate total revenue) = 28 − 2Q/15

Set equal to marginal cost: 15 = 28 − 2Q/15
                            Q = 97.5 (000)

Optimal price: P = 28 − 97.5/15 = £21.5

Question 7.4

(a) Pricing computations for special order of 10,000 AREMAC cameras

(i) Full cost-plus pricing, on current basis:

	£000	£000
Direct costs		
Material	24	
Labour	16	
Prime cost		40
Production overheads (absorbed @ 100% of prime cost):		40
Factory/production cost		80
Administrative and marketing overheads (absorbed at 25% of factory/production cost)		20
Full cost		100
Profit (margin @ 20% mark-up on full cost)		20
Sales price to be quoted for the special order		120

(ii) Pricing decision enabling original budgeted profit to be attained:

	£000	£000
Original budgeted profit	100	
Adjusted budgeted profit @ 75% sales capacity (see supporting calculation[1] adjustment)	25	
Contribution required from special order to subsidise original budgeted profit		75
Marginal costs of producing special order		
Material	24	
Labour	16	
Production overheads ($\frac{1}{2}$ fixed	40	
therefore $\frac{1}{2}$ variable × prime cost above)	20	60
Sales price to be quoted for the special order		135

(iii) Pricing decision using unit overhead absorption rate, with profit applied on current basis:

	£000	£000
Direct costs		
Material	24	
Labour	16	
Prime cost		40

Overheads (see supporting calculation[2] absorption rates)

Production (absorbed @ £5 per unit × 10,000 units):	50	
Administrative and marketing (absorbed @ £2.50 per unit × 10,000 units)	25	75
Full cost		115
Profit (margin applied @ 20% on full cost)		23
Sales price to be quoted for the special order		138

Supporting calculations:
[1]Budget adjusted to 75 per cent sales capacity (i.e. 25 per cent shortfall on sales):

	£000
Direct costs	
Material (£120,000 × 0.75)	90
Labour (£80,000 × 0.75)	60
Prime cost	150
Production overheads	
Variable ($\frac{1}{2}$ of £200,000 = £100,000 × 0.75)	75
Fixed ($\frac{1}{2}$ of £200,000)	100
Factory/production cost	325
Administrative and marketing overheads	100
Full cost	425
Sales revenue (£600,000 × 0.75)	450
Profit (adjustment to original £100,000 budgeted)	25

[2]Unit overhead absorption rate calculations:

Budgeted production overheads = £200,000
Budgeted unit volume = 40,000 units

Therefore:
Production overhead absorption rate

$$= \frac{£200,000}{40,000} = \underline{£5 \text{ per unit}} \text{ (camera)}$$

Budgeted administrative and marketing overheads = £100,000
Budgeted unit volume = 40,000 units

Therefore:
Administrative and marketing overhead absorption rate

$$= \frac{£100,000}{40,000} = \underline{£2.50 \text{ per unit}} \text{ (camera)}$$

(b) Pricing policy for special order of 10,000 AREMAC cameras

Advice to management:

The prices per camera based on the quotations calculated in (a) are

(i) £120,000 ÷ 10,000 units = £12 per camera;
(ii) £135,000 ÷ 10,000 units = £13.50 per camera;
(iii) £138,000 ÷ 10,000 units = £13.80 per camera.

Pricing policy/strategy to be advised is (ii), i.e. sell at £13.50 per camera – see factors below.

Factors to be brought to management's attention:

Both strategies (i) and (iii) above determine prices via policy decisions based on full absorption cost-plus methods/approaches. Neither method (i) which uses budgeted expenditures as the absorption base, nor method (iii) which uses budgeted unit volume to generate an absorption rate upon which the pricing decision is made are suitable. A more appropriate approach is given by strategy/policy (ii) being a marginal/contribution margin pricing method. Decisions made on this basis are more suited to short-run, one-off strategic pricing opportunities such as the one presented by the special order for AREMAC cameras. The approach is a closer approximation to optimal pricing strategies (see section 7.1 of Chapter 7) than the cost-plus/full-cost pricing techniques whose drawbacks are detailed at the end of section 7.2.2. Remember, however, all techniques have a potentially valuable role to play in differing sets of circumstances (see section 7.2.3).

Question 8.1

(a) Computation of expected monetary value (EMV) of annual revenue:

$$EMV = (£20,000 \times 0.5) + (£40,000 \times 0.3) + (£80,000 \times 0.2)$$
$$= £10,000 + £12,000 + £16,000 = \underline{£38,000}$$

(b) Net present value (NPV) calculation:

$$NPV = (£38,000 \times A_{10}) - £95,000 - (£40,000 \times V_{10}) - (£10,000 \times A_{10})$$

Net off the two A_{10} amounts, i.e. deduct £10,000 from £38,000

$$(£28,000 \times 6.145) - £95,000 - (£40,000 \times 0.385)$$
$$= £172,060 - £95,000 - £15,400 = \underline{£61,660}$$

(c) Change in NPV if rock type A is present:

$$NPV = (£20,000 \times 6.145) - £95,000 - (£40,000 \times 0.385) - (£10,000 \times 6.145)$$
$$= £122,900 - £95,000 - £15,400 - £61,450 = \underline{-£48,950}$$

Therefore, NPV change from amount in (b) to (c)

$$£61,660 - (-£48,950) = \underline{£110,610}$$

(d) Maximum amount to pay will be the gross value of the information, *viz.*

Expected net present value (ENPV) *with* information compared with ENPV *without* information. The latter amount is the value already calculated in (b), i.e. £61,660.

With the benefit of information, of rock type A indicated then no investment would be made, resulting in an ENPV with information of:

$$((£40,000 \times 6.145) - £95,000 - £15,400 - £61,450) \times 0.3$$
$$+ \quad ((£80,000 \times 6.145) - £95,000 - £15,400 - £61,450) \times 0.2$$

Therefore ENPV *with* information = £22,185 + £63,950:	£86,135
Compared to ENPV *without* information (see (b) above):	£61,660
Gross value of (i.e. maximum amount to pay for) information:	£24,475

Note: Alternatively a quick solution would be that with information the negative of £48,950 (see (c) above) if rock type A is present could be avoided 50 per cent of the time, i.e. £48,950 × 0.5 = £24,475.

(e) Solution to this part requirement can be extracted from section 5.2.4 of Chapter 5.

Question 8.2

(a) NPV of Projects X and Y:

Year	0	1	2	3	4	5	NPV
	(£000)	(£000)	(£000)	(£000)	(£000)	(£000)	(£000)
Project X:	–200	+(35)(.909)	+(80)(.826)	+(90)(.751)	+(75)(.683)	+(20)(.621)	=+29.13
Project Y:	–200	+(218)(.909)	+(10)(.826)	+(10)(.751)	+(4)(.683)	+(3)(.621)	=+18.53

IRR of Projects X and Y:

Project X: Try 10% (as above)   =+29.13
          Try 20%

(£000)	(£000)	(£000)	(£000)	(£000)	(£000)	(£000)
–200	+(35)(.833)	+(80)(.694)	+(90)(.579)	+(75)(.482)	+(20)(.402)	=–19.03

Project Y: Try 10% (as above)   =+18.53
          Try 20%

–200	+(218)(.833)	+(10)(.694)	+(10)(.579)	+(4)(.482)	+(3)(.402)	=–2.54

Linear Interpolation (mathematically)

Project X:
$$10\% + \left(\frac{29.13}{48.16} \times 10\% \right) = \underline{16.1\%}$$

Project Y:
$$10\% + \left(\frac{18.53}{21.07} \times 10\% \right) = \underline{18.8\%}$$

(b) Recommendation: undertake project X.
Reasons:

▶ Both projects at 10 per cent are acceptable but X has greater NPV.
▶ Although project Y has higher IRR, project X is preferable because NPV is the superior decision technique.
▶ Both projects have IRRs higher than 10 per cent; there is an inevitable consistency with NPV of both being acceptable.
▶ Both projects rejected at 20 per cent – negative NPVs and IRRs lower than 20 per cent.

(c) As projects are mutually exclusive, ranking vitally important as opposed to accept/reject decision. Conflict (at 10 per cent) in ranking: NPV prefers Project X; IRR prefers Project Y. Inconsistency in ranking is explained by the pattern of timing of cash flows. Almost 90 per cent of the cash inflows from Project Y occur in the first year – as the discounting becomes heavier these earlier cash returns, *vis-à-vis* Project X, are rewarded relatively more significantly. At lower discount rates the difference in timing of cash inflows is less crucial. At zero per cent, for example, in £000s:

Project X: (35 + 80 + 90 + 75 + 20) – 200 = 100 net cash flow (undiscounted)

Project Y: (218 + 10 + 10 + 4 + 3) – 200 = 45 net cash flow (undiscounted)

Projects' NPV profiles (see section (d) graph) clearly reflect importance of the timing pattern of cash inflows – Y's 'flatter' line indicates relatively less effect upon its NPV from the process of (heavier) discounting.

(d)

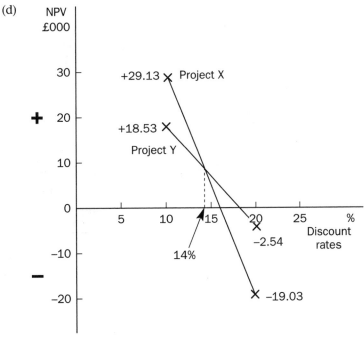

Note: At 14 per cent or above, project Y would be recommended in preference to project X.

Question 8.3

(a) Payback

	Project X	Project Y
Payback period	*4 years*	*5 years*

Project X   *Project Y*

Payback period   *4 years*   *5 years*
(i.e. 2,500 + 1,000 +   (i.e. 1,500 + 2,000 + 2,500
1,000 + 500 = 5,000)   + 1,000 + 1,000 = 8,000)

Project X is to be preferred on the basis of payback

(b) Net present value (NPV)

Project X $-5,000 + (2,500)(.893) + (1,000)(.797) + (1,000)(.712)$
$+ (500)(.636) + (1,500)(.567) + (1,000)(.507) = \underline{417}$

$\text{NPV} = +\,£417$ $\therefore$ project X is *acceptable* on the basis of NPV

Project Y $-8,000 + (1,500)(.893) + (2,000)(.797) + (2,500)(.712) +$
$(1,000)(.636) + (1,000)(.567) + (2,500)(.507) = \underline{-816}$

$\text{NPV} = -£816$ $\therefore$ project Y is *unacceptable* on the basis of NPV

(c) Internal rate of return (IRR)

IRR (by graphical means) for Project X

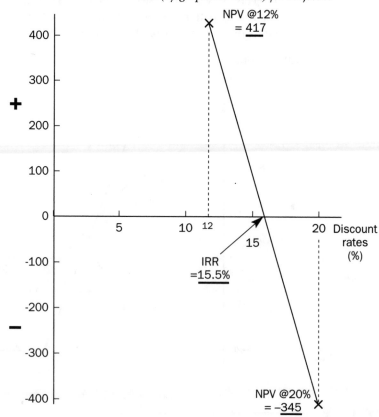

(d) Accounting rate of return (ARR) – not recommended because:
   (i) Profits/income are highly subjective (whereas cash flows are objective);
   (ii) No consideration of time value of money;
   (iii) Different conflicting definitions exist of capital employed (e.g. average or total investment?).

(e) Merits of technique used in (a) to (c):

   (a) *Payback*
       (i) Simple to use/apply.
       (ii) Commonly found in practice.
       (iii) Easy to understand.
       (iv) Emphasis on speedy project returns helps liquidity.

   (b) *Net present value*
       (i) Absolute measure giving monetary result reflecting scale of project.
       (ii) Considers time value of money.
       (iii) Unambiguous decision information even with unorthodox/erratic cash flows.
       (iv) Relatively easy to calculate (compared with IRR).

   (c) *Internal rate of return*
       (i) Considers time value of money.
       (ii) Percentage return figure relatively easy to comprehend by non-financial personnel (compare with NPV).
       (iii) Unlike ARR, uses objective cash flow data.

Question 8.4

(a) Project calculations

(i) ARR: Assuming average profits as a return on average investment:

	Project A (£000)		Project B (£000)	
Year 1	25	Average	10	Average
Year 2	20	profit	10	profit
Year 3	15		14	
Year 4	10		26	
	70 ÷ 4 =	£17,500	60 ÷ 4 =	£15,000

Average investment: (Opening investment value + Closing investment value) ÷ 2

Both projects: (£50,000 + £10,000) ÷ 2 = £30,000

Project A: $\dfrac{£17,500}{£30,000} \times 100 = 58.33\%$

Project B: $\dfrac{£15,000}{£30,000} \times 100 = 50\%$

(ii) Payback period:

As cash flows are the money base for this technique (and for (iii) also) there is a need to calculate them simply by adjusting the profit for depreciation

(£10,000 annual charge: $\dfrac{£50,000 - £10,000)}{4}$

Each year's cash flow, therefore, is the annual profit figure plus £10,000, thus

	Project cash flows	
	A (£000)	B (£000)
Year 1	35	20
Year 2	30	20
Year 3	25	24
Year 4	30	46

(*Note:* Year 4 also includes cash resale value, i.e. cash inflow of £10,000 extra).

	Project A	Project B
Payback (whole years):	2	3
Payback (fractional years):	1.5 (1 + $\dfrac{15}{30}$)	2.42 (1 + $\dfrac{10}{24}$)

(iii) NPV (all values in £000s):

Year	0 (£000)	1 (£000)	2 (£000)	3 (£000)	4 (£000)	NPV (£000)
Project A	−50	+ (35)(.909)	+ (30)(.826)	+ (25)(.751)	+ (30)(.683)	= 45.860
Project B	−50	+ (20)(.909)	+ (20)(.826)	+ (24)(.751)	+ (46)(.683)	= 34.142

(b) Merits of methods

ARR possesses little merit as an investment appraisal decision technique – see solution 8.3, section (d)

Payback and NPV both possess merit – see solution 8.3, section (e).

(c) Recommendation

As NPV is the superior investment appraisal decision technique, then Project A would be preferred as its NPV of £45,860 exceeds that of Project B (£34,142). But note also that A just happens to be preferable to B on the other criteria too (this is coincidental, i.e. it is not necessarily always the case).

Question 9.1

(a) Budget preparation for the month of January

(i) R Limited: Sales budget

Product	Sales quantity (units)	Selling price (per unit)	Sales value (£000)
A	1,000	£100	100
B	2,000	£120	240
C	1,500	£140	210
Budgeted sales	4,500		550

(ii) R Limited: Production units budget

Product	A (units)	B (units)	C (units)	Total (units)
Budgeted sales – from (i)	1,000	2,000	1,500	4,500
Budgeted closing stock	1,100	1,650	550	3,300
(less) Budgeted opening stock	(1,000)	(1,500)	(500)	(3,000)
Budgeted production units	1,100	2,150	1,550	4,800

(iii) R Limited: Materials usage budget

Budgeted production requirement – from (ii)	Units of M1 per product	Units of M1 in total	Units of M2 per product	Units of M2 in total	Units of M3 per product	Units of M3 in total	Total units
Product A (1,100 units)	4	4,400	2	2,200	–	–	6,600
Product B (2,150 units)	3	6,450	3	6,450	2	4,300	17,200
Product C (1,550 units)	2	3,100	1	1,550	1	1,550	6,200
Budgeted material usage		13,950		10,200		5,850	30,000

(iv) R Limited: Materials purchase budget

	M1 (units)	M2 (units)	M3 (units)	Total (units)
Budgeted material usage – from (iii)	13,950	10,200	5,850	30,000
Budgeted closing stock	31,200	24,000	14,400	59,600
(less) Budgeted opening stock	(26,000)	(20,000)	(12,000)	(58,000)
Budgeted material purchase (qty.)	19,150	14,200	8,250	31,600
Unit cost of material	£4	£6	£9	(£)
Budgeted material purchase (£)	76,600	85,200	74,250	236,050

(b) The principal budget factor in part (a) was assumed to be the level of product sales (i.e market demand for R Limited's products) and therefore the primary budget prepared was the sales budget as in (a) (i). Essentially the principal budget factor is given by whatever element or feature places the most important limit upon business operations – indeed it is sometimes alternatively referred to as the 'limiting factor'. In addition to sales demand, other examples include: machine time/hours available; storage capacity; skilled labour necessary.

Question 9.2

(a) Preparation of Squire's cash budget for the four quarters

Quarter ending	31 March	30 June	30 September	31 December	TOTAL
Cash inflows	£000	£000	£000	£000	£000
Sales (debtors)	140	150	145	160	595
Issue of share capital			25		25
Sales of plant and machinery			5		5
	£140	£150	£175	£160	£625
Cash outflows					
Cost of sales (creditors)	87	99	90	104	380
Dividends	40				40
Expenses	23	21	25	23	92
Corporation tax			30		30
Capital expenditure				128	128
	£150	£120	£145	£255	£670
Cash surplus/(deficit)	(10)	30	30	(95)	(45)
Cash balances: Opening	35	25	55	85	35
Closing	£25	£55	£85	£(10)	£(10)

Notes: 1 Debtors (and creditors) outstanding at beginning of quarter are assumed to have (been) settled during the coming three months.
2 Cost of sales includes an adjustment for depreciation (non-cash) item of £5,000.

(b) Comments
Additional financing is going to be necessary in the fourth quarter if it is desired to avoid a cash shortage at the year-end. The deficit is due to the heavy outlay for capital items, which has only been partly financed by measures to raise cash in the previous quarter. A short-term loan of £10,000 would cover the shortfall or, alternatively, perhaps bank overdraft arrangements could be made to allow the cash at bank balances to temporarily go into debit.

(c) The term 'summary budget' also applies, in addition to the cash budget, to:

(i) Budgeted profit and loss account (or income statement);

(ii) Budgeted balance sheet.

Essentially they are budgets which are prepared from, and summarise, the functional/subsidiary budgets of an organisation's budgetary control system.

A functional (or subsidiary) budget is a budget of income and/or expenditure applicable to a particular organisational activity/function. Such a function or activity may refer to a department or a process. When functional/subsidiary budgets have been agreed by management, they provide the budget data for compiling the summary budgets of the organisation.

Examples of functional budgets include: (i) Sales; (ii) Research and Development; (iii) Production (units and cost); (iv) Material purchases; (v) Manpower (labour hours and cost); (vi) Marketing cost; (vii) Administration cost; (viii) General expenses; (ix) Capital expenditure; (x) Manufacturing overhead.

Question 9.3

(a) Preparation of flexible budget for 50 per cent activity level

	£	£
Sales revenue		188,750
Variable costs		
Wholly: Direct materials	31,500	
Direct wages	13,500	
Semi: Production overheads	18,000	
Selling and distribution overheads	9,000	72,000
Contribution		116,750
Fixed costs		
Wholly: Administration overheads	31,500	
Semi: Production overheads	16,000	
Selling and distribution overheads	31,500	79,000
Budgeted profit		£37,750

(b) Three problem areas from decreases in activity level

(i) Break-even point – the firm's margin of safety is eroded by decreasing/contracting activities, eventually to the point where it just breaks even (furthermore, below that activity level losses are suffered);

(ii) Cash flow difficulties (i.e. cash deficits/deficiencies) may arise if industry's current market recession/depression continues;

(iii) Redundancies – rationalisation/cut-back of the labour force, both skilled and unskilled (production, administrative, marketing, etc.) may prove necessary due to contractions in activity level. Added problems of labour unions' opposition, redundancy payments, etc. merely compound recessional difficulties.

Workings

		Exe plc: Flexible Budget			
Activity	Per cent	50%	60%	70%	80%
Level	Units	4,500	5,400	6,300	7,200
Variable costs		(£)	(£)	(£)	(£)
Direct material (@ £7/unit)		31,500	37,800	44,100	50,400
Direct wages (@ £3/unit)		13,500	16,200	18,900	21,600
Semi-variable costs					
Variable	production overhead (@£4/unit)[1]	18,000	21,600	25,200	28,800
	selling and distribution overhead (@£2/unit)[2]	9,000	10,800	12,600	14,400
Fixed	production overhead[1]	16,000	16,000	16,000	16,000
	selling and distribution overhead[2]	31,500	31,500	31,500	31,500
Fixed costs					
Administration overhead		31,500	31,500	31,500	31,500
		151,000	165,400	179,800	194,200
Profit ($\frac{1}{5}$ of selling price = $\frac{1}{4}$ on cost)		37,750			
Sales revenue		188,750			

[1]*production overhead*: High–low estimation:
(1) Highest: £44,800 = a + b 7,200 units
(2) Lowest: £37,600 = a + b 5,400 units

(1) minus (2):   £7,200 =   b 1,800 units

∴ 'b': $\dfrac{£7,200}{1,800}$ = £4 per unit

Substitute in (1):

£44,800 = a + (£4) (7,200)
∴ 'a' =   £44,800 – £28,800 = £16,000 per period

[2]*selling and distribution overheads:* High–low estimation:
(1) Highest: £45,900 = a + b 7,200 units
(2) Lowest: £42,300 = a + b 5,400 units

(1) minus (2):   £3,600 =   b 1,800 units

∴ 'b': = $\dfrac{£3,600}{1,800}$ = £2 per unit

Substitute in (1):

$$£45,900 = a + (£2) (7,200)$$
$$\therefore \text{'}a\text{'} = £45,900 - £14,400 = \underline{£31,500 \text{ per period.}}$$

Question 9.4

(a) (i) Factory unit product costs and production budget:

Factory unit costs for each product manufactured

	Chair (£)	Chair (£)	Table (£)	Table (£)	Bench (£)	Bench (£)
Material – timber		4.00		9.60		20.00
– upholstery		0.80		–		–
– fixing		0.24		0.48		1.00
		5.04		10.08		21.00
Labour – carpenters	4.50		4.80		7.80	
– fixers	1.20	5.70	1.44	6.24	4.80	12.60
Fixed factory overhead		1.00		1.10		2.30
Factory unit product cost		11.74		17.42		35.90

Production units budget

	Chairs	Tables	Benches	Total
Budgeted sales	4,000	1,000	500	5,500
Budgeted closing stock	400	100	50	550
(*less*) Budgeted opening stock	(200)	(300)	(40)	(540)
Budgeted production units	4,200	800	510	5,510

Supporting calculations

	Chairs	Tables	Benches	Total
Labour hours per unit	1	1.1	2.3	(hours)
Budgeted production units	4,200	800	510	
∴ Budgeted labour hours	4,200	880	1,173	6,253

Fixed factory overhead (O/H) absorption rate based on labour hours:

$$\frac{\text{Budgeted o/h}}{\text{Budgeted hours}} \quad \frac{£6,253}{6,253 \text{ hours}} = \underline{£1 \text{ per labour hour}}$$

(ii) Materials purchasing budget in units and cost:

Material units usage budget:

	Timber (ft.³)		Upholstery (yd.²)
Budgeted production unit requirement – from (i)			
4,200 chairs (× 0.5)	2,100	(× 0.2)	840
800 tables (× 1.2)	960		–
510 benches (× 2.5)	1,275		–
Budgeted material usage	4,335		840
Materials purchase budget:			
Budgeted material usage	4,335		840
Budgeted closing stock	650		260
(*less*) Budgeted opening stock	(600)		(400)
Budgeted material purchases	4,385		700

Materials cost budget:

	Total ft.³/yd.²	Price per ft.³/yd.²	Total £
Timber (cubic feet):	4,385	£8	35,080
Upholstery (square yards)	700	£4	2,800
			37,880
Fixing (5% of total cost of material, i.e. £37,880)			1,894
Budgeted materials cost:			39,774

(iii) Direct labour hours and wages budget:

Direct labour hours budget:

	Carpenters (hours)		Fixers (hours)	Total (hours)
Budgeted production unit requirement – from (i)				
4,200 chairs (× 0.75)	3,150	(× 0.25)	1,050	4,200
800 tables (× 0.8)	640	(× 0.3)	240	880
510 benches (× 1.3)	663	(× 1.0)	510	1,173
Budgeted labour hours	4,453		1,800	6,253

Direct wages budget:

	Total hours	Rate per hour	Total £
Carpenters	4,453	£6.00	26,718
Fixers	1,800	£4.80	8,640
Budgeted gross wages to be paid			35,358

(b) Calculation of carpenters and fixers to be employed:

	Carpenters	Fixers
Normal hours per week	40	40
(*less*) absenteeism/lateness	(4)	(6)
Expected hours per week	36	34
Expected hours × 4 weeks	144	136
Budgeted hours – from (iii)	4,453	1,800

∴ Number of workers to be employed:

Carpenters: 4,453 ÷ 144 = 30.9 = 31 employees

Fixers: 1,800 ÷ 136 = 13.2 = 14 employees

(c) Flexed production budget (80%, 90%, 100%, 110%):

	Activity level			
	80%	90%	100%	110%
Budgeted production	(units)	(units)	(units)	(units)
Chairs	3,360	3,780	4,200	4,620
Tables	640	720	800	880
Benches	408	459	510	561
	4,408	4,959	5,510	6,061
	(£)	(£)	(£)	(£)
Variable costs	60,239	67,770	75,300	82,830
Fixed costs	6,253	6,253	6,253	6,253
Total budgeted costs	66,492	74,023	81,553	89,083

Supporting calculations

Variable cost (per unit data from (a) (i))	£	£	£	£
Material				
Chairs @ £5.04	16,934	19,051	21,168	23,285
Tables @ £10.08	6,451	7,258	8,064	8,870
Benches @ £21.00	8,568	9,639	10,710	11,781
Labour				
Chairs @ £5.70	19,152	21,546	23,940	26,334
Tables @ £6.24	3,994	4,493	4,992	5,491
Benches @ £12.60	5,140	5,783	6,426	7,069
Total variable costs	60,239	67,770	75,300	82,830

Note: In the above supporting calculations, the unit variable cost per product is multiplied by the number of product units given at the head of the budget schedule, under budgeted production units, to get total variable costs of production.

Question 10.1

(a) Calculation of variances:

Material variances (analysed as appropriate):

	Powder	Chemicals	Tubes
Actual quantity purchased × actual price	10,000 lb. × 70p. = £7,000	(600ltrs. × £2.3) + (600ltrs. × £2.5) = £2,880	(200 × 40p.) + (5,000 × 30p.) = £1,580
Actual quantity purchased × standard price	10,000 lb. × 75p. = £7,500	12,00ltrs. × £2.4 = £2,880	5,200 × 30p = £1,560
∴ Material price variance	£500 (F)	NIL	£20 (A)
Actual quantity issued × standard price	9,800 lb. × 75p. = £7,350	1,050ltrs. × £2.4 = £2,520	4,520 × 30p. = £1,356
Standard quantity × standard price	9,000 lb. × 75p. = £6,750	1,125ltrs. × £2.4 = £2,700	4,500 × 30p. = £1,350
∴ Material usage variances	£600 (A)	£180 (F)	£6 (A)

(i) Total material price variance   £500 (F) + £20 (A) = £480 (F)

(ii) Total material usage variance   £600 (A) + £180 (F) + £6 (A) = £426 (A)

Direct labour variances:

(iii) Direct labour efficiency variance = £1,125 (A)
(iv) Direct wages rate variance = £315 (F)

Check direct labour variances with formulae:

Rate: $(AR - SR) \times AH = (4.3463 - £4.5) \times 2,050 = £315$ (F)

Efficiency: $(AH - SH) \times SR = (2,050 - 1,800) \times £4.5 = £1,125$ (A)

(b) Possible causes of variances:

Materials:

(i) Not buying in bulk may have caused a few tubes (200) to have been purchased at a price (40p) higher than standard (30p);
(ii) Faulty tubes may have resulted in more being issued/used (4,520) than would have been expected for production of 4,500;
(iii) Efficient use of chemicals;
(iv) Powder bought below standard price may indicate good purchasing performance, however, it may simply be due to cheap/inferior powder being acquired at a lower price;
(v) Inefficient use of powder: may be due to poor production effort, but may result from below-standard powder being used which has been bought cheaply (see (iv) above).

Labour efficiency: A workforce paid below standard wage rate may be of lower quality, inferior in skills, or perhaps average workers demotivated by a lower than average wage. The standard efficiency allowance may be incorrect. Perhaps junior/trainee workers were used, performing below average while learning.

Question 10.2

(a) Calculation of appropriate variances:

(i) *Raw materials:*

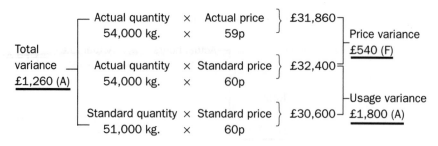

Check with formulae: Price: $(AP - SP) \times AQ = (59p - 60p) \times 54,000 = \underline{£540}$ (F)

Usage: $(AQ - SQ) \times SP = (54,000 - 51,000) \times 60p$
$= \underline{£1,800}$ (A)

(ii) *Fixing items:*

Check with formulae: Price: $(AP - SP) \times AQ = (2.95p - 3p) \times 21,000 = \underline{£10.50}$ (F)

Usage: $(AQ - SQ) \times SP = (21,000 - 20,400) \times 3p = \underline{£18}$ (A)

(iii) *Direct wages:*

	Actual hours	× Actual rate	£40,000
	20,550 h	× £1.95	
Total variance £800 (F)	Actual hours	× Standard rate	£41,100
	20,550 h	× £2	
	Standard hours	× Standard price	£40,800
	20,400h	× £2	

Rate variance £1,100 (F)

Efficiency variance £300 (A)

Check formulae: Rate: $(AR - SR) \times AH = (£1.95 - £2) \times 20,550 = \underline{£1,100}$ (F)

Efficiency: $(AH - SH) \times SR = (20,550 - 20,400) \times £2 = \underline{£300}$ (A)

(iv) *Overheads*:

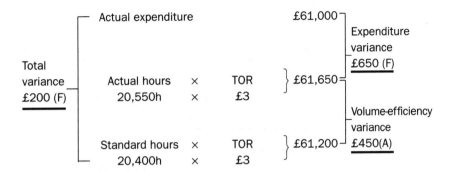

(v) *Sales*:

Note: Detail insufficient to calculate sales volume variance.

Selling price variance:

$$(AP - SP) \times AQ = (£44 - £45) \times 4,500 = £4,500 \text{ (A)}$$

Supporting calculation:

Total overhead absorption rate (TOR): £18 ÷ 6 hours = £3 per hour

(b) A brief comment on direct wages variances:

Rate variance (favourable) may have been caused by strong management negotiations to secure a below-standard wage rate or employment of cheap, sub-standard labour;

Efficiency variance (adverse) may have been the result of poor-quality effort from a below-standard workforce (see rate variance comment above).

Question 10.3

(a) A marginal costing presentation would be a more relevant format for the general manager's information:

MONTH ENDED 31 OCTOBER

Unit standard	Unit value		Fixed budget (original)	Flexed budget (standard)	Actual results	Variance
(u = unit)						
(h = hour)	1	Units	5,000	4,500	4,500	–
	(£)		(£)	(£)	(£)	(£)
1u @ £120	120	Sales	600,000	540,000	550,000	10,000 (F)
		less: Variable costs:				
1u @ £30	30	Direct materials	150,000	135,000	130,000	5,000 (F)
10h @ £4	40	Direct labour	200,000	180,000	189,000	9,000 (A)
10h @ £1	10	Variable production overhead	50,000	45,000	46,000	1,000 (A)
10h @ £1.5	15	Variable selling overhead	75,000	67,500	72,000	4,500 (A)
	95	Total variable cost	475,000	427,500	437,000	9,500 (A)

1u @ £25	25	Contribution	125,000	112,500	113,000	500	(F)
10h @ £0.5	5	*less:* Fixed production overhead	25,000	25,000	29,000	4,000	(A)
10h @ £1	10	Fixed selling overheads	50,000	50,000	46,000	4,000	(F)
1u @ £10	10	Profit	50,000	37,500	38,000	500	(F)

Fixed budget-Flexed budget = Volume variance (sales volume contribution – 500u @ £25):12,500 (A)
Actual-Standard (flexed budget) = Variances (sales price, expenditure and efficiency):   500 (F)

Total variances per original statement   12,000 (A)

(b) Variance calculations:

Variance column (sales price, expenditure and efficiency variances):

	Variances reconciled with (a) (£)

Selling price variance
$(AP - SP) \times AQ = (£122.\dot{2} - £120) \times 4,500 =$ 10,000   (F)

Variable cost variances:
Direct materials [see statement above (no detail
     for further analysis)]   5,000   (F)
Direct labour   (£)
Rate $(AR - SR) \times AH$
     $(£4 - £3.978,947) \times 47,500 =$ 1,000   (F)
Efficiency $(AH - SH) \times SR$
     $(47,500 - 45,000) \times £4 =$ 10,000   (A)   9,000   (A)

Variable production overhead
Expenditure $(AR - SR) \times AH$
     $(£0.968,421 - £1) \times 47,500 =$ 1,500   (F)
Efficiency $(AH - SH) \times SR$
     $(47,500 - 45,000) \times £1 =$ 2,500   (A)   1,000   (A)

Variable selling overhead
Expenditure $(AR - SR) \times AH = (£1.515,789 - £1.5) \times 47,500 = 750$ (A)
Efficiency $(AH - SH) \times SR = (47,500 - 45,000) \times £1.5 =$ 3,750   (A)   4,500   (A)

Fixed overhead variances:
Fixed production overhead
Expenditure (budget – actual)
     $(25,000 - 29,000) =$ 4,000   (A)
Fixed selling overhead
Expenditure (budget – actual)
     $(50,000 - 46,000) =$ 4,000   (F)

Total variances in the variance column   500   (F)

Volume variances:

Sales volume profit (AQ − BQ) × BP		
(4,500 − 5,000) × £10		5,000 (A)
Fixed production overhead		
Budgeted expenditure (50,000 × £0.50)	25,000	
		1,250 (A)
Actual hours × F.O.R. (47,500 × £0.50)	23,750	
		1,250 (A)
Standard hours × F.O.R. (45,000 × £0.50)	22,500	
Fixed selling overhead		
Budgeted expenditure (50,000 × £1)	50,000	
		2,500 (A)
Actual hours × F.O.R. (47,500 × £1)	47,500	
		2,500 (A)
Standard hours × F.O.R (45,000 × £1)	45,000	
Sales volume contribution variance		12,500 (A)

Check variable cost variances with framework:

Direct labour:

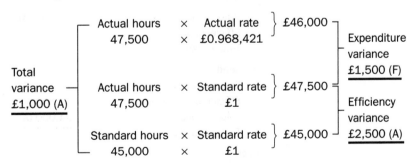

Variable production overhead:

Variable selling overhead:

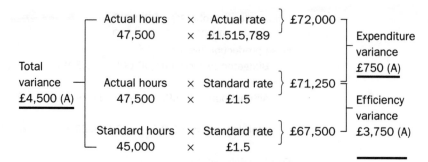

(c) Short report of explanation to the general manager:

Principle:

The report is based on the marginal costing principle rather than the absorption costing technique.

Information content:

For management decision purposes the marginal costing/contribution technique is preferable as it is based on decision-variable information. Fixed overheads will not be affected by decisions to change the level of activity/operations, therefore do not constitute decision-variable information.

Question 10.4

Operating statement for the month:

	(£)	(£)	(£)
Budgeted profit			200,000
Variances			
Direct materials			
Price variance	4,800 (A)		
Usage variance	3,500 (A)		
Total variance		8,300 (A)	
Direct wages			
Rate variance	9,200 (A)		
Efficiency variance	4,500 (F)		
Total variance		4,700 (A)	
Overhead			
Expenditure variance	10,000 (F)		
Efficiency variance	9,000 (F)		
Volume variance	24,000 (A)		
Total variance		5,000 (A)	
Sales			
Selling price variance	95,000 (F)		
Sales volume profit variance	10,000 (A)	85,000 (F)	
Profit variance			67,000 (F)
Actual profit			267,000

Supporting calculations

	£
Standard cost per unit	
Direct material: X (10 kg × £1)	10
Y (5 kg × £5)	25
Direct wages: 5 hours × £3	15
Overhead: 5 hours × £6 (200% of direct wages)	30
	80
Standard profit per unit ($\frac{1}{5}$ on sales = $\frac{1}{4}$ on cost)[1]	20
Standard selling price per unit	100

Note: [1]Required 20 per cent ($\frac{1}{5}$) profit mark-up on sales price is same as 25 per cent ($\frac{1}{4}$) profit mark-up on cost.

Budgeted profit: 10,000 units × £20 = £200,000

Direct material cost variances:

Material X

Check with formulae: Price: $(AP - SP) \times AQ = (£1.20 - £1) \times 96,000 = £19,200$ (A)

Usage: $(AQ - SQ) \times SP = (96,000 - 95,000) \times £1 = £1,000$ (A)

Material Y

Check with formulae: Price: $(AP - SP) \times AQ = (£4.70 - £5) \times 48,000$
= £14,400 (F)

Usage: $(AQ - SQ) \times SP = (48,000 - 47,500) \times £5$
= £2,500 (A)

Total material price variances: £19,200 (A) + £14,400 (F) = £4,800 (A)

Total material usage variances: £1,000 (A) + £2,500 (A) = £3,500 (A)

Direct wages variances:

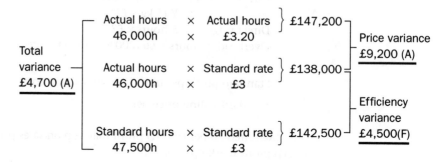

Check with formulae: Rate: (AR – SR) × AH = (£3.20 – £3) × 46,000 = £9,200 (A)

Efficiency: (AH – SH) × SR = (46,000 – 47,500) × £3
= £4,500(F)

Overhead variances:

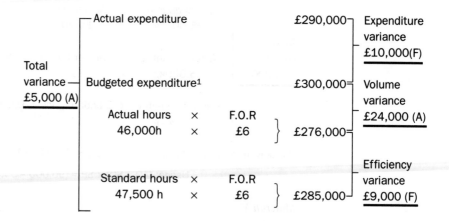

Note:[1] 50,000 hours × £6 fixed overhead rate (FOR) = £300,000

Sales variances:

Selling price variance:

(AP – SP) × AQ = (£110 – £100) × 95,000 = £95,000 (F)

Sales volume profit variance:

(AQ – BQ) × BP = (9,500 – 10,000) × £20 = £10,000 (A)

Actual profit (check/verification):	(£)	(£000)
Sales (9,500 units × £110)		1,045
Direct materials consumed		
X (96,000 kg × £1.20)	115,200	
Y (48,000 kg × £4.70)	225,600	
Direct wages (46,000 h × £3.20)	147,200	
Fixed production overhead incurred	290,000	778
		267

Question 11.1

(a) Calculation of AB Ltd's change in ROCE:

(*Note:* Depreciation charged by AB Ltd on its factory = £150,000 × 1.5% = £2,250 per annum)

CAPITAL EMPLOYED ADJUSTMENT:

	(£)	(£)
Inclusive of factory (£91,000 × 100)		350,000
 26		
deduct written down value of factory:		
10 years depreciation @ £2,250	22,500	
Original value of factory	150,000	127,500
Exclusive of factory:		£222,500

PROFIT ADJUSTMENT:

	(£)	(£)
Unadjusted profit:	91,000	
add depreciation	2,250	93,250
deduct rental @ 10% of revaluation		
(£300,000 × 0.1):		30,000
Profit (adjusted)		£63,250

Revised ROCE calculation:

$$\frac{\text{Revised profit}}{\text{Revised capital employed}} = \frac{£63,250}{£222,500} \times 100 = 28.4\%$$

Change in ROCE: 28.4% − 26% = 2.4% increase

(b) Solution to this part requirement can be extracted from section 11.2.1 of Chapter 11.

Question 11.2

(a) Computation of ROI and NRI for each annual investment level:

Note: The 'annual net income' values given in the table in the question are simply multiplied by the probability of the relevant diesel fuel cost per gallon applying. This calculation provides the *expected annual net income* total figure (i.e. total EV) in the final column of the expected value table immediately below, which is then used to compute ROI and NRI for each annual investment level:

Annual investment level	Expected value (EV) of annual net income at following costs per gallon:					
(£000)	1.20 (£000)	1.25 (£000)	1.30 (£000)	1.40 (£000)	1.50 (£000)	Total EV (£000)
350	5.5	5.2	18.4	12.0	3.0	44.1
400	6.0	5.8	20.8	13.8	3.5	49.9
450	6.8	6.3	22.0	14.1	3.5	52.7
500	7.2	6.8	23.2	14.7	3.4	55.3
550	7.4	6.7	22.4	12.9	3.0	52.4
600	7.5	6.4	21.2	12.0	2.5	49.6

Annual investment level	Total EV of annual net income	ROI $\dfrac{(b)}{(a)} \times 100$	10% p.a. imputed interest charge on investment level in (a)	NRI
(a)	(b)		(c)	(b) − (c)
(£000)	(£000)	(%)	(£000)	(£000)
350	44.1	12.6	35	9.1
400	49.9	12.5	40	9.9
450	52.7	11.7	45	7.7
500	55.3	11.1	50	5.3
550	52.4	9.5	55	(2.6)
600	49.6	8.3	60	(10.4)

(b) Optimal investment level:

As NRI overcomes the potential problem of sub-optimal planning decisions that might result from application of the ROI divisional performance measurement technique it is usually regarded as superior to ROI. The optimal investment level will therefore be taken to be the one showing the greatest NRI. This level is £400,000 which generates a maximum NRI of £9,900. (Notice that use of the ROI divisional investment appraisal technique would have indicated the £350,000 level instead.)

(c) Solution to this part requirement can be extracted from sections 11.2.1 and 11.2.2 of Chapter 11.

Question 11.3

(a) Comparison of companies' performance:

When annualised it can be seen that the estimated ROCE (given in the question as 15 per cent for X and 20 per cent for Y) is equivalent to the actual results for the last month, as follows:

Companies

	X	Y
Monthly profit	£80,000 × 12	£15,000 × 12
Annualised net profit	£960,000	£180,000

$$\text{ROCE} = 100 \times \frac{\text{Net profit}}{\text{Assets employed}} \qquad \frac{£0.96m}{£6.4m} \times 100 \qquad \frac{£0.18m}{£0.9m} \times 100$$

Estimated ROCE (annual basis)	15%	20%

Monthly results (actual) and percentage (%) comparisons:

	X		Y	
	£000	%	£000	%
Sales	600	100	370	100
less: Variable costs	229	38	208	56
= Contribution	371	62	162	44
less: Controllable fixed costs	65	11	28	8
= Controllable profit	306	51	134	36
less: Apportioned group costs	226	38	119	32
Net profit	80	13	15	4

Actual ROCE (annual basis):

$$\text{ROCE} = \frac{\text{Profit}}{\text{Assets employed}} \times 100 = \frac{\text{Sales}}{\text{Assets employed}} \,\% \times \frac{\text{Profit}}{\text{Sales}} \,\%$$

Apply annualised sales and profits:

X			Y		
$\dfrac{£7.2m}{£6.4m}$	×	$\dfrac{£0.96m}{£7.2m}$	$\dfrac{£4.44m}{£0.9m}$	×	$\dfrac{£0.18m}{£4.44m}$
= 112.5% × 13.3%			493.3% × 4.1%		
= 15%			20%		

Discussion points:

▶ Companies X and Y both exceed the target return/cost of capital of 12 per cent for Alphabet Group plc;
▶ Need to know basis for appointment of group costs (– probably arbitrary in nature);
▶ Y's C/S (contribution/sales) ratio of 44 per cent is lower than X's 62 per cent;
▶ Y in comparison to X, produces relatively high sales from a much lower investment base (however, Y's sales generate a significantly lower absolute profit);
▶ *Prima facie*, Y appears to perform better than X on the basis of ROCE.

(b) Redraft of operating statements using alternative of NRI performance measure:

NET RESIDUAL INCOME (NRI) MONTHLY STATEMENT

		X	Y
		(£000)	(£000)
Revenue – sales		600	370
Controllable costs:			
	Variable costs (controlled)	229	208
=	Contribution	371	162
	Fixed costs (controlled incl. depreciation)	65	28
=	Controllable operating income/profit	306	134
	Interest (imputed charge) on company assets employed/investment	64[1]	9[2]
=	Controllable residual income:	242	125
Non-controllable costs:			
	Apportioned group costs	226	119
=	Net residual income	16	6

Note: [1]Company X imputed interest: (£6.4m @ 12% p.a.) ÷ 12 = £64,000.
[2]Company Y imputed interest: (£0.9m @ 12% p.a.) ÷ 12 = £9,000.

Interpretation:

▶ Company Y has lower controllable income/profit compared with X;
▶ Proportionaly less difference in Y's lower NRI compared with relative net profit differences (80:15 in comparison with 16:6);
▶ When interest rates rise then the imputed interest charge will increase in line;
▶ Increasing imputed interest rates/charges will impact upon X significantly more than Y as the former's investment base (£6.4m) is much higher than the latter's (£0.9m);
▶ Up-to-date comparison may be better effected by revaluing company assets at current cost values.

(c) Solution to this part requirement can be extracted from sections 11.2.1 and 11.2.2 of Chapter 11.

Question 11.4

(a) Return on investment (ROI) budgeted for the Solo division:

	(£000)
Contribution budgeted – 30,000 units @ £16 (i.e. £40 – £24)	480
(*less*) Fixed costs budgeted	(200)
Profit budgeted	280

$$ROI = \frac{Profit}{Investment} = \frac{280}{800} \times 100 = 35\%$$

Important note: For the remainder of this question the firm (Chart Products Ltd) requires a 20 per cent ROI. Being the target rate of return, this 20 per cent therefore represents the relevant imputed interest charge to determine (minimum) net residual income (NRI). Current budgeted minimum NRI is calculated thus:

	(£000)
Profit (see above):	280
(*less*) Imputed interest charge (£800,000 @ 20%):	(160)
NRI:	120

(b) Acceptability of order:

	(£000)
Extra contribution from order (10,000 units @ £8 (i.e. £32 – £24))	80
Current contribution (see (a) above)	480
Revised contribution	560
(*less*) Fixed costs revised (current £200,000 + extra £40,000)	(240)
Revised profit	320

Investment level revised to (current £800,000 + extra £140,000)	940
Therefore imputed interest charge revised to (£940,000 @ 20%):	188

Effect of order:

	(£000)
Revised profit	320
(*less*) Imputed interest:	(188)
Revised NRI:	132

Therefore order is acceptable as current NRI (£120,000) will increase by £12,000 (to £132,000).

(c) Worthwhileness of buying-in already made component:

	(£000)
Extra variable cost of buying-in component (30,000 units @ £1 (i.e. £5 – £4))	(30)
Current contribution (see (a) above)	480
Revised contribution	450
(*less*) Fixed costs revised (current £200,000 – £20,000)	(180)
Revised profit:	270

Investment level revised to (current £800,000 – £60,000)	740
Therefore imputed interest charge revised to (£740,000 @ 20%)	148

	(£000)
Revised profit:	270
(*less*) Imputed interest:	(148)
Revised NRI:	122

Therefore buying-in component worthwhile as current NRI (£120,000) will increase by £2,000 (to £122,000).

(d) Most additional investment in assets:

	(£000)
Extra contribution from new product (15,000 units @ £8 (i.e. £20 – £12))	120
Current contribution (see (a) above)	480
Revised contribution	600
(*less*) Fixed costs revised (current £200,000 + extra £80,000)	(280)
Revised profit	320
(*less*) Imputed interest (current £800,000 @ 20%)	(160)
Revised NRI:	160

The revised NRI is £40,000 higher than current £120,000 given a 20% ROI.

Therefore most additional investment in assets is £40,000 ÷ 20%, i.e.

$$\frac{£40,000}{0.2} = \underline{£200,000}$$

(e) Units of existing product necessary to justify new product:

	(£000)
Investment level revised to (current £800,000 + extra £400,000)	1,200
Required (minimum) ROI (i.e. 20% on £1,200,000)	240
Current (minimum) NRI (see (a) above)	120
Revised return (i.e. profit required)	360
Fixed costs revised (see (d) above)	280
Revised contribution required	640

Total requirement of £640,000 comprises:

New product extra contribution (see (d) above)	120
Existing product contribution required	520
	640

Existing product contributes £16 (see (a) above) per unit.

Therefore necessary units of existing product to justify new product

is £520,000 ÷ £16, i.e. $\dfrac{£520,000}{£16}$ = 32,500 units

(f) The main problem in divisional organisations of having multiple goals reflected by performance measured in terms of ROI and NRI is that these two measures can conflict. For example, within Solo division the budgeted ROI (see (a) above) is 35 per cent *but* this reduces, in (b) above, to 34 per cent on acceptance of new customer order, *viz*:

$$\frac{\text{Revised profit}}{\text{Revised investment}} = \frac{£320,000}{£940,000} \times 100 = 34\%$$

However, the budgeted NRI (see (a) above) is £120,000 *but* this changes to a £132,000 revised NRI, in (b) above, from accepting new customer order. Therefore there exists an inherent conflict between the two performance measures here in that ROI *decreases* whilst NRI *increases*. ROI as a relative divisional performance measure is generally considered inferior to NRI's absolute measurement properties. For additional detail see section 11.2.2 of Chapter 11.

Index

Absorption costing 23–35
Absorption of overhead 23–27, 29–35, 216, 222
Accounting 2–3
Accounting rate of return (ARR) 159, 168, 170–173
Accounting Standards Board 42
Activity based costing (ABC) 35–38
Activity based cost-plus pricing 144
Allocation of overhead 27–29
American Accounting Association 1, 3, 13
Apportionment of overhead 27–29, 32–34
Arnold, J. 3–4, 13

Bases of apportionment 28–29
Bounded rationality 106–107
Break-even analysis see cost-volume-profit (C-V-P) analysis
Break-even chart(s) 123–127, 130, 136–137
Break-even point 121–123, 173–174, 198–199
Budget building/preparation 182–192
Budgetary control 12–13, 181–203
Budgeted balance sheet 12, 183, 189, 191–192
Budgeted income statement see budgeted profit and loss account
Budgeted profit and loss account 12, 183, 189, 191
Budgeting see budgetary control
Budgets 12–13, 181–182, 206
Burden 25

Capital budgeting see capital investment appraisal
Capital expenditure budget 183, 188–189
Capital investment appraisal 155–177
Cash budget see cash flow budget
Cash flow budget 12, 182, 183, 189–190
Chartered Institute of Management Accountants (CIMA) 5–6, 13, 91, 115
Computer-aided design and manufacturing (CAD/CAM) 10, 250

Contribution 70–74, 119–121
Contribution margin pricing see marginal pricing
Contribution per unit of limiting factor 75–77
Contribution (-sales/-volume) ratio see profit-volume (P/V) ratio
Contribution variance 216–218, 223–225
Control see management planning and control
Control accounting techniques 6, 179–251
Cost accounting 17
Cost analysis techniques 15–81
Cost ascertainment 17–42, 67
Cost behaviour 43–65
Cost centre(s) 19–21, 232–233
Cost classification 21
Cost driver(s) 36–37
Cost estimation 52–65
Cost of capital 155
Costing see cost accounting
Cost-plus pricing 134, 143–147
Cost structures/build-up 22–23
Cost unit(s) 18–19
Cost-volume-profit (C-V-P) analysis 116–133
Coulthurst, N. 177

Decision accounting techniques 6, 83–177
Decision-making see management decision-making
Decision tree 94–97
Direct cost(s) see prime cost(s)
Discounting see present value
Divisional management performance 8, 230–242
Divisional performance see divisional management performance
Divisionalisation 230–231
Dixon, R. 177
Dun and Bradstreet 2

Expected monetary value (EMV) 89, 91–100
Extel 2

Feedback 6, 9, 12–13, 208
Financial accounting 3–5
Financial Times 2
Fixed budget(s) 193, 195, 197, 206–208
Fixed cost(s) 43, 48–49, 69–70, 195
Fixed overhead(s) *see* fixed cost(s)
Fixed overhead variances 219–223
Flexed/flexible budget(s) 193–199, 206–209
Flexible budgetary control *see* flexible budgeting
Flexible budgeting 193–199
Ford Motor Company 230
Full-cost pricing 134, 143–145
Functional budgets 12, 181–189

General Electric Corporation 238
General overhead budget 183, 188–189
Giffen, R. 135
Goal congruence 238

High-low cost estimation 54–55, 59, 195–196
H. M. Customs and Excise 2
Hope, T. 4, 13
Horngren, C. T. 3, 13

Indirect cost(s) *see* overhead(s)
Industrial Revolution 5
Information analysis 107–111
Information technology 107
Institute of Cost and Management
        Accountants 17
Institute of Cost and Works
        Accountants 5
Internal rate of return (IRR) 159, 162–167
Investment centre(s) 233
Investors Chronicle 2

Jaguar 230
Just-in-time (JIT) 248, 250–251

Labour cost budget 183, 186
Labour cost variances 213–214
Least-squares cost estimation *see* regression
        analysis
Life-cycle 128, 173–174
Limiting factor(s) 74–77, 183–184, 243
Linear programming (LP) 12, 77, 183, 243–247

McIntyre, A. 177
Management accounting 1
Management decision-making 6–12
Management planning and control 6–13
Manufacturing resources planning (MRP 2) 250
Margin of safety 124–125, 198
Marginal cost(s) 45, 67–69, 137–142, 208
Marginal costing 66–81

Marginal pricing 134, 143, 147–151
Marginal revenue 137–142
Master budgets *see* summary budgets
Matching concept 192
Material cost variances 211–213
Materials cost budget 183, 186–187
Materials requirements planning (MRP) 12,
        247–250
Maximin/Maximax 90–91, 93–94
Mixed cost(s) *see* semi-variable cost(s)
Monitoring 13, 181, 207–208
Moore, P. G. 115

Net present value (NPV) 159–161, 164–167,
        173–174
Net residual income (NRI) 233, 237–239

Opportunity cost 18, 150–151
Optimal pricing 130, 134–143
Overhead(s) 22–38

Payback 155, 159, 168–170
Pay-off matrix 92–94
Perfect information 111
Period cost(s) *see* fixed cost(s)
Planning *see* management planning and control
Planning and control accounting techniques
        see control accounting techniques
Present value 155–159
Pricing 134– 154
Prime cost(s) 22–23, 67, 208
Principal budget factor 183–184, 186
Probability analysis 86–90
Product mix 75–77
Production budget 183, 186
Production cost of sales budget 183, 188
Production overhead cost budget 183, 187
Profit centre(s) 233
Profit variance 223–225
Profit-volume (P/V) chart 125–127
Profit-volume (P/V) ratio 127
Purchases budget 183, 186–187

Rate of return pricing 134, 145–146
Rational economic behaviour 106
Reciprocal services 32–34
Regression (least-squares) analysis 57–59
Relevant range 47, 50
Responsibility accounting 230–233
Responsibility centre(s) 28, 205, 232–233
Return on capital employed (ROCE) *see* return
        on investment (ROI)
Return on investment (ROI) 145, 171,
        233–237, 239
Risk *see* uncertainty

Sales budget 183, 185–186
Sales variances 218–219
Satisficing behaviour 107
Scapens, R. W. 115
Scarce resource(s) *see* limiting factor(s)
Scattergraph cost estimation 55–57
Secondary apportionment 29, 32–34
Semi-fixed cost(s) *see* semi-variable cost(s)
Semi-variable cost(s) 51–52, 195
Sensitivity analysis 173–174
Simon, H.A. 107, 115
Sizer, J. 5–6, 13
Standard costing *see* variance analysis
Standards 13, 181–182, 206
Step cost(s) 50, 52, 195
Subjective expected utility (SEU) 100–106
Subsidiary budgets *see* functional budgets
Summary budgets 12, 181–183, 189–192

Thomas, H. 115
Time value of money 155

Uncertainty 10, 85–115
Uniform accounting 235
User cost 187
Utility *see* subjective expected utility

Variable cost(s) 43–48, 195
Variable cost variances 208–218
Variable overhead(s) 67–68, 208
Variable overhead cost variances 215–216
Variance accounting *see* variance analysis
Variance analysis 13, 204–229

Weighted average cost of capital 156
Wright, D. 42